foundations of
economics

third edition

Andrew Gillespie

OXFORD
UNIVERSITY PRESS

OXFORD
UNIVERSITY PRESS

Great Clarendon Street, Oxford, OX2 6DP,
United Kingdom

Oxford University Press is a department of the University of Oxford.
It furthers the University's objective of excellence in research, scholarship,
and education by publishing worldwide. Oxford is a registered trade mark of
Oxford University Press in the UK and in certain other countries

First edition 2007
Second edition 2011
Impression: 2

Published in the United States of America by Oxford University Press
198 Madison Avenue, New York, NY 10016, United States of America

British Library Cataloguing in Publication Data
Data available

Library of Congress Control Number: 2014934365

ISBN 978–0–19–967487–9

Printed in Great Britain by
Bell & Bain Ltd, Glasgow

This book is dedicated to
Tor and John where it all began.

Outline contents

Detailed contents

Preface

This book is intended to provide an introduction to the principles of economics, and to help you to understand many issues that affect businesses and economies around the world: everything from why China has grown so fast, the causes and effects of the recent global recession, to the effects of the eurocrisis, to the minimum wage and whether alcohol should be taxed more heavily to reduce drinking. It will also help you to understand issues that affect your own daily life: Why are houses so expensive in the UK? What determines how much you have to pay to borrow from the bank? How much are you likely to earn in your chosen career? By reading this book, you will develop the tools to analyse these issues from an economist's perspective, and, hopefully, you will soon find yourself talking and thinking like an economist as well! Going to university is an investment decision: is it worth it? Buying this book involves opportunity costs because you could have bought something else: is it worth the sacrifice? (I hope so!) Do the extra benefits from spending an extra hour on your assignment exceed the extra costs? I hope that this book will help you to analyse problems logically and from an economist's perspective and to understand the economic consequences of any decision.

I am assuming no prior knowledge of economics at all. It does not matter if you have no background in economics at this stage. I aim to take you from knowing no economic theory to having a good solid foundation that gives you the knowledge and skills for further, specialized study in economics in higher education. With this background, you can study the subject, or parts of the subject, in much more detail, but will already have an overview of and insight into the key issues. I also aim to show you how relevant this subject is to everything going on around you and how valuable an understanding of economic theory can be.

Do send me feedback on the book: let me know if you enjoy it and find it useful, as well as any ideas on how I can improve the next edition. You can email me at wattgill@aol.com

How to use this book

Gillespie's *Foundations of Economics* offers a range of features carefully designed to help support and reinforce your learning. This guided tour shows you how to utilize these features and get the most from your study.

LEARNING OBJECTIVES

By the end of this chapter, you should be able to:

✓ understand the basic economic problems of d produced, how it is produced, and for whom it

✓ understand the different types of economy, suc market economy, the command (or planned) e mixed economy;

Learning objectives

Every chapter begins with a set of key learning objectives designed to outline the core concepts and ideas you will encounter. This will enable you to connect related topics and plan your revision.

Put into practice

Which of the following statements are true and which are fa

a. A government-run organization is part of the public secto

b. Real wages have taken account of inflation

c. If the marginal cost of an activity equals the marginal ber this activity at all

d. Capital goods are an investment for the future

Put into practice

Test your understanding and problem-solving skills by putting theory into practice. Answers to the put into practice questions are hosted on the book's accompanying Online Resource Centre.

Economics in context

The owner of B&Q, Kingfisher, announced a fall in profits last cold weather. Kingfisher is Europe's largest DIY retailer. As v company was also affected by weak consumer confidence Sales of outdoor products were hit at B&Q and the compa were also damaged by the poor weather. This affected the s

❓ Questions

Economics in context

Explore how economic theory applies to real-world situations and check your understanding using the questions provided.

When the demand curve shifts, this is known as a c change in the quantity demanded).

What do you think?

What do you think will be the big hit in the toy market ne estimate this?

What do you think?

These questions allow you to examine the material presented throughout the chapters, and reflect on your own ideas.

Case study

The following is an extract from the UK government's 'Pla

Britain has lost ground in the world's economy, and needs our country will become poorer and we will find it difficult not wake up to the world around us, our standard of living In the last decade other nations have worked hard to m reduced their business tax rates, removed barriers to en their education systems, reformed welfare and increased

Case studies

Case studies illustrate economic theory in context and are designed to help you apply your learning to the real world.

Examples

Step-by-step numerical examples appear at various points throughout the book, to clearly demonstrate the application of economic theory and support your learning.

> **Example**
>
> Suppose that the quantity demanded of a good rises from 2 from £10 to £6. This means that:
>
> $$\text{Percentage change in the quantity demanded} = \left(\frac{+100}{200}\right) \times 1$$
>
> $$\text{Percentage change in price} = \left(\frac{-4}{10}\right) \times 100$$
>
> $$\text{Price elasticity of demand} = \frac{+50}{-40} = -1.2$$

Review questions

Test and review your understanding of key ideas before you move on to the next chapter.

> **Review questions**
>
> 1 State the three key economic problems facing any
> 2 How do different types of economies try to solve the
> 3 Explain how the government intervenes in your ec decreased in recent years?
> 4 Explore how the concepts of scarcity and choice aff
> 5 Explain the difference between nominal and real w

Assignment questions

Demonstrate your knowledge and practice your exam skills by answering essay style questions at the end of chapters.

> **Assignment questions**
>
> 1 Look in the news this week and identify one key cu another economy. Summarize the issues involved
> 2 Research the jobs market for graduate economist be an economist.

Key learning points

This feature summarizes the core material and ensures you're ready to move on to the next chapter. This is also a useful tool when it comes to organizing your revision.

> **Key learning points**
>
> • Resources in an economy are limited at any mon
> • Economics considers the key economic questions and for whom it is it produced.
> • The key economic questions can be answered by free market), by the government (in a planned ec mixed economy).

Learn more

Signposts at the end of chapters direct you to related content in the book, and to advanced material hosted on the Online Resource Centre.

> **Learn more**
>
> If you read Chapter 29, you can find out more about shows how economies can benefit from free trade a
>
> @ Visit our Online Resource Centre at http://www econ3e/ for test questions and further informat

Advise the government

These questions ask you to think like an economist by drawing together themes from the chapters to advise the government on economic policy. What would *you* do if you were in charge?

> # Advise the Gove
>
> Whichever political party you are, being in governme many competing demands, limited resources, and lot before the next election. In this section we consider so facing governments and ask you to help advise whoe

About the online resource centre

This book is accompanied by a fully integrated Online Resource Centre, providing students and registered lecturers with ready-to-use teaching and learning resources. These supplementary resources are free of charge, and carefully designed to support the learning experience.

www.oxfordtextbooks.co.uk/orc/gillespie_econ3e/

For students

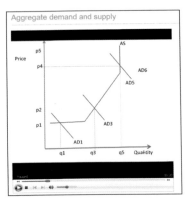

Visual walkthroughs

Develop and reinforce your learning using visual walkthroughs of key concepts from the book, with screen grabs and an audio soundtrack.

Solutions to questions

Check your understanding of key topics from the book with solutions to the 'put into practice' questions.

Self-test questions

Test your knowledge of key themes with these multiple-choice questions linked to each chapter, and receive immediate feedback.

Advanced material

Take your learning further with a range of advanced topics explored in more depth, to supplement the material covered in the book.

Web links

Learn more about those topics that are of particular interest to you, with a selection of reliable and authoritative web links chosen by the author.

Flashcard glossaries

Check your understanding of key concepts using glossary terms in a flashcard format. This is an ideal revision tool when it comes to exam time.

Author blog

Read more about relevant news stories posted with accompanying author commentary by Andrew Gillespie.

Business strategy

Access an additional chapter on business strategy, and learn more about a range of broader business issues.

Business and strategy

- Business as a transformation process
- Forms of business
- Why buy shares?
- Mission statements
- Objectives
- Strategy
- The functions of business
- Business and the environment
- Analysing the micro-environment
- Porter's Five Forces analysis of market structure
- PESTEL analysis of the macro-environment
- Opportunities and Threats
- Using PESTEL analysis
- Influencing the PESTEL environment
- Developing a strategy: SWOT analysis

In this section we consider a number of areas of business activity and consider how an analysis of economic issues fits in with the study of business. To begin with we outline the basic business process of taking resources and transforming them into outputs that hopefully are wanted by the customer. We then consider the various forms of business that exist and the difference between a mission, an objective and a strategy. We then analyse the activities that occur within a business, namely marketing, operations, finance and human resource management. Having looked internally we then consider the factors

Advise the government questions

Additional questions are hosted online, and can be used to draw together your ideas on government policy and contemporary economic issues. How would *you* advise the ruling party?

▇ For registered lecturers

PowerPoint slides

A suite of adaptable PowerPoint slides can be used in lecture presentations. Arranged by chapter, the slides may also be used as hand-outs in class.

Instructor's manual

This resource provides the answers to the 'Put into practice', 'Economics in context', and end of chapter questions set in the book.

Gillespie: Foundations of Economics 3/e
Instructor's Manual

Chapter 1: What is economics?

Activity

Ask students to investigate the costs and benefits of university study. "Is it worth going to university nowadays?"
Obviously this is a highly relevant issue at the moment with fee increases what impact do they think this will have on the number of students going into higher education? What do they think would be the long term impact on the economy if fewer students go to university? How might this affect the production possibility frontier?

Answers to end of chapter questions

1.   How do different economies try to solve the basic economic problem?
2.   In theory this may be through the market mechanism or the government allocating resources or a combination of the two. In reality all economies are mixed. **To what extent does the government intervene in your economy?**
This will be interesting to see and compare what students say - in what sectors is the government intervening? How is it intervening? Is it intervening more or less than before? What do they think determines how much the government intervenes? You could compare and contrast the extent of intervention between countries. You could also discuss how approaches/views have changed over time.
Are there areas where they feel the government intervenes too much, in terms of the economy?

3.   **How does the concept of scarcity and choice affect you in your day to day life?**
This is obviously all about having to make choices. Students like all of us will have limited resources and this limits what they can do. They must decide how to spend their student loan and what their priorities are. This means there is an opportunity cost to everything they do. Think of limited resources in terms of e.g. what they can afford, what is on offer, and what they can do with their time.

Guide to 'Advise the government' questions

Suggested answers to questions from the book, alongside additional questions hosted online, will help guide your discussions with students.

Which of the following is a positive statement in economics?

○ a. The income in the UK needs to be distributed more fairly
○ b. The government needs to put more emphasis on improving UK export levels
○ c. An increase in demand will increase the equilibrium price
○ d. Faster economic growth is more important than a better quality of goods

Test bank

This ready-made testing resource can be imported into your assessment software and customized to meet your teaching needs. Questions are provided for every chapter in the book.

Acknowledgements

Many thanks to everyone at OUP for their support and help in putting this book together. For the first edition, thanks to Kirsty Reade, Fiona Loveday, Nicola Bateman, and Julie Harris. For the second edition, thanks to everyone again at OUP, especially Peter Hooper, Sarah Brett, Philippa Hendry, and Kevin Doherty. For the third edition many thanks to Kirsten Shankland for her endless patience and to Joanna Hardern and Emily Spicer for all their help and support.

All reasonable effort has been made to contact the holders of copyright in materials reproduced in this book. Any omissions will be rectified in future printings if notice is given to the publisher.

New to this edition

The third edition offers extended coverage of globalization, with additional references to developing and emerging economies. It incorporates updated figures and data to support the discussion of the financial crisis, and global steps to recovery. Existing learning features have been developed, and new features have been introduced. These include more questions at the end of every chapter, as well as the addition of new 'assignment' and 'advise the government' questions.

Overview of the book

Microeconomics: Chapters 1–15

The book begins with a discussion of the basic economic problem; in Chapter 1 we look at what studying economics involves, and at some of the key concepts and issues.

In Chapter 2 we examine how resources are allocated within an economy—what determines who works where, what is produced, who earns what, and who gets what. One way of solving these economic problems is to leave it to market forces of supply and demand. In Chapters 3–6 we examine supply and demand conditions, and analyse how the price mechanism brings about equilibrium. Having established how the free market works, we then highlight some of the disadvantages of this approach in Chapters 7 and 8, and consider how the government might intervene to solve these.

Having examined the elements of a market, we then focus on market structure. We begin by developing an understanding of revenues, costs, and profits in Chapters 9 and 10. Once this has been covered, we analyse the different forms of market structure in detail, and the implications of these in terms of price and output decisions in Chapters 11–14.

In Chapter 15 we examine the market for labour and consider how wages are determined for different jobs.

Macroeconomics: Chapters 16–29

In the macroeconomics section, we begin with an overview of the key issues in macroeconomics in Chapter 16. We then analyse what causes equilibrium in the economy in Chapter 17 and whether national income is a good indicator of a country's standard of living in Chapter 18. In Chapter 19 we look at aggregate demand and aggregate supply and analyse the equilibrium output and price level.

We examine consumption and investment in in Chapters 20–21 and then consider apsects of fiscal policy in Chapter 22. In Chapter 23 we examine monetary policy and then consider the use of government policies on growth, inflation, and unemployment in Chapters 24 to 26. We then broaden our analysis to study exchange rates, trade, and globalization in Chapters 27 to 29.

Overall, this book should provide a good introduction to the key issues in economics and provide you with the tools necessary to analyse economics problems. I hope that you enjoy it.

Why study economics?

All around you are issues that an understanding of economics will help you analyse.

- What are the dangers of businesses becoming too powerful and gaining monopoly power?
- If the UK government introduced tariffs and quotas to protect UK businesses from foreign competition would this actually be good for the UK economy?
- Is there more the government could or should do to help the UK economy grow faster?
- What will happen to house prices in the future? Should you buy or rent?
- Why is water which is essential to life relatively cheap whilst diamonds are expensive?
- If a business pollutes, should we just stop it producing?
- Is competition good for consumers?
- Should the European Union intervene in agricultural markets to stabilise prices?

Hopefully the answers to some of these questions will become clearer as you read this book but an understanding of Economics will not just help you understand more about the world around you—it will also help you to make more sense of issues that directly affect you. For example:

- You studied at school. The resources available at your school and factors such as the class size are likely to be determined by how much money the government has available and the extent to which education is its priority.

- You go to university. This used to be free in England but now you have to pay as the government cannot afford to fund universities—its financial position which in turn depends on how well the economy is doing and therefore how much revenue it can earn from taxes affects your fees.

- You have a part-time job. The wage you were paid used to be determined by market forces of supply and demand but now the government has intervened and set a minimum wage.

- You buy food—the price of this is very dependent on supply and demand conditions. A drought, for example, may increase food prices.

- You buy goods and services—the amount you can afford to buy depends on your income and their prices which depend on factors such as the degree of competition in the market and costs.

- You buy petrol. The price of this is influenced by the world supply which in turn is influenced by the cartel of Oil Petroleum Exporting Countries (OPEC) and world demand.

- You go abroad on holiday. The cost of the holiday depends on the exchange rate. Whether you need a visa to travel depends on the extent to which countries are integrated and whether they are part of a union of some form.

- You graduate and apply for a job. The number of vacancies may depend on the state of the economy. The role of banks, the impact of trade, of investment, and of government policy will all have affected this.

- You get a job—how much you earn is likely to be affected by the supply of labour to this industry and the demand for labour. The amount of money you take home depends on the government's taxation policy. The amount you can buy with your earnings depends on the price level. What you spend it on depends on relative prices. The incentive to save depends on the interest rate.

- You want to buy somewhere to live—you need to borrow money. The banking system will affect what funds are available and the cost of borrowing money.

- You put some of your savings into shares—the value of these depend on demand for shares.

You can see from the few scenarios above that economic factors play a big role in everyone's life and that's why studying economics is useful if not essential!

Microeconomics

PART 1

What is economics?

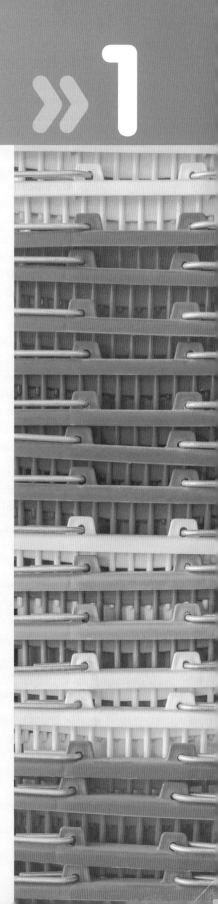

In this chapter, we set out to explain the fundamental issues in economics. These issues centre on the ideas of scarcity and choice. At any moment, there are limited resources available in an economy and so choices have to be made about how to use them most efficiently. This chapter considers how these choices might be made, as well as introducing a number of key economic concepts. Once we have understood the basic concepts of scarcity and choice and the fundamental economic problems this generates we will examine the different ways in which these problems may be solved.

LEARNING OBJECTIVES

By the end of this chapter, you should be able to:

✓ understand the basic economic problems of deciding what is produced, how it is produced, and for whom it is produced;

✓ understand the different types of economy, such as the free market economy, the command (or planned) economy, and the mixed economy;

✓ explain the difference between positive and normative economics;

✓ explain the difference between microeconomics and macroeconomics;

✓ understand some of the key terms and concepts in economics that you will need in your analysis.

▦ The basic economic problem

At the moment, you are likely to have many different things on your 'to do' list, such as write an essay, see friends, or go to a film. The problem is that you do not have enough time to do them all immediately, so you are going to have to make choices about which ones really matter and which need to be done first. You may decide to stay in and study; by staying in and writing your essay, you may get a better degree, and this will benefit you in the long run. On the other hand, maybe you should go out and enjoy yourself now, even though the consequence of this may be that the essay is not handed in, your grades suffer, and you do not do as well as you hoped academically. Which course of action you choose depends on your priorities and your future plans; this will affect how you use your time. Whatever you decide to do is likely to involve sacrificing another option. Going out a lot may mean sacrificing a better grade; staying in all of the time means sacrificing the fun of going out. Faced with the constraint of limited time, you have to make choices; choosing one option involves sacrificing another. Similarly, when you go shopping, there are many things that you might want to buy with your money, but with a limited income, you have to make a decision about what is best for you. You may want the latest iPad, iPhone, Xbox, and Glastonbury tickets, but these may not all be affordable in one go.

In fact, every day in many different situations you are having to choose between alternatives and this highlights the fundamental problem facing not only you as an individual, but also economies as a whole. At any moment in time, the amount of goods and services that an economy can produce is determined by the resources that it has available. These resources include the following.

- **Land** This includes physical land and sea, and the minerals associated with them, such as coal and diamonds. This resource is generally difficult to increase in an economy unless there is a new discovery of a resource such as oil.

- **Labour** This includes the number of people willing and able to work in an economy, and the skills that they have. The size of the workforce will vary if there is immigration into a country or if there is a change in the school-leaving age or retirement age.

- **Capital** This involves the quantity and quality of capital equipment in an economy, such as machinery, offices, and transport. If businesses invest in capital goods, this will increase the capital stock of a country over time.

- **Entrepreneurship** This refers to the ability of managers to think of new ideas, to manage people effectively, and to take risks. The political, legal, and economic environment in an economy can affect the willingness of people to innovate and the ease with which they can turn their ideas into reality successfully.

The quantity and quality of these resources will vary between countries: some countries have bigger populations than others or more natural resources. The resources will also change over time—for example, a higher birth rate or more investment into technology increases the resources available. However, at any given moment, the amount and quality of resources in any region are fixed. This places a limit on what can be produced. With a given number of people, machines, resources, and ideas, there will be a limit to the output that can be produced.

Economics in context — Key UK population data

On the day of the 2011 census

- There were 63.2 million people in the UK
- There were 31 million men and 32.2 million women in the UK.
- The estimated populations of the four constituent countries of the UK were 53 million people in England, 5.3 million in Scotland, 3.1 million in Wales and 1.8 million in Northern Ireland.
- The population of the UK increased by 4.1 million (7 per cent) between 2001 and 2011.
- The population of the UK aged 65 and over was 10.4 million (16 per cent of the UK population) in 2011, 9.4 million in 2001 (16 per cent) and 2.2 million in 1911 (5 per cent).

Latest provisional data show that there was a net flow of 163,000 migrants to the UK in the year ending June 2012, which is significantly lower than the net flow of 247,000 in the year ending June 2011.

- 515,000 people immigrated to the UK in the year ending June 2012, which is significantly lower than the 589,000 who migrated the previous year. This decrease has caused the fall in net migration.
- 352,000 emigrants left the UK in the year ending June 2012, similar to the estimate of 342,000 in the year to June 2011.

Source: ONS

? Questions

What factors do you think influence:

- natural changes in the population?
- net migration into a country?

What impact do these changes have on the economy?
Do you think greater immigration would be good or bad for the UK economy?

Put into practice

Which of the following is not a resource?

- the labour force
- machinery
- natural resources
- finished products

Entrepreneurial culture

The UK is said to have a less entrepreneurial culture than the USA. In the USA, it is not regarded as unusual if business people fail at some point: it is all part of the entrepreneurial learning curve. In the UK, failure is looked on less favourably. Starting up again once you have been made bankrupt has been very difficult in the past in the UK. However, recent changes of legislation have enabled entrepreneurs to get started again and to cancel their debts more quickly. Also, television programmes such as *Dragon's Den* and *The Apprentice* have helped to raise the profile of business, and may lead to more entrepreneurs in the future.

? Questions

Why does it matter whether an economy has an entrepreneurial culture?

How can a government encourage entrepreneurship?

Whilst the amount that can be produced at any moment in an economy may be limited due to limited resources, what we want as consumers certainly is not. We want lots of everything! When we go shopping, for example, we are often tempted by many different things on the shelves even if we know that we cannot afford them all. Similarly, there are many different things that we might want to do with our time, but we cannot fit it all in. The problem is that our resources constrain us. As consumers, we face the problems of scarcity and choice: we would like to do and have everything, but because our resources are scarce, we must make choices. Similarly, within an economy, the scarcity of resources means that choices have to be made regarding how these limited resources are best used.

This concept of scarcity and choice is critical to the study of economics. All of us—whether we are consumers, employees, investors, firms, or policymakers—need to consider how best to use the resources that we have: Which job should we accept? How should we use our time? In which businesses should we invest? What should we buy? These are all decisions that need to be made because of scarcity. Scarcity is a constraint on decision making—the limit on time, people, and other resources—limits what we can do.

In the case of an economy, the constraint provided by the resources available leads to three fundamental questions, as illustrated in Figure 1.1.

- **What is to be produced?** Given that an economy cannot produce everything, decisions have to be made about the right combination of goods and services, given its resources. For example, should an economy's resources be used for the production of flat-screen TVs, hospitals, schools, or smartphones? Do you think that it is better for an economy to produce more cars, more music, or more hotels?

- **How to produce?** The fact that there are a limited number of people and limited amounts of land, capital, and entrepreneurship in an economy means that decisions

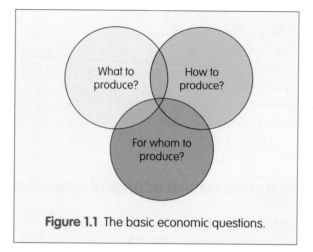

Figure 1.1 The basic economic questions.

have to be made about the best way of producing a given level of output. Given the various products that we want to produce, how should we allocate our employees between different sectors? Should we use the machinery and equipment that we have to produce the houses we want or should we use it to produce the medicines that we want?

- **For whom to produce?** As well as deciding *what* is being produced, an economy needs to decide *for whom* it is producing. Should items produced be distributed equally, so that everyone has the same access to goods and services, or should some people be allowed to have more products than others? How should it be decided who gets what has been produced?

When solving these basic economic problems, we encounter the concept of opportunity cost. Opportunity cost measures what has been sacrificed in the next-best alternative— that is, it considers what is being sacrificed to achieve a particular combination of goods and services.

The concept of opportunity cost is an important one for all of us. When deciding to study at university, you naturally consider the money that you will lose in the short run by not taking a job immediately. Once at university if you spend more time on one topic, you sacrifice time on other ones. By spending more time on your part-time job, you are spending less time studying. Any decision involves a sacrifice and therefore an opportunity cost. In terms of the economy as a whole, if we put more resources into one industry, then those resources are coming out of somewhere else: more resources going into the health service, for example, may mean fewer resources in the defence industry. Similarly, if someone decides to work in the computer industry, then he or she is not working in teaching: we get more computer programmes and fewer lectures (which may or may not be a good thing for the economy as a whole). Economics is therefore based on choices, and this can be seen in government when political parties debate how best to use the resources of an economy and to what extent people should have the same access to products.

What do you think?

Imagine that you have finished your undergraduate degree and are considering studying for a masters.

What would be the opportunity cost of this decision?

What would determine whether studying for a masters would be the right decision for you or not?

▓ Solving the fundamental economic questions

Identifying the fundamental economic questions is one thing; working out the 'best' answers is another and generates much discussion. The way in which these questions of 'what?', 'how?', and 'for whom?' are solved will vary from one economy to another. One option is to have a government take full responsibility for the economy and for the allocation of resources. This is a very interventionist approach and would occur in a planned (or command) economy.

In a planned economy, the government decides:

- what goods and services should be produced—for example, the government may decide that education is a priority and allocate a significant number of resources into this area; alternatively, it might decide that greater manufacturing production is the priority; equally, it may decide not to produce many sunglasses or cosmetics;

- the combination of resources, such as the quantity of machines and people employed in any particular industry, including who works where (jobs would be allocated to workers rather than individuals choosing for themselves what they want to do as a career); and

- the way in which goods and services are distributed—for example, everyone may be given access to free education and health care; prices, wages, and rents may be determined by the government.

In a planned economy, the government takes an overview of the economy and makes the key decisions rather than let these be made by individual consumers, employees, and businesses. Economies in which the government has played a large role include those of North Korea, Cuba, and China.

A completely different approach is to leave the solutions to these questions to free market forces. This means that the government does not intervene, and leaves all decisions to individuals and private firms to work out for themselves. If there is a demand for a particular product and firms can produce it at a profit, then it will be produced, because businesses will want to supply rather than because the government has told them that they must do so. If you want to work in a particular industry, you can do so, and your decision to work there will be linked to the rewards available rather than whether you have been told to by the government. If using more machinery seems to generate a high return, then firms will invest in equipment rather than use labour, because this makes financial sense.

This free market approach has the advantage of not needing a central government to decide everything (which is extremely complex, and may be bureaucratic and inefficient);

instead, decisions are made separately in many millions of individual markets by firms and their customers. Each firm pursues its own objectives and focuses purely on what it wants, as does each individual. There is no need for a central body to make decisions for everyone in the country. This means that a free market can avoid the dangers of a very cumbersome central planning system that needs to gather huge amounts of data and send out millions of directives. A free market approach should also mean that what is produced is definitely in demand (because if it is not demanded, then firms will not produce it), whereas if a government is in control, then it may order certain things to be produced only to find that they are not actually required and that no one wants to buy them. In this case, there would be waste.

In a free market, therefore, there is an incentive for firms to be competitive, and to develop new services and new ways of doing things. Being more efficient and meeting customer needs more precisely can boost profits, which firms or individuals can keep for themselves. The potential benefits from innovating mean that there is likely to be greater choice for customers. In the planned economy, any gains in one industry go back to the government to be used elsewhere, so there is not the same incentive to be efficient because the firm or individual does not personally gain.

However, the free market has many potential failings and imperfections. For example, some goods or services may not be provided because they are not profitable, even if some people might think that they are things that should be provided (for example, educational television programmes, the opera, museums, and libraries). On the other hand, some products, such as guns and drugs, may be openly available because they are profitable, even though society as a whole may think that they are undesirable. In the free market, products are available only if people can afford them; in the case of services such as health and education, this may be felt to be unacceptable. And what about housing? Do you think everyone has a right to somewhere to live even if they cannot afford it in a free market? If so you may need government intervention.

The pursuit of profit may also lead to unsafe products being produced, labour being exploited, consumers being badly informed, and businesses engaging in corruption to win orders. Consumers may be misled as businesses chase sales and don't care how these are achieved. The failings of the free market therefore mean that some intervention by a government is inevitable. The real question is how much intervention there will be—that is, to what extent does a government take responsibility for allocating resources directly, and how much does it regulate the private provision of goods and services? The problems with the free market and the case for intervention are examined in Chapter 7.

What do you think?

Do you think it is a good idea to leave markets to themselves or do you think the government should provide goods and services?

What goods and services do you think should be available free of charge for everyone in an economy? (That is, what products may a government need to provide?)

Can you think of goods and services that may be profitable to provide, but which you think should not be available in an economy? (That is, what goods and services might a government need to intervene to prevent?)

Table 1.1 Comparison of the free market and a planned economy

Free market	Planned economy
Resources allocated by market forces of supply and demand	Resources allocated by government directives
Firms aim to maximize profits	Social objectives; i.e want the best for society
Individuals make decisions to maximize their own welfare	Decisions made by central authority; no incentive for individuals or firms to try to be more efficient or to innovate
Incentive to be efficient to make more profits because businesses keep these	May be bureaucratic; there are huge amounts of information to gather and process, and millions of decisions to be made—all of which could lead to inefficiency
Competition can encourage innovation	May lack competition in markets

Mixed economies

In reality, no economy is completely free market or completely planned. All economies are a combination of the two (see Figure 1.2); this is known as a mixed economy. In a mixed economy, some goods and services are provided by the government, such as education and the police force. Other goods and services, such as mobile phones, laptops, and trainers, may be provided by private firms. However, whilst a mixed economy, in which the government steps in when the free market fails, may be the obvious solution by combining the best of the two systems, this still leaves open many questions, such as the following.

- To what extent should the government intervene?
- In what areas should it intervene? Should it provide transport, energy, and postal services? What about housing, dental care, broadband, and leisure facilities?
- How should the government intervene: does it need to provide products itself? Can it provide products in partnership with private firms? Should it let private firms provide some products, but regulate them, and if so, how?

The trend in many economies for much of the last 30 years has been for governments to intervene less in their economies. In the UK in the 1990s, for example, many companies

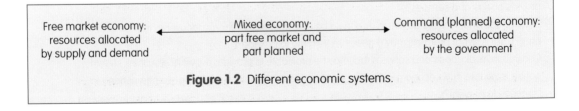

Figure 1.2 Different economic systems.

What do you think?

In a free market, tobacco would probably be widely consumed because people would be willing and able to pay for it. However, we may think that this is wrong and the government should intervene in this market. Do you think that the government should:

a. ignore smoking on the grounds that it is not its role to intervene?

b. ban smoking?

c. tax tobacco more heavily?

d. spend more on anti-smoking promotional campaigns?

e. decide to focus on other issues?

Which of the above do you recommend and why?

such as British Gas, British Steel, and British Airways were taken out of government control and sold to private firms. This process of selling government assets to private individuals and organizations is called privatization. In other sectors, the government has not sold off organizations, but has removed restrictions to allow more firms to compete: this is called deregulation. However, in some economies, notably in South America in recent years, there has been greater government intervention, because electors have felt that their societies would benefit if the government were to take greater responsibility for the provision of goods and services, and reduce the income gap between rich and poor. The global economic crisis in 2008 and 2009 has also made many governments look at whether an approach of privatization and deregulation has been effective. Leaving financial markets unregulated, for example, seemed to have led to speculative high-risk borrowing, which later threatened the banking system and created a strong argument for more intervention.

What do you think?

Would you prefer more or less government intervention in the economy?

Put into practice

Which of the following statements are true and which are false?

a. The free market relies on government intervention.

b. The basic economic problems are: What to produce? When to produce? Why to produce?

c. The free market may lead to income inequality.

The decisions about the extent and method of government intervention are therefore continually being made and reviewed by governments, and their electorate. Almost every day,

In 2013 it was suggested that no-risk shares should be offered to all taxpayers when the government sells its stakes in RBS and Lloyds. The organization, Policy Exchange, recommended that most of the state-owned bank shares are offered to all British residents at no initial cost. The shares would only have to be paid for when they were sold. If the price fell, the government would retain them and bear the loss.

The UK goverment owns 81 per cent of RBS and 39 per cent of Lloyds after the banks were bailed out financially during the recent economic crisis.

Policy Exchange proposed that anyone aged over 18, who was a National Insurance number and registered to vote, would be able to apply for the shares. That would be around 48 million people. The sale of these shares would be the largest public share issue since British Gas and British Telecom were sold off in the 1980s. This proposal would create a whole new generation of shareholders.

However critics argue that as with some previous privatizations shareholders would simply sell these shares the next day.

? Questions

Analyse why the government might want to sell off these shares.

Discuss the factors that might influence the price of the shares.

Do you think the way of selling the shares outlined by the Policy Exchange is a good one?

there are discussions over the appropriate balance between private and public sector, and the extent of government intervention. In the UK in 2009, the government took control of the majority of shares in the Royal Bank of Scotland to protect the banking system. In the USA in 2013, President Obama increased the government provision of health care despite much opposition. In recent years many governments have had to reduce the amount of services they provide because of financial problems. Think about a typical day and you will realize the number of areas in which there are debates over the role of government: Should the government provide more homes? Should it control rents? Should it run the transport system? Should it fund universities and students studying there? Should it control the rate of interest charged on borrowing? Should it control what people eat? Should it regulate whether we can gamble or not?

These questions all require a view about whether the free market is better at allocating resources than a command economy and the extent to which a government is needed. Your role as a voter is to elect a government that has economic policies with which you agree. In part, this depends on whether you trust individuals and firms to make decisions for themselves without government control, or whether you think that the government needs to intervene to make the economy work effectively. If we leave businesses to themselves, will we get better products as they compete amongst themselves, or will we get false accounting, environmentally unfriendly production processes, and unsafe products?

These issues of government intervention, and the benefits and limitations of the free market economy, are examined in more detail in Chapter 7.

What do you think?

What goods and services does the government provide in your economy? How does this differ from another economy with which you are familiar?

Do you think that the government should intervene more or less in your economy? In what way(s)?

What services do you think would be better provided by the government? Why?

What services do you think would be better run by the private sector? Why?

Types of economics

The study of economics is vital to understand the society around you. Whether you like it or not economic decisions are all around you and impact on you as a consumer (the prices and availability of products), an employee (what work is available and what you are paid), and as a taxpayer (how much you pay and what it is used for).

This book will cover many of the essential issues in the study of economics, including an overview of different types of economics, such as those described below.

Economics in context

When the election result in the UK seemed inconclusive in 2010, a Conservative and Liberal Democrat alliance was rapidly agreed because of fears of what would happen to the economy if a government were not quickly elected to start making vital decisions. When Bill Clinton was standing for election as US President in 1992 against George Bush, he reminded all of his team that winning an election was 'all about the economy, stupid'—that is, if you can convince electors that you will look after the economy, and their jobs and incomes, you will win the election. When Pervez Musharraf, became the first ever person in Pakistan to become Prime Minister for the third time, he said his top three priorities were the economy, the economy, and the economy. He argued that getting the economy to grow would reduce unemployment, help growth, and bring more stability to the country. The economy will affect almost every aspect of your own life and the state of the country in which you live. That's why studying it makes sense!

? Question

Why do you think the economy is so important to politicians?

Positive and normative economics

- **Positive economics** examines the different relationships between economic variables and provides an analysis of these that can actually be tested. For example, we may think that an increase in demand for a product will increase its price, that more government spending will lead to faster growth in the economy, or that lower income taxes provide more incentive to work. These relationships can be tested over time to see whether they actually occur. Data can be collected and analysed to assess the validity of such claims, so this is positive economics. The research should show whether any particular claim is correct although identifying the impact of any one individual variable when so much is changing can be difficult.

- **Normative economics**, by comparison, focuses on value judgements about what you think should happen. For example, you might think that the government should spend more money on the health service compared with defence, that it ought to divert resources away from the education sector towards biotechnology, or that it should cut inheritance taxes even if it has to cut spending as a result. These are your opinions; they represent your view of what should be done or what is most important for the economy. You cannot test these ideas, because they are simply opinions of what matters and what you think needs to be done. Not surprisingly, normative economics is the area of economics in which most of the disagreements between policymakers occur! These differences are often at the heart of the manifestos of political parties. Everyone might agree that an increase in spending on health and education could improve the services in these sectors, but they may disagree enormously on which one of these is the priority or exactly how the money should be raised and used or whether these should be the focus of government policy.

What do you think?

Normative economics is based on your views about economic issues. What do you think about the following issues:

Do you think that the government should regulate gambling or should it be left to the free market? Why?

Do you think that medical care should be free or should it be charged for?

Do you think that the government should tax cigarettes and alcohol more heavily?

Do you think that the level of income at which you start to pay income tax should be relatively high or low? Do you think that the rate of income tax should be increased?

Why do you think that the way in which governments deal with the issues above varies from country to country?

Microeconomics and macroeconomics

- **Microeconomics** focuses on the individual decisions of households and firms. It focuses on the demand and supply for goods and services within a particular market, such as the market for housing or labour. It helps to explain the price of a good, your decision whether to work in a particular industry, or the impact of an increase in the supply of a product. Microeconomics might analyse the determinants of the price of oil or a firm's shares, for example.

- **Macroeconomics** analyses the economy as a whole ('macro' means big, whereas 'micro' means small). For example, rather than focus on the price level in one market (micro-economics), macroeconomics considers the general price level in the economy; rather than examine one individual's decision whether to work, it considers the overall numbers employed in the economy. Macroeconomics therefore deals with topics such as inflation, unemployment, economic growth, and international trade, and usually analyses these from a government's perspective.

Put into practice

Are the following micro or macro economic issues?

- The price of fish
- The growth of the UK economy
- The supply of housing in Oxford
- The UK government needs to increase the number of people employed

Are the following normative or positive economics?

- Lower interest rates lead to more spending in the economy
- Higher taxes on alcohol will reduce consumption
- The government should focus more on reducing inflation than growth
- The government needs to spend more on health care

Key terms and concepts in economics

In order to find your way around a foreign country it is often necessary to learn the language to make sure you really understand what is going on. Similarly to study economics effectively, you need to learn the language of the subject. The following are some of the key terms and concepts that you will need to help you on your journey.

Goods and services

- **Goods** are physical products, such as televisions and washing machines. They are tangible—that is, you can see them and touch them.
- **Services,** by comparison, are intangible—for example, education and banking are services.

In reality, most organizations provide a combination of goods and services. When you visit a restaurant, you buy a meal (tangible), but you also receive service and benefit from the experience of the overall environment. In this book, we use the term 'product' to include goods, services, and combinations of the two.

Consumer goods and capital goods

- **Consumer goods** are goods and services that are consumed by the final user—for example, magazines and sandwiches are bought by, or given to, the person who is going to consume them.
- **Capital goods** are goods that are bought to use in the production process—that is, they are bought to produce other goods and services. A production line is used to make products, such as cans of soup, which are then sold to customers to be consumed. A fleet of lorries is bought to distribute products. Lorries and production lines are, therefore, capital goods.

The decision by firms and governments over whether to spend money on consumer goods—which increases today's consumption—or on capital goods—which involves investment for the future at the expense of today's consumption—has important implications for the long-term growth of an economy. Would you buy shares in a business that invested all of its profits into new product development? Or would you prefer no investment in new products? Would you vote for a government that was investing heavily in long-term construction projects if it meant less provision in the short term of benefits to the elderly, ill, or unemployed?

Households also make these choices: do you spend your bonus on a holiday (consumption) or an extension to the house (investment)? Decisions about how much to save and how much to spend have important economic implications for your lifestyle today and in the future.

What do you think?

How important do you think it is to save money for your pension?

If the government were to have £100 billion to spend, do you think that it should use the funds to invest in education or should it be given away in the form of lower taxes?

For many years Apple did not pay dividends to its shareholders; instead managers kept the funds for investment. Do you think this is a good idea for all businesses?

Investment, savings, and consumption

The word 'investment' is often used in the media to mean money that is 'invested' into shares or banks. In economics, however, these are called savings. Savings represent the income of households that is not spent on consumption (that is, on buying goods and services): for example, savings include money put into a bank or into a pension fund. The term 'investment' in economics refers to the purchase of capital goods: for example, firms investing in new equipment that will be used to produce products in the future. Firms may invest in a new factory or information technology systems, for example.

Private and public sector

- The **private sector** is made up of organizations owned by individuals and firms. Companies such as Tesco plc and Barclays Bank plc are owned by private investors, as opposed to the government. Although the plc stands for a 'public limited company', these firms are in the private sector, because they are privately owned by the public. In the private sector, the owners can pursue their own interests; we usually assume that this is to maximize profits. Businesses will seek to produce products where they can make the most profits; if the rewards are not high enough, they will shift resources elsewhere in search of better returns.

- **Public sector** organizations are run by the government—for example, the National Health Service (NHS). These organizations may have social objectives as well as, or instead of, profit targets. The government may measure success in a much broader way than private businesses do: it may consider the effect on jobs, on happiness, on inequality, on the community, and the environment.

Your view of what businesses are there to do and whether pursuing profit is desirable (whether it leads to innovation or to too much power and unethical behaviour, for example) will influence your view of the 'right' mix of the private and public sector.

What do you think?

Identify two organizations run by the government in your economy. Why do you think the government runs these organizations? What are their objectives?

Do you think that all organizations should be owned by the government?

Economics in context   China

China's economy over the past 30 years has changed from a centrally planned system that was fairly closed to international trade to a freer market economy with a rapidly growing private sector. Reforms started in the late 1970s with the reduction of state-run agriculture, more independence for government organizations, less regulation of enterprises and markets, and more free market businesses. This reshaping of the economy and resulting efficiency gains have helped lead to a tenfold increase in gross domestic product (GDP) since 1978, making China the second-largest economy in the world after the USA.

❓ Questions

What is a centrally planned system and what benefits does this have?

Why do you think that China might have moved from a centrally planned system to a freer market economy?

How might this move affect:

- businesses?

- consumers?

Economic models

An economy is made up of millions of households and firms, all of which are making many different decisions in many different markets. Not even the most powerful computer in the world could track all of the decisions and transactions happening in an economy every day. To understand the economy, therefore, economists build models, which make assumptions about how different aspects of the economy work. These are simplifications of reality, but provided that they help to analyse what a particular outcome will be, then they remain useful. We may predict, for example, that a market will move from A to B; in reality, it may move from A to C to B—but nevertheless the model can have some validity because it predicts the end destination. Of course, models of the economy will be continually reviewed, and new theories and approaches are being developed. This is because behaviours alter, the environment in which decisions are being made changes, and we gain new insights into what is determining decision making.

Obviously, economics may not always relate to the specific decisions of a particular individual or business firm; some people and some firms will always act differently from the majority. However, economics focuses on the overall market, sector, region, or country, and seeks to explain the general behaviour within these areas. We assume, for example, that consumers are rational. If a consumer is asked to choose between something that is very good or something that is average, we assume that he or she will choose the very good. Of course, one particular person may be perverse and may not choose this, but it is likely that the vast majority will do as assumed! We also assume that firms try to profit-maximize. This is discussed in detail in Chapter 10 and is open to some debate. However, regardless of whether all firms seek to profit-maximize and even regardless of whether all succeed, if this is what the majority are trying to do, then the model has some value in terms of predicting the price and output outcome in a given market situation.

Economics in context

When retailers want to gain more sales they often cut the price. However according to a recent article in the *Journal of Marketing*, they might be better offering something extra. According to researchers at the University of Minnesota, buyers prefer more benefits to a lower price. This may be because they fail to understand basic mathematics! For example, consumers often struggle to appreciate that a 50 per cent increase in quantity is the same as a 33 per cent cut in price. They almost all think the former is better than the latter. In their study the researchers sold 73 per cent more hand lotion when it was offered in a bonus pack than when it had an equivalent discount. This focus on extra benefits can affect promotional strategies as well—better to stress the extra miles you can get for a fuel-efficient car than the reduction in fuel usage.

Studies have also shown that consumers like double discounts. They prefer a product that has been reduced by 20 per cent, and then by another 25 per cent, to one which has been subject to an equivalent, one-off, 40 per cent reduction.

? Question

Do you think you are rational when making buying decisions? Review some of your recent purchases and decide!

Economic modelling helps us to understand what has happened in a market or economy, and why; this is therefore helpful to analyse what has happened and to predict what will occur in the future, which is essential to managers and policymakers. Economic change affects billions of people in terms of what is produced, the standard of living in a society, the income distribution in an economy, economic growth, and the quality of their lives. Being able to predict the economic environment and to analyse how best to change behaviours is critical to governments.

> **What do you think?**
>
> What do you think is the main economic issue facing your country? Why?

Deciding at the margin

Two of the most important and powerful concepts in economics are those of marginal cost and marginal benefit. Whoever you are and whatever you do, you should consider the marginal (or extra) costs and benefits of your actions. If the extra cost of doing something is less than the extra benefit, then do not do it! By doing it, your overall welfare or happiness will fall. Equally, if the extra benefit from doing something is greater than the extra cost, then do it: if you do, you will gain. This concept of measuring things at the margin in order to work out what is best is important to remember and can be used when analysing any situation. If you do not like something, then this does not mean that you should stop it altogether, but you cut back to the point at which marginal cost equals marginal benefit.

Let us consider air travel: many people claim that this has terrible environmental effects. This is true—but it also brings many benefits: it helps to move supplies around for firms; it creates jobs; and it provides individuals with the opportunity to do business, and to travel and holiday abroad. An economist would argue that air travel should be undertaken up to the point at which the marginal cost equals the marginal benefit. If the marginal benefit of an activity exceeds its marginal costs, do more, because you will be better off; if its marginal benefit is less than its marginal cost, do less, because if you do it, you will be worse off. When marginal benefit equals marginal cost, your welfare cannot increase by consuming another unit and so you have maximized your welfare.

The marginal concept is examined in more detail in Chapter 10.

Real and nominal

- **Nominal** values in economics are those given at the current wages and prices. The amount of money that you receive in your wage packet is a nominal sum. It shows how much you have been given, but does not reveal what you can actually buy with it.

- A **real** figure takes account of inflation. If, for example, you receive a pay increase of 2 per cent, then in nominal terms, you are 2 per cent better off. However, if the prices of items that you buy have generally increased by 2 per cent, then in real terms, you are in the same position in which you were originally; there has been no real increase.

It is always important to think in terms of the 'real' (that is, the inflation-adjusted) effect, not only the nominal.

Put into practice

Which of the following statements are true and which are false?

a. A government-run organization is part of the public sector

b. Real wages have taken account of inflation

c. If the marginal cost of an activity equals the marginal benefit there is no value in undertaking this activity at all

d. Capital goods are an investment for the future

Case study

The following passage is an overview of the UK economy taken from the CIA factbook.

The UK, a leading trading power and financial center, is the second largest economy in Europe after Germany. Over the past two decades, the government has greatly reduced public ownership and contained the growth of social welfare programs. Agriculture is intensive, highly mechanized, and efficient by European standards, producing about 60% of food needs with less than 2% of the labor force. The UK has large coal, natural gas, and oil resources, but its oil and natural gas reserves are declining and the UK became a net importer of energy in 2005. Services, particularly banking, insurance, and business services, account by far for the largest proportion of GDP while industry continues to decline in importance. After emerging from recession in 1992, Britain's economy enjoyed the longest period of expansion on record during which time growth outpaced most of Western Europe. In 2008, however, the global financial crisis hit the economy particularly hard, due to the importance of its financial sector. Sharply declining home prices, high consumer debt, and the global economic slowdown compounded Britain's economic problems, pushing the economy into recession in the latter half of 2008 and prompting the then Brown (Labour) government to implement a number of measures to stimulate the economy and stabilize the financial markets; these include nationalizing parts of the banking system, temporarily cutting taxes, suspending public sector borrowing rules, and moving forward public spending on capital projects. Facing burgeoning public deficits and debt levels, in 2010 the Cameron-led coalition government (between Conservatives and Liberal Democrats) initiated a five-year austerity program, which aimed to lower London's budget deficit from over 10% of GDP in 2010 to nearly 1% by 2015. In November 2011, Chancellor of the Exchequer George Osborne announced additional austerity measures through to 2017 because of slower-than-expected economic growth and the impact of the euro-zone debt crisis. The Cameron government raised the value added tax from 17.5% to 20% in 2011. It has pledged to reduce the corporation tax rate to 21% by 2014. The Bank of England (BoE) implemented an asset purchase program of up to £375 billion (approximately $605 billion) as of December 2012.

Source: CIA Factbook, https://www.cia.gov/library/publications/the-world-factbook/geos/uk.html

? Questions

1 What are some of the key economic issues facing the UK in recent years?

2 Why do think the UK is mainly service based?

3 In what ways does the UK government intervene in the economy?

Review questions

1 State the three key economic problems facing any economy.

2 How do different types of economies try to solve the basic economic problems?

3 Explain how the government intervenes in your economy. Has this intervention increased or decreased in recent years?

4 Explore how the concepts of scarcity and choice affect you in your day-to-day life.

5 Explain the difference between nominal and real wages.

6 Explain the meaning of opportunity cost.

7 Analyse how the concept of opportunity cost relates to your decision to go to university.

8 Explain the difference between the private sector and the public sector.

Put into practice

1 Which activities in the UK are undertaken by the public sector? Compare this with one other economy of your choice. If there are differences in what the government provides in these countries, why do you think this might be?

2 Identify one policy the UK government has introduced recently to affect the economy. Explain what the policy is and why this policy has been introduced.

Assignment questions

1 Look in the news this week and identify one key current economic issue relevant to the UK or another economy. Summarize the issues involved in the debate.

2 Research the jobs market for graduate economists. From this summarize the skills required to be an economist.

Key learning points

- Resources in an economy are limited at any moment; consumer wants are unlimited.

- Economics considers the key economic questions of what is produced, how it is produced, and for whom it is it produced.

- The key economic questions can be answered by market forces of supply and demand (in a free market), by the government (in a planned economy), or by a combination of the two (in a mixed economy).

- Microeconomics focuses on what happens in a particular market.

- Macroeconomics focuses on the economy as a whole.

- Normative economics is based on opinions; positive economics focuses on facts.

 Visit our Online Resource Centre at http://www.oxfordtextbooks.co.uk/orc/gillespie_econ3e/ for test questions and further information on topics covered in this chapter.

The production possibility frontier (PPF)

» 2

The starting point in our economic analysis is to consider what an economy can produce given its resources. As consumers, we may want many things, but there is a limit to what our economy can actually produce to meet these demands. These issues of scarcity and choice can be analysed using the production possibility frontier (PPF). In this chapter, we examine the factors that determine how much an economy can produce and the implications of different output decisions. We then will go on to consider the different economic systems and how they solve the questions of what to produce, how to produce, and for whom to produce.

LEARNING OBJECTIVES

By the end of this chapter, you should be able to:

✓ understand what is meant by a production possibility frontier (PPF), also known as a production possibility curve (PPC);

✓ analyse the shape and the position of the PPF;

✓ understand the concept of productive efficiency;

✓ understand the concept of economic growth.

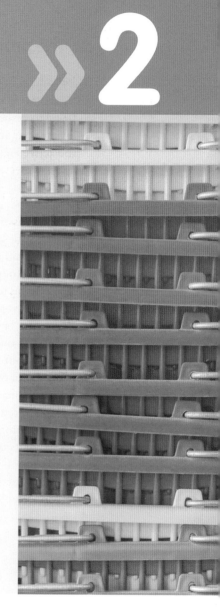

▨ Scarcity and choice

In Chapter 1, we saw how the study of economics was based around the issue of scarcity and choice. As consumers, our wants are unlimited, but there is a limit to what an economy can produce because of a scarcity of resources. What an economy is capable of producing can be shown on a production possibility frontier (PPF), also known as a production possibility curve (PPC).

■ The production possibility frontier (PPF)

The Producton Possibility Frontier shows the maximum output that can be produced in an economy at any given moment, given the resources available. If an economy is fully utilizing its resources efficiently, then it will be producing on the PPF.

To keep our analysis simple, we consider an economy that produces only two products: A and B (see Figure 2.1). Imagine that all of an economy's resources, such as land, labour, and capital, were used efficiently in industry A; then Q0 of A would be produced and no B would be made. Alternatively, if all resources were transferred to industry B, then Q5 of B would be produced and no units of A would be made. If resources were divided between the two industries, then a range of combinations of products is possible. For example, at point X, the economy produces Q1 of product A and Q2 of product B; alternatively, resources could be allocated differently between the two industries and it could produce at point Y, producing Q3 of A and Q4 of B. All of the points on the frontier, such as X and Y, are said to have productive efficiency (that is, to be productively efficient) because they are fully utilizing the economy's resources. This is attractive because it shows that resources are being used properly and not wasted. When an economy is productively efficient, it can only produce more of one product by producing less of another; resources have to be shifted from producing one product to another. The PPF therefore illustrates the concept of opportunity costs. As more units of product B are produced, this involves shifting resources into industry B and out of industry A: this will involve sacrificing some units of A in return for more B. The amount of A sacrificed for extra B is the opportunity cost. For example, the opportunity cost of producing the extra Q4 – Q2 units of B is Q1 – Q3 units of A.

In Chapter 1 we learnt that opportunity cost is the sacrifice made when you choose a particular course of action if you choose to do option 1 and give up option 2 then option 2 is the opportunity cost

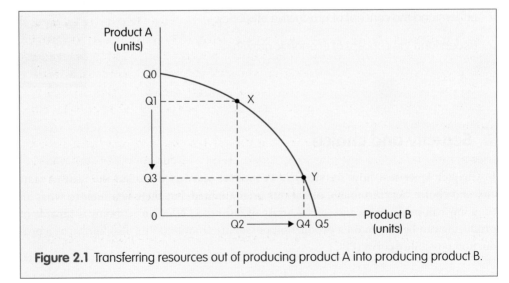

Figure 2.1 Transferring resources out of producing product A into producing product B.

Put into practice

Using Figure 2.2, calculate the opportunity cost of the fifth unit of B in terms of the number of units of A sacrificed.

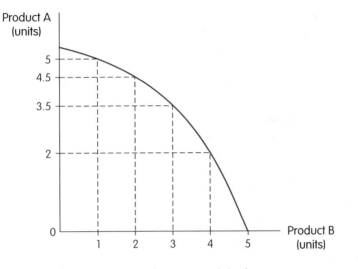

Figure 2.2 A production possibility frontier.

Economics in context

The importance of opportunity cost

The concept of opportunity cost is extremely important in economics and business. It represents the opportunities forgone. Whenever a manager makes a strategic decision, he or she is deciding to lead the business in one direction rather than another. Sometimes this works: for example, Nokia's decision to move out of all of its business areas apart from mobile phones was highly successful for many years. Other times, it is the wrong decision, such as Marks and Spencer's move into the USA, Tesco's launching of Fresh N Easy in the USA, and Walmart's move into Germany. Any decision should be judged not only in terms of what it achieved, but also in terms of what else could have been done with those resources.

Imagine that a firm is earning a return on investment of 0.1 per cent. This means that the profits it earns are 0.1 per cent of the amount of long-term funds in the business. This is clearly better than 0 per cent, but is not better than the rate of interest available in most UK banks. Investors might rightly question how effectively the managers are using the resources available to them.

? Question

If you were to decide to invest money and buy shares in Microsoft, what would the opportunity cost be?

Reallocation of resources

The PPF shows all of the combinations of products that an economy can produce given its present resources. Any combination on the frontier is productively efficient, so to have more of one product produced, there will inevitably be a reduction in the amount of the other produced due to the reallocation of resources. The frontier shows the combinations of products that can be produced efficiently, but which is the right combination? What determines whether an economy should produce at X or Y? Do we want more of product A or more of product B, for example? How do we decide?

Allocating resources in an economy

In a free market economy, the decisions about what to produce are determined by market forces of supply and demand. As these market conditions change the amount of different products produced would change. For example, if there was an increase in demand for product B rather than product A, then it would make this industry more attractive for producers. The greater demand for B would attract firms into this industry and out of A. The firms in industry B would then need more resources, such as labour and materials, to meet the higher demand. This increased demand for resources would increase the price paid for them, attracting resources into this industry and out of industry A. Market forces triggered by an increase in demand for the product would therefore lead to a reallocation of resources from one industry to another. On the PPF shown in Figure 2.3, this can be seen as a movement from X to Y. The demand for digital cameras, for example, has grown rapidly in recent years, whilst the demand for 'traditional' film has declined. As a result, firms have had to move resources out of traditional film and into digital, because that is where the rewards are. Likewise, individuals have had to learn the skills for digital production,

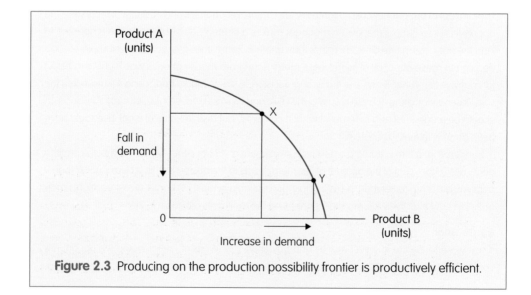

Figure 2.3 Producing on the production possibility frontier is productively efficient.

because that is where the jobs are. Similarly, the music industry has experienced a rapid growth in downloading at the expense of CDs. Companies such as EMI have had to move their resources into these newer areas.

In a planned economy, decisions about what to produce are determined by government instructions and directives. For example, the government may order that more factories and employees are used to produce product B rather than A. In this case, the reallocation from, say, X to Y is not determined by customers' demand, but by government orders.

This intervention may happen if the government does not trust market forces to produce what it regards as the right combinations of products for society. For example, in a free market, consumers may want to consume products today, but may not be very good at thinking about their future—for example, we may not pay enough attention to environmental issues; the government may intervene to ensure that production takes account of these issues.

However, if the instructions given by the government do not match what people are actually demanding, then it can lead to too much of some goods being produced, whilst too few of other goods are available in relation to present demand. The government may decide that resources need to be diverted to defence or nuclear energy, for example, whereas consumers may want more iPads. This can lead to queues and rationing of some products for which demand is high. The lack of the profit incentive may also mean that resources are used inefficiently and that the economy operates within the PPF.

Put into practice

Are the following statements true or false?

a. The PPF shows the amount that consumers want of each product.

b. Any combination of goods inside the PPF is productively efficient.

c. Wants are limited, but resources are unlimited, which means that there is a problem of scarcity and choice.

Economics in context

The following is a description of the North Korean economy from the CIA Factbook.

North Korea, one of the world's most centrally directed and least open economies, faces chronic economic problems. Industrial capital stock is nearly beyond repair as a result of years of underinvestment, shortages of spare parts, and poor maintenance. Large-scale military spending draws off resources needed for investment and civilian consumption. Industrial and power output have stagnated for years at a fraction of pre-1990 levels. Frequent weather-related crop failures aggravated chronic food shortages caused by on-going systemic problems, including a lack of arable land, collective farming practices, poor soil quality, insufficient fertilization, and persistent shortages of tractors and fuel. Large-scale international food aid deliveries as well as aid from China has allowed the people of North Korea to escape widespread starvation since famine threatened in 1995, but the population continues to suffer from prolonged malnutrition and poor living conditions. Since 2002, the government has allowed private "farmers' markets" to begin selling a wider range of goods. It also permitted some private farming – on an experimental basis – in an effort to boost agricultural output.

Source: CIA Factbook

❓ Questions

In what ways are resources being allocated in the North Korean economy?

Discuss some of the problems that centralized control has created for the North Korean economy.

▥ Productive inefficiency

If an economy is producing a combination of products on the PPF, then it is productively efficient. However, an economy may be operating within the frontier (for example, at the point V in Figure 2.4), in which case it is productively inefficient. This is because it could produce more of both products by using the existing resources effectively. Imagine that you are driving around a country and notice lots of factories that are closing down, high levels of unemployment, and shops with very few customers in them; this economy will be productively inefficient. This can be illustrated using a PPF diagram: for example (see Figure 2.4), if an economy were to produce at point W and not V, then it would be making more of both A and B. No

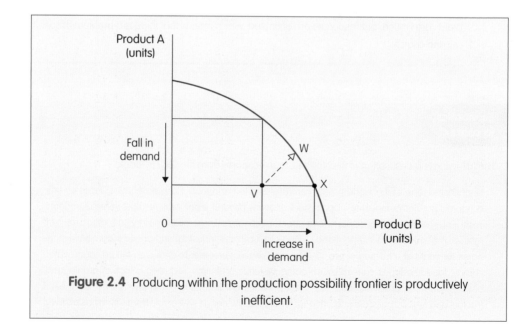

Figure 2.4 Producing within the production possibility frontier is productively inefficient.

economy should be operating within the PPF, because it is wasting its resources. However, this can happen if resources do not reallocate effectively when conditions in an economy alter.

For example, demand for product B may increase, leading to firms wanting to move from A to B. Firms in industry A close down, and, in theory, they and their employees would switch to B. However, if managers and employees lack the necessary skills or experience to work in a different industry they may not be able to move easily. As a result, the economy may get stuck at V which is inefficient. Hopefully, over the long term, employees will be trained and will gain the skills required to take jobs. Firms will therefore be able to produce in industry B, enabling the economy to produce at a point such as X; however, in the short term at least, there is productive inefficiency. Alternatively, there could be a

Economics in context

Over the last 20 years manufacturing in the UK has declined in significance as shown below in Table 2.1. Resources have reallocated into the service sector although they have not all shifted easily and there has been some unemployment as individuals have lacked the right training and skills for the service sector.

Table 2.1 Value of manufacturing output

	2011 prices (£bn)	% change from previous year	% of total economy
1997	186.6	–	18.4%
1998	183.0	−1.9%	17.5%
1999	177.2	−3.2%	16.5%
2000	174.2	−1.6%	15.6%
2001	170.3	−2.3%	14.8%
2002	164.0	−3.7%	13.9%
2003	159.4	−2.8%	13.0%
2004	154.7	−3.0%	12.2%
2005	154.4	−0.2%	11.9%
2006	154.2	−0.2%	11.5%
2007	155.1	+0.6%	11.2%
2008	146.7	−5.4%	10.6%
2009	139.5	−4.9%	10.5%
2010	142.7	+2.4%	10.6%
2011	145.3	+1.8%	10.8%

Source: ONS, series: KKE3 (manufacturing), ABML (total economy)

? Questions

Why do you think manufacturing in the UK has declined?

What do you think are the biggest sectors of the UK economy at the moment?

Using a production possibility frontier diagram, illustrate where the economy might be if resources could not fully reallocate from manufacturing to services.

lack of demand in the economy, so that, although it can produce at W, customers can only afford the combination of products at V. Again, over time, demand will hopefully increase and the economy will end up on the frontier. Another reason for operating within the frontier may be the effect of poor management of the economy, meaning that production is inefficient and people's talents are not utilized fully.

Shifting the production possibility frontier outward

Once on the PPF, an economy can only produce more of both products by shifting the PPF outward—that is, by increasing the amount of both products that can be produced with the economy's resources. This is what happens over time when the capacity of an economy grows. The growth in the potential output of the economy enables more goods and services to become available to consumers. This is known as an increase in the aggregate supply of the economy.

An outward shift of the production possibility frontier might be due to:

- more training and better management of employees, enabling them to be more productive;

- greater investment in capital goods, such as machines and equipment—in the short run, this would mean that resources would have to be shifted from consumption goods toward capital goods, and in the long run, greater investment would enable the economy to produce more products for consumption;

- an increase in the population size, for example through greater net immigration or a rise in the birth rate;

- improvements in technology providing better ways of doing things, such as the improvements in communications technologies in recent years.

Most political parties put forward their policies to help an economy to grow in the future. Voters decide which policies they think are most likely to work. For more about economic growth, see Chapter 21.

What do you think?

How fast is your economy growing at the moment?

What actions would you take to make your economy grow faster if you were in government?

Economics in context

A recent report stated that North America should review its immigration policies with regards to Mexican farmworkers. It claimed that American farms depend on foreign labour and needed Mexican workers. About two-thirds of hired farm workers in America today are foreigners, and America's farms are depending steadily more on hired help and less on family members. Americans are demanding more fresh food products over time and this relies more heavily on manual workers to harvest these labour-intensive crops. North Carolina needs around 6,500 agricultural workers each season. These numbers are unlikely to come from US citizens. In 2011, only 163 people born in the USA showed up for work at the start of the season—and only 7 lasted the whole season!

? Questions

What would the effect of more Mexican immigration be on the Production Possibility Frontier of the USA?

What do you think might be the arguments against allowing more Mexican immigration?

Put into practice

Imagine that technological developments enabled the production of product B to increase for any given amount of other resources, such as land, labour, and machinery. The technology has no impact on the production of A. Draw the new PPF that would occur following the technological development.

Consumption outside the production possibility frontier

The PPF shows what an economy can produce given its available resources. However, it is possible for an economy to consume outside the frontier through international trade. It may well be that another country can produce some items more efficiently than you can and that your economy is able to produce some products more efficiently than your partners overseas; by trading with each other both countries can benefit.

Imagine, for example, that an economy is producing at point W and then gives up ten units of product A (see Figure 2.5). Within its own country, it could produce only five units of B in return. If, however, it were able to find a country that is less efficient at producing A but better at producing B, then it would be able to sell some of its units of A abroad at a profit. For example, it might be possible to sell its ten units of A for 20 units of B; this means that the economy could operate at Z.

The benefits of international trade are analysed further in Chapter 28.

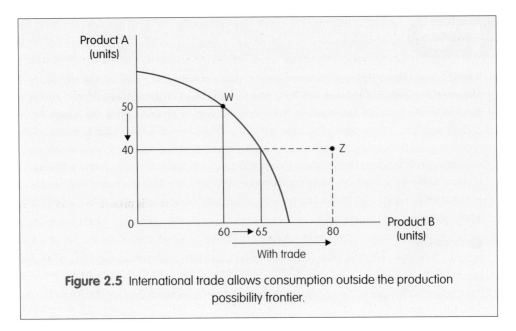

Figure 2.5 International trade allows consumption outside the production possibility frontier.

Put into practice

- Imagine that an economy is at point C in Figure 2.6. Within the domestic economy, what is the opportunity cost of five more units of B?

- Assume that two units of A can be traded abroad for 12 units of B. Then, starting at C, if an economy were to give up two units of A and trade overseas, how many units of B could it now have?

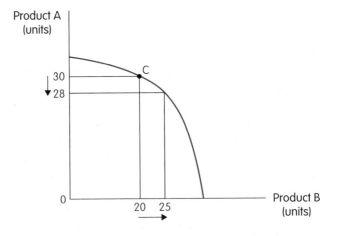

Figure 2.6 The benefits of international trade.

What do you think?

Which countries are the main trading partners of your own? What are the main exports of your country?

Do you think that your economy is very dependent on trade? Is that a good or bad thing?

Present versus future decisions

The PPF is often used to illustrate the extent to which an economy is producing for the present or the future. Economies that focus on capital goods are investing for the long term: they are investing in machines and equipment that will allow the economy to produce more in the future. This will be shown over time by an outward shift of the PPF; when the machines are finished and being used, the economy can produce more. Economies that focus more on the here and now will produce more consumer goods which will be consumed this period; this is likely to lead to a smaller outward shift in the PPF over time, because the investment in the amount of machinery and technology is less.

What do you think?

Is it better for an economy to produce consumer goods—that is, focus on fulfilling people's demands today—or should it invest for the future?

Why might governments be tempted to focus on providing consumer capital goods rather than investing for the future?

Why might managers and consumers in the free market not invest in the future?

The shape of the production possibility frontier

So far, we have drawn the PPF as concave to the origin. This is because of the assumptions that we make about what happens when resources to output are transferred from one industry to another. This depends on what is known as 'the returns to a factor of production'. If there are constant returns to a factor in industries A and B, then this means that every time resources are transferred from one industry to another, there is the same increase in output in B and the same decrease in output in industry A. This would lead to a PPF that is a straight line. For example, in the economy shown in Figure 2.7, every time a given number of resources are shifted from industry A to B, ten units of A are given up in return for 20 units of B.

In reality, resources are unlikely to be equally productive in both industries. Some equipment may be designed specifically for some types of production rather than others; some employees may not be able to transfer their skills easily from one sector to another. This may lead to 'diminishing returns to a factor of production'. This means that every

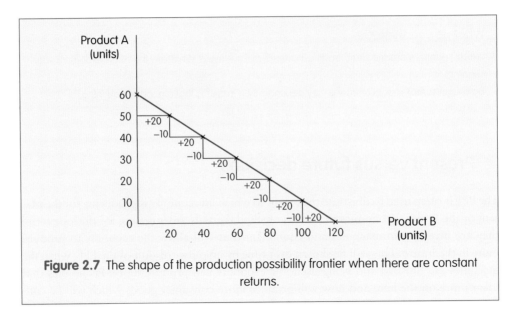

Figure 2.7 The shape of the production possibility frontier when there are constant returns.

time a given number of resources are transferred out of industry B into industry A, successively fewer units of A are produced (for example, see Figure 2.8) because the factors being transferred struggle to keep increasing output at the same rate. This is because if you keep adding labour, for example, to a fixed amount of machinery the extra output starts to fall due to workers getting in each other's way and not having enough equipment to share (see Chapter 9). This means that the PPF is concave to the origin.

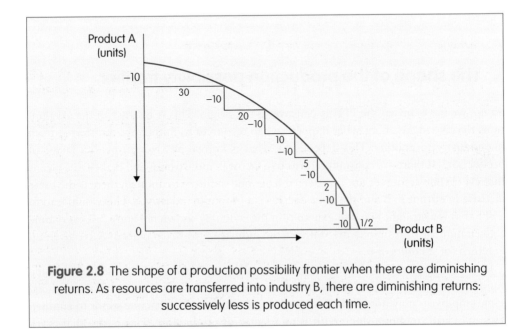

Figure 2.8 The shape of a production possibility frontier when there are diminishing returns. As resources are transferred into industry B, there are diminishing returns: successively less is produced each time.

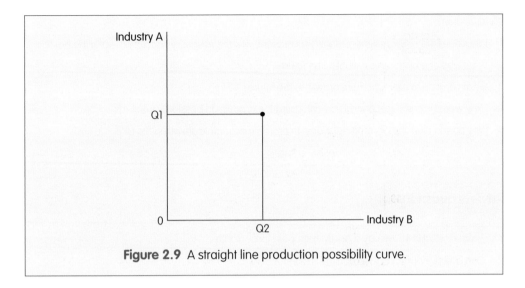

Figure 2.9 A straight line production possibility curve.

If different assumptions are made this will change the shape of the production possibility frontier. If, for example, resources can only be used in one industry or the other but cannot be transferred from one to the other then the PPF would be the shape shown in Figure 2.9. Resources can either be used in industry A and produce Q1 or in industry B and produce Q2 but cannot be transferred between the two.

Case study

The following is an extract from the UK government's 'Plan for Growth'.

Britain has lost ground in the world's economy, and needs to catch up. If we do not act now, jobs will be lost, our country will become poorer and we will find it difficult to afford the public services we all want. If we do not wake up to the world around us, our standard of living will fall, not rise.

In the last decade other nations have worked hard to make their economies more competitive. They have reduced their business tax rates, removed barriers to enterprise, invested in their infrastructure, improved their education systems, reformed welfare and increased their exports. Sadly the reverse has happened in Britain over the last ten years. We literally cannot afford to go on like this. Britain has to earn its way in the modern world. We have to become much more productive so we can be a leading high tech, highly skilled economy. We must build a new model of economic growth – where instead of borrowing from the rest of the world, we invest and we save and we export. Our economy must become more balanced. Private sector growth must take the place of government deficits, and prosperity must be shared across all parts of the UK. We should never again allow our taxes to become uncompetitive, or drive valued entrepreneurs from our shores. If other nations are turning out smarter school and university students, we have to make sure ours are smarter still. We have to tear down the barriers to enterprise and economic development. Britain should be producing businesses that out-compete, out-smart and out-pace the rest of the world.

Source: Plan for Growth, March 2011, https://www.gov.uk/government/publications/plan-for-growth–5

? Questions

1   What does the UK government identify as reasons why the economy has not grown in the past?

2   What type of growth does it want in the future?

3   What can it do to promote more growth in the future?

4   How would you show economic growth using the production possibility frontier?

5   Why do you think the government wants to promote economic growth in the UK?

Review questions

1   Explain what is shown by a production possibility frontier.

2   Can an economy produce outside the PPF?

3   How can an economy consume outside its PPF?

4   Why might an economy end up producing within the PPF?

5   What do you think is the best point at which to be on the PPF?

6   In what way does the PPF illustrate the concept of opportunity cost?

7   Explain what actions a government might take to shift the PPF outwards in the future.

8   How might an increase in demand for one product lead to a movement along the PPF curve?

Put into practice

1   Imagine there an improvement in technology in industry B but this has no impact on production in industry A. Show the effect of this on a Production Possibility Frontier.

2   Imagine that as resources were switched out of one industry and into another, successively more was produced in the new industry. Show this on a production possibility frontier.

Assignment questions

1   Research two economies of your choice. Compare and contrast the extent and nature of government intervention in these economies.

2   Visit the website of the Organisation for Economic Cooperation and Development. Find the country reports and choose a country you wish to report on. Read the report and summarize the actions the OECD think need to be taken to impove economic growth in this country.

Key learning points

- Given the present resources of an economy, there is a maximum combination of products that can be produced. This is shown by the PPF.

- The combination of goods and services produced may be determined, in theory, by the government or by market forces, or, in reality, by a combination of the two.

- If it operates on the PPF it is productively efficient.

- Economic growth can be seen by an outward shift of the PPF.

- By trading abroad, a country can consume outside its PPF.

Learn more

If you read Chapter 29, you can find out more about the principle of comparative advantage. This shows how economies can benefit from free trade and consume outside their PPF.

 Visit our Online Resource Centre at http://www.oxfordtextbooks.co.uk/orc/gillespie_econ3e/ for test questions and further information on topics covered in this chapter.

»3 Demand

In the previous chapter, we examined the maximum output of goods and services that an economy could produce given its resources. However, we did not analyse in detail what would determine which combination of products would be produced and consumed. What makes an economy produce more of some products and fewer of others? This depends on the nature of the economic system. In a free market, the allocation of resources is determined by supply and demand. In this chapter we analyse demand conditions.

LEARNING OBJECTIVES

By the end of this chapter, you should be able to:

✓ explain what is meant by effective demand;

✓ explain what is shown by a demand curve;

✓ understand the difference between a change in the quantity demanded and a change in demand;

✓ explain the possible causes of a shift in a demand curve;

✓ appreciate the difference between marginal and total utility.

▓ Introduction

In a free market economy, the basic economic problems of what to produce, how to produce, and who gets what are solved by market forces.

- The demand and supply of goods and services determine what is produced and sold.
- The demand and supply of resources determine the combination of different resources being used—for example, how much labour and how much machinery are employed in a given industry, and how much people are paid.

- The amount that people earn, their wealth, and the relative prices of products determine who can afford to buy different goods and services.

In these markets individual consumers, businesses and employees are making their own decisions based on a desire to maximize their well-being. The price and wages adjust to bring these decisions together. As supply and demand conditions change the prices adjust to bring about a new equilibrium with a different allocation of resources.

Imagine that changes in technology lead to a greater demand for website designers and less demand for travel agents, because people can search for and book holidays directly online. This should lead to more web design companies setting up and more designers being recruited. Demand for this service, and therefore demand for resources in this industry, increase, highlighting how the markets for products and factors of production are linked. Meanwhile, there will be less demand for travel agency services and these businesses may have to make people redundant. Less demand for the product reduces demand for resources in this industry. The combination of products produced by the economy has moved, so that we are at a new point on the production possibility frontier (PPF). In the market for the different factors of production, rewards will go up for the web designers and down for the travel assistants, bringing about the reallocation of resources as the economy adjusts to change.

An economy is made up of millions of markets, and an understanding of supply and demand conditions is therefore crucial to economic analysis. All markets, whether for housing, oil, shares, labour, property, currencies, or even university places, are influenced by the market forces of supply and demand. We shall therefore begin with an analysis of demand in this chapter, then look at supply in Chapter 5, and finally put the two sides of a market together to examine the concept of equilibrium in Chapter 6.

The demand curve

The demand for a product is the quantity that customers are willing and able to buy at each and every price, all other things being unchanged. This is shown on a demand curve. A demand curve measures the quantity that customers are actually able to buy at each and every price, not only the quantity that they would like to buy. It therefore represents what is called 'effective demand', and depends on what they want <u>and</u> what they can afford. For example, at the price P1, the quantity Q1 is demanded (see Figure 3.1). At a lower price, P2, a greater quantity Q2 is demanded. With a given income customers are able to and want to buy more with a lower price.

The level of demand for a product depends on factors such as the following.

- **The price level** As the price changes, this influences the relative value of the product compared with other goods and services, and the amount that customers want and are able to buy. Higher tuition fees may deter some students from going to university, for example. Lower prices may make a product more affordable and increase the quantity demanded. Given your existing income and preferences, changes in price affect what is affordable and how much you demand.

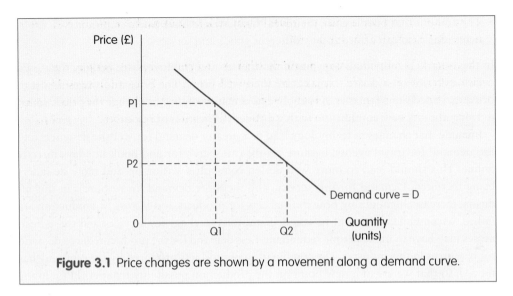

Figure 3.1 Price changes are shown by a movement along a demand curve.

Put into practice

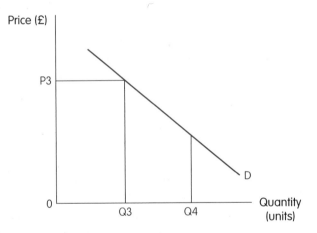

Figure 3.2 Price and quantity combinations.

Consider the demand curve in Figure 3.2.

- What quantity is demanded at price P3?
- What price is necessary for quantity Q4 to be demanded?

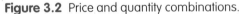

- **The customers' incomes** This influences what customers can afford. If the economy is booming, for example, and people are earning more, this might lead to more spending on many goods.

- **The price of competitors' products (that is, substitute products)** A change in the price of Cadbury's Dairy Milk, for example, may affect the sale of Mars bars. A decrease in the price of satellite navigation devices may reduce demand for maps as customers switch from one product to another.

- **The price of complementary products (that is, products used in conjunction with each other)** For example, an increase in the price of Sony Playstation consoles may affect sales of Playstation computer games. If you cannot afford one part of the overall package, demand for specific elements may fall. If you cannot afford the computer printer you won't buy the ink.

- **The number of customers in the market** For example, a product may be aimed at a new market segment (such as a new country or a new group of buyers), which can boost demand. When several sports clothes manufacturers repositioned many of their products and targeted the leisurewear market, this significantly increased the number of potential buyers for their products. Computer games are now being developed to help to improve the memory and to keep users alert; this is to target the older buyer, because most buyers of computer games at the moment are relatively young. Cereal manufacturers are regularly trying to reposition the product to get customers to view this as a product to eat in the evening as well as the morning.

- **Other factors** The factors affecting the demand for a particular product will, of course, vary. For example, the demand for textbooks will be influenced by the number of students; the demand for sun-cream will be influenced by the weather; the demand for nicotine patches may be affected by anti-smoking laws. In 2013 the birth of Prince George to the Duke and Duchess of Cambridge is estimated to have boosted retails sales by over £240 million thanks to spending on celebrations, souvenirs, toys, books, and DVDs.

The shape of the demand curve

A demand curve is usually downward-sloping. This is because of the law of diminishing marginal utility. This law states that, as buyers consume additional units of a product, the extra satisfaction (or utility) that they gain from each unit will fall. The second cup of tea is not as satisfying as the first in a given time period; the tenth is not as satisfying as the ninth. If the extra satisfaction of a unit declines, then the amount that consumers are willing to pay to buy it will fall as well. For a higher quantity to be demanded, the price must therefore be lower, because the extra satisfaction from these additional units is less according to the law of diminishing marginal utility. We are assuming that consumers are rational and that, given a limited income, they allocate their spending between products to maximize their welfare. If by consuming more of a particular product the extra satisfaction falls, then you will only be willing to buy more units if they become cheaper.

Marginal and total utility

- **Marginal utility** measures the extra utility (or satisfaction) from consuming an additional unit of a product.
- **Total utility** is the total satisfaction from the consumption of a product.

Table 3.1 The relationship between marginal utility and total utility

Units	Marginal utility	Total utility
1	10	10
2	8	18
3	6	24
4	4	28
5	2	30
6	0	30
7	−2	28
8	−4	24

If, for example, the extra utility from consuming another unit of the product is six units of utility (called 'utils'), then the total utility will increase by 6 utils.

Notice in Table 3.1 that the law of diminishing marginal utility operates (see also Figure 3.3). This means that the total utility increases at a diminishing rate. When the marginal utility is 0, this means that there is no increase in total satisfaction from the consumption of that unit (in this case, the sixth unit); at this level of consumption, utility would be maximized. It is possible that you can overconsume some items (for example, eat or drink too much in a given time period and feel ill), in which case the marginal utility might be negative (the seventh unit) and the total utility would then fall.

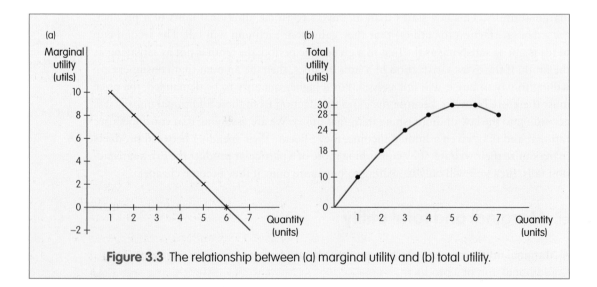

Figure 3.3 The relationship between (a) marginal utility and (b) total utility.

The difference between marginal and total utility is highlighted by the 'paradox of value'. In the case of water, there is a relatively large amount of water available and consumed in the world. This means that, although total utility is high, the extra utility is low and therefore people will not pay much for an additional unit of this, even though it is essential to survival. In the case of diamonds, the availability and consumption is much lower, meaning the marginal utility is high (although total utility is not, compared with water); people will pay a lot for another diamond even though it is not essential to survival.

Put into practice

Quantity consumed	Total utility
1	18
2	38
3	53
4	65
5	75
6	80
7	84
8	86

What is the maximum number of units the consumer will consume if the price of the product is 4 pence (assuming 1 unit of utility is worth 1 pence)?

A movement along the demand curve

The rational consumer will consume any unit shown on the demand curve where the extra utility is greater or equal to the price charged. This means that if the price of a product falls, then there will now be more units that have a higher extra utility than the price, and the quantity demanded will increase. If the price increases, there will be fewer units worth purchasing and the quantity demanded will fall.

A change in the price of a product, such as P1 – P3 (see Figure 3.4), therefore leads to a change in the quantity demanded (Q1 – Q3). This is known as a **movement along** the demand curve.

An increase in the quantity demanded due to a price fall is called an **extension of demand** (Q1 – Q3). A decrease in the quantity demanded is called a **contraction of demand** (Q1 – Q2).

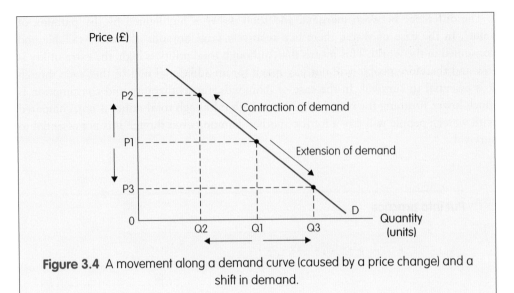

Figure 3.4 A movement along a demand curve (caused by a price change) and a shift in demand.

Example

The equation for a straight-line demand curve can be given in the form:

$Q = a - bP$

For example:

$Q = 80 - 2P$

where

- Q is the quantity demanded; and
- P is the price in £s.

a. If the price is £5, the quantity demanded is:

$Q = 80 - (2 \times 5) = 80 - 10 = 70$ units

If the price increases to £10, the quantity demanded is:

$Q = 80 - (2 \times 10) = 80 - 20 = 60$ units

This shows that, given this equation, the higher the price, the lower the quantity demanded. This is shown as a movement along the demand curve, because the price has changed.

b. If the equation changes to $Q = 150 - 2P$, then the curve will have shifted, because more will be demanded at each and every price.

So, if the price is £5, the quantity demanded is:

$Q = 150 - (2 \times 5) = 150 - 10 = 140$ units

If the price increases to £10, the quantity demanded is:

$Q = 150 - (2 \times 10) = 150 - 20 = 130$ units

c. If $Q = 80 - 2P$ and the quantity demanded is 50 units, then:

$50 = 80 - 2P$

also expressed as

$2P = 80 - 50$

$2P = 30$

$P = \dfrac{30}{2} = £15$

This quantity is demanded at a price of £15.

Put into practice

If the equation for a demand curve is $Q = 50 - 4P$:

- what is the quantity demanded if the price is £5?
- what is the quantity demanded if the price is £10?
- what is the price at which the quantity demanded is 46 units?
- what is the price at which the quantity demanded is 42 units?

Income and substitution effects

Movements along the demand curve can also be explained in terms of income and substitution effects.

- The **substitution effect** occurs when consumers switch towards a relatively cheaper product. If the price of a product falls, we assume that consumers always switch towards it, because it is relatively cheaper than alternatives, and so the substitution effect increases the quantity demanded.

- The **income effect** occurs because, if a good is cheaper, consumers can purchase more products with the same nominal income. Their money can buy more, which means that their real income has increased. In the case of most goods, having more real income increases the quantity demanded.

This means that, with a fall in price, consumers substitute towards the relatively cheaper product; with more real income, they want to purchase more. These two effects increase the overall quantity demanded (see Figure 3.5).

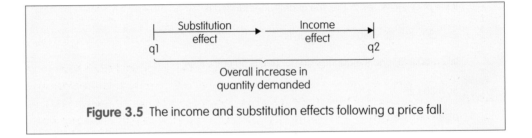

Figure 3.5 The income and substitution effects following a price fall.

Upward-sloping demand curves

In exceptional cases, the demand curve for a product may be upward-sloping (see Figure 3.6). This may be due to one of the following two reasons.

- **The product is a** Giffen good This is a very basic product that is essential to survival in a poor economy, such as rice in a developing country. When the price of this type of product rises, consumers find that they are spending so much on it (because it is essential to survival and one of the few things that they can afford to eat) that they have very little left over for anything else. Given the fact that consumers have so few funds left, they end up buying even more of the original product—that is, the quantity demanded increases when the price increases, because nothing else is now affordable.

- **The product is a** Veblen good Customers believe that the higher price of the product reflects a better quality or has a better image, and therefore want more even though it is more expensive. This type of product was described by Veblen (1899) who highlighted the desire by some customers for 'conspicuous consumption'—that is, they want to be seen to be buying more expensive items! For example, retailers sometimes find that a

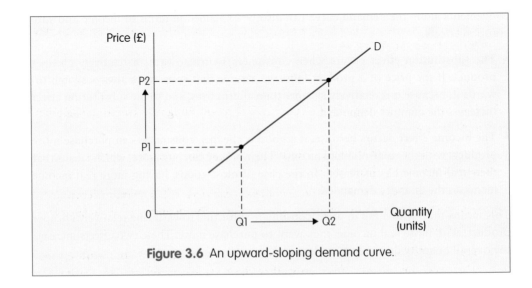

Figure 3.6 An upward-sloping demand curve.

Economics in context

In 2007 two Harvard professors, Robert Jensen and Nolan Miller, analysed the behaviour of poor Chinese consumers and showed that they consume more rice or noodles, their staple food products, as the prices of these products go up. They showed that people need a certain amount of calories to survive—for example, 1600 per day. They could get this by consuming rice and perhaps some vegetables alone, or by eating rice, vegetables, and a few pieces of meat. But meat is expensive and as the price of rice increased the poor Chinese could no longer afford the luxury of cooking meat, so they ate rice instead, which was still relatively cheap compared to meat.

❓ Question

Do you think Giffen goods might exist in the UK? What might they be?

reduction in the price of a bottle of wine leads to a fall in sales, because buyers assume that the quality is worse or do not want to be seen buying cheap wine (or giving it to their guests).

What do you think?

Can you think of products that you buy for which you tend to avoid the cheapest version on the list? Why do you think you do so?

Put into practice

If the equation for a demand curve is $Q = 20 + 2P$, why does this mean that the demand curve for this product is upward-sloping? Show your answer, using calculations to calculate the quantity demanded for different prices.

In terms of income and substitution effects, what is happening with Giffen goods is that a fall in price means that:

• consumers want to substitute towards this product, so this substitution effect increases the quantity demanded; and

• an increase in real income due to the lower price leads to a fall in quantity demanded as consumers switch to more luxurious goods. This is the income effect reducing the quantity demanded.

In the case of a Giffen good the substitution and income effects therefore work against each other, and the income effect outweighs the substitution effect. This means the

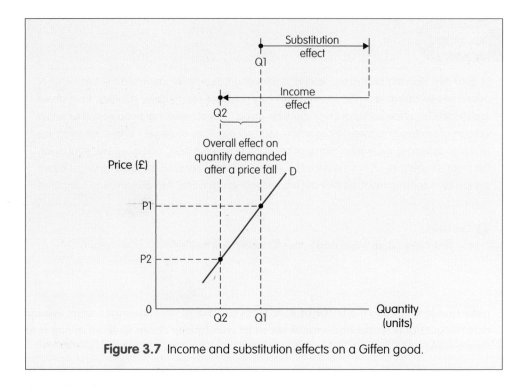

Figure 3.7 Income and substitution effects on a Giffen good.

overall quantity demanded falls with a price fall (see Figure 3.7) and the demand curve is upward-sloping.

A shift in the demand curve

A movement along a demand curve occurs when the price changes and all other things remain unchanged. A shift in demand occurs if these other factors do change. The demand curve for a product will shift if at each and every price customers are willing and able to buy more or less than they did before (see Figure 3.8). If consumers demand more, the curve will shift to the right. If they demand less, then it will shift to the left. When the demand curve shifts, this is known as a change in demand (as opposed to a change in the quantity demanded).

What do you think?

What do you think will be the big hit in the toy market next Christmas? How would you try to estimate this?

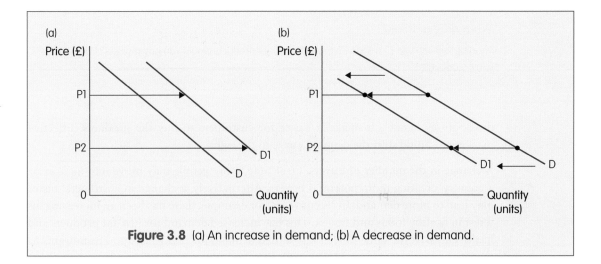

Figure 3.8 (a) An increase in demand; (b) A decrease in demand.

■ The reasons for a shift in demand

The reasons for a shift in demand (that is, a change in demand) include the following.

- **A change in income** If customers have an increase in their incomes, then their demand for products is likely to shift. For 'normal' goods, demand will increase with more income and the demand curve will shift to the right. With more money, you may go on holiday more, eat out more, and go to more concerts. More is demanded at each and every price. The amount by which the demand for a particular product increases depends on how sensitive it is to changes in income. A given increase in income may lead to a relatively large increase in demand for health clubs and fine wines, for example. These goods are known as **income elastic** products. For other goods, demand may not increase so much. An increase in income is unlikely to boost demand for shoe polish or toothpaste very much, for example. These are known as **income inelastic products**. (For more on income elasticity, see Chapter 4.)

  For some goods, demand may actually fall when income increases, because the consumers switch to something that they prefer now that they have more income. Goods for which demand falls in this way are called **inferior goods**. When households' income in developing economies grow, they usually switch from bicycles to motorbikes as a means of transport. The bicycles in this case are inferior and the motorbikes are normal products. However, the status of goods will vary for different people and over time. With even more income growth in developing economies, demand for motorbikes tends to fall as demand for cars increases. Motorbikes have now become inferior over time, as consumers now choose another, 'better', product.

- **A change in marketing policies** Managers of organizations will continually review their marketing strategies to try to boost the demand for their products. Changes to their marketing strategy may include new promotional campaigns or finding new

> **What do you think?**
>
> Imagine that you win £1 million on the lottery. What products would you buy more of? What would you buy less of?

distribution channels to make it easier for customers to buy the products. Effective marketing should shift the demand curve to the right.

- **A change in the number of buyers** Over time, more people may move into an area or a country, creating more potential buyers. Alternatively, a change in customers' tastes may lead to more demand. In recent years, for example, there has been an increasing interest in healthy foods and fitness. This has increased demand for low-fat products and health clubs. At the same time, it has shifted demand for many fast-food restaurants to the left. Companies such as McDonald's have had to reconsider their range of products and marketing strategies.

- **A change in the price of substitute products** Customers have choices when it comes to deciding what to buy. You may be deciding whether to go for a meal out or the cinema, or choosing between decorating the kitchen and going on holiday. This means that all products have substitutes—that is, other products that customers may consider buying as an alternative. If these substitutes become more or less expensive, then this will affect demand for the original product. For example, if the price of football tickets goes up, you may decide to stop going to see the match every week and spend your money on Sky TV instead. The demand for Sky TV would shift to the right, because the price of football tickets increased. Easy, cheap access to reviews of restaurants, hotels, and cities online is leading to a fall in demand for guide books.

- **A change in the price of complements** Complementary products are those that you tend to buy together, for example, writing paper and envelopes, digital cameras and photographic printing paper, and flowers and greeting cards. Changes in the price of one of these items may affect sales of the other. If the cost of filter coffee increases significantly, it may decrease sales of filter coffee machines. If the price of airfares to Spain falls, the sales of suncream may increase as more people go abroad.

- **Weather** Changes in the climate can have a significant effect on the sales of some products. A hot summer boosts the demand for barbecues and lager. Amazingly, it also boosts sales of tanning lotion: office workers want to give the impression that they have been outside or on holiday and so buy fake tan. A wet winter increases the demand for umbrellas.

- **Events** Big events, such as sporting matches, can have a large impact on retail sales. In the build-up to an event such as the Olympics, retail sales are high as people stock up; sales are low during the competition, because people stay at home to watch it.

- **A change in social patterns** Over time, the nature of society will change and this influences demand patterns for different products. In the UK, for example, the average age has been increasing over the last 50 years, the typical family size has been decreasing,

Economics in context

The owner of B&Q, Kingfisher, announced a fall in profits last year due to weak demand caused by cold weather. Kingfisher is Europe's largest DIY retailer. As well as the impact of cold weather, the company was also affected by weak consumer confidence in its main markets.

Sales of outdoor products were hit at B&Q and the company said that sales of building products were also damaged by the poor weather. This affected the share price of the company.

? Questions

Explain the possible effect on B& Q of the fall in profits.

Analyse two factors that might affect demand for B&Q products.

What other products may be vulnerable to changes in the weather?

What could B&Q do to reduce its vulnerability to changes in the weather?

there are more divorces, and there is a greater interest in healthy and organic foods. A noticeable development in the UK has been a change in the way in which we eat. Families are much less likely to sit down together and eat a family meal than they were 20 years ago; Sunday dinners are largely a thing of the past and we tend to eat now by 'grazing'—that is, by eating as we move about. This has helped firms such as Pret A Manger, which sells sandwiches, but negatively affected others such as Waterford and Wedgwood, which make traditional bone china crockery—something for which there is much less need these days, because formal meals are increasingly uncommon.

What do you think?

What do you think are the major determinants of the demand for each of the following?

a. New cars

b. Textbooks

c. Diamonds

d. Health care

e. Flat-screen TVs

f. Eggs

Put into practice

1. Using diagrams, show the effect on demand of the following.

  • The effect on demand for a normal good if income decreases

  • The effect on demand for an inferior good if income increases

- The effect on demand for a product of an increase in the price of a complementary product
- The effect on demand for a product of a decrease in the price of a substitute product

2. What is the only cause of a movement *along* a demand curve for good X?

   a. A change in consumers' tastes

   b. A change in consumers' income

   c. A change in the price of the good

   d. A change in the size of the population

Individual and market demand

An individual's demand curve shows the quantity that a consumer is willing and able to buy at each and every price, other things being unchanged. The market demand is the sum of all of the individual demand curves (see Figure 3.9). To derive the market demand, all of the individual demands are horizontally summated—that is, all of the individual demands are added up at each price.

Whether we are considering individual or market demand curves it is important to remember that a change in price will lead to a change in quantity demanded (a movement along the curve) whereas a change in other factors will change the quantity demanded at all prices and shift the demand curve. These differences are summarized in Table 3.2.

Economics in context

More people living alone in the UK

By 2021, more than a third of the UK population will be living alone. Since 1975, Britain's population has risen by 5 per cent and the number of single-person households has risen by 31 per cent. The proportion of income spent by single-person households on alcohol, tobacco, and recreational drugs is noticeably higher than that of households with two or more people. The top supermarket products bought by people living alone are slimming aids; other products that they are more likely to buy are Marmite and herbal tea.

Supermarkets are now trying harder to target such individuals. Sainsbury's has doubled its range of 25 cl bottles, and has seen strong growth in the sale of its 2 l boxes of wine compared to its 3 l boxes. Its 'Taste the Difference' ready-meal range has also been extended to meals for one. Unilever, meanwhile, is making mini jars of Marmite and single servings of ready-made soups.

❓ Question

The above shows how the existence of more single-person households affects the demand for some products. In the UK, the population is also ageing. List five types of business that might benefit from this and five that might suffer.

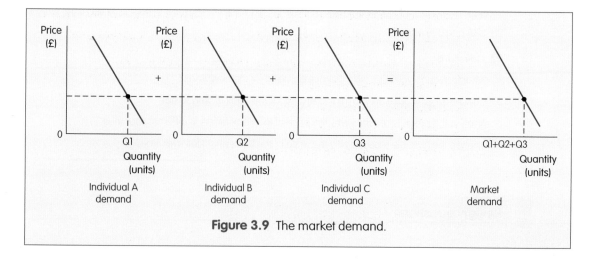

Figure 3.9 The market demand.

Table 3.2 Summary

Change in	Leads to
Price	MOVEMENT ALONG THE DEMAND CURVE
Income	
Prices of other products	
Promotional activities	A SHIFT IN THE DEMAND CURVE
Tastes	
Number of customer	

Case study

In 2013 Microsoft announced the launch date and price for its new Xbox One. It announced that the new console would go on sale in November in that year, with a recommended retail price of £429 in the UK, $499 in the USA, and 499 euros. Rival console manufacturer Sony said its console would be also be out later in 2013.

This was the first time the two rivals had launched their products simultaneously. Previously consoles had been released at least a year apart. Microsoft has announced titles such as Forza Motorsport which involve 'cloud' gaming and others—such as Konami's Metal Gear Solid 5—which may include real-time missions. Even if you are not playing, things will be happening and stories will move on. A good games title can dramatically increase the popularity and sales of a new console. Many commentators claim the success of Microsoft's first console—the Xbox—when it launched in 2001—was due to it securing the exclusive rights to the first person shooter game Halo.

Some people feel the high price of the new Xbox in the UK is an issue but others say the Xbox 360 has so many unique features it will not cause the company any problems. It may be that the initial price is brought down fairly quickly.

When Microsoft launched the Xbox 360 in 2005, it had a launch price in the UK of £279.99, $399 in the USA and 399 euros.

❓ **Questions**

1 What factors do you think will influence demand for the new Xbox?

2 How sensitive to price do you think demand for the Xbox is likely to be?

3 Analyse the possible reasons why the price of the Xbox differs in different countries.

4 Analyse the possible reasons why the price of the Xbox might fall over time.

Review questions

1 Does a demand curve show what a consumer would like to buy at each and every price?

2 Explain the difference between a movement along, and a shift in, a demand curve.

3 Does an increase in income always shift the demand curve outwards to the right? Explain your answer.

4 Does the quantity demanded always fall if the price increases?

5 To what extent do you think a business can control the demand for its products?

6 Explain what might shift the demand curve for a product inwards.

7 If marginal utility is falling does this mean total utiity is falling as well?

8 Explain what happens to the demand for a product if the price of a complement rises.

Put it into practice

1 If the equation for the demand curve is $Q = 300 - 2P$ what is the quantity demanded when the price is £10? £20?

2 The marginal utility for each additional unit of consumption is 12 units of utility then 10, 7, 5, 2, −2, −4. Plot the total utlity derived from the consumptions of these units.

Assignment questions

1 Visit the website of the Advertising Standards Authority. Summarise the role of the authority and analyse the findings in a recent investigation it has undertaken.

2 An increase in the quantity demanded is not the same as an increase in the demand for a product. Explain the difference using diagrams.

Key learning points

- Demand shows what customers are willing and able to purchase at each and every price, not only what they want to buy.

- A movement along a demand curve occurs when there is a change in the price, all other things being unchanged.

- A shift in the demand curve occurs when more or less is demanded at each and every price.

- A demand curve is usually downward-sloping, but in some cases (such as a Veblen or Giffen good), it can be upward-sloping.

- The marginal utility shows the extra utility from consuming a unit; the total utility shows the total satisfaction that a consumer has from consuming a product.

- The marginal utility from consuming a product declines when additional units are consumed.

Reference

Veblen, T. (1899) *The Theory of the Leisure Class*, Macmillan, New York

Learn more

A demand curve can be derived using indifference curve analysis. This analyses the impact of a change in price and income in terms of consumers' utility. To find out more about indifference curve analysis and how a consumer maximizes utility, visit the Online Resource Centre.

 Visit our Online Resource Centre at http://www.oxfordtextbooks.co.uk/orc/gillespie_econ3e/ for test questions and further information on topics covered in this chapter.

»4 The elasticity of demand

In the previous chapter, we examined the factors determining the level of demand for a product, and the differences between a shift in demand and a movement along a demand curve. In this chapter, we examine the extent to which changes in a number of variables can affect demand. For example, how much does demand change when the price or income changes and what determines the scale of these changes? In this chapter we analyse demand in more detail before going on to supply and the interaction of supply and demand.

LEARNING OBJECTIVES

By the end of this chapter, you should be able to:

✓ explain the meaning of the price, income, and the cross-price elasticity of demand;

✓ outline the determinants of the price elasticity of demand for a product;

✓ explain the difference between a normal and an inferior good;

✓ understand the difference between a substitute and a complement;

✓ understand the significance of the concept of elasticity for a firm's planning;

✓ appreciate the limitations of the concept of elasticity of demand.

▦ The elasticity of demand

The managers of a business will naturally be interested in what affects the demand for their products. If they can determine what affects their sales, they can then try to plan accordingly. For example, they can estimate the staff levels that they will need, the stocks that they have to hold, and their projected profits.

To estimate the likely demand for their products in the future, managers may use the concept of the elasticity of demand. This examines the sensitivity of demand to a number of other factors, such as price, income, and the prices of other products.

The general equation for the elasticity of demand is:

$$\text{Elasticity of demand} = \frac{\text{Percentage change in the quantity demanded}}{\text{Percentage change in a variable (such as price or income)}}$$

The following are the two keys to understanding the elasticity of demand.

- **The sign of the answer** If this is a negative answer, then it means that the change in the quantity demanded and the change in the variable move in opposite directions: for example, the answer would be negative if an increase in price were to decrease the quantity demanded or a fall in income were to increase the quantity demanded. A positive answer means that the variable and the quantity demanded move in the same direction—that is, both increase or both decrease: for example, the answer would be positive if an increase in income were to increase the quantity demanded of a product.

- **The size (or value) of the answer** The size of the answer shows how sensitive demand is to the variable. If the value of the answer (ignoring the sign—that is, ignoring whether it is positive or negative) is greater than one (> 1), then it means that the quantity demanded has changed more than the variable, and demand is said to be elastic. (Looking at the equation, if the answer is > 1, then the numerator has changed more than the denominator.) If the answer (ignoring the sign) is less than one (< 1), then this means that the change in the quantity demanded is less than the change in the variable. In this case, demand is said to be inelastic.

For example, if a change in price of 10 per cent were to lead to a change in quantity demand of 20 per cent, the size of the price elasticity would be:

$$\frac{20\%}{10\%} = 2 \, (\text{that is, elastic})$$

If a change in price of 10 per cent were to lead to a change in quantity demand of 5 per cent, the size of the price elasticity would be:

$$\frac{5\%}{10\%} = 0.5 \, (\text{that is, inelastic})$$

Notice that the sign of the answer (positive or negative) tells us nothing about the sensitivity of demand—this is shown purely by the size of the answer. The bigger the number the more sensitive demand is to a change in price and the greater the movement along a demand curve

▩ The price elasticity of demand

The price elasticity of demand measures the change in the quantity demanded of a product relative to a change in price, all other factors unchanged. Basically, this measures how sensitive demand is to price. If the prices at your favourite coffee shop were to go up, would you stop going there completely? Would you go less often? Would you drink less coffee when you are there? Naturally, the coffee shop manager would be interested in the impact of any price change on sales. Would the size of the impact on the quantity demanded be different if your bus fare to get to work were to go up? Would you be likely to switch to another form of transport? What if the price of a haircut at your local hairdresser were to increase? How much would sales fall off there? The answers to all of these questions are linked to the concept of the price elasticity of demand.

The price elasticity of demand is calculated using the following equation:

$$\text{Price elasticity of demand} = \frac{\text{Percentage change in the quantity demanded}}{\text{Percentage change in the price of the product}}$$

In most cases, the price elasticity of demand is likely to be a negative number, because a price increase will reduce the quantity demanded (and vice versa)—that is, the answer is negative because the two variables move in opposite directions—assuming that the demand curve is downward-sloping (see Figure 4.1). If the price elasticity of demand is positive it means that an increase in price increases the quantity demanded; this means the demand curve is upward sloping.

Once the sign (positive or negative) of the price elasticity of demand has been analysed, the next thing to consider is the size of the answer, which shows us how elastic or inelastic demand is in relation to price. For example, if the answer is 3 (ignoring whether it is positive or negative), this means that the percentage change in the quantity demanded is three

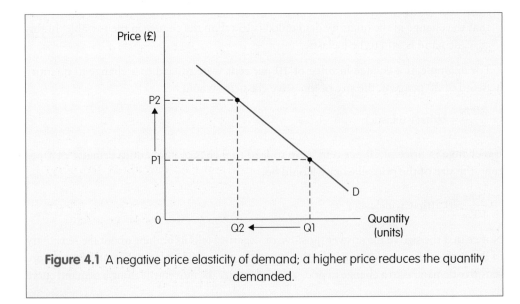

Figure 4.1 A negative price elasticity of demand; a higher price reduces the quantity demanded.

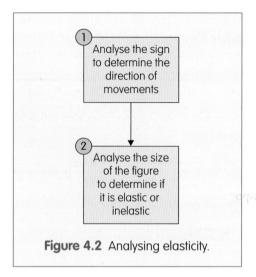

Figure 4.2 Analysing elasticity.

times the percentage change in price. A 1 per cent change in price will lead to a 3 per cent change in the quantity demanded. This means that demand is sensitive to price.

If the value of the price elasticity is 0.5, this means that the quantity demanded changes 0.5 times as much as price (in percentages). This means that demand is not sensitive to price. A 1 per cent change in price will lead to a 0.5 per cent change in the quantity demanded. Whether the answer is positive or negative shows the direction of the relationship between price and quantity demanded, but does not show the strength of the relationship, because this depends on the value of the answer, not the sign (see Figure 4.2).

Any answer (ignoring the sign) that is > 1 is known as a price elastic product: the quantity demanded will change by more than the price (in percentages). If a product has a price elasticity of demand of < 1 (ignoring the sign), this means that demand is price inelastic. The change in the quantity demanded is less than the change in price (in percentages). If a product has a price elasticity of demand equal to one (= 1), this is known as unitary price elasticity of demand. This means that the change in the quantity demanded is equal to the change in price (in percentages). These cases are summarized in Table 4.1.

Table 4.1 The values of the price elasticity of demand

	Value (ignoring the sign)	Meaning
Price inelastic	< 1	The percentage change in the quantity demanded is less than the percentage change in price
Unitary elastic	1	The percentage change in the quantity demanded equals the percentage change in price
Price elastic	> 1	The percentage change in the quantity demanded is more than the percentage change in price

If the price elasticity of demand is zero (0), this means that price changes have no effect on the quantity demanded. If the price elasticity of demand is infinity (∞), this means that a change in price will have an infinite effect on the quantity demanded.

Example

Suppose that the quantity demanded of a good rises from 200 to 300 units when the price falls from £10 to £6. This means that:

$$\text{Percentage change in the quantity demanded} = \left(\frac{+100}{200}\right) \times 100 = +50\%$$

$$\text{Percentage change in price} = \left(\frac{-4}{10}\right) \times 100 = -40\%$$

$$\text{Price elasticity of demand} = \frac{+50}{-40} = -1.25$$

The negative sign in the price elasticity of demand shows that the quantity demanded falls as price increases. The 1.25 shows that demand is price elastic. The quantity demanded changes by 1.25 times as much as price (50 per cent compared to 40 per cent).

NOTE To calculate a percentage change, we use the following expression:

$$\frac{\text{Change in value}}{\text{Original value}} \times 100$$

It should be noted that the price elasticity of demand can also be calculated using the following equation:

$$\text{Price elasticity of demand} = \frac{\text{Change in the quantity demanded}}{\text{Change in price}} \times \frac{\text{Original price}}{\text{Original quantity demanded}}$$

For the example above:

$$\text{Price elasticity of demand} = \frac{+100}{-4} \times \frac{10}{200} = -1.25$$

Example

a. Imagine that the price of a product falls from £10 to £9 and the quantity demanded rises from 400 units to 500 units. This means that the change in the quantity demanded is:

$$\left(\frac{100}{400}\right) \times 100 = 25\%$$

The change in price is:

$$\left(\frac{-1}{10}\right) \times 100 = -10\%$$

The price elasticity of demand is:

$$\left(\frac{25\%}{-10\%}\right) = -2.5$$

This means that demand is price elastic, because its value (ignoring the sign) is > 1. The change in the quantity demanded is 2.5 times the change in price.

b. Imagine that the price of a product falls from £20 to £10 and the quantity demanded rises from 400 units to 500 units. This means that the change in the quantity demanded is:

$$\left(\frac{100}{400}\right) \times 100 = 25\%$$

The change in price is:

$$\left(\frac{-10}{20}\right) \times 100 = -50\%$$

The price elasticity of demand is:

$$\left(\frac{25\%}{-50\%}\right) = -0.5$$

This means that the demand is price inelastic, because the value is < 1.

c. If the price elasticity of demand for a product is –2, then this shows that a change in price has twice the effect on quantity demanded in percentages (because the value is 2) and they act in opposite directions (because the answer is negative). For example, a 5 per cent increase in price leads to a fall in quantity demanded calculated as:

$$-2 \times 5\% = -10\%$$

A 5 per cent fall in price leads to a 10 per cent rise in the quantity demanded of the product.

d. Imagine that the price elasticity of demand is –3 and the price of the product is cut by 10 per cent. The original quantity demanded is 200 units. With the price cut, then, given that the price elasticity of demand is negative, this means that the quantity demanded will now increase. If the price is cut is 10 per cent, then the quantity demanded increases as follows:

$$-3 \times -10\% = 30\%$$

$$30\% \times 200\,\text{units} = \left(\frac{30}{100}\right) \times 200 = 60\,\text{units}$$

So the new quantity demanded is:

$$200 \text{ units} + 60 \text{ units} = 260 \text{ units}$$

NOTE To calculate X per cent of a number Y, we use:

$$\left(\frac{X}{100}\right) \times Y$$

For example, 5 per cent of 200 units is:

$$\left(\frac{5}{100}\right) \times 200 = 10 \text{ units}$$

Put into practice

- If the price changes by 5 per cent and the quantity demanded changes by 2.5 per cent, what is the value of the price elasticity of demand?
- If the price increases from 10p to 12p, and the quantity demanded falls from 50 units to 45 units, what is the price elasticity of demand?
- If the price elasticity of demand is −0.5, what is the effect of a change in quantity demanded of:
    - a 10 per cent rise in price?
    - a 4 per cent fall in price?
- Four hundred units of a product are sold. If the price elasticity of demand is −2 and the price is cut by 5 per cent, what will the new quantity demanded be?

In some cases, the price elasticity of demand may be positive. This occurs when the demand curve is upward-sloping. When the demand curve is upward-sloping, a higher price leads to a higher quantity demanded, meaning that both the denominator and numerator move in the same direction, leading to a positive answer (see Figure 4.3). An upward-sloping demand curve may occur with Giffen or Veblen goods—see Chapter 3

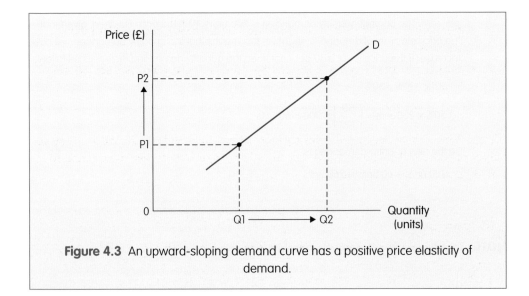

Figure 4.3 An upward-sloping demand curve has a positive price elasticity of demand.

High prices

Holiday companies know that parents are increasingly being prevented by head teachers from taking their children out of school and now fear being fined or taken to court if they decide to do it anyway. This means that there are particular weeks of the year during which families will have to go on holiday. Holiday companies respond to this by putting up prices—much to the annoyance of parents—because they know that, at these times, demand is not very sensitive to price: it is price inelastic.

Motorway cafes and restaurants often charge more for products than their city-centre rivals. This is because once you have decided to stop at a motorway cafe, the choice is limited, and most people cannot be bothered to leave and drive somewhere else to search for a cheaper alternative. Demand is therefore price inelastic.

Printer companies often charge relatively little to get you to buy a particular printer for your computer. After that, you have to buy specific ink cartridges and so demand for these is price inelastic, enabling the companies to make high profits on these. Similarly, what would you pay to restore your hard drive if your computer were to crash? Repairers know that demand for this service will be very price inelastic and charge accordingly.

? Question

Can you think of other situations in which demand is price inelastic, so that firms increase prices?

Put into practice

Calculate the price elasticity of demand for the following examples.

- The price increases from £10 to £12 and the quantity demanded falls from 400 units to 300 units.

- The price increases from £10 to £12 and the quantity demanded rises from 400 units to 500 units.

- The price decreases from £40 to £30 and the quantity demanded increases from 50 units to 55 units.

The price elasticity of demand will vary between products and can change over time for a given product as demand conditions change. For example, firms may take action to try to make demand more price inelastic.

What do you think?

Do you think that firms would prefer demand for their products to be price elastic or price inelastic? Why?

What action might firms take to influence the price elasticity of demand for their products? In 2011–12 Westminster council made £41.6m profit from car parkng charges despite complaints about the higher prices it charged. What do you think this tells us about the price elasticity for parking in Westminster?

Put into practice

The table shows a demand schedule for a product. Within what price range is the price elasticity of demand –2.5?

Price (£)	Quantity demanded
10	40
9	50
8	60
7	70
6	80

a. A price change from £10 to £9

b. A price change from £9 to £8

c. A price change from £8 to £7

d. A price change from £7 to £6

Determinants of the price elasticity of demand

Whether the demand for a particular product is price elastic or price inelastic (that is, how sensitive demand is to price) depends on factors such as the following.

- **How differentiated the product is** If a product has a strong brand image or a unique selling proposition, then customers cannot easily find substitutes and so the impact of a price change on the quantity demanded of this product will be small relative to the price change. The demand will be price inelastic. Visiting the Eiffel Tower in Paris, for example, may be a unique experience and so demand to go up it may not be very sensitive to price.

- **The time period involved** If a firm puts its price up, then customers may find it difficult to find an alternative in the short term. Customers may be used to buying a particular brand, going to a particular restaurant, or using a particular accountant, and so demand for these goods and services is price inelastic at any given moment. With more time, customers may be able to find other providers that are similar, but cheaper, and so demand becomes more price elastic. A price increase by your insurer, or gas or electricity provider, may have a limited impact in the short run because you are locked into a contract or do not have the time to look for alternative providers, but over time, you are likely to search for a cheaper option.

- **Whether the firm has built a relationship with its customers** Some organizations aim to develop loyalty from their customers (for example, supermarket loyalty programmes or frequent flyer rewards); these will make the customer less sensitive to price changes, because they feel loyal to the business. A local newspaper may increase price, for example, if it thinks it has a fairly loyal readership.

- **The breadth of product category being considered** Demand for petrol as a whole is likely to be price inelastic: car drivers cannot easily do without it. However, demand for any one garage's petrol is likely to be more price elastic than for petrol as a whole; this is because drivers can switch to a competitor's garage if there is a noticeable price difference. Similarly, the demand for Marlboro cigarettes is more price elastic than the demand for all cigarettes, the demand for Levis is more price elastic than the demand for jeans, and the demand for Nescafé is more price elastic than demand for instant coffee, because people can switch more easily from the brand than from the product. The wider the category examined, therefore, the more price inelastic demand will be because the less alternatives there are.

- **Who is paying** If you have to pay a bill yourself, you are likely to be fairly sensitive to the price. If, however, someone else is paying (for example, your parents or your company), then you are likely to be less sensitive to price. You may not be so concerned about price increases or search so hard to compare prices, because it is not your money. Demand would therefore be more price inelastic. You can see this when travelling: first-class and business seats are much more expensive, because firms are paying rather than the individuals themselves. How many of those passengers would have travelled economy class if they had been paying themselves?

- **The awareness and availability of substitutes** If customers know that there are many similar substitute products available, then they will be more likely to switch between them if there are noticeable differences in price. The demand will be more price elastic. The growth of the Internet has made it easier to compare prices (not least because there are websites that search for the best deal for you) and this has made demand for many products more price elastic.

- **The percentage of income spent on the product** If you spend a considerable amount of money on an item, then you may be more likely to shop around for the best buy. You may be more aware of the price of a new car or a holiday, for example, than of the price of a pint of milk. Demand for products that account for a high percentage of your income are therefore likely to be more price elastic than those that involve a small percentage of income, because you will compare and look around more for such a big purchase.

- **The nature of the product** If a product is habit-forming or addictive, such as cigarettes, demand is likely to be price inelastic. The impact of a price increase will be relatively small. Similarly, demand for necessities such as bread, coffee, tea, electricity, and gas is price inelastic. If, however, it is a 'shopping good', for which people tend to look around and compare prices between stores (for example, washing machines, dishwashers, and beds), then demand is likely to be more price elastic.

Put into practice

Which of the following statements are true and which are false? Demand is likely to be more price inelastic

a. if there are only a few substitutes.

b. if a large percentage of income is spent on it.

c. if someone else is paying for it.

d. in the short term compared to the long term.

What do you think?

Do you think that people are likely to be more sensitive to prices when the economy is in decline or booming? Explain your answer.
   Under what circumstances might a firm want demand for its products to be price elastic?

Put into practice

1. What do you expect the effect on the price elasticity of demand for a product to be in the following situations?

   • A competitor enters the market with a similar product.

   • A firm invests in a successful advertising campaign for the product.

   • The product is technologically advanced and has **patent** protection, meaning that it cannot be copied by others for several years.

2. Are the following statements true or false?

   a. The price elasticity of demand on a downward-sloping demand curve is negative.

   b. If the price elasticity of demand is –2, this means that demand is price inelastic.

   c. If a 5 per cent change in price changes the quantity demanded by 20 per cent, then demand is price elastic.

   d. If the price elasticity of demand is –0.5, then a 20 per cent increase in price reduces the quantity demanded by 10 per cent.

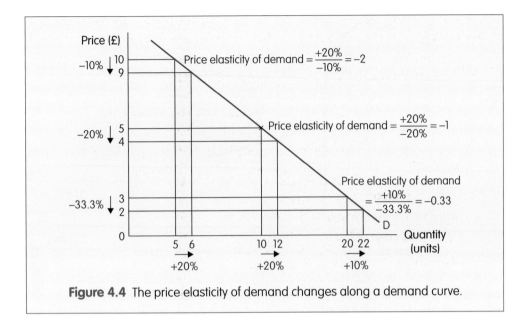

Figure 4.4 The price elasticity of demand changes along a demand curve.

The value of the price elasticity of demand along a demand curve

The price elasticity of demand for a product changes along a downward-sloping straight line demand curve (see Figure 4.4). At the top of the demand curve, the demand is price elastic (see Figure 4.5): a price change leads to a bigger percentage change in the quantity demanded. At the bottom of the demand curve, the demand is price inelastic. In the middle of the demand curve (exactly halfway along the curve between the origin and where it cuts the quantity axis), the price elasticity of demand is unitary.

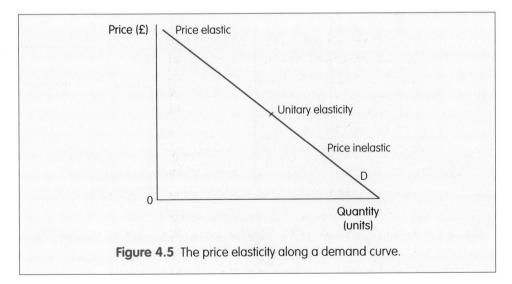

Figure 4.5 The price elasticity along a demand curve.

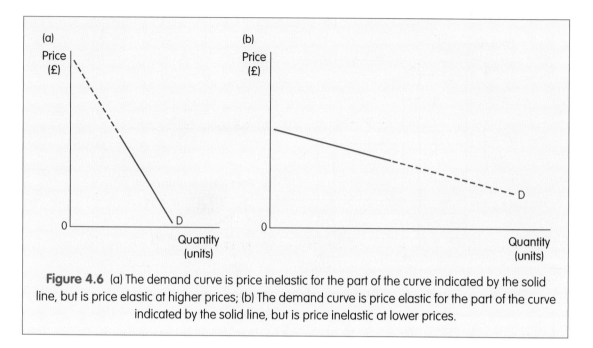

Figure 4.6 (a) The demand curve is price inelastic for the part of the curve indicated by the solid line, but is price elastic at higher prices; (b) The demand curve is price elastic for the part of the curve indicated by the solid line, but is price inelastic at lower prices.

When we talk of a price inelastic demand or a price elastic demand in relation to a downward sloping straight line demand curve, this is because we are focusing on a particular section of a demand curve. Demand may be insensitive to price within a given price band, for example, but if the price continues to increase, then the demand will, at some point, become price elastic (see Figure 4.6).

If demand is completely price inelastic this means the quantity demanded does not change with price as shown in Figure 4.7

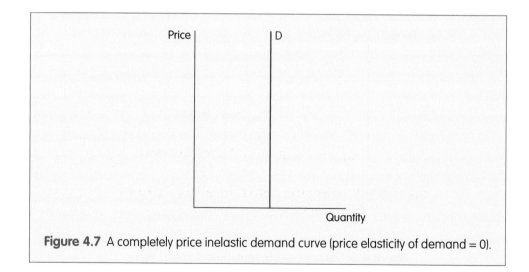

Figure 4.7 A completely price inelastic demand curve (price elasticity of demand = 0).

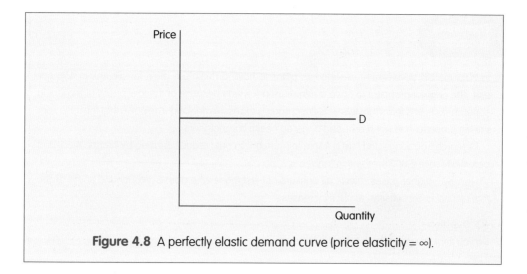

Figure 4.8 A perfectly elastic demand curve (price elasticity = ∞).

If demand is completely price elastic this means that a change in price leads to an infinite change in quantity demanded. This is shown in Figure 4.8.

If demand is unit elastic this means a percentage change in price leads to the same percentage change in quantity demanded. This leads to a demand curve that is known as a rectangular hyperbola as shown in Figure 4.9

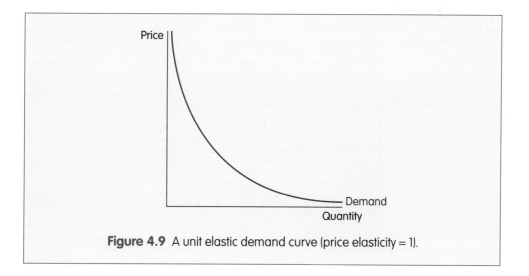

Figure 4.9 A unit elastic demand curve (price elasticity = 1).

In 2013 the UK government dropped its plans to have a minimum price for alcohol of 45p per unit. The original proposal to have a minimum price was because of the low prices of alcohol in supermarkets and fears that this was encouraging excessive drinking. The news that the minimum pricing proposal had been dropped angered health campaigners.

Research had suggested that a 45p minimum price could reduce drinking by around 4.3% and potentially save 2,000 lives within ten years.

However, higher prices affects all drinkers not just those who abuse alcohol and some argue that alcohol is not sensitive to price increases.

? **Question**

Do you think the government should introduce a minimum price for alcohol?

The price elasticity of demand and total revenue

The **total revenue** is the earnings generated from selling a product. It represents the value of sales and does not consider costs. The value of the total revenue depends on the quantity sold and the price per unit, as follows (see Figure 4.10):

Total revenue = Price per unit × Quantity sold

For example, if the price of a product is £10 and the quantity sold is 20 units, then the total revenue earned is:

£10 × 20 = £200

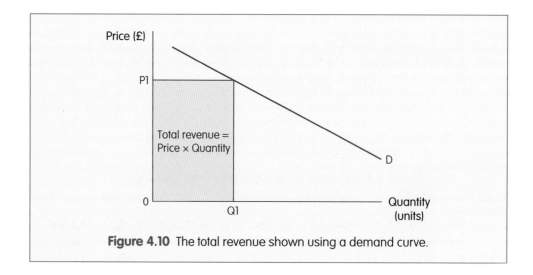

Figure 4.10 The total revenue shown using a demand curve.

Table 4.2 The impact of a price fall on revenue, depending on the price elasticity of demand

	Value (ignoring the sign)	Impact on revenue of a price fall
Price elastic	>1	Revenue increases
Unitary elastic	1	Revenue stays the same
Price inelastic	<1	Revenue decreases

If the demand for a product is price inelastic, then an increase in price will lead to an increase in revenue. Although there will be a fall in the quantity demanded, the higher price per item sold will more than compensate for the loss in the number of products sold. If demand is price inelastic, then a fall in price will lead to a fall in revenue. This is because the quantity demanded will increase, but not enough to compensate for the fall in price per item. If demand is price elastic, then an increase in price will lead to a fall in revenue. The fall in sales outweighs the increase in price per item. However, a fall in price will lead to an increase in revenue; this is because the increase in sales is so great that it outweighs the fall in price per unit.

These statements are summarized in Table 4.2.

If demand has a price elasticity of one (1), then the total revenue will not change when the price changes (see Figure 4.11). The effect of the change in sales exactly offsets the change in revenue from the change in the price per unit.

The estimation of the price elasticity of demand is therefore very important for firms when determining a pricing strategy. Managers will often want to increase the revenue that they generate from sales. To do this, managers should:

- lower price if demand is price elastic; or

- increase price if demand is price inelastic.

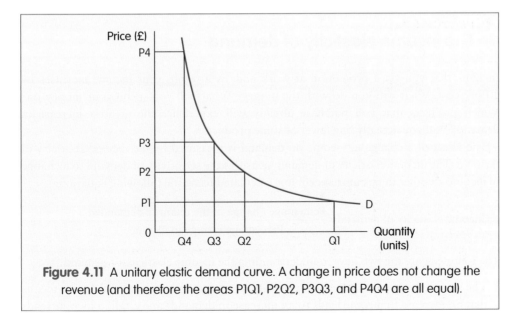

Figure 4.11 A unitary elastic demand curve. A change in price does not change the revenue (and therefore the areas P1Q1, P2Q2, P3Q3, and P4Q4 are all equal).

An understanding of price elasticity and the impact of this on pricing policies can be seen when firms price discriminate; this occurs when they charge different groups of customers different prices for the same product (see Chapter 15).

Put into practice

1. Consider the following two situations.

   a. The price of a product is increased from £10 to £11. The quantity demanded falls from 50 units to 30 units.

   b. The price of a product is increased from £10 to £11. The quantity demanded falls from 50 units to 49 units.

   Answer the following questions for each situation.

   - What is the price elasticity of demand?
   - What is the original total revenue before the price change?
   - What is the new total revenue after the price change?
   - Delete as appropriate in the following: The conclusion is that when demand is price elastic, total revenue will [increase/decrease] following a price increase.

2. Are the following statements true or false?

   a. If demand is price elastic, a price fall increases revenue.

   b. If demand is price inelastic, a price increase decreases revenue.

   c. If demand has unit price elasticity, then a price change has no effect on revenue.

   d. Demand has a constant value along a demand curve.

The income elasticity of demand

Imagine that you get a promotion at work and, as a result, your income increases by 10 per cent. What will you do with the money? What will you spend your money on? Which products that you purchase already will experience the greatest increase in demand? Will you actually buy fewer of some products?

The effect of a change in income on demand is measured by the income elasticity of demand. The income elasticity of demand measures the sensitivity of demand to a change in income all other things unchanged. It is calculated using the following equation:

$$\text{Income elasticity of demand} = \frac{\text{Percentage change in the quantity demanded}}{\text{Percentage change in income}}$$

The following are the two keys to understanding the income elasticity of demand.

- **The sign of the answer** If the income elasticity of demand is positive, then this means that an increase in income leads to an increase in demand (and a fall in income leads

Economics in context

The following table shows estimates of price elasticities of demand for various goods and services.

Goods	Estimated elasticity of demand
Inelastic	
Salt	0.10
Matches	0.10
Toothpicks	0.10
Airline travel, short run	0.10
Coffee	0.25
Tobacco products, short run	0.45
Legal services, short run	0.40
Taxi, short run	0.60
Automobiles, long run	0.20
Approximately unitary elastic	
Movies	0.90
Housing, owner-occupied, long run	1.20
Private education	1.10
Elastic	
Restaurant meals	2.30
Foreign travel, long run	4.00
Airline travel, long run	2.40
Fresh green peas	2.80
Automobiles, short run	1.20–1.50
Chevrolet automobiles	4.00
Fresh tomatoes	4.60

Sources: Bohi (1981); Cheng and Capps Jr (1988); Gwartney and Stroup (1997); Houthakker and Taylor (1970); US Department of Agriculture.

? Questions

a. Based on the estimates above, which is more price elastic?

- Demand for matches or demand for fresh tomatoes.

- Demand for cars in general or demand for Chevrolet cars.

Explain why you think this is.

b. Would an increase in price increase or decrease the total spending on:

- restaurant meals?

- taxis?

Explain why you think this is.

to a fall in demand)—that is, income and the quantity demanded move in the same direction. Products with a positive income elasticity of demand are known as 'normal goods'.

If the income elasticity of demand is negative, then this means that an increase in income leads to a fall in demand (and a fall in income leads to an increase in demand)—that is, income and the quantity demanded move in opposite directions. These products are known as 'inferior goods'. With more income, for example, people may switch from own-brand items to more luxurious brands.

- **The size of the answer** If the value of the income elasticity of demand (regardless of the sign) is > 1, then the product is known as a luxury product: demand is very sensitive to income. For example, a value of +3 means that the percentage increase in demand is three times as much as the percentage increase in income. A 1 per cent increase in income will lead to a 3 per cent increase in the quantity demanded. These may be luxury products such as health clubs, sports cars, and cruise holidays.

If the income elasticity of demand is < 1 (ignoring the sign), then the product is known as a necessity: demand is not particularly sensitive to income. For example, if the income elasticity of demand is +0.5, then this means that the percentage change in demand is 0.5 times as much as the percentage change in income. These may be necessity items such as soaps and shampoos.

Note that the sign of the income elasticity provides information on the direction of the changes; it does not tell us whether demand is income elastic or not—this information comes from the size of the figure.

The different forms of income elasticity can be illustrated on an Engel curve (see Figure 4.12).

Understanding the income elasticity of demand is important to firms because it shows what the effect of income changes might be on demand. If, for example, an economy is expected to grow faster in the future, then the income elasticity should give an insight into what might happen to sales. Sales of luxury normal goods should increase relatively significantly; sales of inferior products should fall. The effect of a change in income on sales would then influence a number of decisions within the business, such as planning staffing levels, cash flow, and profit forecasts.

The income elasticity of demand determines the extent to which the demand curve shifts when income increases; this shows the size of the income elasticity of demand.

The direction of the shift (that is, outward or inward) shows whether the good is normal or inferior (see Figure 4.13). A luxury normal good would shift a relatively significant

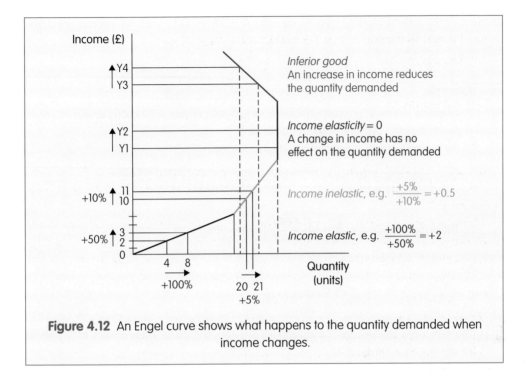

Figure 4.12 An Engel curve shows what happens to the quantity demanded when income changes.

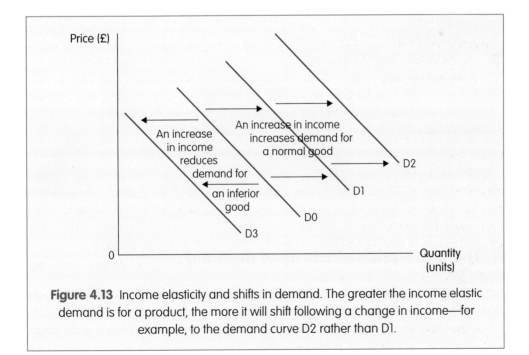

Figure 4.13 Income elasticity and shifts in demand. The greater the income elastic demand is for a product, the more it will shift following a change in income—for example, to the demand curve D2 rather than D1.

distance to the right if income were to increase (e.g. D0 to D2); with an inferior good, the demand would shift inwards (e.g. D0 to D3).

Example

The average income in an area increases from £40,000 per year to £44,000 per year. Membership of local health clubs increases by 20 per cent.

The income elasticity of demand is defined as follows:

$$\text{Income elasticity of demand} = \frac{\text{Percentage change in the quantity demanded}}{\text{Percentage change in income}}$$

$$\text{Percentage change in income} = \left(\frac{4,000}{40,000}\right) \times 100 = 10\%$$

So:

$$\text{Income elasticity of demand} = \frac{+20\%}{+10\%} = +2$$

The demand is positive, which means that it is a normal product. It has a value of > 1, which means that it is income elastic.

Put into practice

- The average income in an area increases from £40,000 per year to £60,000 per year. Sales of carpets increase by 10 per cent. Calculate the income elasticity of demand for this product. Is demand for it income elastic or inelastic?

- What would it mean if the income elasticity of demand for a product were to be zero?

What do you think?

How might an understanding of income elasticity of demand affect a retailer of consumer electrical goods?

▓ The cross-price elasticity of demand

So far, we have examined the sensitivity of demand to a change in price and a change in income. However, demand will also be affected by changes in the price of other products. When you are choosing a new laptop or washing machine, you naturally look at the prices of a range of models. When you are buying a car, you will also consider the other costs associated with running it, such as fuel, insurance, and tax. Changes in the price of other products (both substitutes and complements) will therefore affect demand for any given product. This effect is measured by the cross-price elasticity of demand.

The cross-price elasticity of demand measures the sensitivity of demand of one product to changes in the prices of other goods and services all other things unchanged. It is calculated using the following equation:

$$\text{Cross-price elasticity of demand} = \frac{\text{Percentage change in demand for product A}}{\text{Percentage change in the price of product B}}$$

If the cross-price elasticity of demand is positive, this means that demand for one product increases when the price of another product increases (or one falls when the other falls). These products are substitutes—for example, two brands of coffee. An increase in the price of one brand causes customers to switch to another one.

The size of the answer shows how close the two products are as substitutes: the bigger the answer, the more closely related they are. For example, if the cross-price elasticity of demand is +2, this means that the increase in the quantity demanded of product A is twice the percentage increase in the price of product B. The easier it is for customers to switch between the two and the more similar they think the products are, the greater will be the value of the cross-price elasticity.

If the cross-price elasticity of demand is negative, this means that the products are complements—that is, an increase in the price of one product leads to a fall in the quantity demanded of the other. If the price of Sony Playstation consoles increases, for example, this is likely to reduce the quantity demanded of Playstations and the demand for PS computer games as well. Playstation consoles and PS computer games are therefore complements.

If the cross-price elasticity of demand is −3, for example, this means that a given percentage increase in the price of product B will lead to a fall in demand for product A that is three times bigger (in percentages).

The cross-price elasticity of demand is important because it shows the relationship between price changes of other products and the impact on your demand. In most markets, managers keep a close eye on competitors' pricing strategies; they will be particularly interested in those with a high cross-price elasticity of demand.

What do you think?

What do you think a cross-price elasticity of demand of zero would mean?

What if the value of the cross-price elasticity of demand were infinity?

We have analysed the impact of a change in price, in income, and the price of other firms on a demand curve using elasticity. There are many other factors affecting demand that could be analysed using the concept of elasticity of demand, such as changes in advertising expenditure. Can you think of any more?

Table 4.3   Summary table for price, income, and cross-price elasticities of demand

Type of elasticity of demand	Sign	Size	Type of product
Price	–	>1	Price elastic; downward-sloping demand curve
Price	–	<1	Price inelastic; downward-sloping demand curve
Price	+	Any value	Veblen good or Giffen good; upward-sloping demand curve
Income	+		Normal good
Income	–	Any value >1	Inferior good
Income	+		Luxury
Income	+	Any value <1	Necessity
Cross-price	–	The higher the value, the stronger the relationship	Complements
Cross-price	+	The higher the value, the stronger the relationship	Substitutes

Table 4.3 provides a summary of our discussions of price, income, and cross-price elasticities of demand.

▣ Practical limitations of the concept of elasticity of demand

In theory, the various measures of the elasticity of demand help managers to understand the impact of changes in different variables on their sales. This is important to their planning: for example, when estimating their production and financial requirements, or required staffing and stock levels. However, whilst a knowledge of the price, income, and cross-price elasticities of demand can certainly be useful, in reality using them can be difficult for the following reasons.

- Each of the equations for the elasticity of demand measures the relationship between changes in one specific factor and demand with all the other factors held constant: for example, the price elasticity of demand analyses the impact of a change in price on the quantity demanded with everything else remaining the same. In reality, many factors may be changing at the same time, such as the spending on advertising, competitors' promotional strategies, and customers' incomes, as well as the firm's price. It may therefore be difficult to know what specifically has caused any change in the quantity demanded. A fall in price may be accompanied by an increase in quantity demanded, but this may not be the cause—it could have been due to other factors that also changed at the same time,

Different types of elasticity of demand

The concept of elasticity is very flexible and can be extended to any variable. It is, after all, simply trying to quantify any correlation between a variable and the quantity demanded, which firms can then use in their planning. In some sectors, the weather may have a big impact on the quantity demanded: for example, cold weather leads to fewer people going shopping, whilst it increases the number of people going into hospital. Retail and health-care managers would be interested in the weather elasticity of demand. Umbrella manufacturers may be interested in the rainfall elasticity of demand. Managers will naturally look for the key variables that affect demand for their specific products and calculate their own forms of elasticity of demand. The advertising elasticity of demand, for example, is commonly used because it shows the relationship between advertising expenditure and the quantity demanded. This could be a very important relationship for marketing managers to understand when deciding how to allocate their marketing budget. The greater the advertising elasticity of demand, the greater the effect of any percentage change in advertising spending (see Figure 4.14).

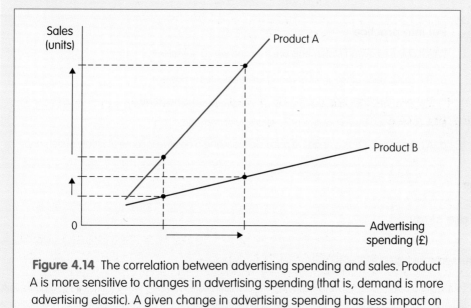

Figure 4.14 The correlation between advertising spending and sales. Product A is more sensitive to changes in advertising spending (that is, demand is more advertising elastic). A given change in advertising spending has less impact on demand for product B.

? Questions

What might be important influences on the demand for each of the following?

• Barbecue sets

• Skis

• Solar panels

- Cosmetics
- University places
- Dentists

such as the weather. A value of the price elasticity of demand that is calculated assuming the change in quantity demanded was all due to the price change may be very misleading.

- To know the elasticity of demand, managers must either look back at what happened in the past when, for example, prices or incomes were changed (but the conditions are likely to have altered since then), or estimate for themselves what the values are now (in which case, they may be wrong because it is an estimate). The value of elasticity is, therefore, not actually known at any moment; rather, it is merely estimated—perhaps based on past data. This means that managers should be careful about basing decisions on their estimates of the elasticity, because the values will be changing all of the time as demand conditions change.

Put into practice

Which of the following statements are true and which are false?

a. The cross-price elasticity of demand for substitutes is positive.

b. The income elasticity of demand for an inferior good is negative.

c. A Giffen good has a positive price elasticity of demand.

d. A normal good has a negative price elasticity and a positive income elasticity of demand.

Case study

The following advice concerns the launch of new products.

Launching a new product always needs careful consideration. However, when launching in a particularly saturated market, your product not only needs to be up to scratch but the other elements of your business must be able to cope too. Last year, when we launched premium mattress brand Dormeo Octaspring, this was an issue we had to face from the get-go. …

We were lucky that our product offering was new and exciting, as this made it easier when speaking to retailers. For years, mattresses have been made with either metal springs or memory foam; we revolutionised this by creating memory foam springs.

We found it important to be confident that our product was market ready before speaking to stockists. To feel confident in working with us, retailers needed to see more of our business processes and proof that we could cope with demand and delivery. Your product may be great, but if retailers are unsure that you have the business function and personnel to deliver their orders, they will be unlikely to work with you. Since launching last year we have secured a total of 280 stockists across the UK, and this was achieved through the combination of forward planning and having a strong product.

Another key to success is getting the product in front of as many people as possible. Showing at trade shows, sharing samples with journalists, or those well known in the industry, will heighten brand awareness and open up dialogue with new customers.

Naturally, when a consumer is looking to purchase a new item, they will only select products from brands that they are already aware of. While people do impulse buy, those long-term investment buys are often well thought out. It's therefore imperative that they know of you to ensure that your product is part of the initial selection process. While exposure isn't an exact science in terms of sales and driving footfall to shop floors, it's extremely powerful, and should be part of a brand's wider strategy.

Product aside, we also thought carefully about how we marketed the brand. Dormeo Octaspring is a modern company, which helped us to stand out in a category that's slow to embrace modern realities. Therefore, our company ethos of offering innovation in our product also had to work across our marketing platforms. We've been quick to embrace digital technologies, and have invested heavily in both digital and social media channels – it's imperative to recognise the importance of social media, or as we call it "social influence"; engaging in conversations your customers are having goes a long way in building brand loyalty and trust. We have found that using online platforms has been one of the most cost-effective and influential ways to engage with potential clients …

Although we have had an extremely successful year, it hasn't all been plain sailing. There have been a lot of barriers to overcome, and equally, a lot of lessons learned. From finding UK specific distribution partners to wholly owning the business and implementing the brand's philosophy to make it a success, it has been a rollercoaster journey. And we are still at the very beginning. It was only by following the advice I have shared with you that we have been able to make the most of having a fantastic product in a heavily saturated market.

Source: John Bramm is managing director of Dormeo Octaspring. Reproduced from Guardian article: http://www. guardian.co.uk/small-business-network/2013/jun/11/successfully-launch-new-product-advice © Guardian News and Media Ltd 2013.

❓ Questions

1　Discuss the factors that might affect demand for this product.

2　Do you think demand for this new product is likely to be price inelastic or price elastic? Why?

3　Imagine that demand becomes more price sensitive over time as competitors improve their offering. How will this affect the pricing of the product?

4　Do you think demand for this product is income elastic or inelastic? Why?

5　Can you think of any products with which this product is likely to have a positive cross-price elasticity? Explain your choice.

6　What about a negative cross-price elasticity? Why?

Review questions

1　Explain what it means if the price elasticity of demand is negative.

2　Explain what it means if the price elasticity of demand equals zero.

3　Explain how a firm can try to make demand for its products more price inelastic.

4　Is it better for a firm wanting to increase prices to have a price elastic or a price inelastic demand?

5　If a firm has a high income elasticity of demand for its products how might this affect its marketing?

6 Explain what it means if the income elasticity of demand for a product is negative.

7 Explain what it means if the value of the cross price elasticity of demand is +2

8 How might an understanding of the cross-price elasticity of demand be useful to business?

Put into practice

The price elasticity of demand is –0.8. The price rises by 5 per cent. Sales were 2,000 units. What was the old revenue and what is the new revenue?

The income elasticity of demand is +1.5. Sales have increased from 4,000 units to 4,500 units following a change in income. Originally the average income was £30,000. What did it change to?

Key learning points

- The concept of elasticity measures how sensitive demand is to a change in a variable.
- The sign of the answer highlights whether changes in quantity demanded and the variable move in the same direction or in opposite directions.
- The size of the answer shows the strength of the relationship between the variable and quantity demanded.
- There are many types of elasticity measuring how different variables such as price, income, and the prices of other products affect the quantity demanded.
- An understanding of the elasticity of demand will help a firm in its planning, for example of stock levels, pricing, and staffing.

References

Bohi, D.R. (1981) *Analyzing Demand Behavior*, Johns Hopkins University Press, Baltimore, MD

Cheng, H.-T. and Capps, Jr, O. (1988) 'Demand analysis of fresh, and frozen finfish, and shellfish in the US', *American Journal of Agricultural Economics*, 70(3): 533–42

Gwartney, J.D. and Stroup, R.L. (1997) *Economics: Private, and Public Choice*, 8th edn, Dryden Press, Fort Worth, TX

Houthakker, H.S. and Taylor, L.D. (1970) *Consumer Demand in the US, 1929–1970*, Harvard University Press, Cambridge, MA

Learn more

The concept of elasticity can also be applied to supply. To find out more about the price elasticity of supply, see Chapter 5.

 Visit our Online Resource Centre at http://www.oxfordtextbooks.co.uk/orc/gillespie_econ3e/ for test questions and further information on topics covered in this chapter.

Supply

The previous chapter examined the factors that influence the demand for products, showing what consumers are willing and able to buy. This chapter examines the factors that influence the supply of a product—that is, what suppliers are willing and able to produce at different prices.

LEARNING OBJECTIVES

By the end of this chapter, you should be able to:

✓ explain what is shown by a supply curve;

✓ understand the difference between a change in the quantity supplied and a change in supply;

✓ explain the causes of a shift in a supply curve;

✓ understand the concept of the price elasticity of supply.

▦ Introduction to supply

The demand curve shows what consumers are willing and able to purchase at each and every price, all others things being unchanged. This is one part of a market. It tells us about the buyers. The other part of any market is the supply curve. This tells us about the sellers. The supply of a product is the amount that producers are willing and able to produce at each and every price, all others things being unchanged. For example, it might show how many houses a construction firm might want to build at different selling prices, or how many live performances a band might want to make at different appearance fees. The amount supplied will depend on factors such as the price, costs, the number of producers, and the resources available.

The supply curve is usually upward-sloping. A higher price is usually needed for firms to be willing and able to produce more, all other things being unchanged; as the price increases, it becomes more feasible and appealing to produce more units. This assumes that to produce more, the extra costs will increase, which means that a higher price is needed by producers to be able to produce.

▓ Movement along the supply curve

Businesses usually need a higher price to cover the extra costs of producing extra units: for example, to extract more oil may require more complex technology, to open more stores may require more land which may be increasingly expensive to get hold of, and to produce more you may need to pay more to keep recruiting staff. If the extra costs of producing increase this means that the supply curve would be usually upward-sloping.

An increase in price (P1 – P2) will usually lead to an increase in the quantity supplied (Q1 – Q2). This is known as an **extension of supply** (see Figure 5.1). A fall in the quantity supplied is called a **contraction of supply** (see Figure 5.2). A change in the price of a product all other things unchanged will therefore cause a change in the quantity supplied; this

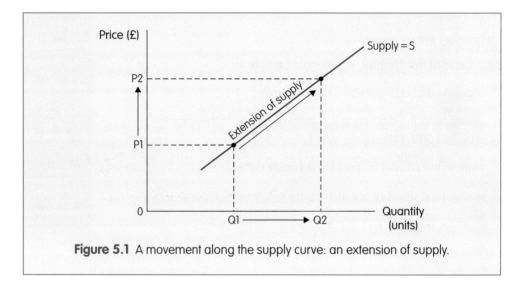

Figure 5.1 A movement along the supply curve: an extension of supply.

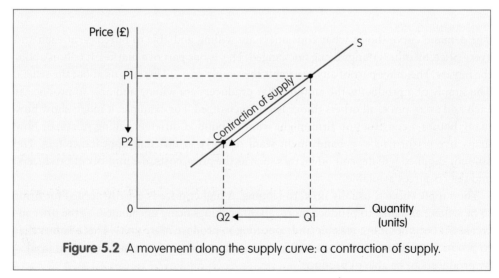

Figure 5.2 A movement along the supply curve: a contraction of supply.

is shown as a movement along the supply curve. The shape of the supply curve is linked to the extra costs of producing a unit; the derivation of the supply curve is examined in more detail in Chapter 9.

Put into practice

Consider the supply curve shown in Figure 5.3. What happens to the quantity supplied if the price increases from £6 to £20?

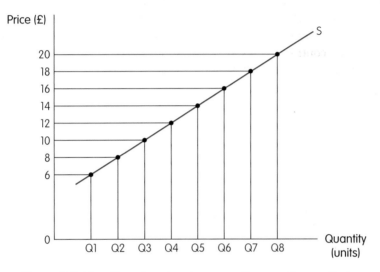

Figure 5.3 The effect of a price change on the quantity supplied.

What would the price have to be for Q7 units to be supplied?

Example

The equation for an upward-sloping, straight-line supply curve can take the form of:

$Q = 20 + 2P$

For example, if the price is £10, the quantity supplied is:

$Q = 20 + (2 \times 10) = 20 + 20 = 40$ units

If the price is £15, the quantity supplied is:

$Q = 20 + (2 \times 15) = 20 + 30 = 50$ units

Put into practice

- If the supply curve is given by the equation $Q = 5 + 3P$, what is the quantity supplied when the price is £10?

- If the supply curve is given by the equation $Q = 5 + 3P$, what is the quantity supplied when the price is £20?

Shifts in supply

A shift in supply means that the supply curve shifts to the right or left (see Figure 5.4). More (or fewer) products are supplied at each and every price. A change in price leads to a movement along the supply curve and assumes all other factors are unchanged; a shift in supply occurs when these other factors do change. An increase in supply is shown by a shift of the supply curve to the right: more is supplied at each and every price. A decrease in supply shifts the supply curve to the left: less is supplied at each and every price.

The reasons for a shift in the supply curve

The reasons for a shift in the supply curve include the following.

* **A change in the number of producers** If there is an increase in the number of producers in an industry, then this should lead to an increase in supply (this is shown by an out-ward shift of the supply curve). More can be produced at each and every price, because there are more suppliers. Producers may be attracted into an industry because they are attracted by the prospect of high returns.

* **A change in technology** New, better technology should enable firms to produce more at any price, thus shifting the supply curve to the right. Technological change might also enable more firms to enter the market. For example, online trading means that new banks, estate agents, or travel agents do not need to establish the same network of high-street outlets that they had to have in the past. Entry into these types of market is therefore easier than it used to be. With more firms in the industry this would increase the quantity supplied at each and every price.

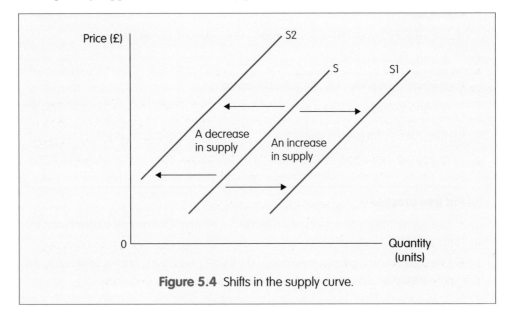

Figure 5.4 Shifts in the supply curve.

- **A change in costs** An increase in wages or the price of raw materials will mean that firms cannot supply as much at a given price because of higher costs. For any given level of output, they will need a higher price. The supply curve will therefore shift to the left (or inwards meaning less is supplied at any given price). In recent years, increases in the price of oil have significantly increased the energy costs of many firms; this has shifted the supply curves in some industries inwards.

- **A change in indirect taxes** If a tax, such as value added tax (VAT), is placed on the sale of goods, then this will increase the selling price of any given output. This type of tax increases the producers' costs because they are liable to pay it to the government and means that they will need a higher price for any given level of output or that less is supplied at any price. (This is analysed in more detail in Chapter 6.)

- **A change in weather conditions** This can be particularly important in agricultural markets, which are very vulnerable to changes in the natural environment. Poor weather can lead to supply shocks shifting supply to the left. Given the time period involved in growing crops, supply cannot quickly be increased again, which means that markets are affected significantly. In 2013, for example, Weetabix which usually prides itself on using locally sourced wheat had to use overseas wheat due to a terrible harvest in the UK.

Put into practice

Using diagrams, illustrate the impact of the following on a supply curve.

- A decrease in price
- A reduction in the number of producers
- A decrease in the costs of raw materials

Economics in context

British scientists recently announced that they have developed a new type of wheat which could increase productivity by 30 per cent.

The Cambridge-based National Institute of Agricultural Botany has combined an older type of wheat with a modern variety to produce a new strain. In the trials so far the new crop appears bigger and stronger than other varieties. It will take at least five years of tests and regulatory approval before it can be harvested. Some farmers argue that the government needs to speed up this process to ensure there is enough food to meet global demand.

Source: NIAB, http://www.niab.com/news_and_events/article/282

? Questions

What would you expect this new type of wheat to do to the supply of wheat? How would you show this on a diagram of a supply curve?

What do you think this will do to the price of wheat? What about farmers' incomes?

Example

If there is a change in supply conditions, the equation might change from:

$Q = 20 + 2P$

to:

$Q = 40 + 2P$

This would mean that more would be supplied at each and every price.
If the price is £10, the quantity supplied is:

$Q = 40 + (2 \times 10) = 40 + 20 = 60$ units (whereas before it was 40 units)

If the price is £15, the quantity supplied is:

$Q = 40 + (2 \times 15) = 40 + 30 = 70$ units (whereas before it was 50 units)

The supply curve has shifted outwards.

Put into practice

1. If the equation for the supply curve changes from $Q = 20 + 2P$ to $Q = 5 + 2P$, what has happened to the supply curve?

2. Which of the following could explain an outward shift in the supply curve for a product i.e. an increase in the quantity supplied at each price?

   a. A decrease in the cost of raw materials

   b. An increase in the cost of raw materials

   c. An increase in the wages paid to the workers

   d. A reduction in the number of firms producing

What do you think?

What do you think are likely to be the main determinants of the amount supplied of the following?

- Personal computers
- Wine
- Wheat
- Diamonds
- Schools

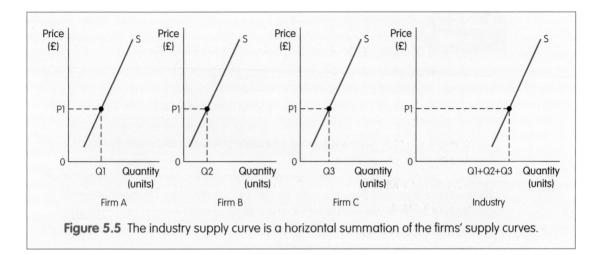

Figure 5.5 The industry supply curve is a horizontal summation of the firms' supply curves.

Industry supply

The industry supply curve is the total supplied by all the firms in the industry at each and every price. It is derived from the horizontal summation of all of the firms' supply curves (see Figure 5.5). At each and every price, the quantity that all of the firms are willing and able to supply are added together. An increase in the number of producers should therefore increase the total industry supply; this occurs when firms enter the industry. This may be because the government removes restrictions on the number and type of firms that can compete in a market, or because higher rewards provide an incentive to enter. In declining industries, firms will leave in search of higher rewards elsewhere and this will shift the industry supply to the left.

What do you think?

In 2013–14 world production of grains rose by 7 per cent to a record 2.5 billion tonnes. This led to end of season stocks of 568 m tonnes—the highest level for 12 years. American farmers have planted the biggest acreage of maize since 1936 and the weather helped create a good harvest. Why do you think farmers might have planted a large crop? What do you think might be the consequences of this for the farmers?

The effect of changes in different variables on supply is shown in Table 5.1.

Table 5.1

A change in	Leads to
Price	A movement along the supply curve
Costs	
Number of producers	A shift in supply
Technology	
Production subsidies	

IGas is one of the businesses that want to extract shale gas from the UK. It believes there may be up to 170 trillion cubic feet (4,810 cubic km) of gas in the 300 square miles where it is licensed to operate in Cheshire. However it is not clear yet how much of this will be economically viable to extract.

Shale gas is extracted by fracking; this means water is pumped with chemicals and sand at high pressure into rock in order to release gas. Critics of this approach claim that it can cause earthquakes.

The UK's gas consumption is currently around 3 trillion cubic feet per year. This means that with fracking the UK may have enough gas for over ten years and not need to import any more, especially given that there are areas of the UK other than Cheshire where extraction is taking place.

The amount of gas that can be extracted will become clearer once a significant number of wells have been drilled and the gas flow rates tested.

? Question

Illustrate the impact on the UK supply of gas in the UK if fracking goes ahead and is successful.

Joint supply

In some cases, products may be supplied together. If we kill more cows in order to eat their meat, then we will also have more leather hides produced. Although demand conditions for leather may not have altered, the supply of leather will shift to the right, changing the equilibrium price and output in this market.

The price elasticity of supply

The slope (gradient) of a supply curve will depend on how sensitive it is to changes in price. Can supply be easily changed in relation to a price increase or decrease, or not? The relationship between changes in price and the quantity supplied is analysed by the price elasticity of supply. The price elasticity of supply measures the extent to which the quantity supplied in a market varies with a change in price. It is calculated using the following equation:

$$\text{Price elasticity of supply} = \frac{\text{Percentage change in the quantity supplied}}{\text{Percentage change in price}}$$

The following are the two key elements to understanding the price elasticity of supply.

- **The sign of the answer** The sign of the answer will usually be positive, meaning that an increase in price increases the quantity supplied (and a fall in price reduces the quantity supplied)—that is, the price and the change in quantity supplied move in the same direction, assuming that the supply curve is upward-sloping.

- **The size (or value) of the answer** The size of the answer measures the strength of the relationship between the price and the quantity supplied. If the answer is greater than one (> 1), then this means that the percentage change in the quantity supplied is greater than the percentage change in price: supply is price elastic. For example, if the price elasticity of supply is +3, it means that a 1 per cent increase in price increases the quantity supplied by 3 per cent. If the price that people were willing and able to pay for a soft drink were to go up by 10 per cent, and producers could increase production by 30 per cent, supply would be price elastic.

If the answer is less than one (< 1), then this means that the percentage change in the quantity supplied is less than the change in price: supply is price inelastic. For example, if the price elasticity of supply is +0.5, it means that a 1 per cent increase in price increases the quantity supplied by 0.5 per cent. If the price that the government is willing to pay to build nuclear power stations were to increase by 10 per cent, then the number available could not increase overnight. It would take several years to build any more nuclear power stations and so the supply is not very sensitive to price in the short term: it is price inelastic. Similarly, supply in agriculture in the short run is usually price inelastic: you cannot quickly grow more crops.

What do you think?

What problems might firms have when trying to make production more flexible?

Economics in context

Flexible production

Many businesses are now focusing on making their production more flexible. They are investing in the latest technology to enable them to respond rapidly to changes in orders—adopting a 'just in time' approach to production, whereby they produce when the order arrives rather than in advance of the order. They are also:

- providing broad job descriptions to enable managers to move staff around the business to different sections as and when help is required;

- spending more money on training staff so that they are multi-skilled and can undertake a range of tasks—this means that they can be moved to where they are needed;

- using flexible suppliers who can quickly increase output if required; and

- employing more people on temporary contracts so that managers can increase or decrease the number of staff as needed.

❓ Question

By being more flexible to demand, manufacturers are trying to avoid producing, and hoping that demand materializes. What are the benefits of producing in response to demand rather than in advance of demand?

The value of the price elasticity of supply

The value of the price elasticity of supply for a product will depend on the following.

- **The number of firms in the industry** The more producers there are in an industry, the more likely it is that the level of output in the industry will change easily with price changes—that is, supply is likely to be more price elastic.

- **The time period** Over a longer period of time, resources can be shifted more easily from one sector to another; this will increase or decrease supply to a greater extent than in the short term, when at least one factor of production is fixed. In the immediate run, it may be impossible to change the quantity supplied at all, because resources are committed to their present use. This means that the supply curve may be totally inelastic and the price elasticity of supply would have a value of zero. Over time, with more resources and more businesses in the industry, the effect of a price increase will be greater, making supply more price elastic.

The price elasticity of supply is illustrated in Figure 5.6.

Extreme cases of price elasticity of supply

Figure 5.7 and Figure 5.8 illustrate extreme examples of the price elasticity of supply.

In Figure 5.7 supply is perfectly inelastic. Whatever the price charged the quantity supplied is the same. This could represent a cinema with a fixed number of seats regardless of the price.

Figure 5.8 illustrates a perfectly elastic supply curve; infinite amounts of the product can be supplied at the given price; for example, it might represent downloads from iTunes.

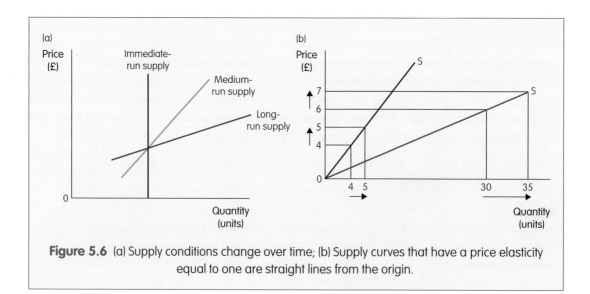

Figure 5.6 (a) Supply conditions change over time; (b) Supply curves that have a price elasticity equal to one are straight lines from the origin.

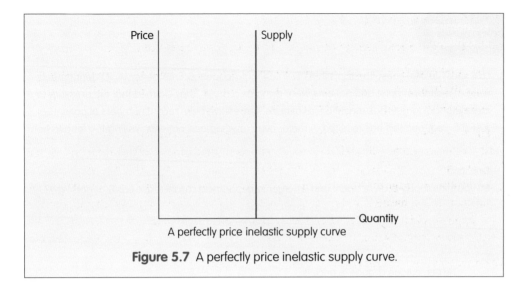

A perfectly price inelastic supply curve

Figure 5.7 A perfectly price inelastic supply curve.

Example

a. The price of a product is £10 and the quantity supplied is 200 units. The price increases to £12 and the quantity supplied increases to 300 units.

The percentage change in the quantity supplied is:

$$\left(\frac{100}{200}\right) \times 100 = +50\%$$

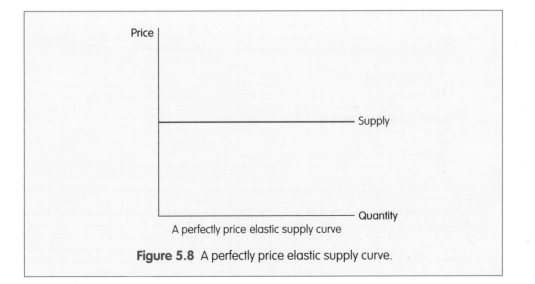

A perfectly price elastic supply curve

Figure 5.8 A perfectly price elastic supply curve.

Last year hospital consultants in Wales warned that Accident & Emergency (A&E) departments were at meltdown point and patients were dying as a result. They claimed that the pressure to meet financial targets has meant a loss of beds. There have been record numbers of patients at A&E this year and this has resulted in major overcrowding and patients waiting too long to be treated.

Question

Do you think supply in an Accident and Emergency department can increase easily or not? Why?

The percentage change in price is:

$$\left(\frac{2}{10}\right) \times 100 = +20\%$$

The price elasticity of supply is:

$$\left(\frac{+50}{+20}\right) = +2.5$$

This is price elastic because the value is > 1.

b. The price of a product is £10 and the quantity supplied is 200 units. The price increases to £12 and the quantity supplied increases to 220 units.

The percentage change in the quantity supplied is:

$$\left(\frac{20}{200}\right) \times 100 = +10\%$$

The percentage change in price is:

$$\left(\frac{2}{10}\right) \times 100 = +20\%$$

The price elasticity of supply is:

$$\frac{+10}{+20} = +0.5$$

This is price inelastic because the value is < 1.

c. The price elasticity of supply is +0.8 and the price of a product increases by 10 per cent. This means that the quantity supplied increases by:

$$0.8 \times 10\% = 8\%$$

d. The price elasticity of supply is +0.2. The price increases from £10 to £12. The quantity supplied was 500 units.

The change in price is:

$$\left(\frac{2}{10}\right) \times 100 = 20\%$$

The change in quantity supplied will be:

$$0.2 \times 20\% = 4\%$$

The quantity supplied is:

$$\left(\frac{4}{100}\right) \times 500 = 20 \text{ units}$$

So the new quantity supplied is:

$$500 \text{ units} + 20 \text{ units} = 520 \text{ units}$$

Put into practice

a. The price of a product increases from £5 to £8. The quantity supplied increases from 200 units to 400 units.

- What is the price elasticity of supply?
- Is supply price elastic or inelastic?

b. The price of a product increases from £5 to £8. The quantity supplied increases from 200 units to 210 units.

- What is the price elasticity of supply?
- Is supply price elastic or inelastic?

c. The price elasticity of supply is +0.1 and the price of a product increases by 10 per cent. How much does the quantity supplied increase?

d. The price elasticity of supply is +0.4. The price increases from £10 to £15. The quantity supplied was 200 units. What will be the new quantity supplied after the price increase?

What do you think?

Can you think of products that would have a price elastic supply? What about ones with a price inelastic supply?

Case study

According to the National Farmers Union (NFU) Britain's wheat harvest this year could be almost 30 per cent smaller than it was last year due to extreme weather. A smaller area was planted last autumn because of the wet soil conditions. However, the NFU said that world prices were unlikely to change as the world price was determined by world production.

The continually wet weather during planting time, between September and December, had resulted in less wheat being planted. Subsequent bad weather, including flooding and snowfalls, had further reduced the yield.

Most of the UK's wheat crop is harvested between July and September and last year's harvest also had lower volumes and quality because of weather extremes, with months of drought followed by downpours and flooding. Earlier this year, breakfast cereal producer Weetabix said it would have to temporarily scale back production of some of its products because of the poor wheat harvest.

This year global production is likely to be higher which may actually reduce prices.

Crops may be helped globally by better crop protection technology which helps the yield potential and grain quality by guarding against pests.

However, if the experts are to be believed and extreme weather is to become more frequent over the coming years, it may be important to look at ways of supporting the industry in the UK, perhaps by allowing more pesticides and possibly through subsidies.

❓ Questions

1 Analyse four factors which affect the supply of wheat in the UK.

2 Discuss whether you think the supply of wheat is likely to be price elastic or price inelastic.

3 Analyse the reasons why changes in UK supply are unlikely to affect the price of wheat in the world.

Review questions

1 Does a supply curve show how much producers would like to supply at each and every price?

2 Why is a change in the quantity supplied different from a change in supply?

3 Explain what might shift the supply curve for a product inwards (i.e. less is supplied at each price).

4 Explain why the price elasticity of supply for a product might be price inelastic.

5 Explain what might shift the supply curve of a product outwards (i.e. more is supplied at each price)

6 What is the effect of an increase in costs on supply?

7 What is the effect of an increase in the number of producers on supply?

8 What is shown by a price elasticity of supply of +0.1?

Put into practice

1 Changes in supply conditions make supply less price elastic. Show the effect of this using a diagram.

2 The price elasticity of supply is +2. The price was £50 a unit and sales were 500 units. The price increases by 10%. What were the suppliers earning before the price increase and how much will they be earning after the price increase if all the output is sold?

Key learning points

- The supply curve is usually upward-sloping.
- The supply curve is derived from the extra costs of production.
- A movement along the supply curve occurs when there is a change in price, all other factors unchanged.
- A shift in the supply curve occurs when there is a change in the quantity supplied at each and every price.
- An increase in supply means that more can be supplied at each and every price.
- A decrease in supply means that less is supplied at each and every price.
- The supply curve shows the decisions of producers; the demand curve shows the decisions of customers.

Learn more

A supply curve is actually derived from a marginal cost curve. To find out why, see Chapter 11.

 Visit our Online Resource Centre at http://www.oxfordtextbooks.co.uk/orc/gillespie_econ3e/ for test questions and further information on topics covered in this chapter.

»6 Market equilibrium

So far we have analysed the basic economic problems and then studied the factors influencing demand and supply conditions in a market. In this chapter we examine how the price mechanism brings about equilibrium and the effects of changes in supply and demand on the market price and quantity. This enables us to examine how the free market solves the basic economic problems. We can then go on to compare this with the planned economy.

LEARNING OBJECTIVES

By the end of this chapter, you should be able to:

✓ explain the meaning of equilibrium in a market;

✓ explain how the price adjusts in a market to bring about equilibrium;

✓ understand the impact on the equilibrium price and quantity of a shift in a supply or demand curve;

✓ understand the effect of indirect taxes and subsidies on the equilibrium price and output;

✓ understand the factors that determine the incidence of an indirect tax or subsidy on consumers and producers.

▓ Markets

A market occurs when buyers and sellers interact to exchange goods and services. This can be a physical market, such as a local farmers' market, in which local producers sell their goods, or an online market, such as eBay, in which the buyers and sellers never physically meet each other. The market may be primarily a local one with regional buyers and sellers, such as a taxi business, a national one, such as the market in the UK for health care, or a global one, such as the world market for oil.

■ Equilibrium

Equilibrium occurs in a market when, at the given price, the quantity supplied equals the quantity demanded and there is no incentive for this position to change. In a free market, the equilibrium output is reached by changes in the price. The decisions of producers and customers are made independently of each other; the price mechanism acts to bring these decisions together, and to equate the quantity supplied and demanded. As demand or supply conditions change the price will adjust to bring about a new equilibrium price and quantity.

How equilibrium is reached in theory in a market is highlighted in Figure 6.1. At P1 in this figure, the price is above the equilibrium level. At this price, the quantity supplied (Q1) is higher than the quantity demanded (Q3). There is excess supply (also known as a surplus) equal to Q1 – Q3. Given the relatively higher price, the amount that producers want to produce is greater than the quantity demanded by customers. This puts downward pressure on the price. To get rid of their stock and boost sales, firms will reduce prices. As the price falls, the quantity that firms are willing and able to sell falls, whilst the quantity demanded increases. This process continues until equilibrium is reached at P2. The price adjusts to equate supply and demand.

At P3 in Figure 6.2, the price is below the equilibrium level. At this price, the quantity demanded (Q3) is above the quantity supplied (Q1). This means that there is a shortage in the market (also known as 'excess demand') equal to Q3 – Q1. This will put upward pressure on the price. As the price increases, firms will be more willing to supply, whilst the

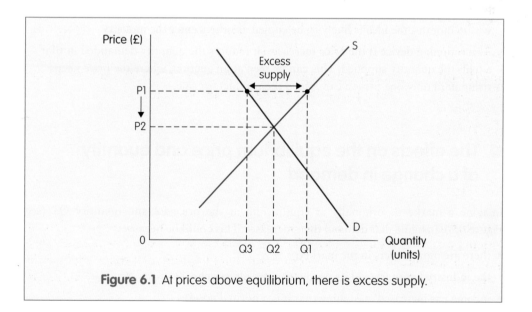

Figure 6.1 At prices above equilibrium, there is excess supply.

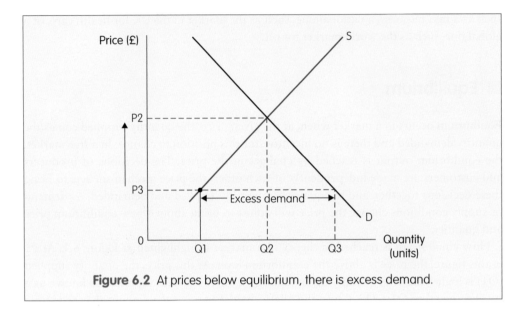

Figure 6.2 At prices below equilibrium, there is excess demand.

quantity demanded will fall. This process continues until the equilibrium price is reached at P2, and again there is no further incentive to change.

In this free market, the price mechanism changes to affect the decisions of producers and consumers. Price acts in the following ways.

- **As a signal and incentive** If the price rises, for example, this acts as a signal to other producers that this is an industry that they might want to enter to earn high profits. The high price acts as an incentive for firms to enter into this industry because of the potential rewards. This can be seen when a new business idea proves to be successful: within months, the idea is likely to be copied as others enter the industry.

- **As a rationing device** If the price increases, it reduces the quantity demanded until it equals the quantity supplied. This can be seen at an auction, where the price keeps rising until only one person can afford the product for sale.

▨ The effects on the equilibrium price and quantity of a change in demand

Imagine a market is originally at equilibrium at the price P2 and quantity Q2 (see Figure 6.3). Imagine that demand then increases. This could be because:

- there are more buyers in the market;
- the industry has marketed its products more effectively;
- income has increased (assuming that it is a normal good);

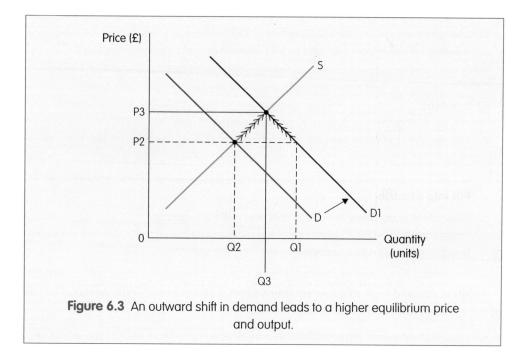

Figure 6.3 An outward shift in demand leads to a higher equilibrium price and output.

- the price of a complement has fallen; or
- the price of a substitute has increased.

As a result of this increase in price, there will be excess demand at the original price. Given that there is now a shortage (equal to Q1 − Q2), there will be upward pressure on the price. The price will increase, leading to a lower quantity demanded and a higher quantity supplied, until the new equilibrium is reached at the price P3 and quantity Q3. An increase in demand therefore leads to a higher equilibrium price and quantity. By comparison, an inward shift in demand will lead to a lower equilibrium price and quantity, assuming that the supply curve is upward-sloping.

Economics in context

Over 15 million plastic surgery procedures are performed around the world each year. This number is increasing by about 4 per cent a year.

The USA accounts for the most cosmetic enhancements, with over 3m procedures performed, or 21.1 per cent of the total. The USA has the largest body of licensed plastic surgeons (nearly 6000 at the last count). Brazil is second, with approximately 1.5m total procedures, and China was third with 1m. The UK has around 211,000 procedures a year. Botox is the most popular procedure, with over 3m injections of botulinum toxin (type A) administered across the world. Lipoplasty, or fat removal surgery, is the leading invasive procedure. Approximately 1.3m lipoplasties were performed,

223,066 of them in the USA, where 35.7 per cent of adults are obese. Breast augmentation procedures were the second most in-demand surgery, followed by eyelid lifts and tummy tucks.

Source: http://www.theguardian.com/world/us-news-blog/2013/jan/30/plastic-surgery-rise-botox-breast-implants

? Questions

What do you think determines demand for cosmetic surgery?

What do you think determines the number of cosmetic procedures that occur each year?

Put into practice

Identify three reasons why demand for chocolate might shift inwards.

Show the effect on the equilibrum price and quantity of an inward shift in demand and explain how the new equilibrium is reached.

A shift in demand leads to a new equilibrium price and quantity in the market. The size of the effect on price and quantity depends on:

• how much the demand curve shifts; this may depend on factors such as the size of the income elasticity of demand and the size of the cross-price elasticity of demand

and

• the price elasticity of supply. The more price inelastic supply is, for example, the more that price will change relative to output. If, however, supply is relatively price elastic, then the effect will mainly be on output rather than price. This is because if supply

---

Economics in context   **A shift in demand for oil**

At 7.45 a.m. on 30 June 2009, the senior trader for PVM Oil Futures was contacted by a clerk questioning why he had bought 7 million barrels of crude in the middle of the night. At first, the trader claimed that he had been buying on behalf of a client, but this could not be substantiated. It soon became clear that Mr Perkins had single-handedly increased the world price of oil to an eight-month high during a 'drunken blackout'. Prices increased by more than $1.50 a barrel in under half an hour at around 2 a.m.—the type of sharp swing usually caused by events of geopolitical significance.

By the time that PVM realized the trades were not authorized and began to try to rectify the positions taken, it had incurred losses of over $9,760,000.

In the early hours of the morning, the trader placed $520 million in orders, gradually edging up the price by bidding higher each time.

He has since told investigators that he has 'limited recollection' of the entire episode, claiming that he had placed the trades during a drink-induced stupor.

Source:http://www.telegraph.co.uk/finance/newsbysector/energy/oilandgas/7862246/How-a-broker-spent-520m-in-a-drunken-stupor-and-moved-the-global-oil-price.html

? Question

Illustrate the effect of the trader's actions in the oil market, using supply and demand curves.

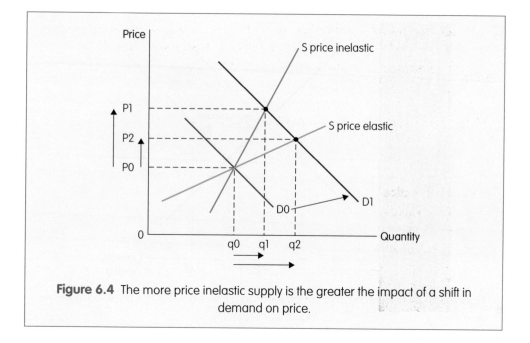

Figure 6.4 The more price inelastic supply is the greater the impact of a shift in demand on price.

is price inelastic it is not very sensitive to price; a given increase in demand will lead to a relatively big increase in price to increase the quantity supplied and bring back equilibrium (see Figure 6.4)

The effects on the equilibrium price and quantity of a change in supply

A market is originally at equilibrium at the price P2 and quantity Q2 (see Figure 6.5). Imagine that supply now increases; i.e. at each and every price more is supplied shifting the supply curve outwards. This could be because:

- there are more producers in the industry;
- technology has improved; or
- the costs of production have fallen.

As a result of this increase in supply, there will be excess supply at the original price equal to Q5 – Q2. Given that there is a surplus, there will be downward pressure on the price. The price will decrease, leading to a higher quantity demanded and a lower quantity supplied, until the new equilibrium is reached at the price P4 and quantity Q4. An increase in supply has led to a lower equilibrium price and a higher quantity supplied than before.

By comparison, a fall in supply (i.e. an inward shift meaning that less is supplied at each and every price) will lead to an increase in the equilibrium price and a reduction in the equilibrium quantity, assuming that the demand curve is downward-sloping.

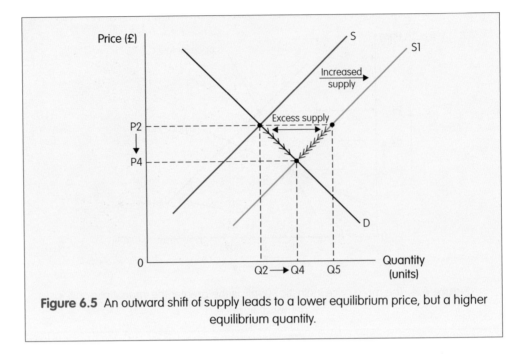

Figure 6.5 An outward shift of supply leads to a lower equilibrium price, but a higher equilibrium quantity.

The effect of a change in supply on the equilibrium price and quantity depends on the extent of the shift in supply and the price elasticity of demand. If demand is price inelastic, then the effect is mainly on price rather than quantity. If demand is price elastic, then the effect is more on the quantity than the price (see Figure 6.6)

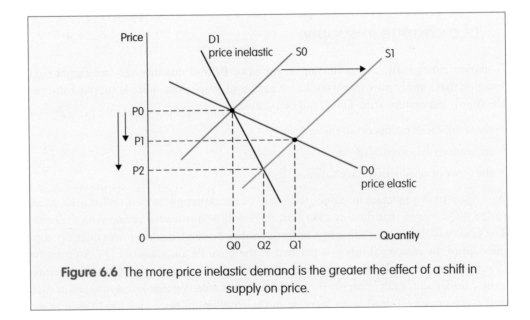

Figure 6.6 The more price inelastic demand is the greater the effect of a shift in supply on price.

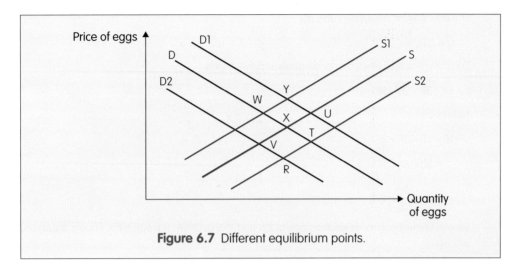

Figure 6.7 Different equilibrium points.

Put into practice

- An increase in the price of complementary products
- An increase in costs
- An increase in income (if it is a normal good)
- An increase in the number of producers

a. Which of the events above could cause the equilibrium price of a product to change from X to W in Figure 6.7?

b. Which of the events above could cause the equilibrium price of a product to change from X to T in Figure 6.7?

c. Which of the events above could cause the equilibrium price of a product to change from X to V in Figure 6.7?

d. Which of the events above could cause the equilibrium price of a product to change from X to U in Figure 6.7?

e. Which combination of the events above could cause the equilibrium price of a product to change from X to Y in Figure 6.7?

f. Which combination of the events above could cause the equilibrium price of a product to change from X to R in Figure 6.7?

Example

Imagine the equation for a straight-line demand curve is given by:

$$Q = 50 - 2P$$

The equation for the supply curve is:

$Q = 20 + 3P$

Equilibrium occurs when demand equals supply—that is:

$50 - 2P = 20 + 3P$

rearranged as:

$50 - 20 = 3P + 2P$

$30 = 5P$

$P = \dfrac{30}{5} = 6$

So equilibrium occurs when the price is £6 and the quantity, if we use the supply equation, will be:

$20 + (3 \times 6) = 20 + 18 = 38$ units

Demand now increases and becomes:

$Q = 80 - 2P$

Equilibrium now occurs when:

$80 - 2P = 20 + 3P$

rearranged

$80 - 20 = 3P + 2P$

$60 = 5P$

$P = \dfrac{60}{5} = £12$

The equilibrium price is £12.
Putting this value back into the demand equation:

$Q = 80 - (2 \times 12) = 80 - 24 = 56$

Equilibrium occurs at price £12 and output 56 units. An increase in demand has led to a higher equilibrium price and output.

Put into practice

Demand is $Q = 40 - P$
Supply is $Q = 6 + P$

- What are the equilibrium price and quantity?
- What would the new equilibrium price and quantity be if demand were to fall to $Q = 10 - 2P$?

Economics in context

In 2013 some of the many Italian restaurants in Sao Paulo in Brazil announced that they would no longer be using tomatoes in their pizzas. This was because tomato prices had risen by over 150 per cent in the last 12 months. This was part of wider price increases throughout the country although things were not as bad as the 1990s when prices generally were growing at over 2000 per cent.

Tomato prices were rising because of heavy rains, high fuel prices, and a reduction in the area used for growing which reduced supply of the product.

? Question

Using a supply and demand diagram show why tomato prices might have increased so much in Brazil.

What do you think?

Can you think of anything that might stop a market adjusting to a new equilibrium following a change in supply or demand conditions?

▤ How can supply and demand analysis help us?

An understanding of supply and demand can help us to analyse many market situations, and to understand why the prices and quantity available in any given market are increasing or decreasing. An understanding of supply and demand will give you an insight into all kinds of markets, from diamonds to housing, from shares to oranges. The following are some examples.

- The UK economy was shrinking in 2008. This reduced demand for many normal goods and led to a switch to inferior products, such as discount brands.

- In recent years, trade between Europe and China has become much more open. This has led to a significant increase in the number of products that are produced in China now being sold in countries such as the UK. This has shifted the supply curve in a number of markets in Europe, such as clothes and footwear, to the right and led to a reduction in the worldwide price of these items.

- Developments in technology in consumer electronics markets have enabled cheaper production. This has shifted supply to the right over time and reduced the price of these products.

- If the grades required to gain a place on a particular course at university are getting higher each year, then this suggests that demand for the course is rising and/or that the supply of places is decreasing. The grades requirement acts as a price of entry.

Put into practice

Which of the following statements are true and which are false?
A fall in price in a market could be:

a. because of a movement along the demand curve.

b. because of an increase in supply.

c. because of a fall in the quantity supplied.

d. because of an increase in the price of a substitute.

Supply and demand analysis can also be used to analyse the impact of the introduction of indirect taxes or subsidies, and the effects of these on consumers and producers.

The introduction of an indirect tax

In some markets, the government may intervene, and this can affect supply and demand conditions. For example, to raise income and/or reduce consumption, a government may impose an indirect tax. An indirect tax, such as value added tax (VAT), is one that is placed on the provider of a good or service. The producer is legally obliged to pay this tax to the government; it has the effect of increasing costs. However, the producer will try to pass this tax on to the customers and make them pay for it. The ability of the producer to do this depends on the price elasticity of demand for the product compared to the price elasticity of supply.

An indirect tax may be a fixed amount per unit (see Figure 6.8a) or a percentage of the price (see Figure 6.8b)—this is called an 'ad valorem' tax. The result of the imposition of an indirect tax is to shift the supply curve as producers add the costs on meaning they need a higher price to sell a given quantity. Producers will add the indirect tax onto the price that they need to supply a given output.

Economics in context

According to the British Retail Consortium, shop prices fell in 2013 compared to the year before mainly due to a decline in the price of clothing, electricals, and DIY products.

Retailers cut the price of products after cold and wet weather at the start of the year disrupted spring sales and led to less demand. Customers seemed reluctant to spend and were looking for good deals. Retailers were helped by a fall in the price of some of their inputs such as cereal and oil costs.

? Question
Using supply and demand analysis show why the price of products in the shops may have fallen.

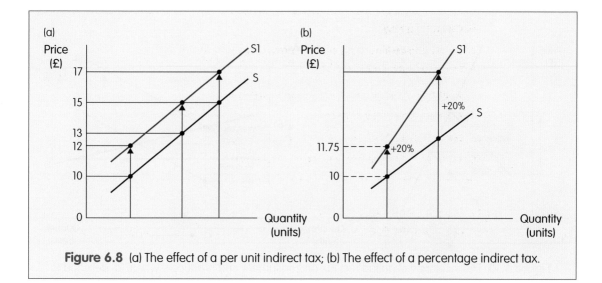

Figure 6.8 (a) The effect of a per unit indirect tax; (b) The effect of a percentage indirect tax.

The effect of the imposition of an indirect tax on equilibrium is to increase the price in the market and reduce the quantity sold. In Figure 6.9, the effect of introducing an indirect tax is to increase the equilibrium price from P1 to P2, and to reduce the equilibrium quantity supplied from Q1 to Q2. An indirect tax therefore shifts the supply curve, and leads to fewer units being bought and sold at a higher price.

However, although the price has increased, this is not usually by the full amount of the tax imposed. The producer can shift some of the tax onto the buyer, but not all of it. In Figure 6.9, the price has risen from P1 to P2, but the tax per unit is P2 – P3.

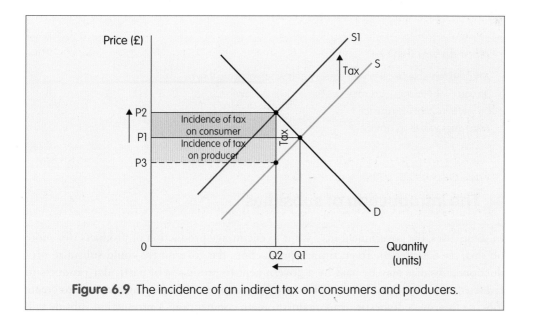

Figure 6.9 The incidence of an indirect tax on consumers and producers.

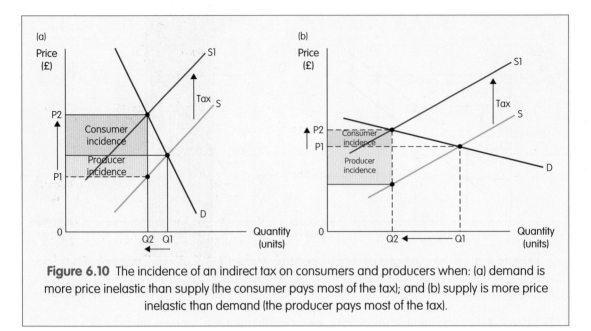

Figure 6.10 The incidence of an indirect tax on consumers and producers when: (a) demand is more price inelastic than supply (the consumer pays most of the tax); and (b) supply is more price inelastic than demand (the producer pays most of the tax).

The amount of the incidence of taxation on the producer and the consumer depends on the relative price elasticity of demand and supply. If demand is more price inelastic than supply, then the consumer will pay more of the tax than the producer (see Figure 6.10a). If supply is more price inelastic than demand, then the producer will pay more of the tax than the consumer (see Figure 6.10b). The amount of tax will only be fully passed on to the customer if demand is completely price inelastic or supply is perfectly price elastic.

What do you think?

What indirect taxes exist in your country and what rates are they?

Do you think that these tax rates are too high or too low?

Do you think that they are fair?

What rates would you impose?

The introduction of subsidies

In some cases, the government may want to encourage production of products (for more on this, see Chapter 8). To encourage production, the government could subsidize production. Subsidies may be paid by a government to producers of particular products to reduce their costs of production. This may be to support a developing industry, to create jobs, or to protect domestic firms against foreign competition. A production subsidy will

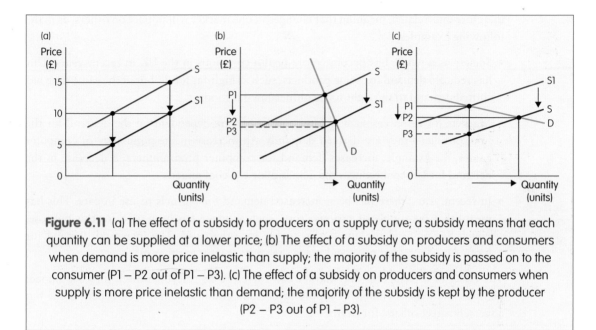

Figure 6.11 (a) The effect of a subsidy to producers on a supply curve; a subsidy means that each quantity can be supplied at a lower price; (b) The effect of a subsidy on producers and consumers when demand is more price inelastic than supply; the majority of the subsidy is passed on to the consumer (P1 – P2 out of P1 – P3). (c) The effect of a subsidy on producers and consumers when supply is more price inelastic than demand; the majority of the subsidy is kept by the producer (P2 – P3 out of P1 – P3).

mean that producers are willing and able to produce any given output at a lower price (see Figure 6.11a). This leads to a downward shift of the supply curve and thus to a new equilibrium at which more is supplied at a lower price in the market. The extent to which the price falls depends on the price elasticity of supply and demand. The more price inelastic demand is relative to supply, the more the subsidy is passed on to suppliers (see Figure 6.11b and 6.11c).

What do you think?

What do you think might be the problems of the government subsidizing producers?

In Chapter 2 we explained how the production possibility frontier shows combinations of products that are productively efficient. However a government may want to influence exactly which combination of products is produced; it may do this through indirect taxes and subsidies.

Interrelated markets

So far, we have analysed the effect of changes in supply and demand conditions in a market on the equilibrium price and output. However, markets rarely exist in isolation; in fact, an economy is a collection of millions of different markets. Many markets are therefore interrelated, meaning that changes in one market will impact on others, as in the following examples.

- Society as a whole has become more health-conscious in the UK in recent years. This has reduced demand for some products, such as high-fat foods, but at the same time has shifted demand to the right for healthier low-fat foods.

- Markets for resources such as land and labour are dependent on the demand for the final product—they are derived demands. An increase in the popularity of computer games, for example, increases demand for computer programmers; a decrease in the demand for UK coal reduces the demand for UK coal miners.

- In recent years, there has been increased demand for biofuels to use in cars. This has meant that the supply of various crops, such as sugar, has been used for this purpose, which has reduced the amount available for other uses. The increased demand for biofuel has increased price and made the crops scarcer in other markets.

The effect of a change in one market can therefore be traced through into the impact on other markets. A change in supply or demand conditions may well benefit some but adversely affect others, for example.

Put into practice

Can you think of examples of how changes in supply or demand may benefit some groups (for example, some firms or households), while others may be worse off?

Case study

UK house prices recently showed a modest rise according to the latest survey from the Nationwide building society. This suggested that the housing market was gradually showing a recovery. The annual rate of price growth rose to 1.1 per cent, the fastest for some time. The increases mean that the average house in the UK now costs £167,912.

Factors affecting the recovery included the greater availability and a reduction in the cost of borrowing for people wanting to buy a house. A short while before, the government introduced the Funding for Lending Scheme which made it even easier for borrowers to access funds. Consumers also seem to be more confident.

The government also introduced a Help to Buy scheme under which borrowers could take out a loan from the government, to allow them to put down a deposit of just 5 per cent on a property. Under this scheme, starting in January 2014 to run until 2017, the government guaranteed up to 15 per cent of a mortgage on homes worth up to £600,000. The scheme was used to support £130bn of mortgages.

Regional house price differences
- London: up 6.2%
- South West of England: up 0.3%
- East of England: down 0.7%
- North West of England: down 3.7%

- South East of England: up 1.4%
- Yorkshire and Humber: down 1.2%
- West Midlands: up 0.5%
- Wales: down 2%
- East Midlands: down 1.2%
- North East of England: down 5.7%

Source: Land Registry. Annual change to end of April

The OECD (Organisation for Economic Cooperation and Development) said that while new housing measures were likely to encourage residential investment and supply in the UK, there could be 'upward pressure on house prices' if builders did not build more homes.

❓ Questions

1 Analyse the factors determining house prices in the UK.
2 Analyse why house prices might differ between different regions.
3 How price elastic do you think the supply of housing is? Why?
4 Does it matter do you think if house prices go up or down?

Review questions

1 What might cause the equilibrium price in a market to increase?
2 Explain how a market returns to equilibrium after an increase in supply.
3 If the demand in a market increases, explain what will happen to the equilibrium price.
4 What might lead to a decrease in the equilibrium price and quantity in a market?
5 Explain how a market returns to equilibrium after an increase in demand.
6 House prices vary tremendously between regions of the UK. Explore why this might be the case by using supply and demand analysis.
7 Explain the circumstances under which most of the incidence of an indirect tax falls on consumers.
8 Explain the circumstances under which the effect of a production subsidy would mainly be on the price rather than the output.

Put into practice

1 Using supply and demand diagrams, illustrate the effect of each of the following.
   - An increase in material costs
   - A decrease in the price of a complementary good

2 Demand is $Q = 60 - 2P$

Supply is $Q = 8 + P$

- What are the equilibrium price and quantity?
- What would the new equilibrium price and quantity be if demand were to fall to $Q = 20 - 2P$?

Key learning points

- When a market is in equilibrium, there is no incentive to change.
- A change in supply and demand conditions will lead to a new equilibrium price and output.
- Supply and demand analysis helps to explain price and quantity changes in a wide range of markets.
- The effect on the equilibrium price relative to the equilibrium quantity of a change in supply or demand depends on the price elasticity of supply and demand.

Learn more

To see how changes in supply and demand affect market equilibrium, visit the Online Resource Centre.

 Visit our Online Resource Centre at http://www.oxfordtextbooks.co.uk/orc/gillespie_econ3e/ for test questions and further information on topics covered in this chapter.

The free market system

So far we have analysed the workings of the free market system and how the price mechanism brings about equilibrium. In this chapter we analyse how the free market system may maximize social welfare but then consider the failures and imperfections of the market system and why governments may need to intervene.

LEARNING OBJECTIVES

By the end of this chapter, you should be able to:

✓ explain the advantages of the free market system;

✓ understand the meaning of consumer, producer, and community surplus;

✓ analyse market failures and imperfections in the free market system;

✓ understand the difference between merit and public goods;

✓ understand the meaning of external costs and benefits;

✓ understand why a government might intervene in a free market.

▦ The free market

In a free market, decisions about what to produce are determined by supply and demand in product markets. The demand for the product will then influence demand for factors of production. The price paid for these resources and the quantity of them used will be determined by supply and demand conditions in the markets for these factors of production. The free market system assumes that consumers and employees are attempting to maximize their utility and that producers are aiming to maximize their profits.

■ Advantages of the free market system

A question facing all societies is the extent to which private individuals and businesses should make the economic decisions, as opposed to the government. To what extent should the basic economic questions of what to produce, how to produce, and for whom to produce be left simply to market forces? Or should a centralized government try to coordinate production and consumption in its country? There are many arguments in favour of the free market approach, at least in theory; one of these is the view that the free market can lead to the best allocation of resources from society's perspective and maximize social welfare. If this is true, then the government should not intervene in a market economy and simply leave the allocation of resources to the forces of supply and demand. In terms of the basic economic questions the issue is whether the free market leads the economy to produce on the production possibility frontier, whether it leads to the right combination of products on the frontier and whether the allocation of products to individuals is efficient.

Maximizing social welfare

In a free market system, the price should adjust to equalize supply and demand and reach equlibrium. At this point of equilibrium, the welfare of society will be maximized. This is due to the following reasons.

- The demand curve is derived from the consumers' extra utility (or satisfaction) from consuming a unit—known as the marginal utility (MU) or benefit (MB) (see Chapter 3). For the moment, let us assume that the benefits to consumers of consuming a unit reflect the extra benefit to society as a whole. This means that the demand curve is derived from the social marginal benefit (SMB).

- The supply curve is derived from the extra costs of producing a unit (see Chapter 11). Let us assume that this shows the extra cost to society of producing a unit—that is, the social marginal cost (SMC).

At equilibrium, the quantity supplied equals the quantity demanded. This means that the extra benefit to society of the last unit produced and sold equals the extra cost to society of that unit—that is:

Social marginal benefit (SMB) = Social marginal cost (SMC)

Therefore the welfare of society will not be increased or decreased by producing another unit, which means that it must be maximized. This is shown in Figure 7.1.

In Figure 7.1, on all of the units up to Q1 the extra social benefit is greater than the extra social cost of providing it:

SMB > SMC

Therefore society as a whole will gain from these units being produced and consumed, because the benefits exceed the costs and so there is extra welfare to be gained. If another unit is produced and sold welfare increases.

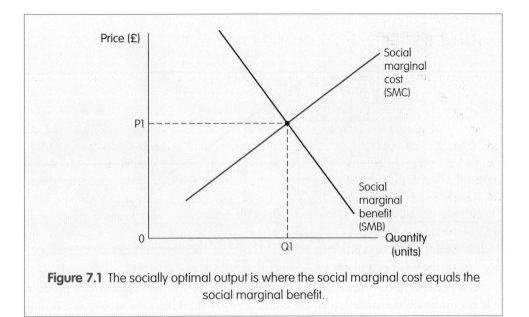

Figure 7.1 The socially optimal output is where the social marginal cost equals the social marginal benefit.

For the units after Q1, the extra social benefits are less than the extra social costs:

SMB < SMC

This means that society would lose out if these units were produced and the total welfare would fall.

At Q1, the extra social benefit of consuming the unit equals the extra social costs of producing it:

SMB = SMC

The welfare to society is therefore maximized by producing at this level of output. This is the output level that occurs at equilibrium in the free market at Q1—that is, in the free market, the equilibrium output maximizes society's welfare.

Community surplus

Another way of analysing the way in which the free market can bring about an optimal allocation of resources is to consider the areas of consumer surplus and producer surplus.

- **Consumer surplus** measures the difference between the price a consumer is willing and able to pay for a product, and what he or she actually pays. It represents utility for the customer for which he or she has not paid.

  Given the law of diminishing marginal utility, the extra satisfaction of each extra unit of a product that is consumed is assumed to fall. This means that the amount that consumers are willing to pay for an additional unit will fall as extra units are demanded. If only one price is paid in a market then the price paid would fall for the extra unit and all of the ones before; this creates consumer surplus (see Figure 7.2).

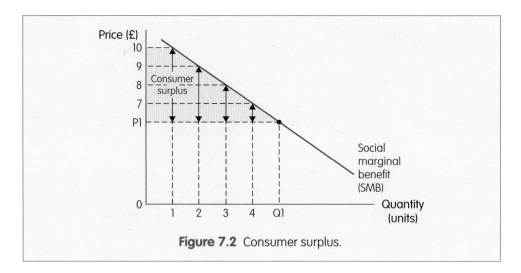

Figure 7.2 Consumer surplus.

For example, a consumer may be willing to pay £10 for the first unit of a product. If two units are demanded, then the consumer may think that the second one is only worth £9, and so in a single price market pays £9 for each of them. This means that, on the first unit, there is £1 of utility that is not paid for; this is consumer surplus. Similarly, if the third unit has a utility worth £8 and the consumer buys three units at £8 each, then there is a consumer surplus of £2 on the first unit and £1 on the second unit—that is, £3 of utility that is not paid for in total.

- **Producer surplus** measures the difference between the price that producers are willing and able to sell at and the price that they actually receive. To sell more units, a firm will want a higher price to cover the higher additional costs. Assuming this higher price is paid on all of the units produced, this creates a producer surplus.

  For example, imagine that a firm is willing to sell one unit at £5, but would need £7 to sell a second unit; if it sells two units at £7 each, then a surplus of £2 is created on the first one. In Figure 7.3, the producer surplus equals the shaded area.

- Community surplus is made up of producer surplus and consumer surplus. This combines the extra utility to consumers for which they do not pay, and the rewards to producers over and above the price that they need to supply these units. Community surplus represents welfare to consumers and producers that has not been paid for, and can be written as:

Community surplus = Consumer surplus + Producer surplus

In Figure 7.4a, in a free market equilibrium at the price P1 and the quantity Q1, the community surplus is equal to the area ABC. This area is the maximum that it can be, so social welfare is maximized in this situation in the free market. No combination of price and quantity would generate as much community surplus as the free market result of the price P1 and the quantity Q1. This is another way of demonstrating that, in theory, the free market leads to the optimal allocation of resources.

Imagine, for example, that the market price was forced up to P2 (see Figure 7.4b). The quantity demanded and therefore sold would be Q2. The consumer surplus would

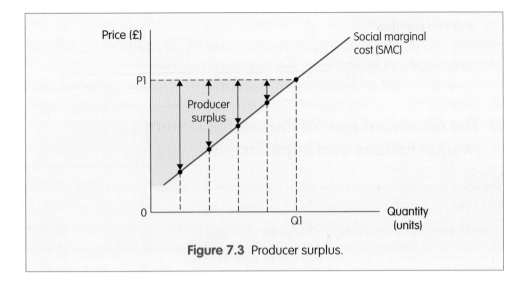

Figure 7.3 Producer surplus.

be equal to the area P2AB and the producer surplus would be equal to the area P2BCF. Overall, the community surplus would be the area ABCF—less than it was at equilibrium by the area BEC.

In theory, then, the free market could lead the economy to an optimal position in equilibrium, maximizing community surplus. In reality, however, there are numerous market failures and imperfections that prevent this optimal allocation being generated. This is why there is a case for government intervention. The issues, then, are how much intervention is justified and what is the best way of intervening.

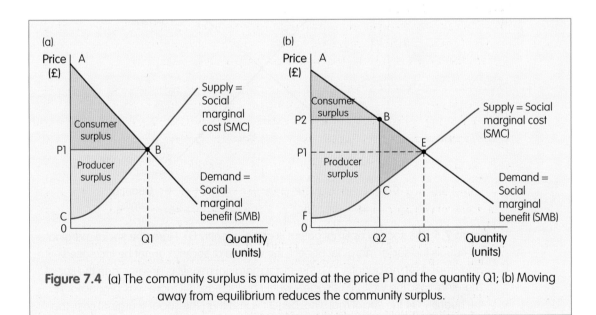

Figure 7.4 (a) The community surplus is maximized at the price P1 and the quantity Q1; (b) Moving away from equilibrium reduces the community surplus.

Put into practice

If a market is producing where the social marginal benefit of a unit is greater than the social marginal cost, should it produce more or fewer units? Explain your answer.

The disadvantages of the market system: Market failures and imperfections

The socially optimal output exists when society is producing and consuming at the level at which

Social marginal benefit (SMB) = Social marginal cost (SMC)

At this output, society's welfare cannot be increased further.

A market failure exists if the market is selling at an output where the marginal cost to society of making a product does not equal the marginal benefit to society of consuming that good or service. i.e. the market does not produce at the socially optimal point.

If a market settles at an output where the social marginal benefit is greater than the social marginal cost (SMB > SMC) (for example, at Q3 in Figure 7.5), then society would benefit from an additional unit being produced. Social welfare would be increased if more units were produced. If, on the other hand, the social marginal benefit of a unit is less than the social marginal cost (SMB < SMC) (for example, at Q4 in Figure 7.5), then

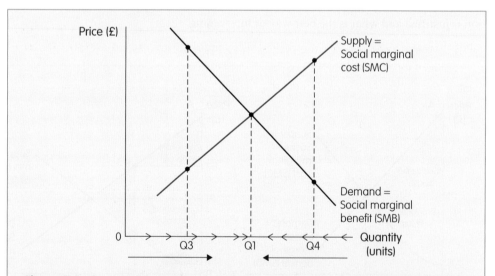

Figure 7.5 The socially optimal output is at the quantity Q1. Here, the social marginal cost equals the social marginal benefit; the welfare of society cannot be increased—it is maximized. At the quantity Q3, the social marginal benefit is greater than the social marginal cost; the welfare of society would be increased if more was produced. At the quantity Q4 the social marginal benefit is less than the social marginal cost; the welfare of society would be increased if less was produced.

producing this unit reduces the total social welfare and this unit should not be produced or consumed.

The causes of market failures and imperfections in the free market include the following.

Monopoly power

So far, we have assumed that market forces are allowed to operate, and that these will lead to an equilibrium price of P1 and an output of Q1. However, in some markets, one or more firms may come to dominate and exert monopoly power. A pure monopoly occurs when one firm has 100 per cent control of a market. In this situation, a monopolist is able to determine how much output it sells and at what price.

A monopolist is a price-setter. For example, it may decide to restrict output and push up the price, selling the quantity Q2 at price P2 (see Figure 7.6). This has the effect of increasing producer surplus from P1AB to P2CDB, which means that producers gain even more than the costs of producing these units. However, the effect of this monopoly action is also to reduce consumer surplus from EAP1 to ECP2. This means that, with monopoly power, producers gain at the expense of consumers (which, of course, is why they do it). In terms of society as a whole there is a reduction in the overall community surplus, which has fallen from EAB to ECDB. This means that there is a welfare loss (also called a deadweight social burden triangle) equal to CAD.

On all of the units between Q2 and Q1 that are not produced by the monopolist, the extra benefit to society is greater than the extra cost of producing them. Society as a whole would therefore benefit from producing these units. However, the monopolist would not benefit, because it would have to lower prices to sell these extra units; this is why it chose to restrict output in the first place.

Monopoly power is therefore likely to lead to a lower output and higher price than would be achieved in a competitive market. The effect of monopoly is to reduce the overall welfare of society. This is examined in more detail in Chapter 12.

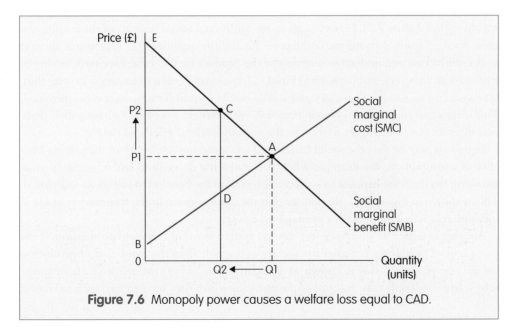

Figure 7.6 Monopoly power causes a welfare loss equal to CAD.

Externalities

In a free market, the amount that customers demand and are willing to pay for products naturally depends on the benefits that they personally receive. Individuals pursue their own interests and aim to maximize their utility. However, the benefit (or utility) that an individual customer derives from consuming a unit is not necessarily the same as the benefit that society as a whole derives from a product. Equally the costs to a producer may not be equal to the costs to society as a whole. These differences between private and social costs and benefits mean that the allocation of resources in the free market may not be the allocation that society as a whole would want, because of the differences between private and social benefits.

For example, when you are considering whether or not to have a flu vaccination, you will think of the personal benefit of not catching flu in the future; you will not think about the benefits to others if you were vaccinated. However, if you do not catch flu, then you are not going to pass it on to others, so this will have a benefit for other people as well as yourself. The social benefits of consumption of the vaccination are therefore greater than the private benefits. This is known as a positive consumption externality: the social benefits are equal to the private benefits plus the external benefits to society. In this case, the demand curve from society's point of view is higher than it would be from a private perspective; this is because the social marginal benefits of each unit are greater than the private marginal benefits.

In a free market, the equilibrium price and output outcomes would be P1 and Q1, respectively (see Figure 7.7). However, given the additional social benefits of these units, the most socially desirable outcome is the price P2 and the quantity Q2. This means there is underproduction and underconsumption of the product (in this case, vaccinations) in the free market. On every unit between Q1 and Q2, the extra benefit to society is greater than the extra cost to society. So society as a whole would benefit if more units were provided. This means that the shaded region in Figure 7.7 represents a potential welfare gain if there was intervention to move the market to the socially optimal price and output.

Equally it may be that the social benefits of consumption are less than the private benefits of consumption; for example when you make the decision to listen loudly to your music on the train the benefits to society are less than the benefits to you as an individual. This is shown in Figure 7.8); this shows that the consumption in the free market at Q1 is too high relative to the socially optimal level at Q2.

Another situation in which the free market system may fail relates to production. If the extra cost of producing is higher for society as a whole than the extra cost of producing for private producers this is known as a negative production externality. Left to themselves, firms will only take account of the costs for which they have to pay, such as labour,

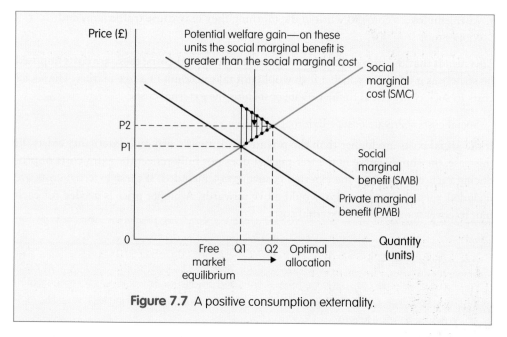

Figure 7.7 A positive consumption externality.

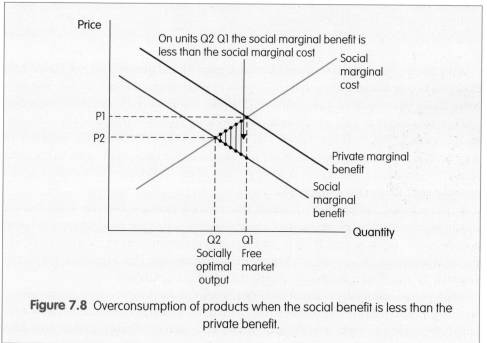

Figure 7.8 Overconsumption of products when the social benefit is less than the private benefit.

land, and machines. These are private costs. They will not take account of other costs that affect society as a whole—for example:

• their factory may be noisy and this may upset local residents;

• the production process may be generating pollution; and

- when employees come to work in the morning they may cause traffic jams and congestion.

This means that the firm's activities are generating external costs; these are costs imposed on society as a whole of which a firm would not take account in a free market. The social costs to society are equal to the private costs *plus* the external costs:

Social costs = Private costs + External costs

If the social costs are higher than the private costs, then a negative externality exists. In this case, the supply curve in the free market does not fully reflect the extra costs of producing each unit because the external costs are not included. If these external costs are included, then the supply curve would move upwards. A higher price is needed for each unit to cover the additional external costs.

What do you think?

Pollution is an external cost. Left to themselves, firms and private drivers would not take account of the costs of pollution. Do you think that, if you were in government, the right thing to do would be to aim to reduce pollution to zero?

At the moment, in the UK, all private drivers pay the same road tax. Should we tax drivers according to how many miles that they drive?

In the free market, equilibrium would occur at price P1 and quantity Q1 (see Figure 7.9). However, taking account of the full social costs of production, the socially desirable outcome would be at price P2 and quantity Q2. In the free market, there is overproduction and overconsumption. This is because the firm does not appreciate the full costs of providing the product. This leads to a welfare loss. On the units Q1 to Q2, the extra social cost of these units is greater than the extra benefit. This means that the welfare of society is being reduced by producing these units. A more socially optimal allocation of resources would be at the price P2 and the quantity Q2.

As you will see, just because a negative external cost exists, it does not mean that we should stop production of the product altogether: this is because producing the product does provide benefits as well. What is needed is intervention to achieve the optimal allocation of resources, which would not happen in the free market. This happens at the output at which the social marginal benefit equals the social marginal cost.

The problems caused by external costs can be seen in the present concerns over global warming. Left to themselves producers and households would not be concerned about the impact for society as a whole of the actions they take even if it leads to greater emissions and environment damage. According to the Stern Review on Climate Change for the UK government in 2006 climate change is the biggest market failure facing the world.

Making businesses and individuals aware of the long-term consequences of their actions and making them take these costs into account is a major challenge facing governments and needs the actions of many countries not just one. For example, the Kyoto Protocol in 1997 involved several governments agreeing to reduce greenhouse gas emissions. However progress has not been particularly successful possibly because the impact

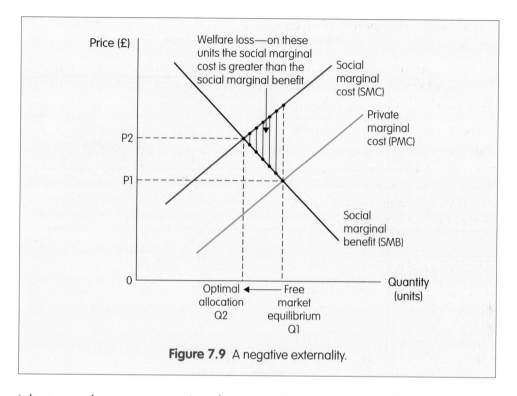

Figure 7.9 A negative externality.

is long term; the present generation of voters may be reluctant to sacrifice present production and consumption for the benefit of future generations.

The global banking crisis of 2008 onwards may also be seen as a failure by banks to appreciate the potential external costs of their actions. They focused on the private benefits and costs and calculated and interpreted the risks on this basis but the collapse of this sector has a major impact on the economy as whole.

However it is also possible that the private costs of production are more than the social costs. If a business switches production away from using a production process that generates high CO_2 emissions to much lower emissions there may be a private cost of switching. However the effect is to reduce the impact on global warming so the cost to society as a whole may be

Economics in context   Chewing gum

In the UK, chewing gum costs local councils well over £4 million per year to clean up from the pavements. It actually costs more to clean up the chewing gum than it does to produce it! The producers and consumers of chewing gum are generating an external cost to society that we have to pay through taxes to clean up.

? Question

Taxes are already placed on many consumers because of the external costs generated by the products that they consume. For example, drivers pay high taxes on petrol and air travellers pay tax on their flights. Do you think that a tax should be placed on chewing gum consumers?

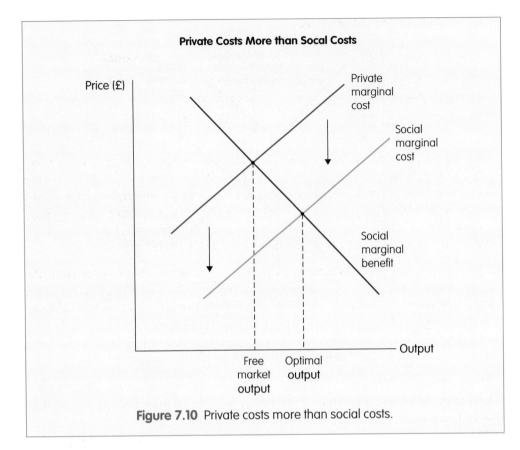

Private Costs More than Socal Costs

Price (£)

Private marginal cost

Social marginal cost

Social marginal benefit

Output

Free market output

Optimal output

Figure 7.10 Private costs more than social costs.

lower than the private cost. This is shown in Figure 7.10. The result is that there is not enough production; the free market leads to an underproduction relative to the socially optimal level.

As we have seen there are several different types of externality—these are summarized in Table 7.1; each of these reduces the overall welfare of society and may justify government intervention.

What do you think?

The increasing number of people being given antibiotics on prescription means that the population as a whole is becoming immune to them. This is leaving many people vulnerable to infection. Individuals are not taking account the social impact of their desire for antibiotics.

What actions do you think the government should take?

Merit goods

- A **merit good** is one that society believes is more beneficial than private individuals do. For example, individuals may not appreciate at the time how important and beneficial education or health care is to them. In one sense, a merit good is like a positive

Table 7.1 Summary table of externalities

Positive consumption externality	Social benefits > private benefits
Negative consumption externality	Social benefit < private benefits
External costs of production	Social costs > private costs
External benefits of production	Social costs < private costs

externality; however, they occur specifically because the government may know more than we do what is good for us (as opposed to positive consumption externalities, the external benefits of which we may know, but about which we may not care). Merit goods would be underconsumed in the free market because we underestimate their benefits. For example, the government might sponsor the arts, opera, museums, and art galleries on the basis that these are good for society as a whole.

- **Demerit goods** are products that we might want to consume without appreciating the harm that they are doing to us—for example, cigarettes. Once again, they arise because the government may know more than we do, or may know what is in our best interests, and may therefore discourage or prevent consumption of them. We may thank the government later on when we appreciate how bad these products were!

What do you think?

What products would you classify as merit goods?

What do you think are demerit goods?

Do you think that society's views of what are and what are not merit goods might change over time?

Public goods

A public good is a product that is non-diminishable and non-excludable. This means that, once it is provided, it does not matter how many people consume it—it will still be available to everyone. In the case of most products if one person consumes more then there is less for everyone else in a given perod. For example, if you buy a pair of Nike trainers in a shop, then you have reduced the number of pairs available at that particular moment for others to buy—you are competing with others to buy this product. However in the case of public goods the addition of extra users does not reduce the amount that others can consume. For example, a lighthouse is a public good. Once it is built, all ships can benefit from it—it does not matter how many ships are passing by, they can all gain from the light being shown. This means that the provision of this service is non-diminishable.

Public goods are also 'non-excludable' because it is difficult to stop people (or ships!) from benefiting from them. Any ship passing by a lighthouse will gain from it. Similarly, if you install a street light or make an area safer by having regular police patrols, then everyone can gain and it is difficult to restrict the service to those who pay. The development of open-access wireless networks has created a public good in recent years. (although many people protect their networks to prevent anyone being able to access them).

Public goods are also non-rectifiable. This means that once provided people will benefit from them even if they don't want to! You may not agree with a nuclear deterrent but once it is provided you benefit from it anyway.

The problem with public goods is that, in a free market, firms will be unwilling to provide them because they cannot restrict consumption to those who pay for them. This means they would be asking households to pay for something that others could then get access to for free. Not surprisingly households will be reluctant to pay for something that everyone has access to. This creates the 'free rider' problem: people will wait in the hope that someone else will pay for the service, so that they can be a free rider and benefit from it as well without actually paying for it. The result is no one will pay for it and so it may not be provided at all. In this case, the government has to step in to provide such products.

A failure to think long term or take account of the effect of your actions on others

One problem in the free market is that businesses and individuals may focus on the short term and not think through or not be interested in the long-term effects of their actions. They might, for example, only consider the short-term costs of any action and not be concerned about the long-term impact on the environment—perhaps through global warming. This may be rational—for example if an individual argues that they will not be around in 100 years' time—but may not be socially desirable. One example of a failure to look ahead is known as The Tragedy of the Commons—a term coined by Garrett Hardin in an article for *Science* journal in 1968. Imagine there is a common area in a village where individuals can let their animals graze. From an individual perspective there is an attraction to let as many animals as you have graze for free. However if everyone does this the animals will soon eat all the grass on the commons leaving no grass for anyone. The pursuit of self-interest has damaged society as a whole over time. Similarly, if fishing fleets are allowed to fish as much as they want in any given area of the sea the dangers are there will be overfishing which will possibly kill off a species of fish. The Tragedy of the Commons therefore refers to a situation where a shared resource may be depleted by individuals pursuing self-interest who are acting rationally even though they might appreciate the long-term impact of this. This effect can be seen in the overuse of water, the deforestation of some areas of the world, and global warming.

What do you think?

Consider the Tragedy of the Commons and with reference to this concept, do you think people should be allowed to have as many children as they want?

Instability

Another problem in the free market is that prices can fluctuate significantly. The fact that the price adjusts to ensure that supply equals demand can lead to major and sudden swings in price as supply and demand conditions change. A fall in supply can lead to a higher equilibrium price and a lower quantity; a fall in demand can lead to a fall in the equilibrium price and sales. This instability can make it difficult for firms and consumers

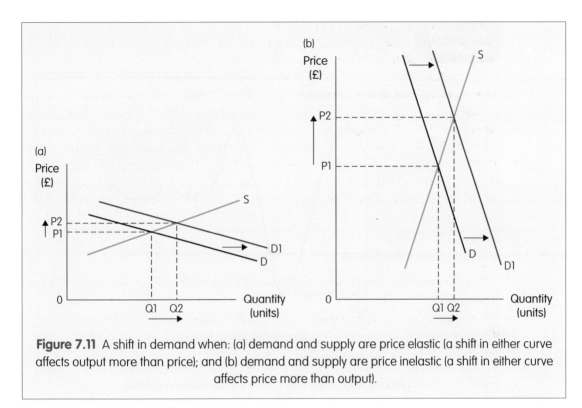

Figure 7.11 A shift in demand when: (a) demand and supply are price elastic (a shift in either curve affects output more than price); and (b) demand and supply are price inelastic (a shift in either curve affects price more than output).

to plan. Price instability can be seen in many sectors, such as the markets for currency, shares, and oil. If the government thinks that instability is undesirable (for example, unstable agricultural prices may deter farmers from continuing production, and problems in planning because of price instability may reduce investment and growth in an economy), then it may intervene to bring about more stable prices. Price instability is a particular issue if supply and demand are price inelastic, because any given shift in the curves has relatively more impact on price than quantity (see Figure 7.11).

Put into practice

- What should happen to the equilibrium price and quantity if the supply curve shifts to the right?
- What if demand shifts to the left?

Income inequality

A free market is likely to lead to income inequality. Some firms and individuals may earn very high incomes if they have products or skills that are in demand; other people's skills may be less in demand and, as a result, they may have lower incomes—for example, a cleaner compared with a Premier League football player. In terms of an economic outcome, this may be efficient, and the labour market may be working perfectly well; however, voters may decide that it is unfair and not a desirable outcome. If this is the

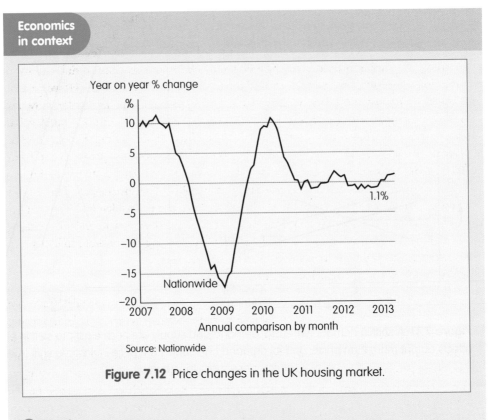

Economics in context

Figure 7.12 Price changes in the UK housing market.

Source: Nationwide

? Question

Using supply and demand analysis show the possible causes of the price changes in the UK housing market shown in Figure 7.12.

case, society may want a government to do something about the income distribution: for example, a government may provide some products freely to everyone so that they can all benefit from them. It may also use taxes and subsidies to redistribute income in the economy. Income inequality is examined in more detail in Chapter 20.

What do you think?

Do you think that the government should intervene to reduce the amount of income inequality in an economy? If so, how much intervention do you think is desirable?
What do you think would be a fair tax rate on people's earnings?
Do you think that people should be allowed to inherit money and property?

Missing information

Problems may occur in the free market due to a lack of information. Buyers may not know what is available or what alternatives they have. Many cinemas and restaurants will be half-empty some of the time and have queues outside them on other occasions. In theory, the price mechanism adjusts to make supply equal to demand. In the case of a cinema, then, given that there is a limited number of seats, when there is a high level of interest in a film, the price should increase to ration demand. On other occasions, if demand for a film is going to be low, then the price should fall to attract more customers. However, cinema managers do not know in advance what demand will be for any particular showing. Therefore they set an average price. Sometimes, this will be too high for the actual level of demand, leading to excess supply and empty seats in the cinema. At other times, it will be too low for the actual level of demand, leading to excess demand and queues outside. For major sporting events, you will usually find ticket touts trying to sell you tickets at a much higher price than that for which they were originally sold. This is because the initial price that was set for these events was too low. Therefore there was excess demand. Ticket touts get hold of the tickets at the original price and sell them on to others who really want them for a much higher price. In this case, the ticket touts are helping the market mechanism to work because the original price was not the equilibrium one.

Other information problems include the following.

- **Asymmetric information** This was examined by George Akerlof in his analysis of the second-hand car market in which he analysed the problem of 'lemons'. A 'lemon' is the name given to a poor-quality second-hand car. Akerlof showed that buyers of second-hand cars are never sure if they will be buying a lemon or not, and so are only willing to offer average prices for what might actually be better-than-average second-hand cars. This then means that people with better-than-average second-hand cars decide not to sell them; therefore the average price becomes too high for what is actually on the market and the price falls. This could potentially lead to the collapse of the market entirely.

- **Adverse selection** This occurs when individuals have inside information and use this to decide whether to accept or reject an offer. Imagine, for example, a medical insurance company that bases its premiums on the typical mortality rate for the country as a whole. Amongst the population there are those who smoke, drink excessively, and do not exercise. These people would regard this premium as very cheap. On the other hand, the very healthy individuals would regard it as very expensive. Unfortunately, the insurance company cannot easily tell who is unhealthy and who is not. The result is that the healthy people will not buy the insurance because it is too expensive, but the unhealthy will, because it is cheap for them. To try to overcome this problem, insurance companies try to gather evidence (for example, medical testing) to prove that the person to be insured is healthy.

What do you think?

Ticket touts are selling tickets for major sports and music events on online auction sites with a typical profit of 59 per cent, according to recent research. Prices are being inflated after touts buy tickets for events that they have no plans to attend. Touts also target fans outside gigs and matches, and charge a huge mark-up.

Do you think that ticket touting should be illegal?

Economics in context

Moral hazard

In 2008, the UK government had to intervene to support the Royal Bank of Scotland and Lloyds Bank to prevent a financial crisis. Some analysts felt that this created a moral hazard issue. This moral hazard arose because, through rapid growth, some banks became so big and so vital to the economy and the financial system that, because they knew that government would ultimately save them, they had less incentive to protect themselves against incurring excessive risk. This problem has posed a major threat to financial stability in the UK, has caused and prolonged the downturn of the economy, and has exposed taxpayers in the UK to more risk. Similarly, there have been worries about subsidizing industries such as the car industry when it is struggling. If a business knows that it will be subsidized, then will it stop trying as hard to be efficient?

❓ Question

How might the government avoid the moral hazard issue outlined above?

Another information problem in the free market is known as moral hazard. Take the case of an insurance company trying to decide on how much to charge people for health care. Someone who has been insured faces a moral hazard, because he or she is likely to be less concerned about his or her health now he or she is insured, and this may bring about more claims. Similarly, a car driver may drive less carefully if he or she is insured because the damage will be covered.

The significance of information problems in markets can be seen in relation to the way in which companies are run. A company is owned by the shareholders and run on a daily basis by managers; in some cases the owners are the managers but in most big organizations they are different. In this relationship the owners are called the 'principals' and the managers are the 'agents'. The difficulty with the 'principal–agent' relationship is that the managers know more than the shareholders about the business. The shareholders fear that managers will actually act in their own interests and not in the interests of the owners and that they will not know what is happening. For example, the managers may want to take over a rival because it its good for their own careers but tell investors it is essential for the success of the business. Investors worry about this lack of information and try to develop reporting controls to monitor what happens as closely as they can. One method used is to reward managers with shares so that managers think more like owners.

Case study

The head of Nestlé, the world's largest food producer believes that high food prices are due to the growing of crops for biofuels. He said that the time of low food prices was over. The growth of production of crops for use as biofuels means these crops and this land is not available for food for human or animal consumption. This is driving up prices. He argued that biofuels were only attractive to suppliers because of the government subsidies available particularly in the USA. When politicians said that they wanted to replace 20 per cent of fossil fuels with biofuels this has meant increasing the production of crops threefold according to the Nestlé spokesperson. Most of the world's sugar production now goes into making biofuels, he said. It also impacts on water. He said that it takes about 4,600 litres of water to produce one litre of pure ethanol if it comes from sugar, and it takes 1,900 litres of water if it comes from palm oil. However, high food prices are also due to increased population growth and greater urbanization which tends to be associated with higher food consumption.

Also with hundreds of millions of people being lifted out of poverty in the decade this leads to more meat being consumed. Another factor has been the weather and environmental factors which have regularly hit supply in recent years. This has led to upward pressure on prices. In some cases the government has responded with maximum prices but this has deterred producers from investing more into the industry.

The solution according to Nestlé is to help farmers become more productive. Better infrastructure, more investment, and more demand would help.

? Questions

1 Discuss the factors which have affected the supply of food in recent years.

2 Discuss the factors which may have affected demand for food in recent years.

3 Discuss whether the government should subsidize the production of biofuels.

4 Discuss the possible effects of high food prices.

Review questions

1 Is a public good any product that is provided by the government?

2 Why might monopolies be undesirable?

3 Should the government ban all smoking because it has negative external costs?

4 Should the UK government subsidize opera? What about football?

5 What problems can imperfect information cause in a free market?

6 Will incomes be equal in the free market?

7 What is meant by consumer surplus?

8 Why does a negative production externality lead to over production in society?

Put into practice

Imagine there was an increase in demand for a product that experienced a negative externality in production. Show the old and new price and output in a free market and highlight the new deadweight social burden triangle.

If the extra cost of providing a public good is zero show using a diagram the price and output that maximizes social welfare occurs.

Assignment questions

1   Research the world price of wheat over the last five years. Analyse the possible reasons for any significant changes in price over that period.

2   There have been several scandals in recent years to do with mis-selling pensions and insurance products. Research one of these scandals; explain what happened and the consequences. Explain how it is linked to market failure.

Key learning points

- In a perfect world, the free market would lead to an optimal allocation of resources. It would maximize community surplus and society would be producing an output at which the social marginal benefit equals the social marginal cost.

- There are many imperfections in the free market that move it away from the optimal allocation of resources. This is why government intervention may be necessary.

- Market failures and imperfections include public goods, externalities, monopolies, instability, merit goods, and information problems.

Learn more

Monopoly power is a major imperfection in the free market system. For a more detailed analysis of the impact of a monopoly on a market, see Chapter 12.

 Visit our Online Resource Centre at http://www.oxfordtextbooks.co.uk/orc/gillespie_econ3e/ for test questions and further information on topics covered in this chapter.

Intervening in the market system

8

We have now analysed the free market and how it works to solve the basic economic questions. However, we have also seen that it can have failures and imperfections. In this chapter we look at how the government might solve such imperfections. We will then go on to analyse the specific issues relating to different types of markets such as monopolies in more detail in the following chapters.

LEARNING OBJECTIVES

By the end of this chapter, you should be able to:

✓ explain how governments intervene in the free market;

✓ understand the impact of maximum and minimum prices;

✓ understand the workings of a buffer stock scheme;

✓ explain the reasons for nationalization and privatization;

✓ explain the problems of privatization.

▨ Intervention in markets

In a perfect free market system, the market forces of supply and demand would lead to the optimal allocation of resources where the social marginal benefit equals the social marginal cost, and community surplus is maximized (see Chapter 7). However, as we saw in the previous chapter, a number of market failures and imperfections exist that may justify government intervention.

The ways in which the government may intervene in a market to achieve a more efficient allocation of resources include the following.

- **The direct provision of goods and services** For example, society may believe that education, police protection, natonal defence, and health care should be freely available to all of its citizens, and therefore the government may want or need to provide these directly. A key political, as well as economic, decision is the extent to which govern-ments should take responsibility for providing goods and services.

- **Legislation and regulation** A government may pass laws to control certain types of behaviour. For example, if it feels that wages are too low in a free market, then it may introduce a minimum wage that employers have to pay. It may also organize stabiliza-tion schemes to prevent price instability in markets such as agriculture. Laws affect a number of areas of business behaviour, such as employment, competition, health and safety, and consumer protection.

> **What do you think?**
>
> Do you think the government should control where casinos are allowed to set up in the UK? What about alcohol and fast food advertising—should this be prevented from happening near schools?

- **Subsidies and taxes** These can be used as 'carrot' and 'stick' policies to encourage cer-tain types of behaviour and to deter other activities. This will change the allocation of resources away from the free market position toward a more socially optimal outcome. For example, undesirable behaviour may be taxed to discourage it; desirable behaviour may be subsidized to encourage it. Higher taxes on producers increase costs and leads the supply curve to shift upwards. Production subsidies lead to more supply at each price.

- **Providing information to promote particular forms of behaviour** For example, the gov-ernment may invest in publicity information to encourage individuals to undertake training, to relocate to get a job, to recycle, or to conserve energy.

> **What do you think?**
>
> In what ways do you think consumers might need protecting from businesses?

▌ Examples of government intervention in the market system

The following are examples of government intervention in the market system.

Regulating monopoly and competitive behaviour

Competition policy aims to prevent anti-competitive behaviour. For example, it is pos-sible that if a few firms dominate a market, then they will charge relatively high prices and provide a poor service to customers. There may be less investment in research and de-velopment (R&D), leading to less innovation and a fall in quality. Producer surplus rises, consumer surplus falls, and there is a welfare loss (see Chapter 7, or for more detailed analysis, Chapter 12). With no pressure to innovate costs may be higher than they would be in a competitive market. This causes 'X inefficiency'. Given that buyers do not have many alternatives, they may have to accept the higher prices and lower quality. To prevent this, the government may decide to intervene.

Other forms of anti-competitive behaviour include:

- colluding and firms fixing prices as part of a cartel;
- firms engaging in price wars (or predatory pricing) to undercut the competition and gain control over a market; and
- firms controlling supply and preventing other firms from gaining access to the market.

The following is a description of competition policy according to the UK government's Department for Business Innovation and Skills:

> Competitive markets provide the best means of ensuring the economy's resources are put to their best use by encouraging enterprise, and efficiency, and widening choice. Where markets work well they provide a strong incentive for good performance—encouraging firms to improve productivity, to reduce prices, and to innovate whilst rewarding consumers with lower prices, higher quality, and wider choice . . . But markets can and do fail. Competition policy is therefore used to ensure the efficient workings of markets, and to avoid market failure, most notably the abuses of market power.

What do you think?

Do you think that greater competition in markets is a good thing?
Can monopoly power ever be justified or desirable?

In the UK, competition policy is regulated by the following organizations.

- **Office of Fair Trading (OFT)** The OFT exists to make markets work better. It deals with anti-competitive practices through enforcement and communication.

- **Competition Commission** The Commission conducts inquiries into mergers, markets, and the regulation of regulated markets if an issue is referred to it by, for example, the OFT or the relevant secretary of state. The Commission can investigate if a merger or takeover leads to a market share of over 25 per cent. It has the ability to force such firms to sell parts of their business or reduce their prices. It can also prevent one firm from buying another (a takeover) or firms joining together (a merger) if it feels that it would lead to too much market power, and to behaviour that would act against the public interest.

- **Restrictive Practices Court** The Court examines agreements between firms supplying goods and services in the UK, such as collusive pricing. These agreements are presumed to be unfair unless they meet one of eight possible 'gateways' or justifications: for example, that they are needed to prevent high levels of unemployment in an area.

UK competition legislation includes the Competition Act 1998 and the Enterprise Act 2002. The UK is also subject to Articles 85 and 86 of the Treaty of Rome—that is, the treaty establishing the European Economic Community (EEC), subsequently the European Union (EU)—which cover restrictive practices and monopolies.

Article 85 states that restrictive practices (for example, when firms collude) must be stated and these are usually prohibited. Article 86 bans the abuse of a 'dominant position' by a firm.

Taxing negative externalities

Negative production externalities occur when the social cost of an activity is greater than the private cost of providing it. Given that private firms do not take account of the external effects of their actions, they will overproduce these products in a free market. To remedy this, the government may place indirect taxes on the products concerned. This will increase their private costs and, ideally, raise them to the level of the social costs. This is

---

Economics in context   **Competition Commission**

The Competition Commission is an independent public body set up to investigate mergers and markets. It describes its role as follows.

> The Competition Commission (CC) is one of the independent public bodies which help ensure healthy competition between companies in the UK for the benefit of companies, customers, and the economy. We investigate, and address issues of concern in three areas:
>
> - In mergers—when larger companies will gain more than 25% market share, and where a merger appears likely to lead to a substantial lessening of competition in one or more markets in the UK.
> - In markets—when it appears that competition may be being prevented, distorted or restricted in a particular market.
> - In regulated sectors where aspects of the regulatory system may not be operating effectively or to address certain categories of dispute between regulators, and regulated companies.
>
> Our inquiries are always initiated following a concern referred to us by another authority: usually the Office of Fair Trading.

Source: Competition Commission

Questions

What do you think are the potential dangers of companies having more than 25 per cent market share?

Can you think of businesses that do have more than 25 per cent market share? How do you think they have achieved this dominance? Do you think that this dominance of a market is likely to be good or bad for customers in their markets?

known as 'internalizing external costs'. Indirect taxes on products such as cigarettes, petrol, and alcohol are to ensure that producers take account of external costs. However, this may be easier to do in theory than in practice; this is because it is often difficult to quantify external costs precisely, and therefore the government may not know exactly what level of taxes to place on selected products to achieve the optimal allocation of goods and services.

What do you think?

Do you think legislation, tax, or subsidies are the best way of changing people's behaviour to make them become more environmentally friendly?

Creating a market in pollution

In a free market, firms do not take account of the pollution that they generate. To make firms take account of these external costs, a government can impose a tax on firms to increase the private costs to the same level as the social costs, as has been suggested above. Alternatively, the government can regulate production by passing laws governing the levels of pollution that are allowed. For example, in the UK, the Clean Air Acts limit the amount of pollution that can be generated. A third option is to create a market for pollution so that firms decide for themselves how much they are willing to pollute. For example, firms are given permits allowing them to generate a certain amount of pollution. They are then allowed to trade these permits. This means that if one firm wants to increase its output, then it can bid for the permit of another firm that does not need to use all of its allowance. If the price is right, then the permit will be sold from one firm to another. Rather than a government deciding who should be allowed to produce and pollute, it sets an overall level of pollution and then the free market decides who pollutes within this.

The Coase theorem

According to Coase (1960), the reason why externalities create a problem is because of a lack of well-defined property rights. In the case of noise pollution, for example, the following are not defined in law.

- **Whether we all have a right to silence** If the right to silence were universally accepted, then, in a free market, the people making the noise would have to pay the rest of us to be allowed to continue. The noisemakers would offer different prices for different amounts of noise and negotiate with the rest of the community to find the equilibrium level.

- **Whether we do not have a right to silence** If the right to make a noise were universally accepted, then, in a free market, the people who want silence would have to pay the noisemakers to reduce their noise. The people wanting quiet would offer different prices to reduce the level of noise. A price and level of noise would be found that suited both parties.

According to the Coase theorem, if we could clearly establish the rights of individuals, then markets could be established to set a price for such things as pollution.

The EU emission trading system (ETS)

The EU emissions trading system (EU ETS) is at the centre of the European Union's policy to combat climate change and is its main tool to reduce industrial greenhouse gas emissions cost-effectively. The EU ETS involves more than 11,000 power stations and industrial plants in 31 countries, as well as airlines and covers around 45 per cent of the EU's greenhouse gas emissions.

The ETS works by setting a cap (a limit) on the total amount of greenhouse gases that can be emitted by factories, power plants, and other installations. The cap is reduced over time so they will be 20 per cent lower in 2020 than 2005.

Within the overall limit companies receive or buy emissions allowances which they can then trade with other firms if they wish. They can also buy limited amounts of international credits from emission-saving projects around the world. The limit on the total number of allowances available ensures that they have a value. At the end of each year each business must have enough allowances to cover its emissions or it will be fined. If it does not use all its allowances it can keep them for the future or sell them. This creates a market for carbon. If the price is high enough this should act as an incentive for businesses to invest in clean, lower carbon technology.

However in recent years the economic crisis has reduced output levels and emissions which means there has been a growing surplus of allowances reducing the price.

Economics in context

The European Parliament recently rejected a plan to rescue the EU's ailing carbon trading scheme. The Parliament members voted against a so-called 'backloading' proposal; this would have cut the huge surplus of allowances that were being traded.

Because this surplus exists the price of carbon on the EU Emissions Trading Scheme (ETS) has fallen to 5 euros a tonne. However opponents of the proposal argued that it would increase energy costs. The price of carbon has fluctuated a lot since the ETS began in 2005. The scheme limits the emissions from around 12,000 power plants and factories across the 27-member bloc. The price of a permit has been above 30 euros per tonne but recently it has fallen as low as 3 euros per tonne. To remove the surplus the European Commission suggested withholding around 900 million allowances from the market over the next two years.

The industries that use a large amount of energy lobbied against the proposal arguing that th low price of permits reflected the reality of a European economy. They argued that higher costs and prices would put European businesses at a competitive disadvantage against US firms.

❷ Questions

Should the European Parliament have pushed through its proposal to reduce the number of permits available?

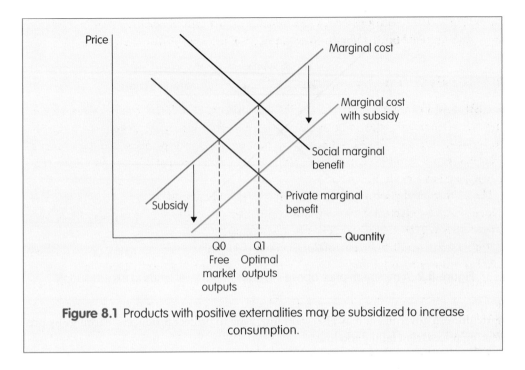

Figure 8.1 Products with positive externalities may be subsidized to increase consumption.

Subsidizing positive externalities

Positive externalities occur when the social marginal benefit is greater than the private marginal benefit. In a free market, products with a positive externality are underconsumed because consumers do not realize how good they are. In this case, the government would subsidize them to encourage consumption. By making them cheaper and more affordable, this can increase the equilibrium quantity (Figure 8.1).

Put into practice

Which of the following statements are true and which are false?

a. In a free market negative externalities lead to overproduction

b. A government is likely to subsidize negative externalities

c. If the social benefit is greater than the private benefit there is a positive externality

d. A monopoly in the UK is defined as a business with more than 50 per cent share of the market

---

Minimum and maximum prices

Minimum prices

A government may intervene in a market to ensure that the price does not fall below a minimum level. For example, in the labour market, the government may believe that the equilibrium wage in some industries is unacceptably low and is unfair (rather than inefficient). The government might therefore introduce a minimum wage to ensure that all employees must earn at least a given amount of money. In other markets, such as

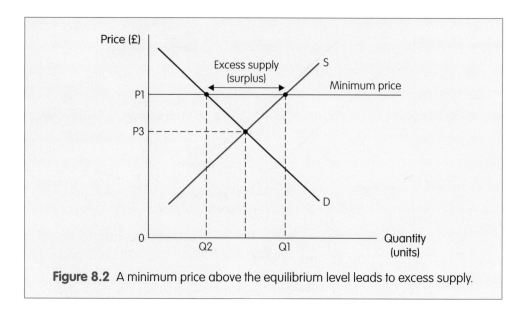

Figure 8.2 A minimum price above the equilibrium level leads to excess supply.

agriculture, a government may also want intervene to protect producers' earnings by preventing prices from falling too low.

If a minimum price is set above equilibrium, then the result is that the quantity supplied will exceed the quantity demanded (see Figure 8.2). At price P1, the amount that suppliers are willing and able to sell exceeds the amount that buyers are willing and able to buy—that is, there is excess supply. This leads to a surplus equal to Q1 – Q2. In a free market, the price would fall to bring back equilibrium at price P3.

Put into practice

Using supply and demand diagrams, illustrate the possible effect on overall earnings of introducing a minimum wage.
What might influence the overall effect on employees' total earnings?

Maximum prices

If a government believes that the equilibrium market price would be too high (for example, the rent being charged for accommodation), then it may intervene to place a maximum level in the market. If this maximum price is below the equilibrium—for example, the price P0 in Figure 8.3—then the impact of this is to create a shortage: the quantity demanded will be greater than the quantity supplied at the given price. There is a shortage equal to Q2 – Q1.

Those who benefit from the limit on the price pay less than they would in a free market. However, the market as a whole has less supplied to it (for example, fewer people would rent out their houses). In a free market, the price would rise to P1 and the quantity supplied would be Q1.

The effect of a maximum and minimum price on the quantity supplied and demanded depends on the price elasticity of demand and supply (see Chapters 4 and 5).

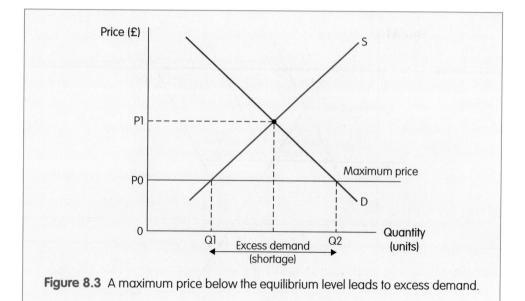

Figure 8.3 A maximum price below the equilibrium level leads to excess demand.

Put into practice

Using a supply and demand diagram, illustrate the effect of a maximum price above the equilibrium price and quantity sold.

Introducing price stabilization schemes

Changes in supply and demand conditions in the free market can lead to major changes in the price level. This can be seen in agricultural markets, in which supply can shift significantly due to changes in weather conditions. The consequent price and income instability

Economics in context

The Venezuelan government recently had to import 39 million rolls of toilet paper because of a major shortage in the country. The government voted to agree to $79m credit for the country's ministry of commerce, for toilet paper, soap, and toothpaste. Venezuela is rich in oil but has to import most other products. The government is very interventionist and controls much of the economy. However its attempts to decide what is produced, for whom, and at what price can cause problems. Price controls that keep prices low act as a disincentive for local producers and creates shortages.

? Question

Draw a diagram to show the effect of placing price controls on food below the market price.

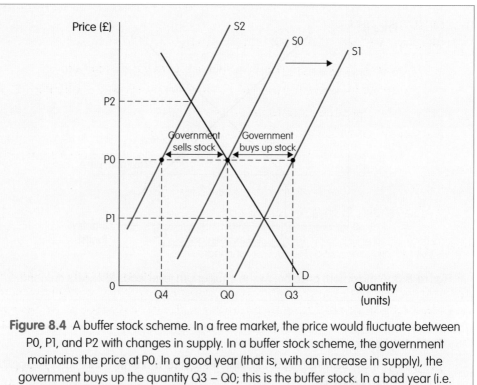

Figure 8.4 A buffer stock scheme. In a free market, the price would fluctuate between P0, P1, and P2 with changes in supply. In a buffer stock scheme, the government maintains the price at P0. In a good year (that is, with an increase in supply), the government buys up the quantity Q3 – Q0; this is the buffer stock. In a bad year (i.e. when supply falls) the government sells the quantity Q4 – Q0 to increase supply and to keep the price at P0.

may discourage farmers from staying in the industry. If the government wants to maintain agriculture as a sector within the economy (perhaps to protect a way of life or, for strategic reasons, to maintain domestic control over some food supplies), then it may use price stabilization schemes.

To stabilize prices, the government can use a buffer stock scheme (see Figure 8.4). If there is excess supply (perhaps due to a good harvest or developments in farming technology), then the price will fall in the free market due to a surplus being created. To stop this from happening, the government can buy up the excess, so that supply equals demand at the original price. This surplus can then be stored for future years.

When there is a fall in supply (perhaps due to a poor harvest), the government can sell the stock that it has built up in the good years (assuming that there have been good years). By selling its stock, the government can increase the supply of the product in the market back to its old level and thereby keep price at its original level.

Such intervention does, of course, incur costs, because the government must pay to organize the stockpiling in the good years. This involves warehousing, security, and possible depreciation costs. Also, if there are continually 'good years', this means that the government will buy up more each year, creating even bigger stockpiles.

Put into practice

Which of the following statements are true and which are false?

a. In buffer stock scheme the government buys up excess demand in a good year

b. In a buffer stock scheme the government sells more when the market supply is limited

c. A minimum price above equilibrium leads to excess supply

d. A maximum price above equilibrium leads to excess supply

Problems of government intervention in the market system

The following are problems that occur during government intervention.

- **Valuation problems** When trying to take account of external costs and benefits, the government will have to try to place a value on things such as the beauty of the countryside, the impact on wildlife activity, the quality of life, the risk to health and personal safety, and the impact of an activity on the environment and future generations. It is obviously difficult to place a monetary value on such items.

- **Bureaucracy** Large organizations such as governments often struggle to respond quickly and efficiently to change. Decisions may involve many different groups and take time. Imagine a government trying to control lots of different markets: by the time a decision is taken and implemented, it may no longer be appropriate or correct.

- **Lack of incentive** The more the government intervenes, the less incentive there is for private firms to innovate and become more efficient. For example, inefficient firms that benefit from subsidies may continue to be inefficient rather than face the harsh realities of competition.

Economics in context — From wine to fuel

A few years ago, nearly a billion bottles of wine were ordered by the EU to be turned into fuel and disinfectant. The EU spent €131 million to distil 430 million bottles of French wine and 371 million bottles of Italian wine into fuel. Nearly a quarter of Spanish wine was also being used for industrial purposes. The European agriculture commissioner said: 'Crisis distillation is becoming a depressingly regular feature . . . Europe is producing too much wine for which there is no market.' Proposals from the EU were likely to put 400,000 hectares under the plough. Farmers would then be paid not for producing wine, but for keeping up environmental standards. One problem was that there were too many small wine makers. In France, there was one worker per hectare of vineyards; in Australia, there was one worker for every 50 hectares.

❓ Questions

In the free market, how would equilibrium be reached in this market?

Why do you think that the EU bought up the excess supply?

▦ Nationalization

Rather than trying to influence market forces of supply and demand through policies such as tax and benefits, a government may decide to take over the provision of some products from private businesses; this is known as nationalization. Nationalized industries are organizations the ownership of which has been transferred from the private sector to the public sector—that is, the government buys the shares of a private company and takes it into state control.

The following are possible arguments in favour of nationalization.

- **Natural monopolies** These occur when the cost advantages of expanding are very high. For example, if there are massive initial costs to set up a gas or electricity network, these fixed costs can be spread over more units as output increases. In this situation, one firm is likely to expand and dominate the industry to benefit from lower unit costs. Other firms entering the market would find it difficult to compete if they were to enter at low levels of output, because their unit costs would be much higher. This means that this industry is likely to be a monopoly. The government may need to nationalize to ensure that this natural monopoly does not abuse its market power.

    It is felt in a number of countries that competition in the utilities (such as gas, electricity, and water) would lead to a wasteful duplication of resources, and that these are better run by the state. Do we need two sets of water or gas pipes, electricity pylons, or roads, for example?

- **Social objectives** Private firms will consider private benefits and costs when making output and investment decisions. The government may believe that there are significant external benefits and costs to consider; therefore a government may want to intervene in this industry to focus on issues such as safety, and ensuring the service is available and affordable for every household.

- **Longer-term objectives** Managers in private sector businesses may plan for the relatively short term. There may be pressure on them from investors to pay dividends which may reduce the funds available for investment and even if projects do go ahead shareholders may want quite quick returns. In addition managers often change jobs every few years so may be interested in projects that generate returns in a few years. However, big infrastructure projects may take many years to bring returns and it may be that a government is needed to nvest on this type of investment

> **What do you think?**
>
> The London Olympics of 2012 involved major investment. This was defended on the basis of the benefits for the UK and the legacy it would leave for sports in the country. Do you think the Olympics were worth it?

▦ Privatization

Although nationalization is occurring in some countries and the effects of unstable economic conditions in recent years have led to greater intervention by many governments, the general trend in the 20 years before this was for the government to intervene less directly

Examples of UK privatizations

The following are examples of privatizations in the UK.

- 1984—Enterprise Oil; Jaguar; British Telecom
- 1986—British Gas
- 1987—British Airways; British Airports Authority; BP
- 1988—British Steel
- 1989—10 water companies
- 1990—12 regional electricity companies
- 1996—HM Stationery Office (HMSO)

? Question

What would you consider before buying a share in a privatized business?

in the provision of goods and services. This led to many privatizations. Privatization occurs when resources are transferred from the public sector to the private sector. In 2013, part of Royal Mail was sold to the private sector.

Forms of privatization may include the following.

- **Denationalization** This occurs when assets that were owned by the government are transferred into private ownership—for example, when a state-owned business is sold to private investors.
- **Contracting out** This involves introducing private contactors to provide some services, such as food in schools, and the transportation of prisoners to and from court.
- **Selling public sector assets** For example, between 1980 and 1983, nearly 600,000 council houses and flats were sold to private individuals in the UK.
- **Selling government shares in private sector businesses**
- **Deregulation** This introduces competition into markets that were previously restricted (that is, opens markets to greater competition).
- **Private finance initiative (PFI)** This occurs when projects are jointly funded by the private and public sectors—for example, the expansion of the London Underground.

▦ Reasons to privatize

The government may privatize an industry for the following reasons.

- **To raise revenue** By selling shares in organizations that were previously state-owned, the government will earn money. This can then be used to finance investment projects or to enable the government to reduce the taxes that it charges. The government can also gain from contracting out by reducing its costs.

- **To free organizations from government control** When firms are government-run, the danger is that they will be run for political means. For example, when elections are approaching, nationalized (state-run) industries may deliberately keep people employed even if it is uneconomic to do so, because the government does not want to lose votes. Privatized businesses may be forced to become more efficient and more innovative to survive; if they cannot compete, they may close.

- **To provide more incentives** If organizations are state-owned, then managers may lack the incentive to run them more efficiently. Given that the profits belong to the state, an increase in profits may simply mean that more funds go to central government rather than are invested back into this particular business or reward those who made them. In private sector organizations, there may be more incentive to provide a better service or be more efficient because this creates more profits that are kept by the owners. Managers may be more interested in understanding and meeting customer needs.

- **To create more competition** When transferring resources into the private sector, the government will often open up that market for other firms to compete in, which should provide more choice for consumers. Greater competition should encourage more innovation and more efficiency, leading to better products at lower prices. Greater efficiency can stimulate further economic growth.

- **To provide firms with more access to finance** Once firms are privatized, they are able to sell shares to investors to raise finance. When they are nationalized, they rely on the government for funding and, given that the government has many demands on its funds, they may not get the long-term investment that they need to be competitive. With access to private finance, they may be able to raise more money for investment.

- **To enable firms to have access to private finance** The government has many different demands on its funds. This may lead to underinvestment in some sectors. By privatizing, firms can sell shares to raise the finance needed for investment and modernization.

- **To create more share owners in the economy and raise the general level of awareness in the economy regarding investment** This may then lead to more investment in other firms, helping firms to finance expansion.

> **What do you think?**
>
> Do you think that privately owned motorways in the UK would be a good thing?
> In 2013 the government sold shares in Royal Mail. Do you think this was a good idea?

■ Problems of privatization

The following are problems associated with privatization.

- Privatization may create private monopolies that abuse their power (in which case, privatized organizations may need to be regulated by the government).

- Privatized firms are likely to pursue private objectives rather than social objectives. This may mean that the needs of society are not met as effectively as they were when the industry was nationalized; the socially optimal price and output decisions may not be achieved. Privatized business may also pursue profit at the expense of safety or quality. There is a danger that private businesses may drop standards in an attempt to boost short-term profits.

- Some people criticize privatization on the basis that it is selling the nation's assets back to the nation—that is, in some ways, it is selling what we already own.

- If the public sector industries were making profits, then by privatizing them, the government will lose this income.

- The industry may be a natural monopoly. This means that the economies of scale are so great that one firm is bound to expand and dominate to benefit from the cost advantages. By splitting up this industry into smaller firms, the unit costs of smaller firms will be higher and this may lead to higher prices.

- It may lead to job losses as managers find more efficient ways of undertaking tasks. This may be efficient but politically unpopular.

Problems of intervention

Whilst there are undoubtedly numerous reasons why a government might want to intervene in a market this also brings problems. These include:

a. information problems. In the free market the price mechanism operates in billions of markets to equate supply and demand. Producers and consumers act rationally and make their own decisions to pursue their own interests. If the government intervenes it is trying to take control of a market and this involves massive informational issues. This can lead to slow and inaccurate decision making

b. shortages and surpluses. If the government misjudges what consumers want or decides they should have something different this is likely to lead to overproduction of some products and underproduction of others. The government may end up providing some products that customers do not want; for other products there may be queues and rationing because of too much demand and not enough supply.

c. Lack of incentive. Given that profits belong to the government rather than investors this might lead to a lack of incentive to be efficient or to innovate. This may affect the competitiveness of the economy and long-term growth.

Regulatory capture

Regulatory capture occurs when the regulating body identifies so much with the industry that it is regulating that it protects its interests rather than monitors the industry. Those involved in the regulated industry will devote a great deal of time, effort, and resources to protecting their own interests, and may well influence the regulator to see these from their own perspective.

Put into practice

Which of the following statements are true and which are false?

a. A nationalized organization is in the public sector

b. A privatized business is likely to have social objectives

c. Regulatory capture reduces the effectiveness of the regulators

d. One reason for privatization is to create natural monopolies

Economics in context

Network Rail was recently informed by the rail regulator that it needs to cut costs by £2bn over the next five years as well as improve punctuality. The Office of Rail Regulation (ORR) said the cost cuts must not come at the expense of safety and said that at least 9 out of 10 trains must run on time on all routes by 2019.

The ORR said Network Rail had missed all of its punctuality targets for England and Wales last year. Along with the price of a ticket, punctuality is a major issue for train passengers.

Network Rail has another year to improve significantly or face a fine from the regulator, which could run to about £75m.

During the 2014–2019 period, the ORR said Network Rail must:

- Improve punctuality—an average of 92.5 per cent of trains on all routes across the UK must arrive on time, compared with its target of just over 90 per cent now

- Complete projects to increase capacity and improve service as fast as possible

- Provide better and more up-to-date data on the condition of its tracks, bridges, and other assets, so problems can be fixed before they occur

- Improve safety for passengers and workers—the ORR has approved £67m of funding to upgrade and close level crossings in England and Wales

According to the ORR's assessment the cost between next year and 2019 of running the rail network should be £21.4bn—nearly £2bn lower than proposed by Network Rail.

The savings will be made through new technologies, improved management, and more efficient ways of working but will not come at the expense of safety, the ORR said. The general secretary of the Rail, Maritime and Transport workers' union, said it would mean massive cuts to renewals and maintenance, compromising safety and leading to more breakdowns, failures, and delays.

❓ Questions

Why does Network Rail need to be regulated do you think?

Why might Network Rail oppose some of the regulator's recommendations?

Case study

The International Energy Agency (IEA) says that climate change could pass a critical level if the world waits until 2020 for the planned comprehensive UN deal to cut emissions.

It therefore recommends some short-term measures.

These include action on energy efficiency, coal-fired power stations, and fossil fuel subsidies.

The IEA authors believe governments will find it easier to take smaller focused measures than to change their entire economies to cleaner energy systems.

The agency repeats its warning that two-thirds of existing fossil fuel reserves cannot be burned if emissions are to be held within the projected danger threshold of a 2 C° rise.

It believes it is necessary to have major investment in carbon capture and storage technology to enable more fossil fuels to be used. However this technology is years behind schedule and still untried in power stations on a large scale.

The recent report, *Redrawing the Energy Climate Map*, tries to appeal to politicians' self-interest by suggesting such measures could lead to a competitive advantage to nations that can save more energy and cut emissions cheaply.

Its latest tactic offers by 2020 to reduce emissions by 3.1 gigatonnes of CO_2 equivalent (3.1 Gt CO_2-eq) at what it says will be no net economic cost.

Limiting the use of old polluting coal-fired power stations is another idea, which the IEA says will also combat air pollution. However, new plants are expensive if they are the most efficient type recommended by the IEA.

Dirty fossil fuels receive $523bn a year in subsidies—six times more than clean renewables. Another suggestion is the removal of these subsidies but this tends to provoke a sharp political response.

Overall, global emissions rose 1.4 per cent despite the economic slowdown. On current trends, the world is moving further away from its target of limiting global temperature rise to 2 C°, the report says.

Source: http://www.bbc.co.uk/news/science-environment-22845425

? Questions

1 Analyse the reasons why businesses do not take account of their emissions in a free market economy. Show the effect of this using diagrams.

2 Analyse the reasons why controlling emissions matters to society.

3 Discuss the ways in which the government might intervene to reduce emissions

Review questions

1 If a monopoly develops, what is the likely impact on the price charged and the quantity available compared with the free market?

2 Travelling by air has a major negative environmental impact. Do you think that air travel should be stopped completely?

3 What action would a government that is operating a buffer stock scheme take if there were a surplus of a product?

4 Explain two reasons for privatizing a business.

5 Explain two arguments against privatization.

6 Explain how a government might deal with the problem of a negative externality.

7 Explain how a government might deal with the problem of a positive externality.

8 Why might a government want to nationalize an industry?

Put into practice

1 Show the effect of a minimum price set below the equilibrium price using a supply and demand curve diagram.

2 Show the effect of an indirect tax imposed on a market on the equilibrium price and quantity. Show the tax revenue for the government. Assume demand is relatively price inelastic and supply is relatively price elastic.

Assignment questions

1 The Common Agricultural Policy (CAP) is the European Union's buffer stock scheme for agriculture. Research the CAP and present a case to show that it needs reform.

2 Should the government subsidize windfarms? Research the case for and against this and make a justified recommendation.

Key learning points

- In theory, a free market may provide an optimal allocation of resources; in reality, there are many market failures and imperfections

- A government can intervene in a number of ways to try to remedy market failures and imperfections, such as through legislation, price fixing, indirect taxes, subsidies, and direct provision.

- A buffer stock scheme can be used to stabilize good prices.

- Nationalization occurs when a government takes firms under its control.

- Privatization occurs when assets and contracts are transferred to the private sector.

- Privatization can lead to greater efficiency and innovation, but may need regulation to ensure that customers are not exploited.

Reference

Coase, R. (1960) 'The problem of social cost', *Journal of Law, and Economics*, 3(Oct): 1–44

 Visit our Online Resource Centre at http://www.oxfordtextbooks.co.uk/orc/gillespie_econ3e/ for test questions and further information on topics covered in this chapter.

Costs: Short run and long run

9

In the coming chapters we will analyse different market structures such as competitive and monopoly markets in detail and examine their impact on efficiency and community surplus. To do this we need to build our understanding of costs, revenues, and profits. In this chapter we consider different types of costs and how costs may vary in the short and long run. We will then bring in revenues in the next chapter to analyse profits.

LEARNING OBJECTIVES

By the end of this chapter, you should be able to:

✓ distinguish between short-run and long-run costs;

✓ explain the law of diminishing returns;

✓ understand the difference between marginal, average, and total product;

✓ understand the difference between marginal, average, and total cost;

✓ understand the significance of economies and diseconomies of scale;

✓ understand the difference between internal and external economies of scale;

✓ understand the meaning and significance of the minimum efficient scale.

The importance of costs

To be able to decide on the appropriate price and output required to maximize profits, managers need a detailed understanding of the level of costs at different levels of output and how costs might change over time. They will be interested in factors such as the total cost of producing, the cost per unit (average cost), and the extra costs of producing another product (marginal cost). This unit examines the factors that determine the nature of costs in both the short run and the long run. Managers will aim to achieve the lowest possible cost per unit for any given level of output given a quality level they are trying to achieve for their product and this involves getting the most efficient combination of resources. Their ability to do this varies from the short run to the long run. In the short run, there will be more constraints than in the long run and this will affect the costs of producing any level of output.

The pressure on firms to be efficient has generally increased with greater worldwide competition, and the ability of consumers to search more easily and compare prices via the Internet. This makes it even more important for firms to look for the best way of producing. It may also lead to undesirable behavior—in 2013 some producers of beefburgers were found to be using horsemeat instead. The pressure on suppliers to keep prices down leads to unethical actions. Similarly Foxconn, which supplies Apple, was criticized recently for the conditions and treatment of staff in an attempt to keep costs low.

The costs structure in an industry is also important because it influences the number of firms that can survive within it. If costs are very high to start up or at low levels of output, for example, then it is likely that established firms or large producers will face limited competition. Consider the oil, pharmaceutical, and banking industries. By comparison if start-up costs are relatively low for example with cafes, hairdressers and florists we expect quite a competitive industry with many producers.

Economics in context

More than two thirds of the income of Premier League's football clubs £2.4bn income was paid out in wages. Most of this £1.6bn was spent on players' wages.

In 2013 the wage bill accounted for 67 per cent of clubs' turnover. The clubs do not separate the wage bill in their annual accounts between players, senior employees, and other staff but the players certainly account for the majority of their spending. Manchester City's wage bill of £202m was the Premier League's highest, almost £30m more than the £173m paid by Roman Abramovich's Chelsea. Carlos Tevez was paid £198,000 a week but many other employees such as the catering or shop staff are still paid the minimum wage.

❓ Questions

Why do you think players in the Premier League are paid so much?
Why do the cleaners and shop staff earn so much less?
Should the clubs pay players less and pay the cleaning staff more?

▇ Short-run costs

The short run in economics is the period of time during which there is at least one factor of production fixed. This means a business faces a resource constraint. In the short run, at least one of the resources cannot be changed—for example, a firm cannot recruit the staff that it wants, cannot acquire new equipment, or cannot find new premises. This means that, in the short run, a firm cannot necessarily find its optimal mix of resources. As a result, there are fixed costs in the short run. For example, you may have rented premises and be committed to a contract for a period of months or years, or you may be repaying a loan on equipment for a five-year period.

Short-run total costs are therefore made up of fixed costs and variable costs.

- **Fixed costs (FC)** These are costs that a firm has to pay, but which are not dependent on the level of output. For example, the interest on a loan is related to the size of the loan and the interest rate, not the level of output. Even if output is zero, a firm must pay its fixed costs. High levels of fixed costs represent a high level of risk for a business because the firm still has to pay these costs even if sales fall.

- **Variable costs (VC)** These are costs that are directly related to the level of output, such as the costs of materials and components used in the production process. As output increases, variable costs will increase as well.

How long the short run lasts will vary from industry to industry. If it is easy to sell and buy land and equipment, for example, the short run may be months, or a year or so. If, however, expansion involves a major investment—for example, in a new airport terminal—then it may take five to ten years to expand capacity.

> **What do you think?**
>
> In what ways do you think firms might be able to shorten the short run?

The law of diminishing returns

In the short run, a firm's ability to produce will be constrained by its fixed factors of production. For example, a business may be constrained by its equipment or office space. Although it will be able to change these factors over time (for example, invest in new equipment or buy new office space), in the short term it cannot do so. Therefore, to increase production, it can change some of its factors of production (for example, managers could ask employees to work overtime or the business might recruit more employees), but not others; expansion involves adding variable factors of production to fixed factors to increase output. As a result, the business will experience the law of diminishing returns. Under the law of diminishing returns, the extra output produced as more units of a variable factor are added to fixed factors will decrease. This means that the total output increases at a decreasing rate.

The extra output produced by the variable factor is known as the marginal product. If labour is the variable factor, then we measure the marginal product of labour (MPL). If capital is the variable factor, then we measure the marginal product of capital (MPK—where K is used to represent capital).

The marginal product (MP) can be calculated using the following equation:

$$\text{Marginal product} = \frac{\text{Change in the total output}}{\text{Change in the variable factor of production}}$$

Imagine increasing output by adding additional people to an office environment with a given amount of equipment. There will simply not be enough computers or telephones for them all to use if you keep adding staff; they will begin to get in each other's way. The first person you employ could be very useful and productive; the sixth or seventh employee may add little to the overall output of the office if you cannot increase the fixed factors, such as office equipment.

The law of diminishing returns is illustrated in Figure 9.1.

Short-run marginal costs

The marginal cost curve shows the extra cost of producing a unit. The marginal cost is calculated as follows:

$$\text{Marginal cost} = \frac{\text{Change in the total cost}}{\text{Change in output}}$$

The short-run marginal cost (SRMC) curve is inversely linked to the marginal product curve. As each additional factor of production is added to the business, the extra output of each employee diminishes in accordance with the law of diminishing returns. Assuming that the employees are all being paid the same amount of money, this means that you are paying the same for each extra worker who is adding fewer extra units of output; therefore the extra cost of these units in terms of labour is increasing. So, when a firm experiences the law of diminishing marginal returns, its short-run marginal costs are increasing assuming wages stay the same. If extra workers are less productive, then the extra output that they are producing is becoming more expensive. The relationship between the marginal product and the marginal cost is shown in Figure 9.2. The SRMC curve is usually a 'tick' shape.

What do you think?

If the wage rate were to be increased to attract more employees, what would this do to the marginal cost curve?

Put into practice

1. If marginal product is rising what is happening to total product?
2. If marginal product is falling what is happening to total product?
3. If marginal product is 0 what is happening to total product?
4. If marginal costs are falling what is happening to total costs?
5. If marginal cost is increasing what is happening to total costs?

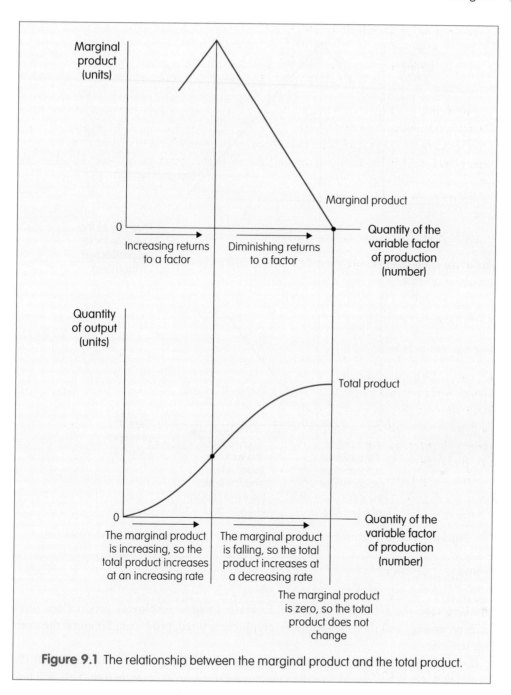

Figure 9.1 The relationship between the marginal product and the total product.

Marginal product and average product of labour

The average product of labour is the output per employee (often called labour productivity).

If the marginal product of labour is greater than the average product, this means that the extra employee is more productive than the employees were, on average, before. This will pull up the average—that is, if the marginal product is greater than the average

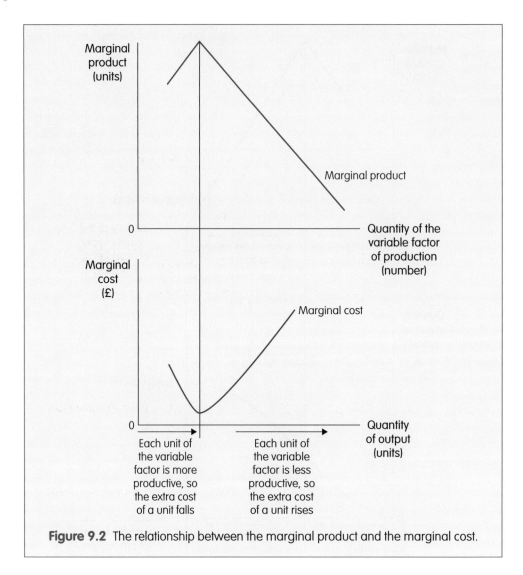

Figure 9.2 The relationship between the marginal product and the marginal cost.

product, then the average product will increase. Imagine employees produce ten units each on average and then an additional employee is hired, producing 20 units: the average will rise.

If the marginal product of labour is less than the average product, this means that the extra employee is less productive than employees were, on average, before. This will pull down the average—that is, if the marginal product is less than the average product, then the average product will fall. If employees are producing ten units each and then an additional employee is hired producing two units, the average falls.

This means that the marginal product will cross the average product at its maximum point (see Figure 9.3).

The relationship between marginal, average, and total product is shown in Table 9.1.

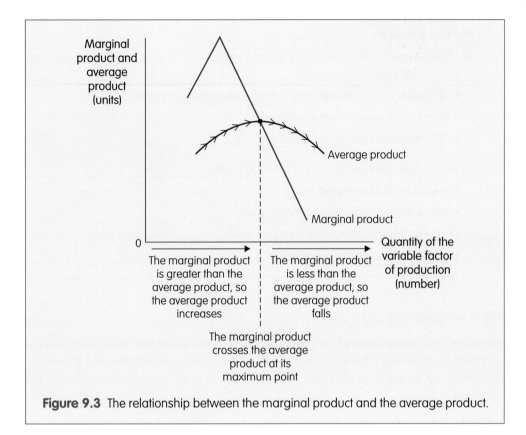

Figure 9.3 The relationship between the marginal product and the average product.

Table 9.1 The relationship between the marginal product, the average product, and the total product (output)

Number of employees	Total output (units)	Average product of labour = $\dfrac{\text{Total output}}{\text{Number of employees (units)}}$	Marginal product of labour = $\dfrac{\text{Change in total output}}{\text{Change in number of employees (units)}}$
1	10	10	–
2	30	15	20
3	60	20	30
4	76	19	16
5	80	16	4

Put into practice

a. Employees are hired at a wage of £200 each per week. You have four employees producing a total of 400 units.

- What is the total cost of production? (assume labour is the only cost)
- What is the average output per employee?
- What is the average cost of a unit?

b. You hire a fifth employee and output rises to 450 units.

- What is the total cost of production?
- What is the marginal product of the fifth worker?
- What is the average output per employee now?
- What is the average cost per unit now?

Short-run average costs

The short-run average cost (SRAC) curve shows the lowest cost per unit for any level of output given the fixed factor(s) of production. The SRAC curve is generally U-shaped. It is made up of the average fixed costs and the average variable costs. Using the equation:

Total cost = Fixed cost + Variable cost

we divide by the output level to obtain:

$$\frac{\text{Total cost (TC)}}{\text{Output (Q)}} = \frac{\text{Fixed cost (FC)}}{\text{Output (Q)}} + \frac{\text{Variable cost (VC)}}{\text{Output (Q)}}$$

which means that:

Average cost (AC) = Average fixed cost (AFC) = Average variable cost (AVC)

The average fixed cost curve will fall continuously as the fixed costs are spread over more units. The average variable cost curve is usually U-shaped and is the inverse of the average product curve.

Assume that the variable factor is labour and the wage rate is constant. When, on average, labour is less productive, then the average cost of a unit in terms of labour will rise. When, on average, labour is more productive, then the variable cost per unit in terms of labour will fall. (This is similar to the inverse relationship between marginal product and marginal cost.) The relationship between productivity and costs is shown in Figure 9.4.

The average cost and average variable cost curves converge (that is, get closer) as output increases, because the average fixed cost becomes less significant. The overall costs per unit are increasingly dominated by variable costs as the fixed cost per unit becomes smaller (see Figure 9.5).

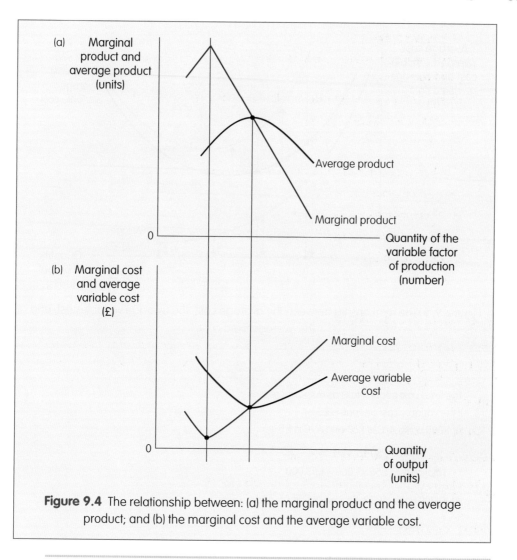

Figure 9.4 The relationship between: (a) the marginal product and the average product; and (b) the marginal cost and the average variable cost.

Example

The fixed costs of a business are £50,000. This means that the fixed cost per unit will be as follows.
At 1,000 units:

$$\frac{£50,000}{1,000} = £50 \text{ a unit}$$

At 10,000 units:

$$\frac{£50,000}{10,000} = £5 \text{ a unit}$$

At 50,000 units:

$$\frac{£50,000}{50,000} = £1 \text{ a unit}$$

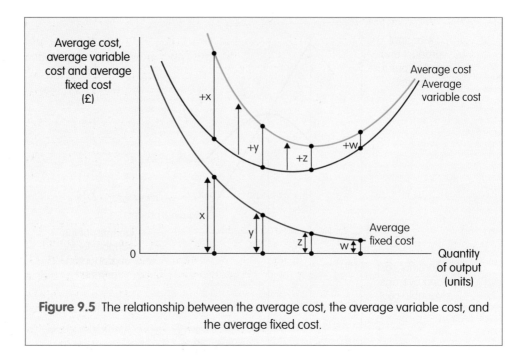

Figure 9.5 The relationship between the average cost, the average variable cost, and the average fixed cost.

The fixed cost per unit falls as output increases.

If the variable cost per unit is £5—

At 1,000 units, AFC is £50 and AVC is £5, so:

$$AC = £50 + £5 = £55$$
$$\text{Total costs} = £55 \times 1,000 = £55,000$$

At 10,000 units, AFC is £5 and AVC is £5, so:

$$AC = £5 + £5 = £10$$
$$\text{Total cost} = £10 \times 10,000 = £100,000$$

At 50,000 units, AFC is £1 and AVC is £5, so:

$$AC = £1 + £5 = £6$$
$$\text{Total costs} = £6 \times 50,000 = £300,000$$

Put into practice

- The fixed costs of a business are £10,000. What is the average fixed cost if output is i. one unit, ii. ten units, iii. 100 units, or iv. 1,000 units? What is happening to the average fixed cost as output increases?

- Suppose that the variable cost per unit is £2. Calculate both the total cost and the average cost for one unit, ten units, 100 units, and 1,000 units.

Table 9.2 Output and costs

Output (units)	Total cost (£)	Marginal cost (£)	Average cost (£)
3	30	–	10
4	80	50	20
5	150	70	30

The relationship between marginal cost (MC) and average cost (AC)

The marginal cost is the extra cost of producing a unit. The average cost is the cost per unit. If the marginal cost is greater than the average cost, then this will pull the average cost up. For example, if a firm produces three units at an average cost of £10 and then it produces a fourth unit for £50, then this will pull the average cost up (see Table 9.2).

Conversely, if the extra cost of a unit is less than the average cost, it will pull down the average cost. For example, if a firm produces three units at an average cost of £10 and then it produces a fourth unit for £6, then this will bring the average cost down. The total cost of three units is:

$$3 \times £10 = £30$$

So the total cost of four units is:

$$£30 + £6 = £36$$

This means that the average cost is:

$$\frac{£36}{4} = £9 \text{ a unit}$$

Put into practice

Fill in the two blank cells in the table below.

Output (units)	Total cost (£)	Marginal cost (£)	Average cost (£)
3	30	–	10
4	36	6	9
5	40	?	?

This relationship between marginals and averages means that the marginal cost will cross the average cost at its minimum point. This is shown in Figure 9.6.

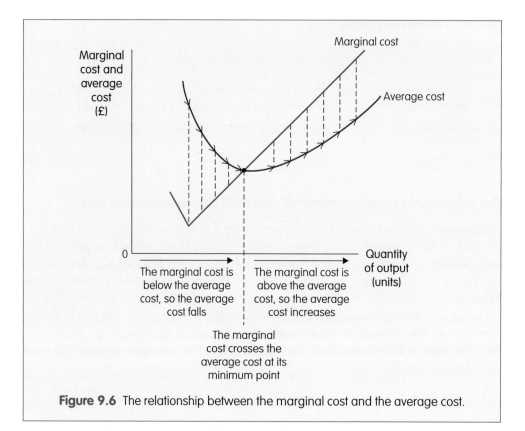

Figure 9.6 The relationship between the marginal cost and the average cost.

Put into practice

1.

- The average cost of ten units is £6. What is the total cost?

- The marginal cost of the 11th unit is £17. What is the total cost now? What is the average cost? What does this show in terms of the relationships between marginal costs and average costs?

- The marginal cost of the 12th unit is £7. What is the total cost now? What is the average cost? What does this show in terms of the relationships between marginal costs and average costs?

2. Which of the following statements are true and which are false?

   a. The short-run average cost and short-run average variable cost converge as output increases.

   b. Costs are zero when output is zero.

   c. If marginal costs are positive, total costs are increasing.

   d. If average costs are £25, average fixed costs are £15, and output is 20 units, then variable costs are £200.

Table 9.3 Summary table of key terms

Item	Description
Marginal product (MP)	Extra output from employing an extra factor of production
	$= \dfrac{\text{Change in the total output}}{\text{Change in the variable factor of production}}$
Average product (AP)	$= \dfrac{\text{Total output}}{\text{Number of factors of production}}$
Total cost (TC)	Fixed cost + Variable cost
Marginal cost (MC)	$= \dfrac{\text{Change in the total cost}}{\text{Change in output}}$
Average variable cost (AVC)	Variable cost per unit
	$= \dfrac{\text{Variable cost}}{\text{Output}}$
Average fixed cost (AFC)	$= \dfrac{\text{Fixed cost}}{\text{Output}}$
Average cost (AC); also known as average total cost (ATC)	$= \dfrac{\text{Total cost}}{\text{Output}}$
	$= $ Average fixed cost + Average variable cost

A summary of the key terms covered so far is shown in Table 9.3.

Put into practice

a. Which of the following statements is true? The law of diminishing returns:

- applies in the long run.
- shows that utility falls as more units of a product are consumed.
- states that, after a point, each additional unit of a variable input produces less than the previous unit.
- shows that revenue falls as the price is reduced to sell more units.

b. In the short run, as output is increased, more variable inputs are added to a given amount of fixed inputs. After some point, which of the following do we expect?

- no change in average fixed costs.
- average variable cost to stop falling and to begin rising.
- average total cost to stop rising and begin falling.
- marginal cost to decline throughout all ranges of output.

The orange producers in Brazil have recently been struggling due to stagnant world demand, rising production costs, and the power of the businesses that process the oranges.

Brazil produces over 1.4 million tons of oranges a year and is one of the world's largest producers and exporters.

Production costs have soared and even though prices have also tripled most producers have found it difficult to make a profit. Costs are higher due to an increase in minimum wages plus higher land prices and pesticide costs. Some estimates are that the production costs are around 5 dollars per crate (40.8 kilograms or 90 pounds) whilst the selling price is between 3.5 to 4 dollars.

In the citrus region of Sao Paulo, half of the orange farms have disappeared over the past 10 years, and only the most productive survive. The other producers have switched to sugar cane, corn, and soybean.

According to data from the government's crop supply agency Conab, 36,700 hectares of orange trees were uprooted between 2012 and 2013.

Source: Adapted from http://en.mercopress.com/2013/06/10/brazil-world-s-top-orange-juice-exporter-conditioned- by-rising-labour-costs

? Questions

Explain why costs have increased for Brazilian orange growers.

Discuss the possible effects of this increase in costs.

c. Which one of the following is incorrect?

- $AVC = AC - AFC$
- $AFC = AC + AVC$
- $AC = AVC + AFC$
- $AFC = AC - AVC$

Long-run cost curves

Long-run average costs

The long-run average cost (LRAC) curve shows the lowest possible cost per unit for any level of output when all factors of production are variable.

In the long run, managers are able to change all of their resources to find the optimal combinations. If, as a result of changing its combination of resources, the firm is able to reduce its unit costs when it produces more, then this means that the firm is experiencing internal economies of scale.

Imagine that a firm has a fixed amount of machinery K1 (see Figure 9.7). The lowest cost per unit for any level of output given this level of machinery is shown by the short-run average cost curve SRAC1. For a particular level of output there will be one optimal

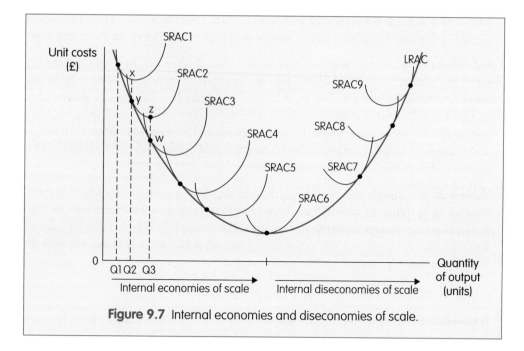

Figure 9.7 Internal economies and diseconomies of scale.

amount of capital —in this case, Q1. With K1, the unit cost at Q1 is the lowest it can possibly be; even in the long run, this is the amount of capital that would be chosen. However, for any other level of output, K1 would not be the optimal amount of capital—it would not be the amount of equipment, for example, that you would want in the long run. If K1 is the most efficient level of capital to produce Q1 then to produce any other output it will be too much or too little. If we choose another output such as Q2, for example, then K1 will no longer be the amount of machinery or equipment the business might want in the long run. In this case K2 may be the optimal amount of capital. If in the short run, the firm is committed to K1 capital the lowest unit costs achievable in this period are shown at 'x'.

In the long run, however, the firm is able to change the level of equipment and can find the optimal level of machinery K2. This means that it can move onto a new short-run average cost curve SRAC2 and that unit costs fall to 'y'. In the long run, it can produce more cheaply. The unit costs have fallen as the firm has increased the scale of production. This means that the firm is benefiting from **internal economies of scale**.

Similar observations can be made if the firm expands further to Q3. In the short run, it is now constrained by the level of equipment K2. The lowest unit costs possible in the short run with this level of equipment are 'z'. In the long run, the amount of capital can be changed, and, as a result, the firm moves onto a new SRAC curve and unit costs fall to 'w'.

Types of internal economy of scale

The reasons for internal economies of scale include 'plant economies'. These specifically refer to lower unit costs as a result of a larger size of factory and include the following.

- **Technical economies** With larger production levels, it may be possible to adopt production techniques that are more efficient on a large scale within the plant, such as mass production. At large volumes, such techniques lead to lower unit costs. These techniques require heavy investment that can be spread over high volumes to reduce the unit cost.

- **Indivisibilities** Some machines are indivisible—that is, they can be used on a certain scale, but cannot be split up or divided—so to produce on a small scale is relatively expensive. Imagine that you buy an excavator; this may be cost-effective if used on a regular basis, but not if used only once a month. Similarly with a small farm you may not be able to afford a tractor and therefore plant and harvest your crops by hand or with basic tools which is an expensive method for production. As your scale increases a tractor becomes more viable and more efficient.

- **Volume** If you double the height, width, and depth of a container (such as a lorry, warehouse or transport vessel), then the volume that it contains will increase more than proportionately compared to the surface area. For example, a box that has six sides of 1 m × 1 m has six sides each with an area of 1 m²—that is, 6 m² overall (see Figure 9.8). The volume is:

$$1\,m \times 1\,m \times 1\,m = 1\,m^3$$

If the measurements are doubled, then the area is now 24 m²—that is, six sides each with an area 4 m² (see Figure 9.8)—and the volume is:

$$2\,m \times 2\,m \times 2\,m = 8\,m^3$$

So a four-times increase in surface area has led to an eight-times increase in volume. This will reduce the average storage or transportation costs per unit. By spending four times as much to build a container, you can carry eight times as much, so the transport

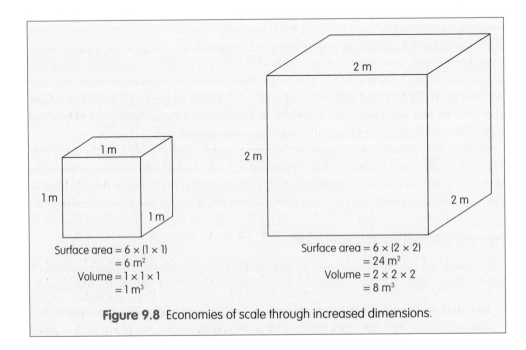

Figure 9.8 Economies of scale through increased dimensions.

Economics in context

Global container shipping companies are expanding rapidly despite overcapacity in the industry because they are aiming for greater economies of scale.

In 2013 total container shipping fleet capacity was expected to grow by 5.9 per cent even though the amount of container capacity being scrapped is a record high.

The order books of the three largest carriers, Maersk Line, Mediterranean Shipping Company and CMA, currently stands at 15.6 per cent of their current fleet.

Maersk Line has recently taken delivery of five mega ships with a capacity of 18,270 twenty foot container units. The average size of container ships on the busy routes between ports in Asia and Northern Europe exceeded 10,000 TEU earlier this year. The average age of scrapped container ships has fallen to around 22 years from around 30 years a few years ago.

? Questions

How might larger container ships benefit from economies of scale?

Why might shipping companies be pursuing economies of scale even if there is overcapacity in the industry?

costs per unit will be lower. Think of how many products are shipped worldwide these days and the appeal of volume economies becomes clear.

- **Specialization and division of labour** As firms produce on a larger scale, the production process can be divided into a series of clearly and narrowly defined jobs. This means that employees do not need extensive training. By undertaking tasks again and again, they may become more productive, making production more efficient. This approach reduces recruitment and training costs.

Other types of economies of scale are known as 'firm' or 'enterprise' economies. These include the following.

- **Purchasing economies** When a firm operates on a larger scale, it will need to purchase more, such as components, materials, and advertising space. Being larger puts the firm in a better bargaining position with suppliers, and should mean that it is possible to negotiate better payment terms and lower prices for these resources, thereby reducing unit costs. One of the reasons for the success of the US retailer Walmart is its sheer size; this enables it to buy products from suppliers at much better prices than many competitors and to pass these cost savings on to consumers. This makes it difficult for smaller firms to survive. Similarly, discount retailers such as Aldi and Lidl focus on a limited range of products, which they then buy in bulk to enable them to buy relatively cheaply.

- **Managerial economies** As an organization expands, it may be able to employ specialist managers to undertake various functions, such as marketing, human resources, and the purchasing of resources. By having specialists dedicated to these tasks, this should lead to better decision making and less waste. Another managerial economy occurs because the rate of increase in the number of managers required by an organization is not as fast as the rate of growth of the organization itself. For example, if there is a manager of a department of 8 people, then it could probably grow to, say, 12 without a new manager being appointed; the costs of the existing manager can therefore be spread over more staff up to a point.

- **Financial economies** A larger firm with more assets, such as land and equipment, may be able to borrow money from a bank at lower rates of interest than a new firm starting up, because it has more collateral. It is a lower risk to the banks because its assets can be seized. This greater level of security should reduce the level of interest payments that need to be made, thereby reducing costs.

The importance of economies of scale can be seen with businesses such as Amazon and Wal-Mart which operate on a huge scale; their economies of scale enable them to drive down the price relative to their rivals and yet still be profitable.

Internal diseconomies of scale

If a firm grows too large, then it may find that the average costs begin to rise. This is because of internal diseconomies of scale. These include the following.

- **Motivation issues** When a business is too large, employees may no longer feel part of the organization as a whole. They may lack a sense of connection to the overall business. Low motivation can lead to mistakes being made, low levels of attendance, and low productivity; all of these tend to increase unit costs. Firms will try to overcome these problems in a variety of ways, such as introducing mission statements to provide a sense of direction for employees. A mission statement sets out the purpose and values of the business.

- **Management problems** Managing a larger business is a more complex process than running a small business. For example, you are likely to be controlling a wide range of products, communicating between many different sites or outlets, and coordinating many different departments. This can be very difficult, and may lead to inefficiency, mistakes being made, and higher unit costs. Firms may try to overcome these problems with budgets, regular meetings, and review sessions called appraisals.

Returns to scale

Increasing, decreasing, and constant returns to scale are described as follows.

- **Increasing returns to scale** occur when an increase in *all* of the factors of production leads to a more-than-proportionate increase in output. For example, if doubling the amount of labour, land, and capital leads to a tripling of output, then this is known as increasing returns to scale. This leads to a fall in the average costs and is another example of internal economies of scale.

- **Decreasing returns to scale** occur when an increase in *all* of the factors of production leads to a less-than-proportionate increase in output. For example, if tripling the amount of labour, land, and capital leads to a doubling of output, then this is known as decreasing returns to scale. This leads to an increase in average costs and is an example of internal diseconomies of scale.

- **Constant returns to scale** occur when an increase in *all* of the factors of production leads to a proportionate increase in output. For example, if doubling the amount of labour, land, and capital leads to a doubling of output, then this is known as constant returns to scale. Average costs stay constant.

Minimum efficient scale

The long-run average cost may have a variety of shapes depending on the industry and the revelant cost conditions.

The minimum efficient scale (MES) is the first level of output at which the long-run average costs of a firm are minimized—that is, at which internal economies of scale are no longer being experienced. This is illustrated in Figure 9.9. The MES may be significant in determining the structure of an industry. If, for example, the MES is relatively high compared to demand in the industry, then this suggests that only a few firms could operate efficiently (at the lowest unit cost) within it—that is, the industry may be more likely to be an oligopoly (see Chapter 13).

The existence of significant economies of scale explains why there are relatively few firms in industries such as banking, oil, cars, gas, water, and tobacco

What do you think?

Following numerous mergers and takeovers, the UK pharmaceutical sector is now dominated by relatively few businesses. To what extent do you think this is desirable?

If, however, the MES occurs at very low levels of output compared to the total demand in the industry, then this suggests that many firms could operate efficiently. This suggests that the market may be much more competitive, with more smaller firms operating in it at the same time and providing more choice for customers. In markets such as hairdressing,

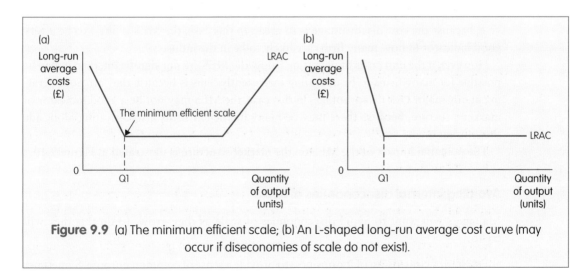

Figure 9.9 (a) The minimum efficient scale; (b) An L-shaped long-run average cost curve (may occur if diseconomies of scale do not exist).

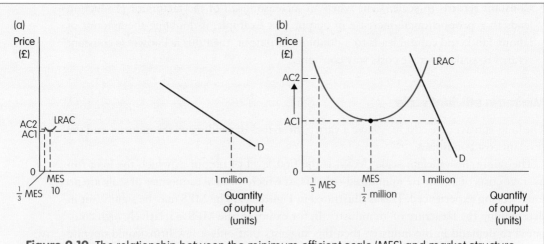

Figure 9.10 The relationship between the minimum efficient scale (MES) and market structure: (a) The MES is low relative to the market demand and the cost disadvantage of operating below the MES is also low. This means that this market is likely to be very competitive, with many firms competing. (b) The MES is high relative to the market demand, and the cost disadvantage of not operating at the MES is also high. This industry is likely to be dominated by a few firms, probably two given that the MES is half of the market demand.

advertising, and plumbing significant economies of scale do not exist which helps to explain why there are many small businesses in these sectors.

However, the precise impact of the MES on the market structure also depends on the cost disadvantage of operating below this level of output—that is, it depends on what happens if a firm enters and produces below the MES (for example, at one-third of the MES). If the consequences of this are that this firm would have much higher unit costs, then it will clearly struggle to compete with the bigger firms; for example, it would be likely to suffer in a price war. In this situation, it is unlikely that inefficient firms will survive, because the cost disadvantage is so great. In this case, the MES is likely to be a very good indicator of how many firms are likely to be in the industry.

However, if the unit costs of operating below the MES are not significant, then it may be possible for many firms to be operating inefficiently. This is because they are not operating at any major cost disadvantage. In this case, the MES may not be a good indicator of market structure, because there may be many inefficient firms also operating alongside the efficient ones.

The potential impact of the MES on the market structure is illustrated in Figure 9.10.

Avoiding internal diseconomies of scale

Managers will want to avoid diseconomies of scale as they grow. To do this they will try to:

- Establish a clear vision of the business to provide a sense of common purpose. Sometimes businesses produce vision statements setting out where they are going and mission

Concentration ratios of top five UK businesses as a percentage of total output in 2004

Market	Concentration ratio (%)
Sugar	99
Confectionery	81
Tobacco products	99
Soft drinks and mineral waters	75

Source: ONS.

? Question

The concentration ratios above measure the market share of the largest five companies in the market. How might these concentration ratios be linked to the concept of the MES?

statements defining what they think the purpose of the business is. The aim is to unite employees and develop a sense of shared purpose

- Review the organizational structure. For example, managers might decentralize enabling local managers to make more decisions and operate as semi-independent units. Employeees in these smaller decision making units may have a stronger sense of identity and this can avoid diseconomies of scale

Over the last 20 years Taiwanese firms have invested billions into China; probably over $120bn. However increasingly they seem to opening factories in Taiwan now rather than China. One major reason is the increasing wage costs in mainland China. These have nearly doubled in a few years. Chinese companies now have to pay money into health care and pensions plans as well. Other investors into China also seem to be looking for alternative production locations such as Vietnam.

Last year, Taiwanese investments in China fell 12 per cent whilst investment in Malaysia, Vietnam, and Thailand increased by 44 per cent, doubled, and quadrupled, respectively.

The world's biggest contract electronics manufacturer, Taiwanese-owned Foxconn, employs about one million people in China, but it is slowing the speed with which it recruits new workers there. It recently announced plans to hire 5,000 technicians to work in two plants in Taiwan.

? Questions

Explain why the costs of producing in China might be increasing.
In what ways does the item above highlight the importance of costs to businesses?

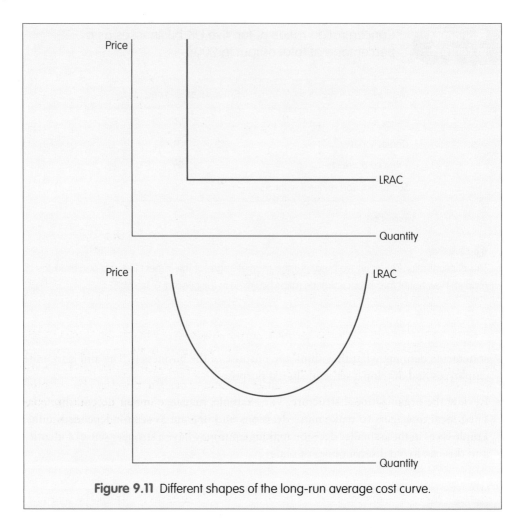

Figure 9.11 Different shapes of the long-run average cost curve.

- Develop control and review mechanisms such as budgets to monitor what is happening within the business.

If these approaches work the long-run average costs curve may be L shaped rather than U shaped (Figure 9.11).

Internal versus external economies of scale

Internal economies of scale refer to cost advantages that a firm experiences when it grows—that is, the average cost per unit falls in the long run as the scale of production expands.

External economies of scale occur when changes outside the firm reduce the unit cost of it operating at all output levels.

This may be because there are government subsidies in the area that reduce the costs. Governments sometimes target areas that they want to develop and so provide incentives to firms wanting to set up or grow there. Also, other firms in the same industry may have

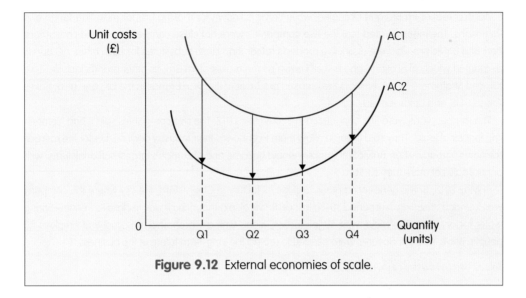

Figure 9.12 External economies of scale.

located there, encouraging the development of a local supplier network that reduces transport costs. The close proximity of several firms in the same industry may lead to a pool of labour with relevant skills that can make recruitment and training cheaper. These cost benefits of location near other firms are called '**economies of agglomeration**'. For example, in the UK, Northampton has traditionally attracted shoe firms; in the USA, Silicon Valley has attracted computer businesses; northern Italy has attracted clothing companies.

External economies of scale are illustrated in Figure 9.12.

The significance of economies of scale

The drive for economies of scale is a very important one as firms seek to reduce their unit costs and increase their efficiency. This enables them to offer lower prices to consumers and/or benefit from higher profit margins. This is also how they can compete against other firms worldwide. With more free trade worldwide, local producers are now facing much greater competition and need to be as efficient as they can. You will often see economies of scale given as the reason behind a takeover or merger as firms join together to benefit from shared resources and reduce the unit costs. Industries such as banking, music, insurance, car production, and pharmaceuticals have seen major restructuring as firms join to gain economies of scale and be more competitive.

Case study

The Competition Commission can investigate mergers if it thinks they will lead to monopoly power and harm the public interest. However, it may allow a merger if it thinks there are no competition issues. It recently cleared a planned merger between drinks makers AG Barr and Britvic. The Commission said the proposed integration of the two companies would not harm competition or cause prices to rise significantly.

AG Barr makes Irn Bru and Orangina, while Britvic is known for making brands including Tango and Robinsons. The inquiry stated that the two companies were not close competitors. It said consumers' Barr and Britvic brands were distinctive products rather than close substitutes for each other. AG Barr is distributed widely in Scotland and is well known as the maker of Irn Bru. Its other brands include Tizer, KA, and Strathmore Water. Britvic is the licensed producer of PepsiCo brands in the UK, and also makes Tango, 7UP, and Lipton Ice Tea.

The merger plans were first announced in September 2012. The two companies said it had 'compelling industrial logic'. They said it would allow them to enhance their industry position. Under the merger, the new company—Barr Britvic Soft Drinks—would become one of Europe's largest soft drink firms, with annual sales of more than £1.5bn.

In May 2013, Britvic announced plans to close its factory in Chelmsford, the city where the company was founded, resulting in around 230 job losses. Britvic also announced it was to close its Pennine Spring water factory in Huddersfield, with 40 job losses, along with a warehouse in Belfast that employs 20 people. Britvic said the closures were needed to protect the long-term future of the business.

Source: http://www.bbc.co.uk/news/business-22852442

? Questions

1 Analyse the potential costs savings as a result of the AG Barr–Britvic merger.

2 Analyse the possible diseconomies of scale that might occur as a result of the deal.

3 Discuss whether the price is likely to fall or increase for consumers following this merger.

Review questions

1 Explain what is meant by the law of diminishing returns.

2 If the marginal cost of producing another item is positive and increasing, what is happening to the total costs?

3 If the marginal costs of producing a unit are below the average costs, explain what will happen to the average costs. Why?

4 Explain the relationship between short-run average costs and long-run average costs.

5 Can you explain three types of internal economy of scale?

6 Can you explain two types of internal diseconomy of scale?

7 Is a competitive market more likely if the minimum efficient scale is high or low relative to the level of demand in the industry? Why?

8 Does expansion inevitably reduce unit costs?

Put it into practice

1 Marginal costs of production for each extra unit is £5, £3, £7, £12, £20, £35. Plot this and then below plot the total costs showing the relationship between the marginal and total costs.

2 Draw a diagram showing Average Fixed Cost, Average costs, and marginal costs. Show the effect of an increase in fixed costs.

Assignment questions

1   Some regions of the world such as Silicon Valley and Hollywood have become hubs for particular industries. Choose a region of your choice that is well known for a particular industry and present a pitch to explain to investors of a business in the same industry why they should locate there.

2   Productivity is a key factor in business affecting costs. Research factors that affect productivity and recommend three actions the UK government should take to help UK firms be more productive.

Key learning points

- There is a difference between the short run and the long run: in the long run, all of the factors of production are variable; in the short run, at least one factor of production is fixed.

- It is important to distinguish between the marginal product (or costs) and the average product (or costs).

- The law of diminishing returns states that, as additional units of the variable factor are added to a fixed factor of production, the marginal product of the variable factor falls.

- In the long run, a firm may benefit from internal economies of scale if it increases the scale of its production, but if its size increases too much, then it may experience diseconomies of scale.

Learn more

Firms will want to identify the minimum cost combination of resources for any level of output. This can be analysed in more detail using what is called 'isoquant analysis'. To learn more about this, visit the Online Resource Centre.

 Visit our Online Resource Centre at http://www.oxfordtextbooks.co.uk/orc/gillespie_econ3e/ for test questions and further information on topics covered in this chapter.

» 10 Revenues, costs, and profits

A great deal of economic analysis is based on the assumption that firms want to maximize their profits. Profits occur when a firm's revenue is greater than its costs. In this chapter, we examine the determinants of a firm's revenue and its costs, and analyse the price and output decisions that will maximize profits. We also examine how low the price level must fall before firms will shut down in the short run and in the long run. An understanding of all of these issues will help us to predict how firms will behave in a particular market situation, and analyse the price and outcome results in perfect competition.

LEARNING OBJECTIVES

By the end of this chapter, you should be able to:

- ✓ explain the difference between revenues and costs;
- ✓ outline the difference between marginal and total revenue;
- ✓ explain the difference between marginal and total costs;
- ✓ explain the difference between normal and abnormal profits;
- ✓ appreciate the difference between profits and profitability;
- ✓ explain the output level at which firms profit-maximize;
- ✓ understand the decision regarding whether or not to produce in the short run and the long run.

▦ Introduction

An important element of economic analysis involves examining the structure of a market and the behaviour of firms within it. Doing this requires an understanding of revenues, costs, and profits. This chapter examines these topics in detail.

Total revenue

The total revenue (TR) of a firm measures the value of its sales. If a car dealership sells ten cars at £30,000 each, then its total revenue is £300,000. The total revenue of a business equals the price of the products multiplied by the number sold:

Total revenue (TR) = Price of a unit (P) × Quantity sold (Q)

The total revenue is also called 'sales', 'sales revenue', and 'turnover'. The total revenue may not be the same as the cash received at that particular moment because a sale may be on credit, but it represents what the sale is actually worth. The cash may be paid later and controlling cash flow effectively is an important business activity.

On a demand curve, the total revenue is illustrated by the area under the curve for any price and quantity combination (see Figure 10.1).

What do you think?

Why do you think that many firms sell their products on credit rather than insisting on cash being paid?

Marginal revenue

The marginal revenue (MR) is the difference in the total revenue when an additional unit is sold:

$$\text{Marginal revenue} = \frac{\text{Change in total revenue}}{\text{Change in the number of units sold}}$$

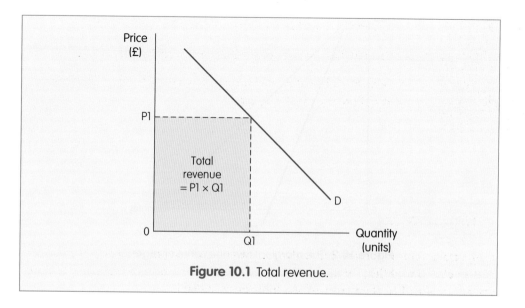

Figure 10.1 Total revenue.

Assuming that the firm faces a downward-sloping demand curve, to sell another unit it may have to reduce the price not only on the last unit, but also on all of the ones before. For example, imagine that one unit is sold for £10, but to sell another, the price of both must be reduced to £9. This means that:

(One unit) Price per unit = £10; Total revenue = £10

(Two units) Price per unit = £9; Total revenue = £9 × 2 = £18

The marginal revenue for selling the second unit is £8. Although the second unit sells for £9, the price of the first one has been reduced by £1, so the gain in revenue is:

£9 − £1 = £8

Thus we have:

Marginal revenue = Price of the last unit − Reductions in price on the units before

Now, imagine that to sell a third unit, the price is reduced to £8. This means that:

(Two units) Price per unit = £9; Total revenue = £18

(Three units) Price per unit = £8; Total revenue = £24

The marginal revenue for selling the third unit is £6.

This is because the price of the last unit is £8, whilst the price of the previous two units has been reduced by £1 each. So the marginal revenue = Price of the last unit − Reductions in price on the units before = £8 − £2 = £6.

As the number of units being sold increases, then, to sell another one, the price must be reduced on an increasing number of previous units. This means that the difference between the marginal revenue and the price becomes ever greater as more units are sold. The marginal revenue curve therefore diverges from the demand curve (Figure 10.2).

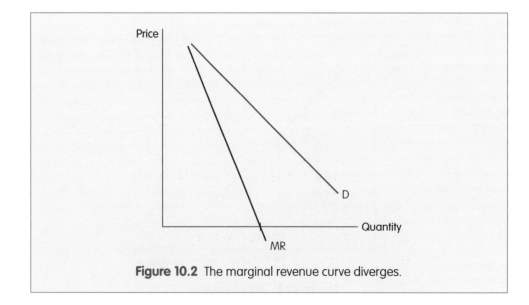

Figure 10.2 The marginal revenue curve diverges.

At some point, the price cut will not change the total revenue. This means that the extra revenue (the marginal revenue) is zero. The effect of higher sales on revenue is exactly cancelled out by the lower price per unit. This occurs when the price elasticity of demand is equal to one (= −1; see Chapter 4). This is at the midpoint of the demand curve. The relationship between the price, the marginal revenue, and the total revenue is highlighted in Tables 10.1–10.3.

It is also possible that the total revenue can fall following a price reduction. This is because of the price cut on so many previous units that is required to sell one more. If the total revenue falls, then this means that the marginal revenue is negative. It also means that the price elasticity of demand is price inelastic (see Chapter 4).

The relationship between demand, the marginal revenue, and the total revenue is shown in Figure 10.3.

Put into practice

a. Ten units are sold at £15 each. To sell an 11th unit, the price must be reduced to £12.

- Calculate the old and new total revenue.
- Calculate the marginal revenue of the 11th unit.

b. To sell a 12th unit, the price must be lowered to £10 for all units.

- Calculate the marginal revenue of the 12th unit.

Table 10.1   The relationship between the marginal revenue and the total revenue

Quantity (units)	Price (£)	Total revenue = Price × Quantity sold (£)	Marginal revenue = Extra revenue from selling an additional unit (£)
1	10	10	–
2	9	18	8
3	8	24	6
4	7	28	4
5	6	30	2
6	5	30	0
7	4	28	−2
8	3	24	−4

Table 10.2   The effect of marginal revenue on total revenue

Marginal revenue	Effect on total revenue
Positive, but falling	Increasing at a slower rate
Zero	Unchanged
Negative	Falling

Table 10.3   The effect of a price cut on total revenue

Price elasticity of demand	Effect of a price cut
Price elastic	Increases revenue
Unit elastic	Revenue does not change
Price inelastic	Revenue falls

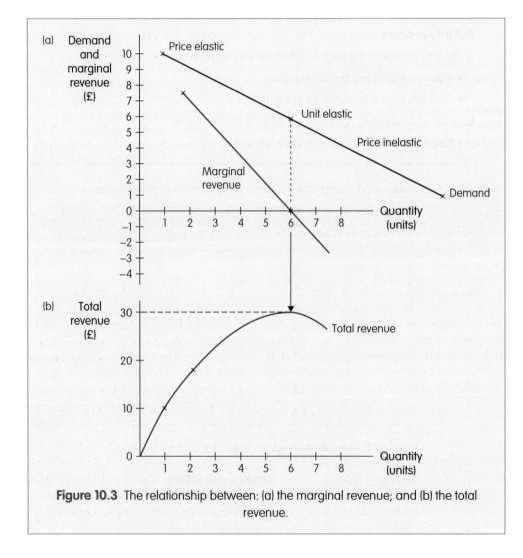

Figure 10.3 The relationship between: (a) the marginal revenue; and (b) the total revenue.

Marginal revenue and total revenue

The marginal revenue shows the change in the total revenue. If the marginal revenue is positive following a cut in price and the sale of an extra unit, then this means the total revenue increases: demand is price elastic. If the marginal revenue is zero when another unit is sold, then the total revenue does not change: demand is unit-price elastic. If the marginal revenue is negative when another unit is sold, then the total revenue falls; this means that demand is price inelastic.

Put into practice

The total revenue from selling 20 units is £300. Imagine that the marginal revenue from selling the 21st unit is either £30, £100, £0, or –£50.
What is the total revenue from 21 units for each of these four situations?

Total costs

The total costs (TC) of a firm represent the value of the resources that have been used up in the production and sale of the products. These include the costs of labour, land, materials, and machinery, and are written as follows:

　Total costs = Fixed costs + Variable costs

The total costs will increase as more output is produced because there will be more variable costs—for example, more materials will be used up.

Marginal costs and total costs

The marginal cost is the extra cost of producing a unit. For example, if the cost of making four units is £1,000 and the cost of making five units is £1,200, then the marginal cost of the fifth unit is £200. The relationship between the fixed costs, the variable costs, the total costs, and the marginal costs is shown in Figure 10.4.

The relationship between the different types of cost is also highlighted in Table 10.4.

If the marginal cost is positive, then this means that the total costs must have increased. For example, a marginal cost of £300 means that the total costs have gone up by £300 when another unit is made. If the marginal cost is £400, then the total costs will rise by this amount. If the marginal cost is £0, then this means that the total costs do not change when an extra unit is produced. The marginal cost therefore shows the rate of change of the total costs. The relationship between the marginal costs and the total costs is shown in Figure 10.5. The effect of marginal cost on total cost is shown in Table 10.5.

Put into practice

Complete the following table.

Output (units)	Fixed costs (£)	Variable costs (£)	Total costs = Fixed costs + Variable costs (£)	Marginal costs = Change in total costs / Change in output (£)	Average cost (£) = Total costs / Output
0	?	?	10,000	–	–
1	?	1,000	?	?	?
2	?	?	13,000	?	?
3	?	4,000	?	?	?
4	?	?	?	3,000	?
5	?	?	?	?	4,500
6	?	22,250	?	?	?

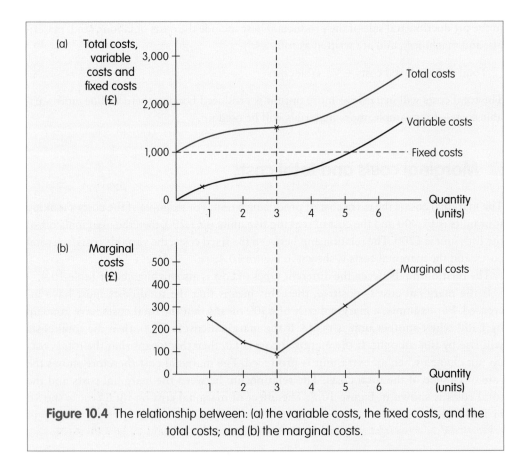

Figure 10.4 The relationship between: (a) the variable costs, the fixed costs, and the total costs; and (b) the marginal costs.

Table 10.4 The relationship between the total costs, the marginal costs, and the average costs

Output (units)	Fixed costs (£)	Variable costs (£)	Total costs = Fixed costs + Variable costs (£)	Marginal cost = Change in total costs / Change in output (£)	Average cost (£) = Total costs / Output
0	1,000	0	1,000	–	–
1	1,000	250	1,250	250	1,250
2	1,000	400	1,400	150	700
3	1,000	500	1,500	100	500
4	1,000	800	1,800	300	450
5	1,000	1,200	2,200	400	440
6	1,000	1,700	2,700	500	450

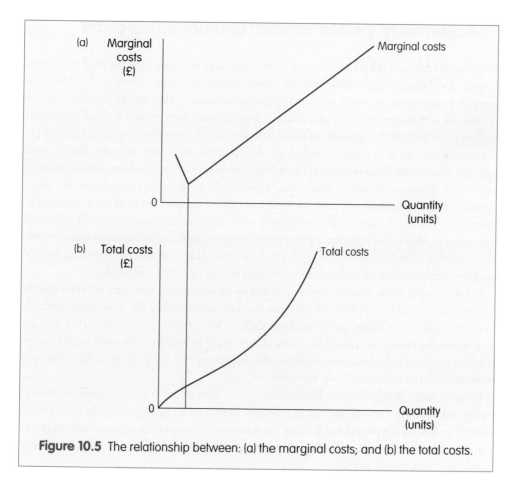

Figure 10.5 The relationship between: (a) the marginal costs; and (b) the total costs.

Table 10.5 The effect of marginal cost on total cost

Marginal cost	Effect on total cost
Positive, but falling	Increasing at a slower rate
Positive, but rising	Increasing at a faster rate

Profit and loss

The profit of a firm measures the difference between the value of what has been sold and the value of what has been used up to provide these goods—that is:

Profit = Total revenue − Total costs

If the total costs are greater than the total revenue, then a loss is made.

The difference between accounting profit and economists' profits: Normal and abnormal profit

When an accountant thinks of costs, he or she measures the costs of items used up to produce and sell the products; these include labour, materials, components, land, and equipment. An economist, however, will add opportunity costs to this list. This means that an economist will estimate how much a firm's inputs could have earned if used in another industry and include this as a cost of being in business in a particular market. As a result, in economics, when a firm is only covering its costs, it is earning a sum of money that it could earn elsewhere with these resources. Therefore there is no incentive to move these resources into other industries. In accounting terms, a profit will be declared to investors, but to an economist, this simply means that the firm has earned the amount of money required to keep resources where they are; if less than this were earned, then resources would be shifted into other sectors of the economy. When revenue equals costs (including opportunity cost), an economist calls this normal profit; if all of the firms in an industry were earning normal profit, then there is no incentive to move resources into or out of this industry.

If a firm earns more than the costs included by an economist, then this is called abnormal profit, or supernormal profit. This means that the resources are generating rewards that are higher than those needed to keep them in this particular industry. This will act as a signal for resources to shift into this sector to try to benefit from such high returns. Abnormal profit will attract other firms into this sector and act as a signal for resources to be reallocated and move from their existing use,

If the revenue does not cover economists' costs, then a loss is made; resources should be moved out of this sector and into a more profitable one. The resources are not earning enough to justify keeping them in their present use. In accounting terms, the firm could still be declaring a profit, but to an economist, if this does not justify the resources being in this industry, then it is a loss.

Standardized metal containers were developed by Malcom McLean who ran an American trucking business in 1956. Until then products had been simply put into a ship however they would fit. This took time and was very inefficient. The introduction of containerization made loading and unloading quicker and cheaper. The cost of moving cargo fell from $6.62 a tonne to $0.16 per tonne. It also meant far less stock was held waiting in ports and far less was stolen reducing insurance costs. The use of containers also meant more cargo could be moved. Until then labour could only move 1.7 tonne per hour; within 5 years workers were moving 30 tonnes an hour. Containerization has been an important factor in the growth of world trade; in fact a recent study claimed that containerization was a more important factor than all the trade agreements of the last 50 years in encouraging world trade.

? Questions

Analyse the way in which containerization reduced costs.

Analyse how contanerisation should affect the profits of companies

Profits versus profitability

The profit made by a firm is measured as an absolute amount, such as £X million. However, this does not show an analyst what funds were invested to generate such a return. A £3 million profit earned in a year may be a high sum for a small business, but is not so impressive for a very large organization such as Tesco plc. We may therefore want to measure profit in relation to the amount of long-term funds invested in the business. This is known as the return on capital employed (ROCE).

The ROCE is a very common measure of a firm's financial performance and can be written as follows:

$$\text{Return on capital employed} = \frac{\text{Profit}}{\text{Capital employed}} \times 100\%$$

Managers and investors will usually seek to generate the highest possible ROCE. This will mean that they are using their resources to generate a relatively high level of profit.

What do you think?

Do you think profit is a good measure of business success these days?

Profit-maximization: The marginal condition

To maximize their profits, firms must sell the number of units for which there is the largest positive difference between the total revenue and the total costs. To identify this level of sales, economists often use the marginal condition, also known as the

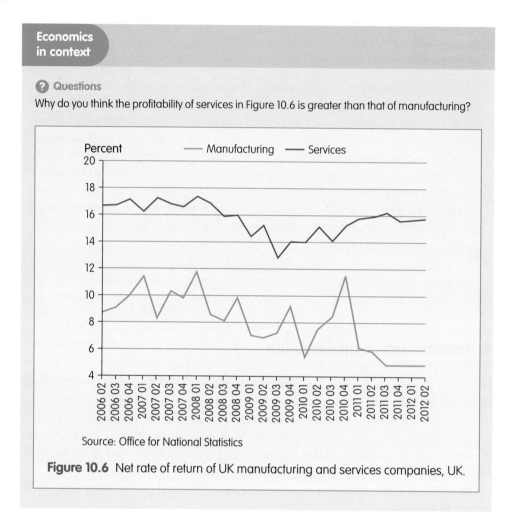

Economics in context

? Questions

Why do you think the profitability of services in Figure 10.6 is greater than that of manufacturing?

Source: Office for National Statistics

Figure 10.6 Net rate of return of UK manufacturing and services companies, UK.

profit-maximizing condition. This means that they look for the highest level of sales at which the marginal revenue from selling an extra unit equals the marginal cost of producing and selling another unit.

If the marginal revenue from selling a product is greater than the marginal cost of producing it, then the extra unit will make a profit and total profits will go up. The extra revenue is greater than the extra costs, and so profits increase by producing and selling it. The firm should therefore produce all of the units for which the marginal revenue is greater than the marginal costs because, by doing so, profits will rise.

The profit-maximizing firm should stop producing when the marginal revenue equals the marginal costs. At this point, no extra profit can be made, which means that profits must be maximized. They cannot be increased further. A firm will therefore profit-maximize if the marginal revenue equals the marginal costs.

If the marginal revenue is less than the marginal costs, then a loss will be made on the extra unit. These units should not be produced.

So the profit-maximizing output occurs when:

Marginal revenue (MR) = Marginal costs (MC)

The profit-maximizing output in terms of the total revenue and the total costs, and the marginal revenue and the marginal costs, is shown in Figure 10.7 and summarized in Table 10.6.

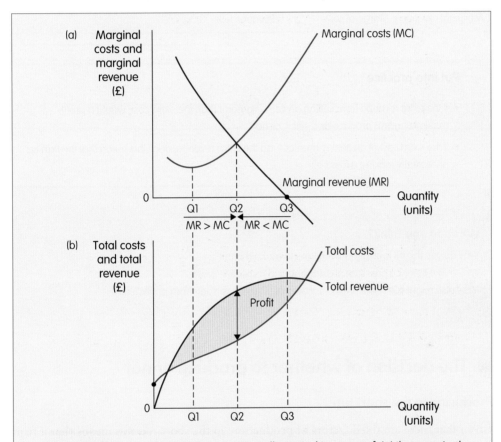

Figure 10.7 The profit-maximizing output, illustrated in terms of: (a) the marginal revenue and the marginal costs; and (b) the total revenue and the total costs. The marginal costs fall up to Q1 and therefore the total costs rise at a decreasing rate. After Q1, the marginal costs increase, so the total costs increase at an increasing rate. At Q3, the marginal revenue is zero, so the total revenue does not increase. After Q3, the marginal revenue is negative, so the total revenue falls. Up to Q2, the marginal revenue is greater than the marginal costs, so by selling more the profits will increase. At Q2, the marginal revenue equals the marginal costs, so no extra profit can be generated; this means that profit is maximized. At output levels beyond Q2, the marginal revenue is less than the marginal costs, so the firm makes a loss on these extra units; profit would increase by cutting output back to Q2. The profit-maximizing output is Q2; this is also shown by the largest positive difference between the total revenue and the total costs.

Table 10.6   The profit-maximizing output decision

MR and MC	Output decision
Marginal revenue > Marginal cost	Produce more because there is extra profit to be made
Marginal revenue = Marginal cost	Profit-maximizing because there is no extra profit to be made
Marginal revenue < Marginal cost	Produce less

Put into practice

- If the extra revenue from selling an item is greater than the extra cost, would a profit-maximizing firm produce and sell it, or not?

- If the extra cost of an item is greater than the extra revenue, does this mean that the firm is necessarily making a loss?

What do you think?

Why do you think it is important for firms to make a profit?
Why might there be pressure on managers to maximize profits?
How else might you measure the success of a business apart from profits?

■ The decision of whether to produce or not

Producing in the short run

Given that there are fixed factors of production, in the short run this means that a firm must pay fixed costs even if output is zero. For example, if you have rented a building then for the period of the contract you will need to pay this rent whether or not you actually produce. This means that a firm will lose an amount equal to the fixed costs even if it does not sell anything. The decision of whether it is financially viable to produce will therefore depend on the variable costs (the costs incurred by producing, such as materials and components), because the fixed costs must be paid anyway. The fixed costs are 'sunk costs' and should not affect a decision about whether to continue to produce in the short run.

If the revenue earned from making and selling the units can at least cover the variable costs, then this means that it is financially worth producing them. Anything earned over and above the variable costs is called a 'contribution'; it contributes towards the fixed costs. For example, if the revenue is £200 and the variable costs are £180, then there is a £20 contribution towards the fixed costs. Figure 10.8 shows a contribution

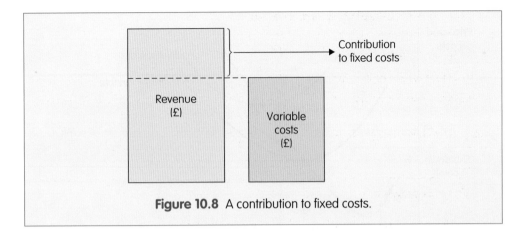

Figure 10.8 A contribution to fixed costs.

being made to fixed costs. This does not mean that the firm necessarily makes a profit (this depends on the relative size of the contribution to the fixed costs), but the loss will be less than it would be by not producing. (Remember that fixed costs must be paid anyway.)

For example, imagine that the fixed costs are £100. If the firm does not produce, then it makes a loss of £100. If it does produce and gains a £20 contribution towards the fixed costs, its losses are only £80. This means that it is better to produce than not to produce even if a loss can be made. The firm should therefore continue in production even though it makes a loss, because the revenue at least covers the variable costs. When the revenue only equals the variable costs, the loss will be the same whether producing or not producing. This is known as the **shutdown point**. If the revenue is less than the variable costs, then the firm should not produce. For example, if the revenue is £150, the variable costs are £180, and the fixed costs are £100, then, by producing, the firm will make a loss of £130. Not only are fixed costs being paid, but there is also another £30 of variable costs that cannot be covered by the revenue. In this situation, the firm would reduce its loss by not producing.

So, in the short term, a firm should only produce provided that its revenue at least covers its variable costs.

This analysis can also be undertaken on a 'per unit' level. If the price per unit more than covers the variable costs per unit, then the sale generates a contribution per unit that can be put towards the fixed costs and so production should continue. If the price per unit cannot cover the variable cost per unit, then not only do fixed costs have to be paid, but also variable costs cannot be covered either, so the firm should shut down.

Thus, in the short run, we have the following two possibilities.

- **A firm should produce if the price is greater than or equal to the average variable costs** This means that a contribution is being made on each unit towards the fixed costs and so production should continue. Even if a loss is made, then it is less than the loss that would be made if the firm were to shut down and still had to pay the fixed costs.

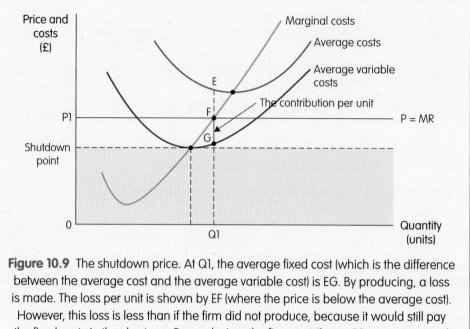

Figure 10.9 The shutdown price. At Q1, the average fixed cost (which is the difference between the average cost and the average variable cost) is EG. By producing, a loss is made. The loss per unit is shown by EF (where the price is below the average cost). However, this loss is less than if the firm did not produce, because it would still pay the fixed costs in the short run. By producing, the firm contributes FG per unit toward the fixed costs. The firm will not produce if the price is less than the average variable cost. We have assumed all units are sold at the same price, so the extra revenue (MR) equals the price. Firms produce where MR = MC.

- **A firm should not produce if the price is less than the average variable costs** This means that the firm cannot pay its variable costs and has fixed costs to pay as well. The firm should shut down. The shutdown point is illustrated in Figure 10.9.

The long run

In the long run, a firm will not continue producing at a loss. It is not constrained by resources and so is not committed to fixed costs. The firm will produce only if it breaks even—that is, if all of its costs can be covered—and at least a normal profit is made. This means that the total revenue must at least cover total costs.

Looking at this on a 'per unit' level, this means that the price per unit needs to be at least equal to the average cost per unit. If the price were less than the average cost, then this means that a loss would be made on each unit and so the firm would not produce.

The break-even point is illustrated in Figure 10.10. Again we have assumed that every unit is sold at the same price, so the extra revenue (MR) equals the price. Firms produce where MR = MC to profit-maximize.

Table 10.7 defines some of the key terms used in this section.

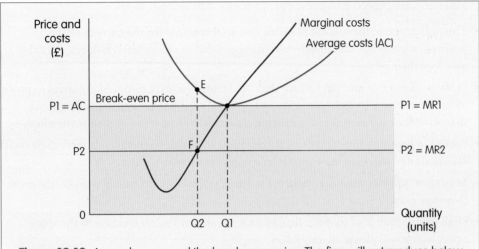

Figure 10.10 A supply curve and the break-even price. The firm will not produce below the price that equals the minimum of the average costs curve, because then a loss would be made. For example, at P2, the loss per unit is EF (the price is less than the average costs). In the long run, the firm will not produce if the price is below P1 as a loss is made.

Table 10.7 Summary table of key terms

Term	Description
Total cost	= Fixed cost + Variable cost
Marginal cost	Extra cost of an additional unit
	$= \dfrac{\text{Change in total cost}}{\text{Change in output}}$
Total revenue	Revenue earned from sales
	= Price × Quantity sold
Marginal revenue	Extra revenue from selling an extra unit
	$= \dfrac{\text{Change in total revenue}}{\text{Change in the number of units sold}}$
Abnormal profit	Total revenue > Total cost
Normal profit	Total revenue = total costs

Business objectives

The classical assumption in economics is that managers will aim to maximize profits. This means that firms will produce an output where the marginal revenue equals the marginal costs. At this level of output, no further profit can be made, and so there is the largest possible positive difference between the total revenue and the total costs.

Managers are expected to pursue profit for the following reasons.

- This will generate the highest possible financial rewards for the owners of the business, such as the shareholders. If managers fail to satisfy shareholders, then they may lose their jobs.

- Profit is a source of internal finance that can be used for expansion. Alternatives to profit include borrowing (which incurs interest charges) or, if it is a company, selling more shares (which can mean that the existing shareholders lose some of their ownership).

- Profit is a common benchmark of success, and so enables managers to meet their own ego needs and measure their own effectiveness relative to others.

- Managers' salaries may be connected to profits: the more profits they make, the more they may earn.

- High profits may lead to more demand for the shares and an increase in the share price, which will please shareholders.

However, the profit-maximizing assumption has some limitations—not least the difficulties that managers have knowing exactly what the revenues and costs would be at different levels of output. Without perfect knowledge, it is unlikely that managers could identify the actual profit-maximizing price and output, even if they were trying to do so.

Furthermore, a business is actually made up of many different interest groups, all of whom may be pursuing slightly different objectives: for example, the marketing department, the production department, the human resources department, the finance department, and the administrative staff (see Figure 10.11). The finance department may well be focused on profit, but the marketing team may be more concerned with the level of sales,

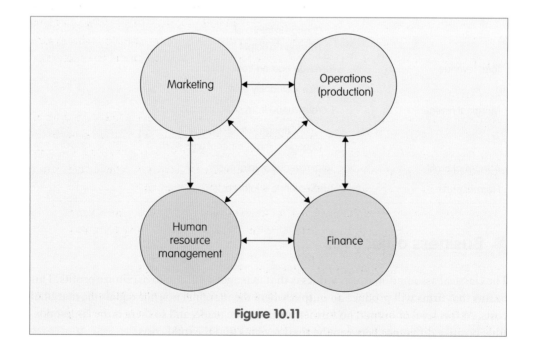

Figure 10.11

even if boosting sales requires higher expenditure and less profit. The human resources department may be reluctant to make people redundant, even if this increases efficiency and profit.

All of these different interest groups will be bargaining and negotiating over every decision made within a business; it is therefore likely that the actual pricing and output decisions that are made are a compromise between them. A business may well 'satisfice' its different stakeholders rather than profit-maximize. This idea was put forward by Simon (1947), and stems from Cyert and March (1963); it suggests that managers are satisfying different needs and trying to balance their demands.

There may also be a difference between the objectives of the managers and the owners. For example, the owners may want high profits so that they can receive higher dividends, whereas the managers may want the following.

- Some managers may want to control larger departments or want faster growth. They may be more interested in the scale of their operations and the power that they have than they are in achieving the most profitable outputs.

- Some managers may have environmental or social concerns that lead to more expensive production methods or not producing in the least-cost location.

- Some managers and employees may be interested in job security and the quality of their working life. They may wish to be paid more, even if profits are reduced.

■ Other objectives

As we have seen, there are many groups within an organization, all with their own agenda. Although shareholders are the owners of a company and are likely to want the business to maximize profits, managers may not necessarily pursue the objectives that the shareholders want. There are a number of theories that economists have developed about possible objectives other than profit-maximization. The following are two possible alternative theories.

Sales revenue maximization

According to Baumol (1959), managers may want to maximize the revenue earned from sales even if profits are not maximized (although a minimum level of profit must be made to satisfy the owners). For example, a firm may invest heavily in advertising to boost revenues, and may end up with lower profits than it could have achieved otherwise because of the advertising costs. Managers may want high revenues because:

- it means that the business has a higher profile, which gives the managers a sense of achievement (and may be good for their future careers if they move on to other firms); and

- their salaries may be linked to the firm's income rather than its profit.

To maximize revenue, a firm should produce at a level of output where the marginal revenue is zero. At this output, no extra revenue can be earned. This occurs at the output Q3 in Figure 10.12. Notice how the focus is on revenues, not costs.

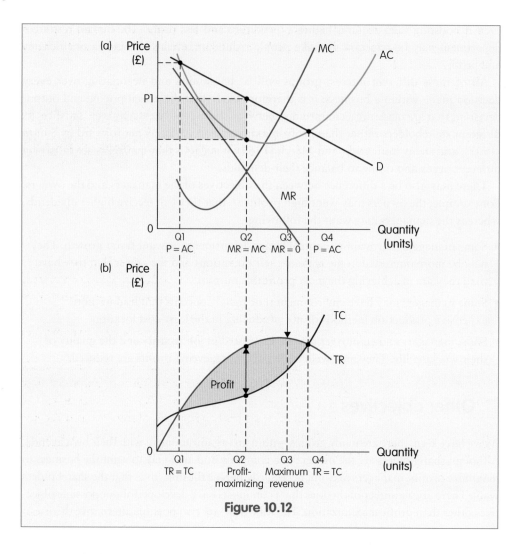

Figure 10.12

Growth maximization

According to Marris (1964), managers may seek to make the business as large as possible in terms of its output, provided that they do not make a loss and that they meet some minimum profit requirement to satisfy investors. The reason why growth may be important is to make the business more difficult to take over. By increasing the size of the organization, managers are possibly protecting their own jobs by making the firm more expensive to buy and therefore less likely to be bought. Growth also makes the business more visible because it is selling a lot of products and therefore the organization has a higher profile. Once again, this may be good for the managers' own careers. The Royal Bank of Scotland in the 1990s and 2000s undertook a rapid expansion plan led by (the then) Sir Fred Goodwin that raised his profile and that of the company; at the time both regarded as very successful.

The highest possible level of output at which a firm can produce without making a loss is where the average revenue (price) equals the average cost. This is shown at the output Q4 in Figure 10.12.

What do you think?

What other objectives might managers have apart from maximizing profits, growth and sales?

■ How to grow

Growth is a common objective of businesses. This can be achieved by selling more of your own products—this is called organic growth—or by joining with or buying another business which is called external growth. External growth leads to much faster growth as the size of a business can increase dramatically with one deal.

Growth can be achieved through a number of different strategies which were outlined by the business writer Ansoff (Table 10.8):

When deciding on a strategy a business will have to consider the risks and rewards. Diversifiying can be very risky for example, in that you do not have experience of these products and markets, Tesco recently had to withdraw from America when it sold its Fresh and Easy company – it was experimenting with a new type of store in a new country and could not make sufficient returns. On the other hand if it is successful it does spread the risk – problems in one market may be offset by gains in another.

Table 10.8 The Ansoff matrix

	Existing products	New products
Existing markets	MARKET PENETRATION Sell more in existing markets to existing customers e.g. through greater advertising	NEW PRODUCT DEVELOPMENT Develop new products for existing customer e.g. extend the product range or widern your offering to customers. Consider how Tesco has moved from food to clothes to electrical products
New markets	MARKET DEVELOPMENT Offer existing products to new market segments e,g different age groups or different countries. Jaguar is trying to target younger buyers nowadays and Tesco operates in many countries other than the UK now	DIVERSIFICATION Offering new products to new customers

Why grow?

Businesses may want to grow:

A. to benefit from internal economies of scale. This may enable them to lower prices and be more competitive—for example, in international markets

B. to be safer from takeover. Some managers believe that if the business becomes larger it will be more expensive to buy and therefore it may be less vulnerable to takeover bids which may protect their jobs.

C. to achieve monopoly power which will give them power over consumers. The producers will be able to fix prices—they wll be price makers not price takers. This means there is producer sovereignty not consumer sovereignty.

However, growth can bring with it the problems of diseconomies of scale such as communication, motivation and control problems as there are more employees and processes to manage and more decisions to make (see Chapter 9).

Mergers and takeovers

Mergers occur when two or more firms join together and create a new combined business. This has happened a great deal in global industries such as cars and pharmaceuticals. GlaxoSmithKline, for example, is a major pharmaceutical company brought about as smaller companies joined together to share resources and expertise. British Airways joined together with Iberia Airlines to create IAG in 2011 and became the world's third largest scheduled airline. In theory mergers can bring economies of scale and the benefits of sharing skills and resources which is known as synergy (this means that $2 + 2 = 5$ i.e. combined the businesses are stronger than they are individually). A merger may enable one business to gain access quickly to markets it had little presence in whilst providing the other with research and development facilities. Takeover can provide similar benefits but occurs when one business buys control of another. In a merger, business A and business B join to create a new business C; in a takeover B becomes part of A.

Although in any given deal the managers of the merging businesses or the acquiring business will talk greatly about the benefits that will occur, the evidence suggests that in reality most mergers and takeovers are not successful. Rather than adding value they tend to reduce it; combined A and B become worth less than they did separately. This is often due to the problems in managing larger businesses and to culture clash. When News International bought MySpace, for example, the two styles of management clashed badly and the different teams could not work together effectively. They had different priorities, objectives, and values, and cooperation and compromise did not occur. This clash of cultures has been seen in many deals such as AOL Time Warner, Daimler Chrysler, and HP and Autonomy. Getting people from different businesses to work well together seems to be a real problem.

Takeovers have an additional problem in that the bid may not be welcomed by the victim company's shareholders. When Kraft bid for Cadbury in 2010 there was fierce opposition from Cadbury shareholders who feared what would happen to jobs, the brand, and Cadbury's values if the American business took it over. This means that information about the victim business may not be readily forthcoming, increasing the risk and danger of problems if the deal does go ahead. Furthermore, the buyer may need to pay a premium to make the other company's shareholders sell. This means it has a cost burden from the minute the deal succeeds and needs to make profit just to recover these takeover costs.

External growth may be popular on a personal level with managers—undertaking a deal is exciting and if you win it looks good on your CV; however it is not always profitable.

What do you think?

Do you think a culture clash is inevitable if two businesses join together? What do you think could be done to reduce the risk of such a clash?

Case study

Sir Richard Branson who founded the Virgin Group and Kering director Jochen Zeitz have recently launched a non-profit group to encourage global businesses to focus on more than short-term profit.

This group, known as the B Team, said it would champion a new way of doing business that prioritizes people and planet alongside profit. Branson said that business needed to be a 'force for good'. The team consists of 14 global business leaders including Arianna Huffington and Ratan Tata. According to Branson business has previously been too concerned with profits and has not got involved enough in society or with the wider issues of the world.

The B Team aims to work together with politicians, the social sector, and other organizations.

Sir Richard said the group would be looking at specific issues, such as quarterly reporting on profits to investors and subsidies for fossil fuels, and big global problems such as unemployment and inequality.

Jochen Zeitz was previously Chief Executive of Puma. As well as turning Puma into one of the biggest sportswear firms in the world, Mr Zeitz has argued for the use of environmental profit and loss (EPnL) accounting, where companies put a cost on their impact on the environment.

Other companies are also looking at putting a value on their environmental impact with a view to incorporating these external costs into their annual accounts. They argue that natural resources, such as clean water should not be regarded as free and businesses will have to pay to protect them, for example through pollution taxes. Companies that are taking action to reduce their environmental impact now, argue they will benefit in the long term.

Questions

1 Explain what is meant by profit.

2 Analyse the reasons why businesses might want to make a profit.

3 Do you think business should focus on people and the planet as well as profits?

Review questions

1 Explain the profit-maximizing condition.
2 Explain what is meant by normal profit.
3 What is shutdown point?
4 What is the break-even point in the long run?
5 Explain what is meant by fixed costs.
6 If the marginal cost is positive but falling, what is happening to the total costs?
7 If marginal revenue is zero explain what is happening to total revenue.
8 If marginal revenue is positive but falling explain what is happening to total revenue.

Put into practice

1 If marginal revenue is constant at £10 a unit, draw the total revenue curve.
2 The marginal revenue from selling each extra unit is £10, £8, £6, £3, £0, −£2. Show this on a diagram and below plot the total revenue associated with this, showing the links between the two.

Assignment questions

1 The banks have been blamed for causing the recent financial crisis. Some have argued that banks should be taxed heavily as a result. Research the case for and against taxing banks' profits heavily. Recommend whether taxes on banks should be increased and justify your answer.
2 Many businesses now argue that Corporate Social Responsibility (CSR) is an important aspect of their behaviour. This view seeks to act in a socially responsible way over and beyond the legal requirements—for example in the way they treat suppliers, the community, and employees. Research the arguments for and against CSR and assess the view that CSR can lead to longer term profits.

Key learning points

• Profit is the difference between total revenue and total cost.
• There is a difference between an economist's view of profit and an accountant's view of profit.
• Profit is maximized at an output for which the marginal revenue equals the marginal cost.
• Normal profit occurs when the total revenue equals the total cost.

- Abnormal profit occurs when the total revenue is greater than the total cost.

- A loss occurs if revenue is less than total costs.

- In the short run, a firm will produce only if the price is equal to, or greater than, the average variable cost.

- In the long run, a firm will produce only if the price is equal to, or greater than, the average cost.

References

Baumol, W. (1959) *Business Behaviour, Value, and Growth*, Macmillan, New York

Cyert, C.M. and March, J.G. (1963) *A Behavioral Theory of the Firm*, Prentice Hall, New Jersey

Marris, R. (1964) *The Economic Theory of 'Managerial' Capitalism*, Macmillan, London

Simon, H.A. (1947) *Administrative Behaviour*, Macmillan, New York

Learn more

The relationship between short-run and long-run costs can be analysed in more detail using isoquant analysis. To learn more about this, visit the Online Resource Centre.

 Visit our Online Resource Centre at http://www.oxfordtextbooks.co.uk/orc/gillespie_ econ3e/ for test questions and further information on topics covered in this chapter.

Perfect competition

An important part of economic analysis is to consider how firms behave in different types of market and the impact of this on consumers. Perfect competition is one form of market structure. In this chapter, we examine the features of a perfectly competitive market, and the consequences of this form of market structure in terms of price, output, and efficiency. In the following chapters, we then examine other market structures and compare them with perfect competition.

LEARNING OBJECTIVES

By the end of this chapter, you should be able to:

✓ understand the key features of a perfectly competitive market;

✓ analyse the price and output decisions in the short run and the long run in a perfectly competitive market;

✓ explain why the supply curve is the marginal cost curve in perfectly competitive markets.

▪ Why study market structures?

Not all markets are the same. Some are dominated by a few firms; some have many competitors in them. In this chapter and the following three, we examine different types of market to consider how the structure affects firms and consumers within them. This is an important aspect of economic analysis because it helps us to decide whether one form of market structure is better than another; this has implications for government policy. Microsoft has a high market share of the PC market at the moment; Intel dominates the microprocessor market; and Wrigley's is a big producer in the market for chewing gum: is this desirable or should governments intervene to limit the firms' power and encourage more competition? By comparison, the market for fruit and vegetables is usually divided between hundreds of thousands of farmers: should the government intervene to encourage the growth of a few big farmers or not? Is it better to have one business responsible for delivering the mail or many? Is it dangerous, inefficient, or desirable to have a few firms dominating the sale of food, petrol, banking services, and insurance in the UK, or should the government leave them to it?

In the following chapters, we consider these issues, as well as think about why markets differ in the first place. There are many providers of kennels, there are thousands and thousands of pubs in the UK (although the number is declining), and there are lots of hairdressers, plumbers, and taxi firms. There are far fewer energy companies, airlines, private medical care firms, and electrical goods retailers. In the following chapters, we examine why this might be and the effects of these differences.

We begin by analysing a market structure known as perfect competition.

What do you think?

Think of three different markets such as banking, hairdressing and energy supply—how do they differ in terms of the number of firms competing in them? What impact do you think this has on consumers? Why do you think these differences exist?

Introduction to perfect competition

A perfectly competitive market is one in which:

- there are large numbers of buyers and sellers;
- products are homogeneous (that is, exactly the same);
- there is perfect knowledge (so buyers know what all firms are charging and firms know what profits are being made in the industry); and
- there is freedom of entry into, and exit from, the market, so that firms can easily move into and out of the market.

In reality, all of these conditions are unlikely to be met; the closest are likely to be commodity markets, such as wheat, which have millions of small farmers operating in a global market with a world price for their products. Even though it may be extreme, by analysing the model of perfect competition, it is possible to decide whether society should attempt to move towards this market situation or not.

What do you think?

What impact do you think the Internet is having in terms of the information that customers have?

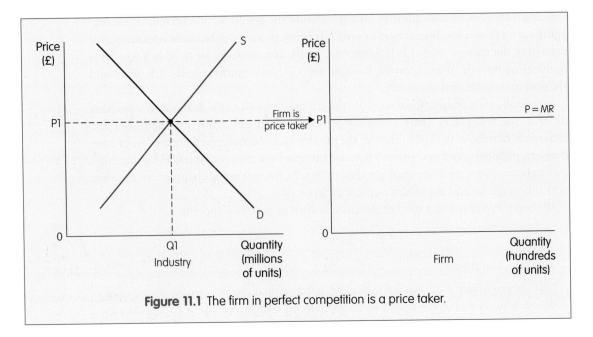

Figure 11.1 The firm in perfect competition is a price taker.

Perfectly competitive firms as price takers

In a perfectly competitive market, there are many firms. One firm's output decisions cannot influence the overall market supply to any noticeable extent. If one firm changes its output level, then this has such a small effect on the industry supply that the market price does not alter.

Each firm is therefore a 'price taker'—that is, it is so small that its actions cannot influence the market price. A firm can sell as much as it wants without bringing down the market price. This means that every unit can be sold at the market price. For example, every unit can be sold at £10, so the extra revenue generated from a sale is the same as its price. This means that:

Marginal revenue (MR) = Price

This is illustrated in Figure 11.1.

If a firm tried to increase the price above the market level it would lose all its demand as customers would switch to alternative providers. The demand curve in perfect competition is therefore perfectly elastic.

Short-run equilibrium in perfect competition

- A profit-maximizing firm in perfect competition will produce at the highest output where the marginal revenue equals the marginal cost. This is the marginal condition.
- The amount of profit being made will depend on the average revenue (price) compared to the average costs. This is the average condition.

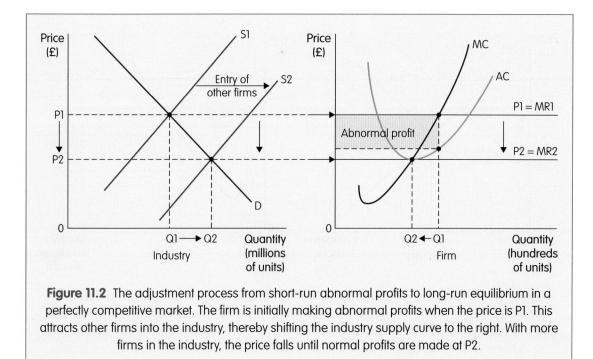

Figure 11.2 The adjustment process from short-run abnormal profits to long-run equilibrium in a perfectly competitive market. The firm is initially making abnormal profits when the price is P1. This attracts other firms into the industry, thereby shifting the industry supply curve to the right. With more firms in the industry, the price falls until normal profits are made at P2.

In the short run, firms in perfect competition are able to make abnormal profits (when the price is greater than the average cost) or losses (when the price is less than the average cost). However, this situation will not continue in the long run.

If firms are making abnormal profits, then this acts as a signal for other firms to enter the market to benefit from this. The entry of more firms will lead to more being supplied and this will shift the industry supply curve to the right; this will reduce the market price. (Although one firm cannot shift the industry supply on its own, the entry of many firms will shift the curve to the right.) This process will continue until only normal profits are being made (the price equals the average cost), as shown in Figure 11.2. When normal profits are being made, there is no incentive for more firms to enter or leave the industry and the market and business is in long-run equilibrium.

If firms are making losses, then this means that businesses will leave the industry. This shifts the industry supply curve to the left and increases the market price. This will continue until only normal profits are being made, as shown in Figure 11.3. At this point, there is no further incentive for firms to enter or leave the industry.

What do you think?

Why are the assumptions of perfect information, freedom of entry and exit, and a homogeneous product important to reach the long-run equilibrium of normal profits in perfect competition?

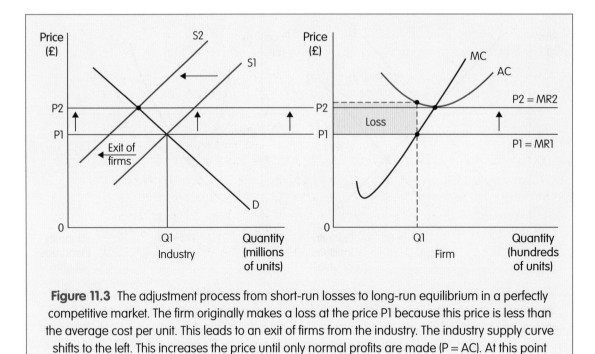

Figure 11.3 The adjustment process from short-run losses to long-run equilibrium in a perfectly competitive market. The firm originally makes a loss at the price P1 because this price is less than the average cost per unit. This leads to an exit of firms from the industry. The industry supply curve shifts to the left. This increases the price until only normal profits are made (P = AC). At this point there is no further incentive to leave the industry.

Put into practice

Which of the following defines:

a. normal profits?

b. break-even point?

c. shutdown point?

d. abnormal profit?

- Price equals average fixed cost.
- Price equals average variable cost.
- Price equals average total cost.
- Price equals average revenue.
- Price is greater than average cost.
- Price is greater than average variable cost.

The most commonly traded commodities are crude oil, natural gas, base metals such as iron and zinc, precious metals such as gold and silver, sugar, coffee, wheat, corn, soybeans, cotton, and livestock

Recently nearly all commodity prices fell. Much of this price fall was due to disappointing growth figures from China. The rapid growth of the Chinese economy has helped to fuel demand for commodities in recent years but slower growth recently has had the opposite effect,

However, there are also supply-side factors that may bring prices down. Since the early 2000s commodity prices have typically been rising at around 20 per cent a year. The effect of such high prices has been to encourage more production—more mining and drilling, for example. Commodiy traders talk of a super cycle when prices go up, this leads to more supply and then they come down again. Supply can take a long time to come onstream but when it does it may bring prices down for some time.

? Question

Using supply and demand diagrams illustrate why the changes in commodity prices above might have happened.

◾ Long-run equilibrium in perfect competition

The long-run equilibrium in perfect competition is shown in Figure 11.4. In the long run, in perfect competition, firms can only make normal profits. Assuming that they are profit-maximizers, they will produce when the marginal revenue equals the marginal cost (MR = MC) (see Chapter 10).

Given that each firm is a price taker, the marginal revenue will equal the price (P = MR). This means that firms will produce when the price, the marginal revenue, and the marginal cost are all equal. As a result, firms will be allocatively efficient. Allocative efficiency occurs when the extra benefit to society (as shown by the price that consumers are willing to pay) equals the extra costs—that is, the price equals the marginal cost. In the long-run equilibrium of perfect competition, firms are producing all of the units for which the price (which represents the extra benefit or utility to the consumer) is greater than the extra cost of producing it, up to the point at which the extra benefit equals the extra cost. At this point, the community surplus is maximized (see Chapter 7).

In the long run, firms in perfect competition are also productively efficient. **Productive efficiency** occurs when firms are producing at the minimum of the average cost curve; they have the lowest unit cost possible and therefore they are not wasting resources.

To summarize, in the long run, in perfect competition:

- firms earn normal profits;
- the industry is allocatively efficient (the price that represents the marginal benefit of a unit to a consumer equals the marginal cost); and

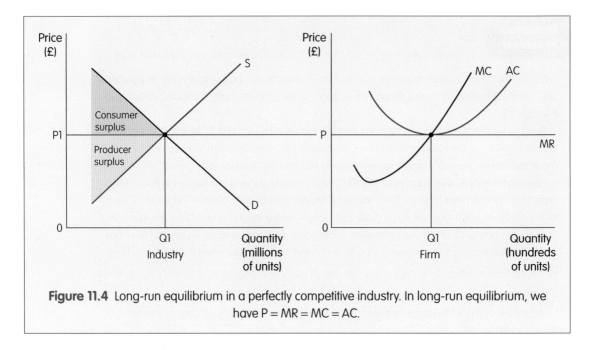

Figure 11.4 Long-run equilibrium in a perfectly competitive industry. In long-run equilibrium, we have P = MR = MC = AC.

- the industry is productively efficient (firms are producing at the minimum of the average cost curve).

Put into practice

Imagine that a perfectly competitive market is in long-run equilibrium. Show the impact of a fall in demand in the short run and the long run on both the industry and a firm.

■ Deriving the supply curve in perfect competition

The supply curve of a firm

A supply curve shows the quantity that a firm is willing and able to produce at each and every price, all other things being unchanged. Assuming that a firm wants to profit-maximize, it will produce when the marginal revenue equals the marginal cost (MR = MC). In perfect competition, because firms are price takers and every unit is sold at the same price, then the price equals the marginal revenue. As a result, firms will produce when the price equals the marginal cost (because the price equals the marginal revenue and the marginal revenue equals the marginal cost). Therefore the marginal cost curve shows the quantity that will be supplied at any given price. This means that the marginal cost curve is the supply curve for a business, as shown in Figure 11.5.

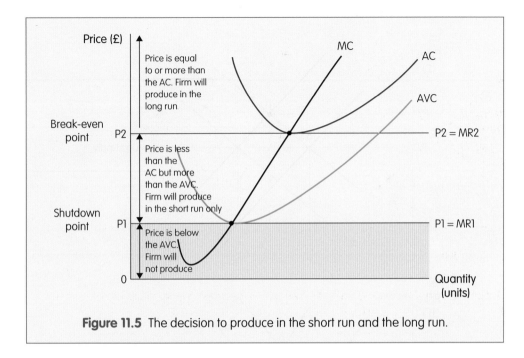

Figure 11.5 The decision to produce in the short run and the long run.

In the short run, a firm will supply provided that the price is at least equal to the average variable cost (because this means that the revenue is at least making a contribution to the fixed costs), so the supply curve is the marginal cost curve above the minimum average variable cost.

In the long run, a firm will supply only if the price covers the average costs (otherwise a loss would be made), so the supply curve is the marginal cost curve above the average cost curve.

The short-run and long-run industry supply curve

The short-run supply curve in perfect competition is derived from the marginal cost curve. In the short run, an increase in demand leads to a movement along the supply curve from equilibrium at 'a' to 'b' (Figure 11.6). This increase in price will lead to higher profits and lead to entry of other firms into the industry. The short-run supply shifts to the right. If the price falls back to its existing level, this would mean that firms are making normal profits at the same level of average costs as before (see Figure 11.6a). If, however, entry into the industry bids up the price of inputs, such as employee wages, this means that normal profits would be earned only with a higher price and the long-run supply curve would be upward-sloping (see Figure 11.6b).

If the expansion of the industry leads to lower average costs—perhaps because of the build-up of specialist support services—a normal profit will be made at a lower price in the long run. This means that the long-run supply curve is downward-sloping (see Figure 11.6c).

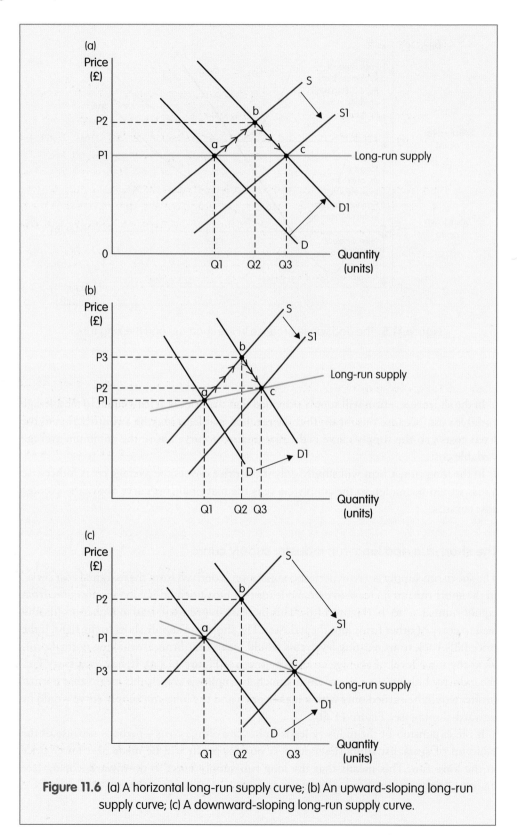

Figure 11.6 (a) A horizontal long-run supply curve; (b) An upward-sloping long-run supply curve; (c) A downward-sloping long-run supply curve.

Put into practice

a. In perfect competition, which of the following statements is true?

- Each firm in the market has some, but not complete, control over the price of its product.
- Firms are completely free to enter or leave the market.
- There are many producers producing similar, but not identical, products.
- Firms in the market advertise in order to shift the demand curve for their product.

b. The demand curve for the perfectly competitive firm is determined by:

- the firm's marginal cost of producing an extra unit of output.
- the price that is established by the firm.
- the market demand for, and supply of, the good.
- the average total cost of producing a particular level of output.

▪ Summary

Perfect competition may or may not exist in reality as a market structure, but it provides a benchmark against which to judge other forms of market. It highlights the benefits of competition, and this may well influence government policy regarding helping start-up firms and limiting the power of firms to dominate an industry.

Case study

Global cocoa production

Global cocoa production is over 3 million tonnes per year. The production of cocoa is undertaken by thousands of small producers in countries such as Ghana, the Ivory Coast, and Cameroon. Although there are a few big farmers, almost 90 per cent of production is by small producers with farms of less than 5 hectares.

These producers produce similar crops and have no power to control prices on the international markets. The world price is determined by the industry supply and the level of demand from the huge multinationals, such as Cadbury and Mars. The small firms are often said to be exploited by the larger confectionery companies. Fairtrade organizations attempt to rectify this by guaranteeing a reasonable price for their crops. The underlying principle of Fairtrade is that the product must have been traded in such a way that:

- the primary producer gets a fair deal;
- the primary producer receives a proportion of the price in advance to enable it to pay for its inputs; and
- the Fairtrade company enters into a long-term relationship with the supplier.

The Fairtrade Labelling Organizations International standard for cocoa outlines the calculation of Fairtrade cocoa prices. The prices are calculated on the basis of world market prices plus Fairtrade premiums.

? Questions

1 What factors do you think determine the supply of cocoa?

2 What factors do you think determine the demand for cocoa?

3 Do you think that the price of cocoa is relatively stable or unstable? Why?

4 In what ways is the market for cocoa like perfect competition? In what ways is it different?

5 Do you think that the Fairtrade scheme is desirable? Why is it needed?

@ Web

For more information on Fairtrade, visit http://www.fairtrade.org.uk

Review questions

1 How many firms are there in a perfectly competitive market?

2 Explain why firms in perfect competition are price takers.

3 Can firms in perfect competition make abnormal profits?

4 Explain why the absence of barriers to entry is an important assumption in perfect competition?

5 Why is the fact that firms offer homogeneous products an important assumption in perfect competition?

6 Explain what happens in the long run if a firm in a perfectly competitive market is making a loss.

7 In the long run is a firm in perfect competition allocatively efficient?

8 Expain how the supply curve in perfect competition is derived.

Put into practice

1 Imagine a business is making a loss in the short run in a perfectly competitive market. Using diagrams for the industry and the firm show how the industry adjusts to long-run equilibrium.

2 Imagine a perfectly competitive market is in long-run equilibrium. Show the effect of a fall in fixed costs using industry and firm diagrams.

Key learning points

- A firm in perfect competition is a price taker.
- Firms profit-maximize where Price (P) = Marginal revenue (MR) = Marginal cost (MC).
- In the short run, in perfect competition, firms can make abnormal profits or losses.
- In the long run, due to the entry and exit of firms, only normal profits are made.
- In the long run, in perfect competition, firms are allocatively and productively efficient.

 Visit our Online Resource Centre at http://www.oxfordtextbooks.co.uk/orc/gillespie_econ3e/ for test questions and further information on topics covered in this chapter.

»12 Monopoly

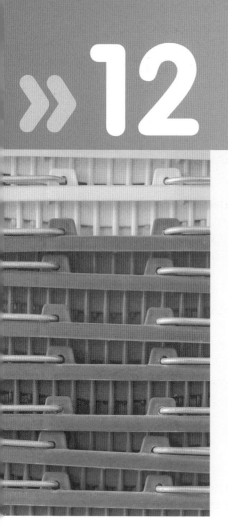

Monopoly is a very different form of market structure from perfect competition. This chapter outlines the nature of a monopoly, and examines the price, output, and efficiency outcomes in this type of market. Governments are often concerned about the effects of monopoly power; in this chapter, we outline the arguments for and against monopoly power.

LEARNING OBJECTIVES

By the end of this chapter, you should be able to:

✓ explain the key features of a monopoly;

✓ explain the price and output decisions in a monopoly;

✓ discuss the efficiency of a monopoly;

✓ explain the theory of contestable markets.

▓ Introduction to monopoly

A monopoly occurs when a firm dominates a market. This means that the firm determines the price in the market rather than accepts the industry price. It is a 'price maker' rather than a 'price taker'.

A 'pure' monopoly occurs when one firm has a market share of 100 per cent: for example, in nationalized industries, the government might allow only one state-owned firm to provide a particular service, such as health care or electricity. More generally, a monopoly exists when a firm exerts a major influence over a market. Under UK competition law, a monopoly occurs when a firm has a market share of 25 per cent or more—that is, its sales are over 25 per cent of the total sales in a market. In a monopoly the consumer lacks choice and the producer has the power. The monopolist has 'producer sovereignty' because it dominates the market and is a price maker.

Note that when assessing whether a business is in a monopoly position or not you may want to consider what is an appropriate definition of the market involved. A retailer with 100 supermarkets spread across Europe will not dominate any one region so is not in a monopoly position in the European market as a whole. However, a retailer with 100 supermarkets in a small part of the UK may dominate that particular local market. The only nightclub in your town is not a monopoly of the UK market but may have a dominant position if the only competitor is 30 miles away. It may also be important to consider the alternatives available—a theme park may be the only one of its kind in the area but it may be competing against leisure centres, cinema complexes, and wildlife parks; if it is operating in the market for family days out then even if it is the only one in the area it may not be appropriate to regard it as a monopoly in terms of its behaviour because it may be competing vigorously against these rivals.

Demand and marginal revenue for a monopolist

A monopolist faces a downward-sloping demand curve. To sell more units, it must lower the price. If products are sold at a single price this will involve lowering the price on the additional unit and on all of the units before. As a result, the marginal revenue diverges from the demand curve (see Chapter 10).

Price and output decisions in a monopoly

A monopolist is assumed to be a profit-maximizer. This means that it produces at the highest output when the marginal revenue equals the marginal cost (see Chapter 10). In Figure 12.1, this occurs at the price P2 and the quantity Q2.

At this price and quantity combination, the firm will make an abnormal profit—that is, the price is greater than the average cost at that output. This means that the firm is

Economics in context

In 1623 Avedis Zildjian founded a cymbal-manufacturing company in Istanbul. This business is now run by the 14th generation of the family and has around 65 per cent of the world's cymbal sales with revenues of more than $50m last year. The company's cymbals have been used by many famous drummers such as Ringo Starr. One reason why Zildjian has been able to maintain a high market share is the secret mixture of copper, tin, and silver that gives the Zildjian cymbals their world famous sound.

? Question

One reason for Zildjian's high market share is the sound its cymbals produce. What other factors might enable the business to dominate the market?

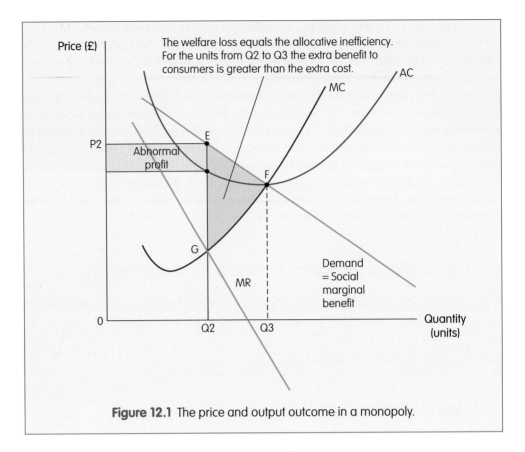

Figure 12.1 The price and output outcome in a monopoly.

earning more with its resources in this industry than it could earn with them elsewhere. Its revenue is more than covering the costs including the opportunity costs of the resources involved. This abnormal profit will attract other firms into this industry from other sectors. They will want to shift resources into this industry to share the abnormal profits. However, unlike firms in a perfectly competitive industry, a monopolist can continue to make abnormal profits in the long run because it can prevent other firms from entering the market to erode its profits. This is because barriers to entry exist.

Put into practice

Which of the following are true and which are false?

a. A monopolist faces a perfectly elastic demand curve

b. A profit-maximizing monopolist produces where marginal revenue equals marginal cost

c. A monopolist can make abnormal profits in the short run only

d. A monopolist is a single seller of a product

Unlike the firms in the long-run equilibrium position in a perfectly competitive market, a monopoly is allocatively and productively inefficient.

It is allocatively inefficient because the price paid by consumers for the last unit produced is greater than the marginal cost of providing it. Customers are paying more for the last unit of the product than the extra cost of producing it. Society would like more units to be produced and sold.

For the units from Q2 to Q3, the extra benefit of these units to society (as shown by the price that the consumer is willing to pay) exceeds the extra cost of providing them. Therefore, if these units were to be produced, then society's welfare would increase. The monopoly price and quantity outcome has led to a welfare loss. The triangle EFG in Figure 12.1 is a welfare loss area (also called a deadweight social burden triangle) that exists because the firm is allocatively inefficient. The monopolist does not produce these units because to sell them requires a reduction in price on all previous units, which means that marginal revenue would be below the marginal costs and profits would fall. What is in the interests of society is not in this case in the interests of the business.

A monopolist is also likely to be productively inefficient because the firm may not be producing at the minimum average cost. To benefit from the lowest possible average costs, the firm would have to sell more and produce at Q3. This would involve reducing the price because the demand curve is downward-sloping and the firm's profits would fall (because the marginal revenue is less than the marginal cost on these additional Q3 – Q2 units). Although the monopolist is maximizing its profits, it is not usually producing at the most efficient output level. The unit costs are minimized at Q3, but because the price would have to be lowered so much, the overall profits would fall.

A monopolist may also suffer from:

- X inefficiency. With a lack of competition there may be no pressure to keep costs down and so they may drift upwards.

- According to Leibenstein (1966), a monopoly situation leads to 'X inefficiency'; with less competitive pressure on firms due to barriers to entry, costs will drift upwards, and this wastes resources. This means that costs in a monopoly may be higher than in a competitive market and so monopolies are bound to be inefficient.

- Dynamic inefficiency. If a monopolist feels protected by barriers to entry it may lack any incentive to develop new technology. There will be a lack of innovation into new processes and new products. Over time therefore costs will not fall in the way they might in a more competitive situation meaning prices are higher and consumers may not have the same amount of choice of new products. This is known as 'dynamic inefficiency'.

Put into practice

Imagine that demand for a monopolist's products increases. Show the effect of this on the price, quantity, and profits of the firm, using a diagram.

Which of the following statements are true and which are false?

a. In a monopoly the marginal revenue is below and diverges from the demand curve

b. In a monopoly the average revenue is upward sloping

c. In a monopoly one firm dominates the market

d. In a monopoly there is freedom of entry and exit in the long run

---

Monopoly compared to perfect competition

Perfect competition and monopoly are two market structures at the opposite ends of the competitive spectrum. However, a comparison of the two structures may influence our view of which structure is more desirable, and therefore our view of how they should be treated by the government and the types of competition policy that the government should adopt.

In both types of market, we assume that the firms are profit-maximizers. Apart from this, there are many differences, as shown in Table 12.1.

Table 12.1 A comparison of a firm operating in a perfectly competitive industry and a monopoly

	Perfect competition	Monopoly
Price taker	Yes	No
Barriers to entry	No	Yes
Long-run abnormal profits	No	Yes
Differentiated product	No	Yes
Allocatively efficient	Yes	No
Productively efficient	Yes	No

Economics in context

The UK Competition Commission recently ruled that Eurotunnel would not be able to continue to offer ferry services from Dover. The channel tunnel operator began operating a ferry route between Dover and Calais in 2012. The Commission claimed that the firm's large market share was likely to lead to price rises for passengers and for freight customers. Eurotunnel already runs the channel rail tunnel, including the Le Shuttle Dover to Calais car rail service and has over 40 per cent market share. It will appeal the decision.

The company acquired three ships from Sea France, which went into liquidation and leased them to LD Lines. The Competition Commission argued that Eurotunnel bought the ferries in order to prevent its rival, DFDS, buying them and then driving down the price of cross-channel travel. The only other independent operator on the route is P&O.

❓ Questions

Do you think Eurotunnel should be made to stop offering its cross Channel service?

Should we prevent monopolies?

There is much debate regarding monopolies. Some commentators argue that they need to be regulated and controlled for the following reasons.

- They can abuse their market power to restrict their output and to force up prices for the customer relative to a perfectly competitive situation. Given that there are limited substitutes available, the customer may be forced to pay more than he or she would in a competitive market. This reduces the community surplus in a market and creates allocative inefficiency.

- Producers do not produce at the minimum point of their long run average costs curve so are productively inefficient.

- The lack of competition in a market may reduce the pressure on firms to innovate and be efficient. This may lead to a cutback in research and development spending, and less new product and process development. This is known as dynamic inefficiency.

If monopolies do behave in the ways described above, then a government may want to prevent them from occurring. If they already exist, it may want to regulate them.

Economics in context

Since the late 1990s the European Commission has been trying to prevent Microsoft abusing its market power. In 2009, the European Commission investigated Microsoft's practice of bundling its own browser, Internet Explorer, with new copies of Windows. It found that this was an abuse of market power and created an unfair barrier to entry of other browsers, such as Firefox. An agreement was reached that Microsoft would include a 'choice screen' in which users in the EU would be given a full list of alternative browsers and asked which they would like to install. This screen was supposed to be available until 2014. Between March 2010, when the choice screen was first provided and November of the same year, 84 million browsers were downloaded through it.

In May 2011, however, the screen was no longer present on new Windows 7 purchases. The screen reappeared some 13 months later, after some 15m copies of Windows software had been sold.

In 2013 Microsoft was fined €561m for failing to stick to the earlier judgment to allow Windows users to choose their web browser.

❓ Questions

Do you think the European Commission was right to fine Microsoft?

Micosoft has a large market share. How might it defend this legally from competition?

In the UK, the Competition Commission has the powers to:

- prevent takeovers or mergers that would lead to a monopoly position if it can show that this would act against the public interest; and

- investigate any firm with more than 25 per cent market share and force it to sell off parts of its business or reduce its prices.

What do you think?

If a government were to tax monopoly profits, it would not affect the profit-maximizing price and output; these would still be the best financial outcomes for the monopolist although the monopolist would obviously keep less of the profits. Do you think that it would be a good idea therefore to tax monopoly profits heavily?

However, in the UK, monopolies are not automatically assumed to be undesirable. The following are some arguments in favour of monopolies.

- As a monopoly firm dominates the industry, it may be bigger than any individual business in a more competitive industry. This means that it is more likely to benefit from internal economies of scale. Its unit costs may be lower than they would be for firms in a competitive market. This could lead to lower prices and higher output than in a competitive market situation. The ability to benefit from economies of scale may be essential to compete in global markets such as cars and pharmaceuticals; a monopoly may enable the cost savings required to compete internationally.

- The ability to make monopoly profits provides dominant firms with the funds that they need to invest in more research and development. As a result, they can afford to take risks, and to invest in more long-term research and development projects than firms in a competitive industry. This may lead to greater efficiency and more choice for customers.

- A firm may have achieved its monopoly position because it is so innovative and/or so efficient. In this case, splitting it up would work against the public interest. Most governments allow firms to protect inventions with patents. These are intended to reward innovation, and to encourage other firms to develop new products and new ways of doing things. The patent system highlights that governments think that monopoly power can be justified in certain circumstances.

- Any abnormal profits that are made will either be invested in the business or paid out to shareholders in the form of dividends. These shareholders will often be individuals or financial institutions, such as insurance companies and pension funds. This means that the abnormal profits of monopolies may be redistributing money from customers to investors. The money is not disappearing from society altogether; rather, it is simply moving from one group to another.

- The fact that monopolies can make high levels of profits is an incentive for other firms to be innovative and to establish a monopoly position. This is known as the Schumpeter effect (named after Joseph Schumpeter). Monopoly profits may therefore encourage innovation as other firms try to gain control of a market for themselves. Schumpeter (1942) described this as 'the perennial gale of creative destruction'. Barriers to entry may exist at some point, but new firms will find ways of overcoming these to gain from the abnormal profits—that is, by creating new markets to replace the old ones. Monopoly profits therefore act as a beacon to encourage the development of new products and new ways of doing things, and this stimulates economic growth.

- A monopoly may establish a common system that makes it easier for users and other businesses. Microsoft might argue, for example, that by establishing Office as a dominant software system it has made it easier for users to share documents. By establishing Internet Explorer as a major browser this helps developers know how to develop their programmes so that they are compatible. A range of different technical systems may make buyers uncertain what to buy, may hinder the communication between users and may make it difficult for businesses to design their products.

- In some cases, the existence of a monopoly may rectify another market failure. For example, in a freely competitive market, firms may create negative externalities, such as pollution, and overproduce relative to the socially optimal position (see Chapter 7). A monopoly, by comparison, may cut back on output, which in this case might move the economy nearer to the socially desirable level of output. Given that a First-Best World (in which there are no market failures and no imperfections occur) does not exist and therefore we are operating in the Second-Best World (in which failures and imperfections do exist), a monopoly may actually be desirable in some circumstances to offset some other failures.

- Monopolies might prevent wasteful duplication. For example, if there are several gas, telecommunications, electricity, or railway companies, then they might simply be investing in unnecessary infrastructure that duplicates the resources of other firms.

What do you think?

Should monopolies be allowed? What do you think is the best way of regulating them? Intel is the world's largest producer of computer processors. Do you think that governments should allow Intel to be this big?

It is clear then that arguments exist for and against monopolies and these are summarized in Table 12.2.

◼ Contestable markets

Traditional economic theory examines monopolies in terms of the existing market share of the dominant firm in an industry—that is, it focuses on whether a firm already has a market share of over 25 per cent. However, the theory of **contestable markets** considers

Table 12.2 Summary table of monopoly

Possible advantages	Possible disadvantages
Abnormal profits may encourage innovation by others ('creative destruction')	Higher price and lower quality than a perfectly competitive industry
May lead to economies of scale	Allocatively inefficient
May remedy another market failure e.g. lower output may remedy a negative externality	Productively inefficient
May avoid wasteful duplication of resources	Dynamically inefficient
	X inefficient

the likelihood that other firms will enter the market in the future. This recognizes that a firm that has, say, 25 per cent of a market with no threat of others entering is in a very different position from a firm that has 25 per cent of a market with a high threat of others joining. In the former situation, the established firm is indeed in a strong position and there is the possibility of sustained long-term abnormal profits. In the latter situation, short-term abnormal profits are likely to attract more firms into the industry and this will compete away the abnormal profits over time. To avoid this happening, the established firm may deliberately avoid profit-maximizing in the first place.

In a perfectly contestable market, the costs of entry and exit are zero, so any abnormal profits could quickly be eradicated by others coming in and competing them away. The threat of this happening will mean that the existing firm will:

• keep prices down so that only normal profits are made; and

• have to be as efficient as possible so that entrants do not come in and undercut it.

The theory of contestable markets highlights the dynamic nature of monopolies and the importance of barriers to entry in terms of influencing monopoly behaviour.

▨ Barriers to entry

The monopoly power of a firm or group of firms can be sustained only if there are barriers to entry. Otherwise any abnormal profits that they earn will be competed away by new firms entering the market. Firms that operate within a market with barriers to entry are protected from the effects of competition, and the impact of this on price and output. In some cases, the barriers may exist because the government has granted exclusive rights to provide a service. In other instances, firms will set out themselves to devise ways of preventing others from coming in. In its competition policy, a government must decide whether barriers to entry do exist in a market and whether customers suffer as a result. Even if barriers to entry do exist, they can be removed or reduced over time: for example, with the signing of treaties opening up new markets, or with new technology making it easier or cheaper for others to enter a market.

Types of barrier to entry include the following.

- **Legislation** A firm's monopoly power may be protected by law. For example, it may gain a patent; this prevents other firms from making, using, or selling its invention for a given period.

It generally takes three to five years to obtain a patent. Patent protection gives firms 20 years' protection. IBM spends over $5 billion per year on research and development to develop its products and new technology. It earns over $1.2 billion by licensing its intellectual property—for example, selling the rights to use its technology.

Alternatively, barriers to entry exist if a government controls an industry itself and passes legislation to prevent other firms from competing in it.

- **The learning experience** Existing firms have the benefit of experience when operating in an industry. They know what to do, how to do it, how not to do it, and how to put things right. They have the contacts, and an understanding of what works and what does not work. This means that they will benefit from this experience, and tasks can be completed more effectively and efficiently. This makes it more difficult for new entrants to compete. Remember how difficult it was when you first learned to drive; now you can change gears without even thinking. A learner driver will find it difficult to compete with your skill. The same is true when a firm considers entering a new market; it must be aware of the expertise of those already in it and how this can give them a competitive advantage. The management consultancy Boston Consulting Group argued that the learning (or experience curve) was so significant that it should drive business strategy. By growing and dominating a market, a business can achieve significant cost advantages over competitors because of its greater experience in operating in that environment.

- **Technology** Existing firms may have a technological advantage that new entrants cannot easily imitate. This may be a way of producing or organizing things that others do not know how to imitate.

- **Internal economies of scale** If there are high levels of economies of scale in an industry, then those firms that are producing on a larger scale will have much lower unit costs than new entrants, which are likely to be producing on a smaller scale. It will therefore be difficult to enter a market that has a high minimum efficient scale (MES) relative to demand and there is a significant cost disadvantage in operating below the MES (see Chapter 9). In this situation, if a firm does enter the market, it is most likely to focus on a niche; this enables it to charge a higher price for a specialist product.

- **Entry costs** The initial costs of starting up in an industry can be high: for example, to buy equipment or to promote the product nationally. This can make entry prohibitive for small firms. For example, imagine the costs involved in establishing a national network (or even an international network) for a mobile phone operator.

- **Fear of retaliation** If existing firms have reacted in a hostile way to new entrants in the past (for example, by starting a price war), then this sends out a signal to others that may deter them from entering.

Registering a patent

The following is information from the Patent Office.
To be patentable your invention must be the following.

- **Be new** The invention must never have been made public in any way, anywhere in the world, before the date on which an application for a patent is filed.

- **Involve an inventive step** An invention involves an inventive step if, when compared with what is already known, it would not be obvious to someone with a good knowledge and experience of the subject.

- **Be capable of industrial application** An invention must be capable of being made or used in some kind of industry. This means that the invention must take the practical form of an apparatus or device, a product such as some new material or substance, or an industrial process or method of operation.

Patents are one form of protection for intellectual property. Others include trade marks for logos and designs, and copyright for books and music. Well-known legal cases relating to intellectual property include the following.

- *James Dyson v Hoover* This was an action by Dyson against Hoover for allegedly infringing a Dyson patent for bagless vacuum cleaners.

- *Elvis Presley Enterprises Inc v Sid Shaw Elvisly Yours* This case concerns the rights of well-known celebrities to exploit their names as trade marks.

- *Michael Baigent, Richard Leigh v The Random House Group Ltd (The Da Vinci Code case)* This case was concerned with the alleged infringement by Dan Brown in his book *The Da Vinci Code* of the claimants' copyright in their work *Holy Blood, Holy Grail*.

- *R Griggs Group Ltd and Others v Ross Evans, Raben Footwear Pty Ltd (The Doc Martens case)* This case relates to the question of beneficial ownership or ownership in equity of all aspect of the copyright in a logo.

Source: UK Patent Office

? Question

What do you think are the benefits of protecting intellectual property rights through systems such as patents?

- **Brand loyalty and product differentiation** Existing firms in an industry will try to make their products different, in the eyes of the consumer, from competitors' products. If they can do this successfully, then they can generate brand loyalty; this makes it difficult for potential entrants because it will be more difficult for them to win new customers.

Economics in context

Apple recently lost a ruling in the USA over a patent dispute with its rival Samsung. The International Trade Commission (ITC) stated that Apple infringed a Samsung patent; this could mean some older models of the iPad and iPhone will be banned from sale in the USA.

The patent relates to 3G wireless technology and the ability to transmit multiple services correctly and at the same time. Apple said it would appeal. Samsung argued that the judgement proved that once again Apple had used its technology. In a separate patent fight in the US federal court last year, Samsung was ordered to pay more than $1bn for patent infringement, an award that was later slashed to $598.9m.

? Questions

Do you think the patent system is useful?

- **Control supplies or distribution** If a firm can gain control of the major supplier or a significant distributor, then this can make it difficult for newcomers to get into the market.

The higher the level of barriers to entry, the more protected existing firms are from competition; this means that they have more power over the market and are more likely to be able to earn large abnormal profits in the long run.

Price discrimination

If barriers to entry do exist in a market, then firms may have some form of monopoly power and be price makers. This may enable them to price-discriminate. Price discrimination occurs when a firm offers the same product to different customers at different prices. For example, a nightclub might charge different prices depending on what time of the evening or what day you enter; the price of a train ticket may vary depending on what time of day you travel.

By price-discriminating, a firm can increase its own profits; at the same time, it reduces the amount of consumer surplus (utility that is not paid for). In our earlier analysis of monopoly, the firm profit-maximized at the price P1 and the quantity Q1 in Figure 12.2, when the marginal revenue equalled the marginal cost. It charged one price for all of its units. If it were able to price-discriminate, then it might sell some of these units for a higher price. For example, imagine that the output Q2 was sold at the price P2, whilst the remainder (Q1 – Q2) was sold at P1 (see Figure 12.2). The firm is now earning more revenue from its sales and therefore more profits. At the same time, consumer surplus has been reduced from ABP1 to the shaded areas in Figure 12.2. Price discrimination therefore enables the firm to make more profits, but the customer is worse off.

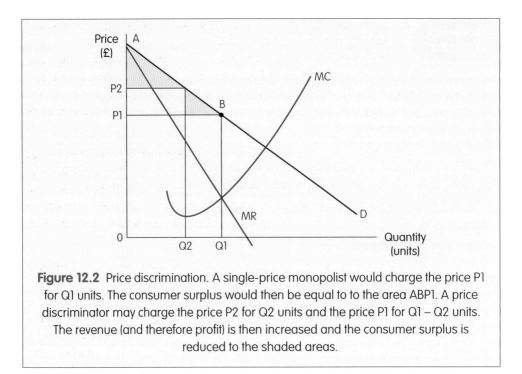

Figure 12.2 Price discrimination. A single-price monopolist would charge the price P1 for Q1 units. The consumer surplus would then be equal to to the area ABP1. A price discriminator may charge the price P2 for Q2 units and the price P1 for Q1 – Q2 units. The revenue (and therefore profit) is then increased and the consumer surplus is reduced to the shaded areas.

▥ Conditions for effective price discrimination

To price-discriminate effectively, a firm must be able to identify different demand conditions: for example, demand may be different between different groups of customer. It will then charge a higher price when demand is price inelastic and a lower price when demand is price elastic. This leads to different prices in different market segments.

To be successful, a policy of price discrimination requires the following.

- The first requirement is that buyers in one market cannot switch easily to another market—that is, that those being asked to pay a high price cannot switch to the low-price market (because this would undermine the policy).

Markets can be separated in many ways, such as the following.

- **Time** This means that people pay different prices at different times of day (for example, peak and off-peak travel).
- **Age** For example, old-age pensioners or children pay less than other people on the bus; their age can be verified by travel cards.
- **Region** For example, charging different prices for the same model of car or the same beer in different parts of the world; the transport costs to buy the cars in the cheaper market and bring them back can ensure that it is not worth trying to buy in the lower-priced market.

- **Status** For example, some firms may have customer clubs or loyalty schemes, and charge different rates to members and non-members.
- **Income** The price charged may vary according to how much you earn. Some private schools offer bursaries to subsidize students who come from low-income backgrounds. However, for this to work, the business must be sure that it can tell accurately what people earn; otherwise, everyone will pretend to be on a low income to try to obtain a bursary!

- The second requirement for effective price discrimination is that the price elasticity of demand is different—that is, that demand is more price inelastic in one market segment than another, enabling prices to be increased in some sections of the market and reduced in others. The fact that demand conditions vary enables different prices to be charged. The higher price will be in the more price inelastic segment(s) of the market, because this will increase revenue.

In Figure 12.3, the demand and marginal revenue in the two markets (A and B) have been added together at each price (that is, horizontally summated) to give the total market demand and the market marginal revenue. The profit-maximizing output, as ever, occurs when the marginal revenue equals the marginal cost. This determines the profit-maximizing output level for the market as a whole. For each market, the marginal revenue must be equal to MR1. If the marginal revenue in one market were greater than in another, then it would make sense to switch output to the one in which the extra revenue is higher, because this would boost profit. To sell this output, the price would need to fall in this market, and this would reduce the marginal revenue. This should continue until the marginal revenue is the same in both markets. Thus,

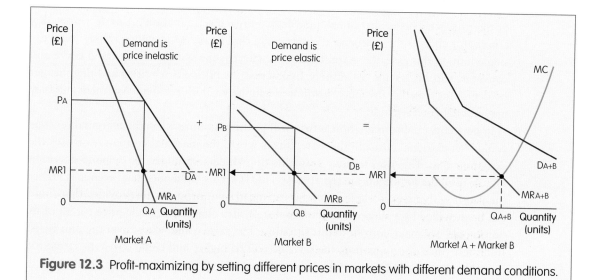

Figure 12.3 Profit-maximizing by setting different prices in markets with different demand conditions.

to profit-maximize, the marginal revenue in market A must be equal to the marginal revenue in market B.

Given that the marginal revenues are equal in both markets, the relevant price and output in each one can then be identified. The price will be higher in the price inelastic market and lower in the price elastic market (PA > PB in Figure 12.3).

Put into practice

Which of the following are true and which are false?

a. When price discriminating a business will charge a higher price in the market where demand is price elastic

b. Price discrimination involves charging different prices for the same product

c. Barriers to entry enable a monopolist to earn normal profits in the long run

d. Brand loyalty makes demand more price elastic

What do you think?

In 2012 a European court ruling meant that it was illegal to charge different prices to men and women for car insurance. This increased the costs of insurance for many female drivers. Do you think it makes sense for male and female drives to be charged the same?

▉ Perfect price discrimination

Perfect price discrimination occurs when a different price is charged for every single unit of the product. This is also called 'first-degree price discrimination'. A perfect price discriminator charges the customer the maximum that he or she is willing to pay for every single unit. In this case, the marginal revenue curve is the same as the demand curve and consumer surplus is removed entirely. In practice, the difficulty for firms in doing this lies in identifying exactly how much customers genuinely value each item. Ask them and they may not tell you the truth!

In perfect price discrimination, a firm will profit-maximize when the marginal revenue equals the marginal costs; in this case, this is where the marginal cost curve crosses the demand curve. The total revenue earned is the whole area under the demand curve. In Figure 12.4, the total costs are the area AC1EQ1O. This highlights that revenue is higher than costs with price discrimination; this can mean some products are provided that could not be provided by a single price monopolist. A firm charging a single price for all of its units could not make a profit in this situation. The price could never cover the unit costs. In perfect price discrimination, the revenue will be higher and could cover the costs: for example, the area OFGQ1 may be greater than AC1EQ1O.

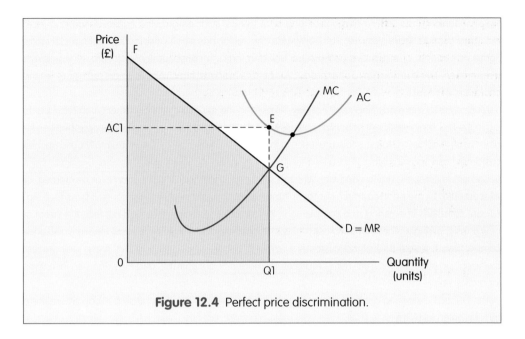

Figure 12.4 Perfect price discrimination.

The benefits of price discrimination

Price discrimination increases a firm's profits and reduces consumer surplus. The in-crease in profits may be seen as undesirable (an abuse of monopoly power); however, it may provide more funds for investment and innovation, leading to lower costs in the long term.

Price discrimination may also enable some goods and services to be produced that would not otherwise be provided. By price-discriminating, a firm may be able to make enough profits to want to stay in the industry when otherwise it would make a loss and leave.

Case study

The retail banking sector, supplying services to households and small and medium-sized businesses, is at the core of the UK's financial system and the wider economy. It provides essential services, including the means to make payments, deposit funds and access credit. In doing so, it supports the economy and society as a whole, forming a critical part of the investment chain, linking savers with borrowers, and helping people and businesses manage financial risks. The efficiency of the retail banking sector is therefore an important contributor to economic growth and productivity in the UK.

Retail banking has seen a number of long-term trends, such as growing consolidation and technological change. From summer 2007 onwards, the sector has been affected by the financial crisis. Some well-known brands have exited retail banking through consolidation or failure, or – perhaps temporarily – by choosing not to offer products in certain markets, leaving consumers with more limited choices of provider.

More recently there has been entry of new firms, and the expected entry of others, into retail banking in the UK. The divestment of banking assets by State-aided banks may also create opportunities for other firms to achieve a large-scale presence in the sector without having to incrementally build up their customer base from scratch.

Barriers to entry, expansion and exit, which can be a natural feature of the market or be created, or exacerbated, by the behaviour of incumbent firms, are critical to these developments. If firms face significant difficulties in entering and competing in the market, incumbent firms will not face the threat of new firms challenging them for business and will have little incentive to reduce costs, innovate and price competitively to retain and attract customers. Similarly, if there are barriers to exit, these may prevent inefficient incumbent firms from being replaced by more efficient entrants and thus dampen incentives for market entry.

The OFT has examined aspects of personal and Small Medium size Enterprise banking where there may be potential barriers:

- regulatory requirements and processes access to essential inputs, such as IT systems, payment schemes, information and finance needed to offer retail banking products
- the ability of new entrants to attract customers and achieve scale, and
- issues around exiting the market.

The OFT has found that new entrants face significant challenges in attracting customers and expanding their market shares in retail banking. Most firms are able to achieve the necessary regulatory authorisations to accept deposits and extend credit. They are also able to gain access to the necessary infrastructure to offer retail banking products… However, the OFT has found that new entrants face significant challenges in attracting personal and SME customers through a combination of low levels of switching, high levels of brand loyalty and consumers' preference for providers with a branch network. These challenges pose the greatest barriers and can have the effect of deterring firms from entering the market in the first place if they do not believe they will be able to attract sufficient numbers of customers to recover start-up costs, grow market share and maintain a successful presence in the market.

Source: OFT http://www.oft.gov.uk/shared_oft/personal-current-accounts/oft1282

❓ Questions

1 Why does the banking system matter to the economy?

2 Analyse the potential barriers to entry in the banking system. What does the article suggest is the key barrier?

3 What might be the consequences of barriers to entry in the banking system?

Review questions

1   Explain two types of barriers to entry.

2   What is meant by abnormal profit?

3   Explain why a monopolist can earn abnormal profits in the long run.

4   Explain why a monopolist is allocatively inefficient.

5   Why is a monopolist likely to be productively inefficient?

6   Why may a monopolist be X inefficient?

7   If a business is price-discriminating, explain why the price will be higher in the more price inelastic market segment.

8   Explain one benefit of price discrimination.

Put into practice

1   Explain, using a diagram, the effect of an increase in variable costs on the price and output outcomes in monopoly.

2   Show the effect of an increase in marginal costs on the pricing outcomes in a price inelastic and price elastic market for a price discriminating business.

Assignment question

1   Visit the Competition Commission website and summarize a recent investigation into monopoly power. Why did it occur and what were the findings?

Key learning points

- A monopoly is a dominant firm in an industry.

- In a monopoly, it is possible to earn abnormal profits, even in the long run, due to barriers to entry.

- A monopolist faces a downward-sloping demand curve; the marginal revenue curve is below the demand curve and diverges from the demand curve.

- In the long run, monopolies may be allocatively and productively inefficient.

- When analysing a monopoly market, it may be important to consider the possibility of entry in the future as well as the existing levels of competition.

- The theory of contestable markets considers the likelihood of entry by other firms as well as the number of rivals in the market at present. Price discrimination occurs when different prices are charged for the same product.

- Price discrimination reduces consumer surplus, but increases producer surplus.

- Price discrimination may enable some products to be produced that it would not be financially feasible to produce otherwise.

- When price-discriminating, a higher price is charged where demand is more price inelastic.

- With perfect price discrimination, consumer surplus is reduced to zero.

References

Leibenstein, H. (1966) 'Allocative efficiency, and *X*-efficiency', *The American Economic Review*, 56(3): 392–415

Schumpeter, J.A. (1942) *Capitalism, Socialism, and Democracy*, Harper and Row, New York

 Visit our Online Resource Centre at http://www.oxfordtextbooks.co.uk/orc/gillespie_ econ3e/ for test questions and further information on topics covered in this chapter.

Oligopoly

So far, we have examined the market structures of perfect competition and monopoly. Another type of market is oligopoly. This has elements of monopoly power, but also involves some degree of competition. An oligopoly is a relatively common form of market structure, and therefore an important one to study and understand. In particular, governments are interested in the impact on prices and output. We then go on to examine other imperfect market structures in the next chapter.

LEARNING OBJECTIVES

By the end of this chapter, you should be able to:

✓ explain the meaning of oligopoly;

✓ understand the significance of interdependence in an oligopoly;

✓ outline different models of behaviour in an oligopoly;

✓ explain the meaning of cartel.

▨ Introduction

An oligopoly occurs when a few firms dominate a market. This is a common occurrence in many markets; in the UK, for example, the car industry, the petrol market, the airline industry, the banking sector, and the supermarket sector are all oligopolies. In these industries, the largest few firms have a large market share. Economists often measure the four-firm or five-firm **concentration ratio**; this shows the combined market share of the largest four or five firms.

Oligopolies are particularly interesting markets to analyse because the firms involved are interdependent. The actions of one business will clearly affect the others. As a result of this interdependence, oligopolistic firms have to decide on how they want to behave in relation to others in a market. In a monopoly, one firm dominates and so it does not have

Competitive	⟵		⟶	Uncompetitive
Perfect competition	Monopolistic competition	**Oligopoly**	Monopoly
Many firms producing identical products	Many firms producing differentiated products	**A few firms dominating a market**	A single firm dominating a market

Figure 13.1 Different forms of market structure.

to consider what others might do; in perfect competition, there are so many other firms that it is impossible to take into account how they might all react. Only in an oligopoly is the number of firms competing so few that decisions have to be made regarding how to work with them. For example, before cutting the price of its major brands, Cadbury will consider how Nestlé and Mars might react. The relationship between oligopoly and other forms of market structure is shown in Figure 13.1.

One strategy that the major firms in an oligopoly might adopt is for all those involved to join together and act as if they were a monopoly. When this happens, it is called a **cartel**; the firms collude to set the price and agree how much each one is going to produce (this is called a quota). Alternatively, the firms may decide to compete against each other, in which case this is likely to drive prices down (in what is known as a price war). In between these two extremes of cartel and price war, there are many different possible outcomes, depending on how firms decide to act. The range of options open to firms in oligopoly is shown in Figure 13.2. The importance of the interdependence of firms has led to the development of game theory, in which the strategic planning of one firm depends on its assumptions about the behaviour of others.

The study of oligopolies is extremely important because so many markets have this structure; as a result, governments, regulators, member firms, and would-be entrants are

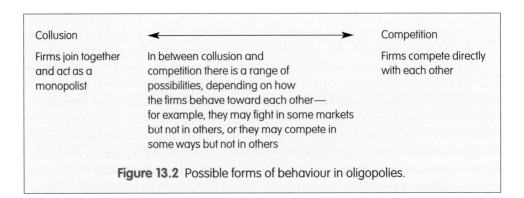

Collusion	⟵	⟶	Competition
Firms join together and act as a monopolist	In between collusion and competition there is a range of possibilities, depending on how the firms behave toward each other— for example, they may fight in some markets but not in others, or they may compete in some ways but not in others		Firms compete directly with each other

Figure 13.2 Possible forms of behaviour in oligopolies.

interested in knowing what determines the behaviour of the firms involved, and the possible consequences of the different strategies that they adopt.

Put into practice

Which of the following statements are true and which are false?

a. An oligopoly occurs when many firms dominate a market

b. A cartel is a collusive oligopoly

c. A price war occurs when firms compete with each other

d. Game theory occurs when one business plans ahead based on the predicted actions of others

▨ The kinked demand curve model

The kinked demand curve model of oligopoly developed by Hall and Hitch (1939), and by Sweezy (1939), is based on the following two key assumptions.

- If the firm being considered increases its price, then the other firms in the market will not follow. This means that the fall in the quantity demanded is likely to be relatively high because customers will switch to other firms; demand is therefore price elastic.

- If the firm being considered decreases its price, then the other firms will follow this price cut (because they do not want to lose sales). This means that the increase in the quantity demanded will be smaller than the price change (in percentages); demand will therefore be price inelastic.

Put into practice

Can you remember the following?

- The equation for the price elasticity of demand

- The difference between price elastic demand and price inelastic demand

- The effect of a price change on revenue when demand is price elastic or price inelastic

These assumptions take a pessimistic view of how others might react (that is, they assume that you will not get away with a price cut, and that if you increase price, then you will be on your own). It is a non-cooperative model of oligopoly because firms are assumed to compete with each other. Given these assumptions, the firm being examined is likely to leave price where it is. An increase in price will lead to such a fall in demand that the overall revenue will fall. A decrease in price will lead to such a small increase in sales that, again, revenue will fall. If revenue is going to fall whatever you do with the price, then why not leave it where it is?

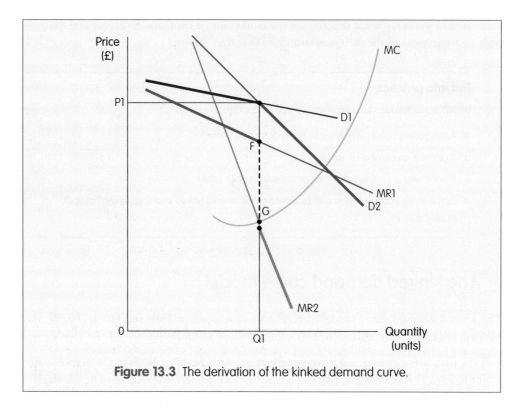

Figure 13.3 The derivation of the kinked demand curve.

The kinked demand curve

The demand curve D2 in Figure 13.3 is price inelastic; it assumes that a price change will have relatively little effect on the quantity demanded because any price change by one firm will be followed by the others, and so there will be little difference between them. By comparison, the demand curve D1 is price elastic; it assumes that a price change will have a relatively large effect on the quantity demanded because any price change by one firm will not be followed by the others.

Starting from P1Q1 in the kinked demand curve model, it is assumed that a price increase will not be followed—so D1 is relevant—but a price decrease will be followed—D2 is relevant. This gives the kinked demand curve indicated by the thicker line in Figure 13.3.

The marginal revenue linked to this kinked demand curve is also indicated by a thicker line. You will notice a gap in this curve; marginal costs can move between F and G, and the profit-maximizing output (where the marginal revenue equals the marginal costs) is still at the price P1 and the quantity Q1. This shows that costs can change without affecting the profit-maximizing price and quantity in this model of oligopoly.

The kinked demand curve that is derived from the two demand curves in Figure 13.3 is shown in Figure 13.4.

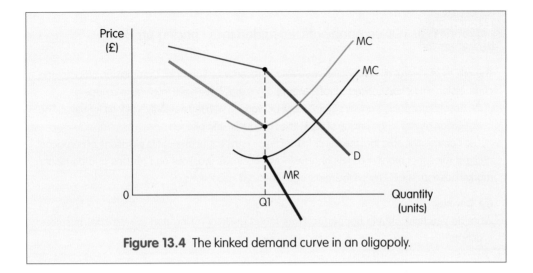

Figure 13.4 The kinked demand curve in an oligopoly.

The kinked demand curve model provides an explanation of why prices in oligopolistic markets are often 'sticky'—that is, they do not change very much. Price competition is not common in many markets because it is relatively easy for a firm to copy another firm's price cut. Many firms prefer to try to differentiate their products—for example, by building a brand or developing some unique selling point—and using this as a means of competing rather than the price. It is much more difficult for competitors to imitate a brand image than it is for them to follow a price cut.

Economics in context

The main supermarkets dominate the food retail industry but seem to compete aggressively with each other. Tesco offers to give you vouchers if your shopping costs more than it would have been at Asda. Sainsbury's gives you vouchers if any branded good you buy would have been cheaper at Tesco or Asda. Asda give you vouchers if your shopping is not 10 per cent cheaper than Tesco, Sainsbury's or Morrisons and you use its Price Guarantee application online. But can they all really be cheaper than each other? Possibly yes! Given that customers are drawn to discounts and offers your basket of goods at say Tesco is different from the basket you would have bought at Asda. So the Tesco basket is filled with offers and is cheaper than competitors. Market researchers Kantar WorldPanel say that more than 40 per cent of groceries are bought on special offer, so regardless of what we think we are going to buy when we enter the shop we end up buying things on special offer.

❓ Question

How much competition do you think there is in the supermarket industry?

The offices of several oil companies were raided recently by European Commission officials. The commission said it had concerns that the companies may have been involved in colluding.

BP, Royal Dutch Shell, Norway's Statoil were all working with the authorities in their inquiries. The investigation relates to the pricing of oil, refined products, and biofuels.

The Commission said that the behaviour of these firms might amount to violations of European antitrust rules that prohibit cartels and restrictive business practices and abuses of a dominant market position. The EU called the raids 'unannounced inspections'.

❓ Question

What do you think should happen to firms found guilty of taking part in restrictive business practices?

◼ Cartels

A cartel occurs when the firms in an oligopoly work together to agree on the price and output that are set in a market. This agreement may be explicit (that is, they may formally agree) or implicit (that is, both sides may agree without anything actually being said or written down). The aim of a cartel is to maximize the profits of its members by restricting the amount available and pushing up price. Cartels may decide on who sells to whom, and what the terms and conditions are, as well as price and output levels. Cartels occur between countries as well as firms. For example, the Organization of the Petroleum Exporting Countries (OPEC) is a cartel of petroleum-exporting countries and has a huge influence on the price of oil.

What do you think?

What factors might influence whether a firm decides to join a cartel?

However, the basic problem with cartels is that it is in the interest of individual firms to cheat! By producing more than the amount agreed with the other members of the cartel (the quota), an individual firm can make more profit at the expense of its 'associates'. On the other hand, if everyone is cheating, then the market supply gets ever higher, and this brings the price down; the group as a whole therefore ends up worse off. Cartels may therefore self-destruct even if it is in their interests to keep together.

In Figure 13.5a, the industry profit-maximizes at the price P1 and the quantity Q1. This determines the price and quantity that should be set. Each member of the cartel is given

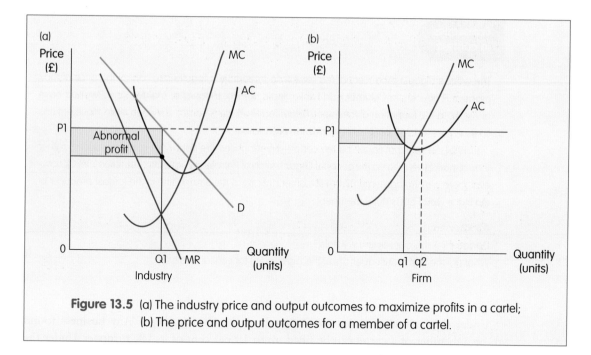

Figure 13.5 (a) The industry price and output outcomes to maximize profits in a cartel;
(b) The price and output outcomes for a member of a cartel.

a quota: for example, q1 to be produced at the set price (see Figure 13.5b). Each member is making an abnormal profit. However, the individual firm is not profit-maximizing; it would profit-maximize when the price equals the marginal revenue at the quantity q2. Therefore there is an incentive for an individual firm to produce more to increase its own rewards. However, if all of the members of the cartel were to do this, then it would drive up industry output and bring down the industry price, moving the industry as a whole away from its profit-maximizing position.

To make a cartel work, it therefore requires the member firms to trust each other, and, if necessary, to be able to check easily how much each member is producing and at what price. Policing the agreement becomes very important; otherwise, it is likely to fall apart.

What do you think?

KPMG, Deloitte, PwC, and Ernst & Young are accounting forms that audit 90 per cent of the UK's largest stock-market-listed companies (i.e. check their accounts to confirm they represent 'a true and fair view' of the company's financial position). What might be the dangers of this type of market structure?

In the UK until 2001, manufacturers of certain products, such as pharmaceuticals and books, were allowed to set the price at which they were sold in shops rather than retailers being allowed to determine their own prices (this was called resale price maintenance). What arguments might have been used to justify such price fixing?

The world's biggest producers of tea recently agreed to join together, to control the price of their product. Producers in Columbia, Sri Lanka, India, Kenya, Indonesia, Malawi, and Rwanda have announced the formation of the International Tea Producer's Forum. Between them these nations control more than 50 per cent of worldwide production.

In 1994, Sri Lanka proposed a tea cartel—where prices are set by the major producers rather than a market—similar to the oil cartel Organization of Petroleum Exporting Countries (OPEC); however there was no agreement from the other nations at the time. China is the largest producer of tea in the world but is not a member.

❓ Questions

Do you think this agreement will hold?

What are the likely consequences of this agreement for consumers?

Under the Competition Act 1998, cartels in the UK are illegal. Any business found to be a member of a cartel can be fined up to 10 per cent of its UK turnover. Under the Enterprise Act 2002, it is a criminal offence for individuals dishonestly to take part in the most serious types of cartel. Anyone convicted of the offence could receive a maximum of five years' imprisonment and/or an unlimited fine.

Put into practice

Which of the following are true and which are false?

a. In the kinked demand curve model it is assumed that a price increase is not followed by other firms

b. In the kinked demand curve model it is assumed that a price decrease is not followed by other firms

c. A cartel profit maximizes when marginal revenue equals total costs

d. A cartel acts liked a monopolist

▓ Game theory

The interdependence of firms within an oligopolistic market and the importance of considering the reactions of other firms is highlighted in **game theory**. This highlights how the strategy of one business is likely to depend on its assumptions about the behaviour of other firms. Game theory examines different strategies based on different assumptions about the actions and reactions of other firms. Different assumptions will lead to different outcomes in the market. A 'game' involves two or more individuals or organizations.

An example of game theory is known as the 'prisoner's dilemma', in which two individuals have both been arrested for a crime. The question is whether they should confess to the crime or not and that, in turn, depends on what they think the other person will do. Unfortunately, they are locked up in separate rooms and cannot communicate, so they have to make assumptions about the other person's behaviour. It is assumed that if they both confess, they will be imprisoned for a long time; if they both refuse to confess, the police cannot prove anything and they will be released. The problem comes if one person refuses to confess and the other one does so: the latter person gets a light sentence and the one who refused to talk gets a very long sentence for non-cooperation. The ideal solution, from the prisoners' point of view, is not to confess and then they would both get off. But if you do not trust your fellow prisoner and think that he or she will confess, you are better confessing as well. On this basis, they will both confess because they do not trust each other.

The prisoner's dilemma highlights how your decisions about what to do depend on your relationship with other prisoners (or businesses in an oligopoly) and your view of whether you think you can trust them or not. You can imagine the manager of one business thinking carefully about what a major competitor might be about to do and trying to work out the best action in different situations. The prisoner's dilemma shows the dangers of oligopoly from a manager's view: a lack of trust may lead to an outcome in which firms are worse off than if they trusted each other.

The prisoner's dilemma in a business context is highlighted in Figure 13.6. Two businesses are considering what level of output to produce: high or low. If they both produce

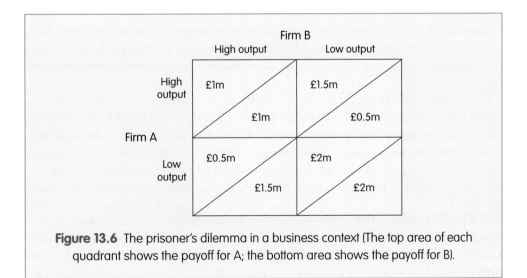

Figure 13.6 The prisoner's dilemma in a business context (The top area of each quadrant shows the payoff for A; the bottom area shows the payoff for B).

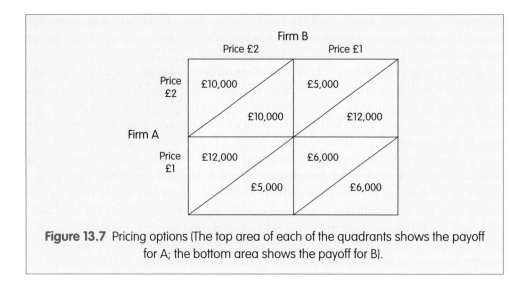

Figure 13.7 Pricing options (The top area of each of the quadrants shows the payoff for A; the bottom area shows the payoff for B).

low outputs, this will push the price up and both will win. But if one produces relatively little and its competitor produces a lot, this will increase supply and drive the price down; the first producer will do badly because its rival wins the market and is selling more. As a result, both producers might flood the market fearing that each other will do this anyway; the total output in the market ends up very high and the market price is low, meaning that both are both worse off compared to a situation in which both had restricted their output.

Figure 13.7 shows the financial results of each possible outcome: if both firms produce high levels of output, they will gain £1 million each; if both restrict output, they will earn £2 million each.

This model shows the importance of managers' assumptions about what other businesses will do. The past behaviour of businesses becomes very important here: how they have behaved in the past may influence assumptions about what they will do in the future.

Game theory can become much more complex depending on the assumptions that are made. Imagine that, in relation to Figure 13.7, you are the manager of Firm A thinking about your pricing options. Assume that you are pessimistic and look at the worst possible outcome of any decision. If you choose a price of £2, the worst that can happen is that B will charge £1 and you will make profits of £5,000. If you were to charge £1, the worst that could happen is that B would do the same and you would end up with £6,000. If you decide to choose the 'best of the worst', then you choose a £1 price. This is called a '**maximin**' strategy because you are maximizing the minimum outcomes. If Firm B were to do the same, it would choose £1 as well and you would both end up with £6,000, when you could have had £10,000 had you agreed to charge £2 and believed each other.

		Firm B	
		Increase promotional spending	Do not increase promotional spending
Firm A	Increase promotional spending	£4m / £3m	£5m / £1m
	Do not increase promotional spending	£2m / £5m	£6m / £2m

Figure 13.8 Deciding whether to increase promotional spending.

A '**maximax**' strategy occurs when a manager is optimistic and bases decisions on the 'best of the best' outcomes. The best outcome if you choose a price of £1 is that your rival chooses £2 and you earn £12,000. The best outcome if you choose a price of £2 is that your rival chooses £2 and you end up with £10,000. To maximize the maximum outcomes you would choose £1.

In this case the best strategy whether you adopt a minimax or a maximax approach is the same—the business should set the price at £1. Because both assumptions give the same solution this is known as the '**dominant strategy**'.

Now let's look at Figure 13.8 which considers whether a business should increase its promotional spending or not.

If A assumes B will increase its spending then its best strategy is to increase its spending and earn £4m. If A assumes B will not increase its spending then its best strategy is not to increase its own spending (which would earn £6m). This means there is no dominant strategy for firm A.

If B assumes A will increase its spending then its best strategy is to increase its spending to earn £3m. If B assumes A will not increase its spending then its best strategy is to increase its spending and earn £5m. This means B does have a dominant strategy which is to increase its spending.

This means that the best strategy for B is to increase its promotional spending regardless of what A does. If A realizes this it will also increase its promotional spending so both will end up increasing their spending. This is known as the **Nash equilibrium.** A Nash equilibrium occurs in a game involving two or more players, in which each player is assumed to know the equilibrium strategies of the other players. If each player has chosen a strategy and no player would benefit by changing his or her strategy while the other players keep theirs unchanged, then the current set of strategy choices and the corresponding payoffs represent a Nash equilibrium.

Put into practice

Imagine a business (business A) is deciding whether or not to increase its promotional expenditure. It is concerned about how its main rival B will react. The expected outcomes are shown in Figure 13.9:

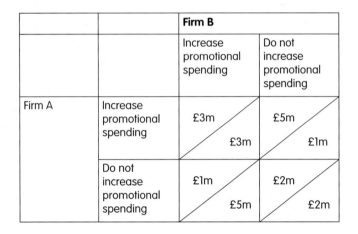

		Firm B	
		Increase promotional spending	Do not increase promotional spending
Firm A	Increase promotional spending	£3m £3m	£5m £1m
	Do not increase promotional spending	£1m £5m	£2m £2m

Figure 13.9 Deciding whether to increase promotional spending.

What is the best strategy for firm A if B increases promotional spending?
What is the best strategy for firm A if B does not increase promotional spending?
What is the best strategy for firm B if A increases promotional spending?
What is the best strategy for firm B if A does not increase promotional spending?

Game theory has many possible applications—for example thinking about whether to lower price, increase advertising, enter a market or whether to launch a product. In each of these cases it is worth considering the possible reactions of competitors. Game theory can, of course, become far more complex as it includes multiple stages considering how A might react once B has acted in a certain way in response to an initial move by A and so on!

Price war

If the firms in an oligopolistic market do not agree to collude, then they may compete. The most aggressive form of competition is a price war (also called predatory pricing), whereby one firm undercuts the others in an attempt to remove them from the market. The ability of a business to survive a price war depends on how much the price needs to be cut and its own resources compared with the finances of its competitors. Although customers may benefit in the short term from lower prices in a price war, in the long term

Economics in context

In 2013 BT announced it was going to to offer free Premier League football coverage to its broadband customers. This was part of its challenge to BSkyB's dominance of the UK's sports pay-TV market. BT had recently won a three-year deal to show 38 Premier League games a season at huge expense. BT had 6.3 million broadband customers, but only 750,000 pay-TV customers, compared with Sky's 10 million subscribers. This move by BT was part of its attempt to establish itself as a major multi-platform provider, offering TV, Internet, and telephone in one package. Customers who wanted to access the sports channels needed to pay for a set top box, or pay an extra £5 per month for the basic television package. This compared with Sky's offer of 116 Premier League matches, as part of a six-channel sports package that costs £42.50 per month for the first six months, and included broadband Internet. BT Sport's channels would also show 69 live Aviva Premiership rugby matches per season, plus live football from leagues in Germany, France, Italy, and Brazil.

BT Sport is also taking on BSkyB in pubs and clubs, with an offer of 12 months' subscription for the price of nine, and a free installation offer. Analysts say the entry into the market by BT represents a serious challenge, despite Sky's success in fighting off previous competition from the likes of ITV Digital, Setanta, and ESPN.

? Question

How do you think Sky should respond to BT's challenge?

the firm that wins may exploit its market power and push up prices even higher than they were originally.

Put into practice

Which of the following statements are true and which are false?

a. A business would be more likely to cut price if demand was price elastic

b. If products are close substitutes they have a high positive cross price elasticity

c. A strong brand is likely to be price elastic

Summary

Oligopolistic markets are very common. They involve a few dominant firms. The price and output outcomes in an oligopoly depend on the behaviour of the firms involved; this, in turn, can depend on their assumptions about what the other firms will be doing. Oligopolistic firms are often involved in complex strategic planning in which they try to determine what other firms might do.

Case study

Authorities in Canada recently accused the large food companies Nestlé and Mars, as well as a network of independent wholesale distributors of being involved in an alleged conspiracy to fix prices of chocolates.

Nestlé Canada, Mars Canada, and the distributors ITWAL have been charged by Canada's Competition Bureau. Officials said Hershey Canada, an alleged co-conspirator, is expected to plead guilty at a hearing in exchange for leniency.

A spokesperson for the Competition Bureau said it was fully committed to pursuing those who were involved in anti-competitive behaviour that harms Canadaian consumers. The Bureau stressed that price fixing is serious criminal offence and that is was determined to stop cartels.

Hershey said it would plead guilty to one count of price fixing, dating from 2007, blaming previous management.

? Questions

Using the text above and data provided:

1 Why might companies such as Mars and Herhsey become involved in price fixing?

2 Discuss the possible consequences for the consumer if there was collusion in the chocolate confectionery market.

3 Discuss the actions the Competition Bureau might take if it found there was a cartel in the chocolate confectionery market.

Review questions

1 Explain how an oligopoly differs from perfect competition.

2 In what ways does an oligopoly differ from a monopoly?

3 Why is the kinked demand curve kinked?

4 What is meant by game theory?

5 Explain what is meant by a cartel.

6 Explain what is meant by a 4 firm concentration ratio.

7 How might firms compete if they do not use price?

8 Are firms in an oligopoly most likely to collude or compete?

Put into practice

1 Draw a Kinked Demand curve and show how a change in marginal costs may not affect the price in the market.

2 Draw a diagram to show a cartel acting like a monopolist and the price and output of a member firm.

Assignment question

1　OPEC is a cartel of Oil Petroleum Exporting Countries. Research OPEC and discuss the case for and against such a cartel.

Key learning points

- An oligopoly occurs when a few firms dominate a market.
- The price and outcome results in an oligopoly depend on the assumptions that are made regarding the way in which firms behave toward each other (for example, whether they compete or collude).
- Oligopoly highlights the significance of interdependence in business. One firm's decisions about how much to produce and what price to charge are linked to its assumptions about how other firms will behave.

References

Hall, R. and Hitch, C. (1939) 'Price theory and business behaviour', *Oxford Economic Papers*, 2(1): 12–45

Sweezy, P.M. (1939) 'Demand under conditions of oligopoly', *Journal of Political Economy*, 47(4): 568–73

Learn more

To learn out more about game theory and the strategies that firms might adopt, visit the Online Resource Centre. To learn more about non-price competition, read Chapter 14.

 Visit our Online Resource Centre at http://www.oxfordtextbooks.co.uk/orc/gillespie_econ3e/ for test questions and further information on topics covered in this chapter.

Monopolistic competition and non-price competition

We have now examined the following market structures: perfect competition; monopoly; and oligopoly. Another form of market structure is monopolistic competition. In this chapter, we examine the features of monopolistic competition, and the implications of this market structure for customers and firms.

LEARNING OBJECTIVES

By the end of this chapter, you should be able to:

✓ explain the key features of monopolistic competition;

✓ consider the efficiency of monopolistic competition;

✓ outline non-price forms of competition that are experienced in many markets;

✓ outline Porter's five forces analysis;

✓ understand how firms might try to influence these forces.

▦ Introduction

Monopolistic competition occurs in a market in which there are many firms competing and each one offers a differentiated product. There are, for example, many thousands of cafes and restaurants in the UK. Whilst they all compete in the same market, there are differences between them: for example, they have different menus, different themes, and different locations. These factors can influence your decision when choosing between them; this means that the cafes involved have some control over their market and the ability to decide what prices to charge.

Firms in monopolistic competition face a downward-sloping demand curve. If they increase the price, they will lose some customers (but not all) to competitors; if they reduce prices, they should gain some customers from competitors (but not all). As in a monopoly, the marginal revenue is below the demand curve and diverging; to sell more, the price has to be lowered on the last unit and all of the ones before.

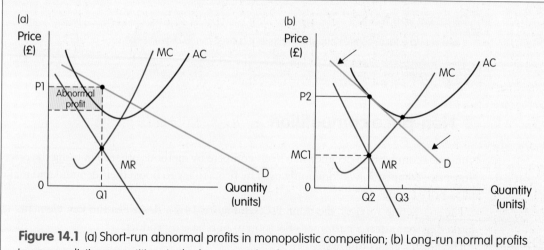

Figure 14.1 (a) Short-run abnormal profits in monopolistic competition; (b) Long-run normal profits in monopolistic competition. In the long run other firms enter the market, reducing demand for any individual firm until normal profits are made.

Firms in monopolistic competition are assumed to be profit-maximizers. This means that they will produce the highest output at which marginal revenue equals the marginal cost (see Figure 14.1a). The difference between this type of market and a monopoly is that there are no barriers to entry. This means that if firms are making abnormal profits in the short run, then this will attract other firms into the industry. This will cause the demand for any one firm's products to fall. It will cause an inward shift of the firm's demand curve until only normal profits are made (see Figure 14.1b).

If losses were being made, then firms would leave the industry, so demand for a particular firm's products would increase until normal profits were made.

Put into practice

Draw a diagram that illustrates a firm in monopolistic competition making a loss in the short run and then, following the departure of other firms, the firm making normal profits in the long run.

In the long run in monopolistic competition, a firm is:

- allocatively inefficient because the price that it charges is greater than the marginal cost (P2 > MC1 in Figure 14.1b); this means that the extra benefits of a unit to society are greater than the extra costs but the business will not produce these units because it reduces their profits and

- productively inefficient because the firm does not produce at the minimum of the average cost curve (Q2 not Q3 in Figure 14.1b). Again the business does not produce this output because it would involve a lower price and less profit.

▇ Non-price competition

Non-price competition occurs when firms compete by methods other than using the price. Non-price competition is commonly used by firms to try to boost their demand and make it less price elastic.

The marketing mix, or the 'four Ps' (see Figure 14.2), describes the key elements in marketing that affect a customer's decision to purchase a product.

The four Ps are as follows.

- **Price** This involves not only the price, but also the payment terms—for example, whether you can pay over time and how payments can occur.

- **Product** This encompasses all of the different elements of a product, including the features, the specifications, the after-sales service, and the brand. For example, Apple has long been admired for the design of its products; Dyson won a significant market share in the vacuum cleaner market with its innovative technology.

- **Promotion** This includes all of the different ways in which a firm communicates about its product, such as advertising, the sales force, sponsorship, public relations activities, and sales promotions (for example, offers and competitions).

- **Place** This refers to the distribution of the product—that is, how it gets to the market. For example, whether it is sold through wholesalers and retailers or direct to customers.

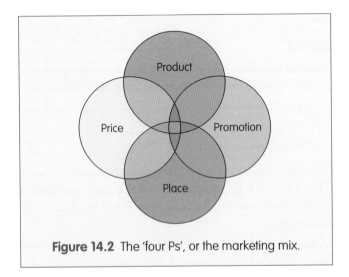

Figure 14.2 The 'four Ps', or the marketing mix.

Economics in context

In a search for new distribution channels JD Wetherspoon announced in 2013 it would open its first motorway pub after being given permission to set one up at the services on the M40.

The bar and restaurant opened at Extra in Beaconsfield, Buckinghamshire, after a successful application to the local council. Its licence allows it to serve alcohol between 08:00 and 01:00.

The £2m development created around 50 jobs. The Wetherspoon chairman, Tom Martin, said that the company had always been innovative and that he hoped it would be one of many others in the future. Critics argued the opening of a Wetherspoons would encourage drink driving.

Source: http://www.bbc.co.uk/news/uk-england-beds-bucks-herts-22760874

? Questions

Can you think of other new types of locations where you might open a new pub?

Can you think of other businesses that have done well by developing new distribution channels?

If a firm is not competing on price, then it can use other elements of the marketing mix to win customers. For example, firms might do the following.

- Firms may use their promotional activities to develop a strong brand image. Companies such as Virgin, Microsoft, Nike, and Coca-Cola all have very strong brand names. Customers associate these names with certain values. This brand image has been created by the way in which the company advertises, the quality of its products, the way in which its employees behave, and the types of sponsorship that its undertakes. By differentiating their products, firms may develop their customers' brand loyalty, which means that new entrants to the market will have to fight harder to get buyers to switch to them. Brand loyalty also means that the customer may be less sensitive to price (that is, demand is more price inelastic) and that customers would be more likely to accept new products launched by a business. This can make product launches cheaper and more likely to be successful.

What do you think?

How do you think the following brands differ?

a. Costa, Starbucks, and Caffè Nero

b. Pepsi and Coca-Cola

c. French Connection and Next

d. Nike and Umbro

e. The *Daily Telegraph* and The *Daily Mail*

- Firms may develop the product to create a unique selling point—that is, something that makes it stand out from the competition. This could be the recipe for the product or a special feature, such as rapid delivery times or an extended warranty.

- Firms may develop more distribution channels to make the product more widely available and easier for customers to buy.

What do you think?

The markets for many consumer products, such as DVD players and digital cameras, are very competitive. Is it better to compete in these markets using price or using other factors?

▨ Porter's five forces analysis of market structure

We have now considered four different types of market: perfect competition; monopoly; oligopoly; and monopolistic competition. Each one has its own characteristics, and its own price and output outcomes. A comparison of these helps us to predict what might happen in different markets and to consider what policies we might want to introduce as a government.

In 1985, Michael Porter, a business analyst, produced his study of market structure. According to Porter, the likelihood of making profits in an industry depends on the following five factors (known as Porter's five forces—see Figure 14.3).

- **The likelihood of new entry** This refers to the extent to which barriers to entry exist. The more difficult it is for other firms to enter a market, the more likely it is that

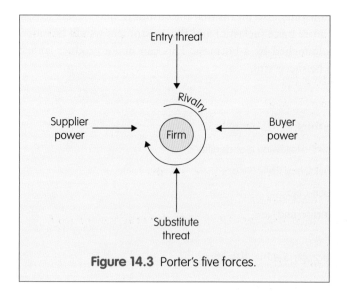

Figure 14.3 Porter's five forces.

existing firms can make relatively high profits. In a monopoly, for example, these would be high, whereas in a competitive market, it would be easier to enter.

- **The power of buyers** The stronger the power of buyers in an industry, the more likely it is that they will be able to force down prices and reduce the profits of firms that provide the product. Buyer power will be higher if:
  - there are relatively few buyers;
  - the buyers can easily switch to other providers; or
  - the buyers can threaten to take over the firm.

- **The power of suppliers** The stronger the power of suppliers to an industry, the more difficult it is for firms within that sector to make a profit. Suppliers will be more powerful if:
  - there are relatively few of them (so that the buyer has few alternatives);
  - switching to another supplier is difficult and/or expensive; or
  - the supplier can threaten to buy the existing firms.

- **The degree of rivalry** This measures the degree of competition between existing firms. The higher the degree of rivalry, the more difficult it is for existing firms to generate high profits. Rivalry will be higher if:
  - there are a large number of similar-sized firms (rather than a few dominant firms);
  - the costs of leaving the industry are high (for example, because of high levels of investment), which means that existing firms will fight hard to survive because they cannot easily transfer their resources elsewhere; or
  - the level of capacity underutilization is high—if there are high levels of capacity being underutilized, then the existing firms will be very competitive to try to win sales to boost their own demand.

- **The substitute threat** This measures the ease with which buyers can switch to another product that does the same thing: for example, aluminium cans rather than glass bottles.

Using Porter's analysis, an industry is likely to generate higher profits if:

- the industry is difficult to enter;
- there is limited rivalry;
- buyers are relatively weak;
- suppliers are relatively weak; and
- there are few substitutes.

On the other hand, profits are likely to be low if:

- the industry is easy to enter;
- there is a high degree of rivalry between firms within the industry;
- buyers are strong;
- suppliers are strong; and
- it is easy to switch to alternatives.

The implication of Porter's analysis for managers of firms is that they should examine these five factors before choosing an industry into which to move. They should also consider ways of changing the five factors to make them more favourable. For example:

- if firms merge together, then this can reduce the degree of rivalry;
- if firms buy up distributors (this is called forward vertical integration), then they can gain more control over buyers; and
- firms may differentiate their product, perhaps by trying to generate some form of unique selling proposition (USP) that makes them stand out from the competition.

The five forces will change over time as market conditions alter. For example, the Internet has made it easier for customers to compare prices and therefore this increases buyer power in many markets, including travel and consumer products, such as fridges and televisions. The Internet has also made it easier for producers to access customers, making it easier to enter many markets, such as finance, book retailing, and clothes retailing. As ever, the business world is not static and the conditions in any industry will always be changing to some extent.

What do you think?

Do you think the Internet is good for business? How does it change the five forces? What about customers—is it good for them?

Case study

The nightclub business in the UK is very fragmented with many providers. Demand has fallen in recent years (see Figure 14.4).

Despite recent discounting at non-peak times (e.g. early in the evening and on week nights), the total number of admissions into clubs has continued to fall. Occasional visitors appear to be moving further away from clubs with many preferring hybrid bars, which may offer anther attraction such as a tribute band or stand-up comedy and not have entry fees.

? Questions

1. Why do you think the nightclub business is quite fragmented with many small providers in the industry?

2. Analyse the factors that might have led to a fall in admissions for nightclubs.

3. If you were setting up a nightclub in your city, how would you differentiate it from your rivals?

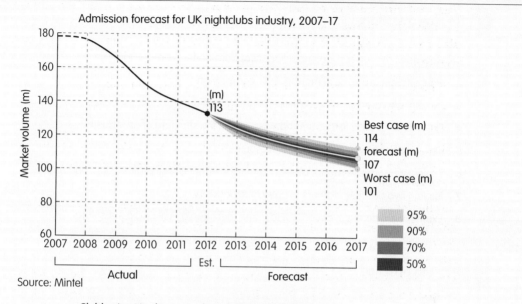

Admission forecast for UK nightclubs industry, 2007–17

Source: Mintel

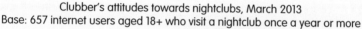

Clubber's attitudes towards nightclubs, March 2013
Base: 657 internet users aged 18+ who visit a nightclub once a year or more

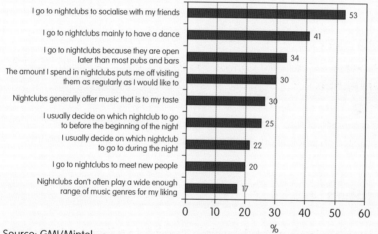

Source: GMI/Mintel

Leading UK nightclub operators, by number of clubs, April 2013	
	Number of clubs
The Luminar Group	56
Novus Leisure	30
Tokyo Group	20
Yellowhammer	17
Eclectic Bars & Clubs	16
Fever Bars	15
G1 Group	14

Source: Operators/Mintel

Figure 14.4 Admission forecast for UK nightclubs industry, clubbers attitudes, and leading nightclub operators.

Review questions

1 How does monopolistic competition differ from perfect competition?

2 How efficient are firms in monopolistic competition?

3 Explain two common forms of non-price competition.

4 Explain Porter's five forces and how they affect the structure of an industry.

5 How can firms try to influence the five forces?

6 Explain why firms in monopolistic competition earn normal profits in the long run.

7 Explain two possible barriers to entry to an industry.

8 Explain the difference, according to Porter, between a rival and a substitute.

Put into practice

1 Imagine a firm is in long-run equilibrium in monopolistic competition. Show the effect of an increase in costs.

2 Imagine a firm is in long-run equilibrium in monopolistic competition. Show the effect of a fall in demand.

Assignment question

1 'Advertising is a waste of resources' Research the case for and against advertising. Reach a justified conclusion on whether advertising is a waste of resources in the economy.

Key learning points

* In markets that are monopolistically competitive, there are many competitors, but each firm attempts to differentiate its products.

* In monopolistic competition, firms face a downward-sloping demand curve.

* In the short run, firms in monopolistic competition may make a loss or abnormal profit; in the long run, firms make normal profits due to entry or exit.

* Price changes are relatively easy for competitors to follow and therefore firms often use non-price methods of competing, such as advertising.

* The structure of a market may be analysed using Porter's five forces analysis.

 Visit our Online Resource Centre at http://www.oxfordtextbooks.co.uk/orc/gillespie_econ3e/ for test questions and further information on topics covered in this chapter.

The labour market 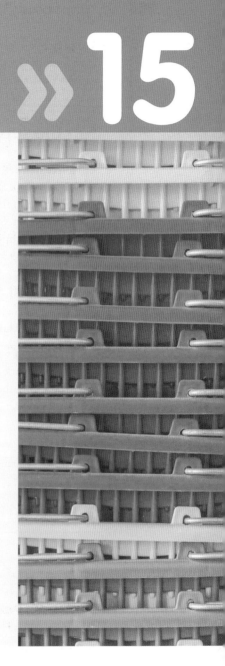 » 15

So far we have analysed the free market system and how it might allocate resources. We have focused on product markets, but now consider one of the key factor markets: the labour market. In this market we analyse market forces again but in relation to a factor of production. This will end our analysis of micro economics. Labour is a vital resource in business. An understanding of the labour market will help us to understand why wage levels differ between jobs and regions, and what determines the number of people working in a particular industry. In this chapter, we consider the determinants of supply and demand for labour, and examine how changes in wages bring about equilibrium in the market.

LEARNING OBJECTIVES

By the end of this chapter, you should be able to:

✓ understand why labour is a derived demand;

✓ explain the factors that affect the demand and supply of labour;

✓ explain the profit-maximizing condition for hiring labour;

✓ understand the role of a trade union;

✓ explain the factors influencing the powers of trade unions.

▨ The labour market

Most of us are interested in the wages that we might earn in different jobs. What is also interesting is how the wages vary between industries and why the earnings of, say, a cleaner can be so different from those of a merchant banker. We all think that nurses, police, and firefighters do a valuable job, and yet their pay is relatively low. Some footballers seem to play relatively few games per season and yet earn vast sums of money. In this chapter, we look at the labour market and consider why wages differ so much, and examine the impact of changes in market conditions.

The supply of and demand for labour

In a free market, the wages of employees will be determined by the supply of and demand for labour in a given industry. In just the same way that the price adjusts to bring about equilibrium in the product market, the wage will adjust to bring about equilibrium in the labour market. So, to understand why some jobs pay so much more than others, we must examine the supply and demand of labour.

Labour supply

The supply of labour to a particular industry will depend on the following.

• **The level of wages** The higher the wages being paid, then the more people are likely to want to work in an industry, all other things being unchanged. This will cause a movement along the supply curve for labour (see Figure 15.1a).

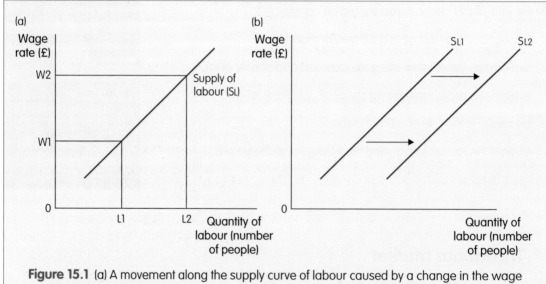

Figure 15.1 (a) A movement along the supply curve of labour caused by a change in the wage rate; (b) A shift in the supply of labour curve means that more (or less) is supplied at each and every wage rate.

- **The value of the benefits available from the government if people are unemployed** If these benefits are relatively low, then there will be more incentive for people to work. This will increase the supply of labour at any wage level and shift the supply curve of labour to the right (see Figure 15.1b).

- **The training period** If there is a long training period for a particular industry (perhaps because the work requires highly specialist skills, such as being a surgeon), then this will reduce the number of employees who can work in this sector at any moment and shift the supply of labour to the left.

- **The overall appeal of the job** If the job itself is unappealing (perhaps because working conditions are unpleasant or even dangerous—think of night work, working on an oil rig, or being a firefighter), then this will reduce the supply of labour to it.

- **The number of people in the labour force** This will determine the overall size of the labour pool and therefore the number that can work in any industry. The working population will depend on what the working age is (for example, at what age people leave school and at what age they retire), and demographic factors such as birth and death rates, and migration rates. Out of this labour force, the number of people willing to work will depend on the unemployment benefits available relative to the wages offered.

- **Trade unions** Trade unions represent employees and bargain with management to protect their interests. Unions may take industrial action (such as a strike) as a bargaining tool. In some countries, unions can affect the supply of labour by restricting jobs to union members.

- **The time period** In the immediate run, the supply of labour will be fixed. You will have a certain number of employees available. In the short and medium terms, you can attract people with the right skills into your industry from other sectors. Over time, however, people can be trained to accept jobs and this will increase supply.

What do you think?

What job do you want to pursue as a career? Why?

Why might the quantity of labour supplied not increase if the wage goes up?

What do you think?

- What jobs could you apply for tomorrow?
- What jobs would you need extensive training for before you could apply?

Wanted: secret service officer

The following is an extract from an advert for an operational officer for the UK Secret Intelligence Service.

The role of the Operational Officer is to plan and execute covert intelligence operations overseas. Working in London and abroad, Operational Officers gather the secret intelligence which government needs to promote and defend UK national interests.

The work calls for men and women who combine exceptional interpersonal skills with a strong intellect and a high degree of personal integrity. The successful Operational Officer will be someone able to influence and persuade others, and to do so across cultural and linguistic boundaries. Candidates who are bilingual or who come from ethnically diverse backgrounds are welcome for the particular skills and insights they bring. Regardless of their background and experience, Operational Officers will be energetic and resourceful, motivated by the challenge of solving complex problems. Resilience is important, as is the ability to deliver results under pressure, often in difficult and stressful environments. To become an Operational Officer requires a keen interest in international issues and a curiosity about other cultures, along with an appetite for living and working overseas.

Successful candidates for this special and demanding role will need a strong academic record to degree level or beyond, a history of personal achievement and influence in extra-curricular activities, and experience of independent travel. They will also have a demonstrable commitment to public service.

❓ Question

Do you think that the supply of labour for this position is likely to be high or low? Why?

▨ Transfer earnings and economic rent

The wage level at which an employee needs to work (as shown by the supply curve in Figure 15.2) is known as transfer earnings. It is the amount of money that means that labour is willing and able to supply its services to this industry rather than another. If an employee earns transfer earnings he or she will stay in this industry (in this sense it is like normal profits). If however an employee is paid more than he or she needs to work in this industry this is known as economic rent. Imagine the 10th employee needs £200 a week to work in this industry, To attract an 11th employee the wage may have to increase to £220. This means the 10th employee is now earning economic rent (like abnormal profit).

▨ The wage elasticity of supply of labour

The elasticity of supply of labour shows how responsive the supply of labour is to changes in the wage rate, all other factors being unchanged.

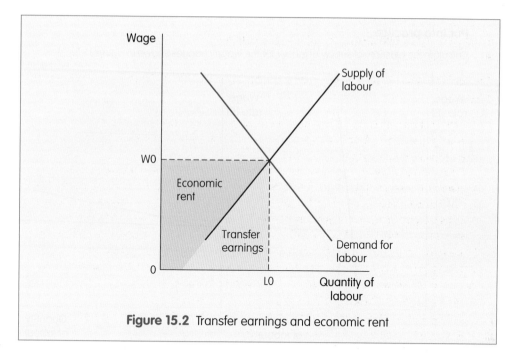

Figure 15.2 Transfer earnings and economic rent

The elasticity of supply of labour is measured as follows:

$$\text{Elasticity of supply of labour} = \frac{\text{Percentage change in the quantity of labour supplied}}{\text{Percentage change in the wage rate}}$$

The elasticity of supply of labour depends on factors such as the following.

- **The geographical mobility of labour** This refers to how easy it is for people to change location to get a job. This depends on:
  - the availability of information (do employees know that jobs are available in the first place?);
  - the costs of moving—for example, transport costs, removal costs, and the costs of finding accommodation in different areas (house prices in some areas can be a major barrier to location);
  - the upheaval involved in moving location—for example, changing children's schools, interrupting their education, and leaving friends and family; and
  - the willingness of people to take risks and move to a new area.
- **The occupational mobility of labour** This refers to how easy it is for employees to change professions if wages change. This depends on factors such as the training involved, the qualifications needed, the skills required, and the awareness of the availability of jobs.

Put into practice

Calculate the elasticity of supply of labour for the wage changes shown in Figure 15.3.

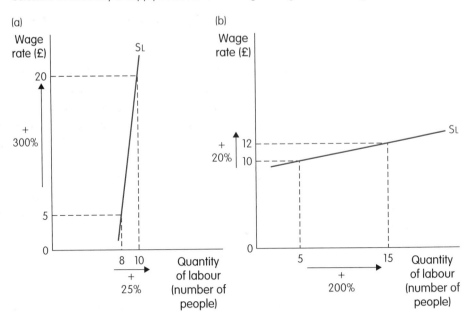

Figure 15.3 (a) A labour supply that is not responsive to changes in the wage rate (the supply of labour is wage-rate inelastic); (b) A labour supply that is responsive to changes in the wage rate (the supply of labour is wage-rate elastic).

What do you think?

What do you think makes people go out to work?

Economics in context   **An ageing population**

One of the key issues facing European business in the future is the increasing average age of the population. This means that firms will need to consider how to recruit older workers and how to retain their younger ones. It also means that many organizations will have to review their pension arrangements. Their existing pension schemes are simply not viable. In recent years, nearly all large firms have ended their final-salary pension schemes. These give employees a proportion of their final salary during every year of their retirement; the amount of pension that they receive depends on how many years they had worked.

? Question

How might an ageing population affect a firm's approach to recruitment and the management of staff?

◼ The demand for labour

The demand for labour measures the number of employees that a firm is willing and able to employ, all other things being unchanged.

The demand for labour is a 'derived demand'. This means that employees are demanded because there is a demand for the final good or service. The demand for employees is derived from the demand for the product. Employees are needed to produce the output, so an increase in the demand for the product increases the demand for labour.

The demand for products was examined in Chapter 3. This highlighted how changes in factors such as income, prices of substitutes and complements, number of customers, and marketing activities.

The demand for labour is determined by the value of each employee's output. This is measured by the marginal revenue product of labour (MRPL). The MRPL depends on how much output is produced by an additional employee and the value of that output when it is sold—that is:

Marginal revenue product of labour (MRPL) = Marginal product (MP)

× Marginal revenue (MR)

For example, if an additional employee produces ten units that can sell for £5, then the marginal revenue product of labour is £50.

The demand for labour will depend on the following.

- **Wages** At higher wages, fewer employees will be demanded because they are more expensive, all other things being unchanged. This is shown by a movement along the demand curve for labour and a change in the quantity of labour demanded.

- **The stock of capital equipment and technology** The level of investment in capital goods will affect the productivity of employees and therefore their MRPL. Better capital equipment and technology should enable staff to produce more, and this will lead to an increase in their MRPL.

- **Working practices and management approaches** Better management and better ways of organizing people can lead to improvements in the levels of output produced by employees.

- **Training** If employees are better trained, then they should be more able to do their jobs and be more productive; this will increase their MRPL.

> **What do you think?**
>
> What do you think influences the levels of investment and training within an industry or economy?

The MRPL is downward-sloping because:

- the marginal product (extra output) of extra employees falls due to the law of diminishing returns (see Chapter 9); and

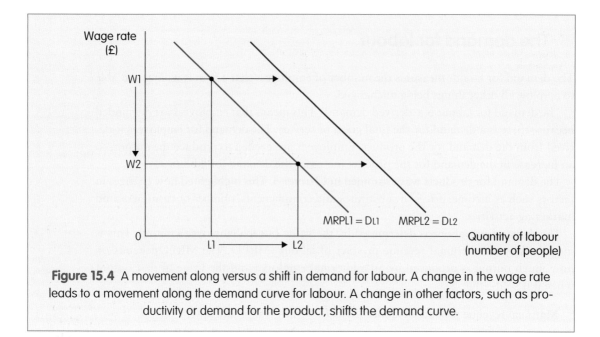

Figure 15.4 A movement along versus a shift in demand for labour. A change in the wage rate leads to a movement along the demand curve for labour. A change in other factors, such as productivity or demand for the product, shifts the demand curve.

- the marginal revenue (extra revenue) generated from selling units will either:
  - fall if the products are sold in monopoly markets (this is because the price has to be lowered to sell more—see Chapter 10); or
  - be constant if the product is sold in perfectly competitive markets in which the price is constant (see Chapter 11).

Changes in the wage rate are shown as a movement along the demand-for-labour curve. Changes in any of the other factors above will lead to a shift in the curve as the value of the MRPL for any number of employees changes. The difference between a movement along, and a shift in, the MRPL is shown in Figure 15.4.

■ The wage elasticity of demand for labour

The wage elasticity of demand for labour measures how sensitive the demand for labour is in relation to changes in the wage level. It is calculated as follows:

$$\text{Elasticity of demand for labour} = \frac{\text{Percentage change in the quantity demanded of labour}}{\text{Percentage change in the wage rate}}$$

The demand for labour is wage inelastic if the percentage change in the quantity demanded is less than the percentage change in the wage level (see Figure 15.5a). This means the elasticity of demand for labour would be less than 1. The demand for labour is wage elastic if the percentage change in the quantity demanded is greater than the percentage change in the wage rate (see Figure 15.5b). In this case the wage elasticity of demand will have a value that is greater than 1.

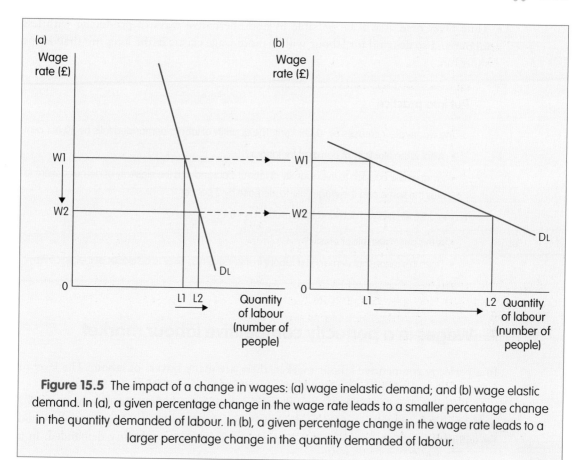

Figure 15.5 The impact of a change in wages: (a) wage inelastic demand; and (b) wage elastic demand. In (a), a given percentage change in the wage rate leads to a smaller percentage change in the quantity demanded of labour. In (b), a given percentage change in the wage rate leads to a larger percentage change in the quantity demanded of labour.

The elasticity of demand for labour will depend on the following.

- **How easy it is to replace labour with other factors of production** For example, is it easy to replace people with machines? The easier it is to replace staff, the more elastic the demand for labour will be. When economies are industrializing, the elasticity of demand for labour can be relatively high, because there is plenty of scope for investment in capital equipment to do the work that people are doing at present.

- **The price elasticity of demand for the final product** An increase in the wage rate will increase a firm's costs and therefore the price of the product; this will lead to a fall in sales. The greater the price elasticity of demand for the product, the greater the fall in sales, and therefore the greater the fall in the number of staff needed—that is, the more price elastic demand for the product is the more wage elastic the demand for labour is likely to be.

- **Wages as a proportion of total costs** If wages are a high proportion of total costs, then an increase in wages will significantly increase the overall costs. This is likely to lead to a relatively large fall in the quantity of labour demanded—that is, the demand for labour will be wage elastic.

- **Time** Over time, it will be possible to find alternative ways of producing with less labour and so demand for labour will be more wage elastic in the long run than in the short run.

Put into practice

a. The wage rate increases by 10 per cent. The quantity of labour demanded falls by 20 per cent.

- What is the elasticity of demand for labour?
- What would happen to the quantity of labour demanded if the elasticity of demand were to stay the same and the wage rate to increase by 2 per cent?

b. The price elasticity of demand for a product is −0.1.

- Is this price inelastic or elastic?
- Does this mean that demand for labour in this industry is likely to be elastic or inelastic? Why?

▦ Wages in a perfectly competitive labour market

In a perfectly competitive labour market, there are many buyers of labour. The level of wages in an industry is determined by the supply of labour and demand for labour.

If the wage was set at a wage rate above the equilibrium—for example, the wage W2 in Figure 15.6—then this would lead to an excess supply of labour. More people would be willing and able to work at this high wage rate than the quantity demanded. In a

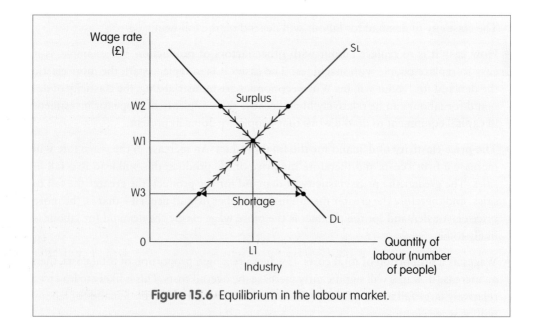

Figure 15.6 Equilibrium in the labour market.

free market, the wage rate would fall, leading to an increase in the quantity of labour demanded and a fall in the quantity supplied. This process continues until equilibrium is reached at W1, where the quantity of labour supplied equals the quantity demanded. At this point, there is no incentive for the wage rate to change given the supply and demand conditions. If the wage rate was originally at W3, which is below the equilibrium rate, then there would be excess demand. The number of workers willing and able to work at this wage is less than the number demanded. In a free market, this will lead to an increase in the level of wages until it reaches W1, where the labour market is in equilibrium.

A firm's decision to hire employees

A firm in a perfectly competitive labour market is small relative to the industry. It can hire as many employees as it wants and it will not have any noticeable impact on the overall demand for labour in the industry. This means that the firm is a **wage taker**: it can hire as many people as it wants at the given wage. This means that the extra cost of an employee is the wage (the marginal cost of labour equals the wage rate), as shown in Figure 15.7.

A profit-maximizing firm will employ workers up until the point at which the marginal revenue product of an employee is equal to the marginal cost of employing that worker—that is, the extra amount of revenue that they generate is equal to the extra cost of employing them.

If the marginal revenue product of labour is greater than the marginal cost of labour, then the extra revenue generated by hiring someone is greater than the extra cost of employing them—that is, profits increase by employing that person, so he/she will be hired.

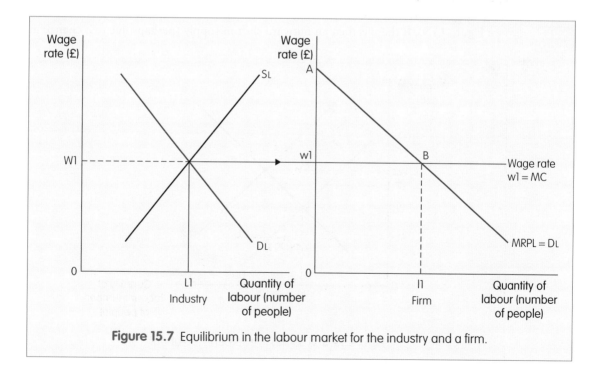

Figure 15.7 Equilibrium in the labour market for the industry and a firm.

If the marginal revenue product of labour is less than the marginal cost of labour, then the extra revenue earned by hiring someone is less than the extra cost of hiring them—that is, profits will fall if that person is employed, so they will not be recruited.

The area w1Bl10 in Figure 15.7 shows the wages earned by employees. A profit-maximizing employer hires l1 employees (i.e. where MRPL = MC). The area Aw1B represents the surplus (the difference between the marginal revenue product of labour and the marginal cost of labour) earned by the firm.

■ Changes in demand and supply conditions in the labour market

The effect of an increase in demand for labour

Imagine that the market is at equilibrium at the wage W1 and the quantity of labour L1 (see Figure 15.8). If there is then an outward shift in the demand for labour (perhaps due to an increase in demand for the final product), then this will lead to an excess demand at the given wage. This, in turn, will lead to an increase in wages. As wages increase, the number of people willing to work will increase (that is, there will be an increase in quantity supplied) and the quantity of labour demanded will fall. This will continue until a new equilibrium is reached with higher wages, and more people employed at the wage W2 and the quantity of labour L2.

The effect of an increase in the supply of labour

Imagine that the market is at equilibrium at the wage W1 and the quantity of labour L1 (see Figure 15.9). If there is then an outward shift in supply (perhaps due to a change in

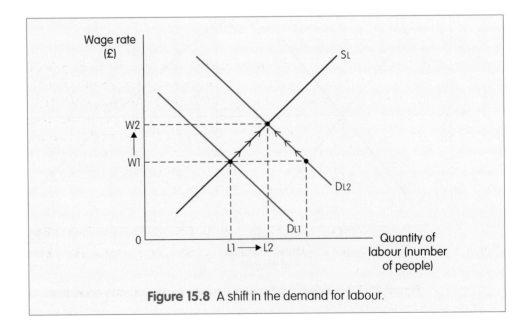

Figure 15.8 A shift in the demand for labour.

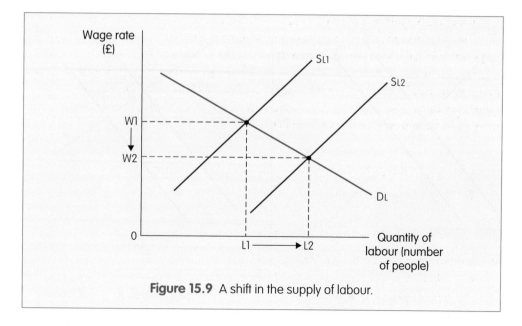

Figure 15.9 A shift in the supply of labour.

income tax rates that makes working more financially rewarding), then this will lead to an excess supply at the old wage rate. This, in turn, will lead to a fall in the market wage rate. As this happens, the quantity of labour supplied will fall, whilst the quantity demanded will rise. This will continue until a new equilibrium is reached with a lower wage rate, and a higher number of people employed at the wage W2 and the quantity of labour L2.

▓ Wage differentials in labour markets

If all labour markets were perfectly competitive, then all employees would be paid the same. This is because if the wages were higher in one industry than another, then the employees in the lower-paid industry would move to the higher-paid one, attracted by the greater rewards. This would decrease the supply of labour in the lower-paid sector and bring up the equilibrium wage in that market (see Figure 15.10a), whilst increasing the supply of labour in the higher-paid sector and reducing the equilibrium wage in that market (see Figure 15.10b). This process continues until the wages are equal and there is no further incentive for labour to move between industries.

This assumes that:

• the movement of employees between industries is easy (that is, there is no immobility);
• employees are aware of what is being paid elsewhere and want to move to gain the highest possible wage; and
• employees have equal abilities, and there are no barriers to prevent them moving and entering another industry.

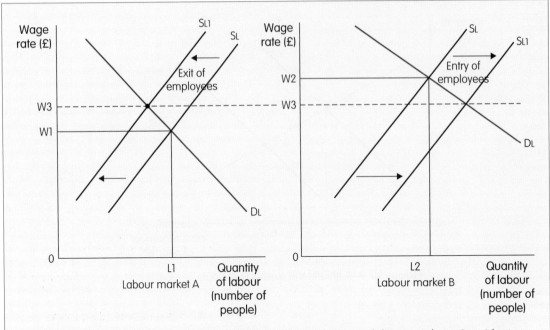

Figure 15.10 Shifts in supply bringing about equilibrium between labour markets. Consider two labour markets that are in equilibrium: market A is in equilibrium at the wage rate W1 and the quantity of labour L1; market B is in equilibrium at the wage rate W2 and the quantity of labour L2. If there was perfect mobility, then employees would leave market A and enter market B, attracted by the higher wages. The supply curve for labour in market A would shift to the left; the supply curve for labour in market B would shift to the right. This process would continue until the wages were equal and there was no further incentive for movement.

In reality, wage differences obviously do exist, for the following reasons.

- Movement between industries is limited by geographical and occupational immobility. For example, there can be significant differences in the workforce in terms of skills and natural abilities; this can prevent employees moving easily from one market to another. Also differences in the cost of living in regions can make moving from one area to another difficult.

- Jobs differ significantly in terms of working conditions and job satisfaction; this naturally affects people's willingness to do them.

- Lack of information can be a factor, because employees may not know what jobs are available elsewhere and so wage differences may continue.

These reasons mean that some people earn considerably more than others. If, for example, the supply of labour is limited (perhaps because of the need for special skills, talents, or specialized training) and/or demand for labour is high, then the equilibrium wage rate is likely to be high (see Figure 15.11a). If, however, the supply of labour is high (perhaps because it is an unskilled job) and the demand for labour is low (perhaps because it does not generate high revenues for the firm), then the wage rate will be much lower (see Figure 15.11b).

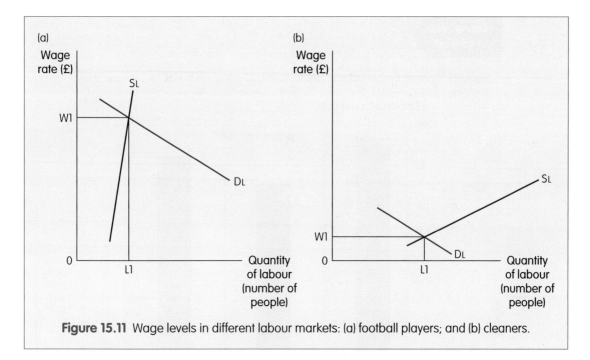

Figure 15.11 Wage levels in different labour markets: (a) football players; and (b) cleaners.

What do you think?

Men and women still tend to follow very different career paths. Approximately 25 per cent of female employees undertake administrative or secretarial work, whilst men are most likely to be managers, senior officials, or in skilled trades. Why do you think this is?

Monopsony in the labour market

The analysis so far has assumed a competitive labour market in which an individual firm is able to hire as many employees as it wishes at the given wage rate. This is because a firm is so small relative to the industry that however many people it employs, it does not affect the industry demand for labour and therefore does not affect the equilibrium wage rate.

However, in some markets, one or more firms may dominate the recruitment and employment of staff. In this case, the employer has what is called **monopsony** power, and this will alter the equilibrium wage and employment level.

Imagine that there is one employer in an industry facing an upward-sloping labour supply curve. To employ more, the employer must offer higher wages. We assume that this higher wage will have to be offered to the additional employee and all previous employees. The extra cost is therefore higher than is suggested by the supply curve for labour.

Imagine you hire one person for £10 an hour, then increase the wage to £11 to recruit a second. The marginal cost of labour is now the additional £11 plus the £1 to the first employee—that is, the marginal cost is £12. As more employees are recruited, the marginal

Figure 15.12 shows the annual earnings for men and women in the UK for 2011 and 2012.

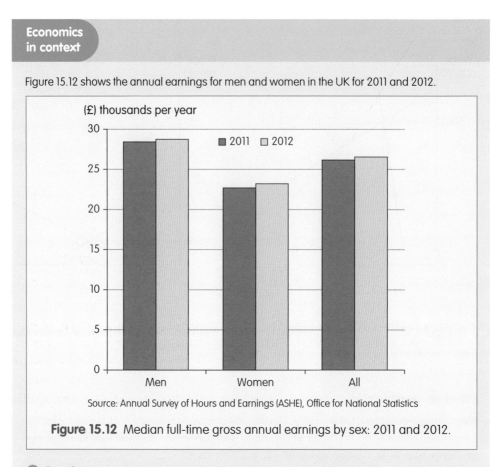

Source: Annual Survey of Hours and Earnings (ASHE), Office for National Statistics

Figure 15.12 Median full-time gross annual earnings by sex: 2011 and 2012.

② Questions

Why do you think earnings for men and women increased from 2011 to 2012?

Why do you think that men earn more than women on average? Is this evidence of sex discrimination?

Twenty-seven EU governments recently agreed to cap bonuses at 100 per cent of a banker's annual salary, or 200% if shareholders approve. The aim is to curb the sort of high-risk lending linked to bonuses that contributed to the financial crash in 2008. Banks will also have to hold more money in their reserves. The UK government has been more reluctant to limit bankers' bonuses as it was worried that bankers might seek work outside the UK and that it might have a limited effect because banks might simply increase the basic salary, for example. The UK's financial sector has a dominant position in Europe, handling by far the highest number of trades daily.

② Question

Why do you think some bankers receive high earnings?

Do you think bankers' bonuses should be taxed?

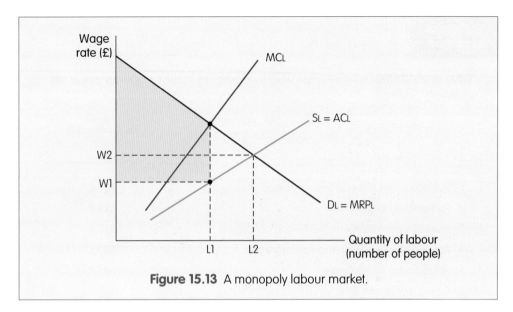

Figure 15.13 A monopoly labour market.

cost will diverge from the supply curve (which basically shows the average cost of employees—that is, the wage rate paid to each one). This is illustrated in Table 15.1 below.

Put into practice

Explain why the marginal cost of the fifth worker in Table 15.1 is £18 when the average cost (the wage) is only £14.

A profit-maximizing employer will employ staff up to the level at which the marginal revenue product of labour (MRPL) equals the marginal cost of labour. This is where L1 employees are employed at a wage rate of W1. Employees beyond L1 are not employed because the extra cost (taking account of the fact that wages would have to be increased not only to the additional worker, but all those before) exceeds the value of their additional output.

As we might expect, the effect of monopsony power is to push down wages below the level that they would achieve in the free market (W2); also, fewer people are employed (L1 compared to L2). The shaded area in Figure 15.13 represents the difference between the wage that each worker is receiving and the value of his or her additional output.

Table 15.1 Illustration of monopsony in the labour market

Number of employees	Wage rate per hour (£)	Total cost of labour per hour (£)	Marginal cost per hour (£)
1	10	10	–
2	11	22	12
3	12	36	14
4	13	52	16
5	14	70	18

Table 15.2   Median full-time gross weekly earnings by major occupation group; UK, April 2012

Major occupation group	All £ per week
All	505.9
1 - Managers, directors and senior officials	738.4
2 - Professional occupations	694.3
3 - Associate professional and technical occupations	575.0
4 - Administrative and secretarial occupations	393.1
5 - Skilled trades occupations	465.7
6 - Caring, leisure and other service occupations	332.7
7 - Sales and customer service occupations	323.3
8 - Process, plant and machine operatives	426.4
9 - Elementary occupations	333.0

Source: ONS

? Question

Using supply and demand analysis explain the differences in wages shown in Table 15.2.

If employees were well organized, perhaps in a trade union, they would try to recover some of the shaded area that represents a 'zone of bargaining'. If employees could exert their power and be rewarded fully for the additional revenue that their extra output generates, then each one would be paid a wage suggested by the MRPL curve. Their ability to do this depends on their power, which in turn depends on factors such as the effect of any strike action and how easy it would be to replace them.

▦ Limitations of the marginal revenue product model of wage determination

Whilst using supply and demand analysis in the labour market provides some very useful insights into why certain jobs pay more than others, it does not fully explain wage levels in a mixed economy. This is because of the following reasons.

- In some sectors—particularly the service sector—the actual productivity of an employee cannot easily be measured. What is the productivity of a receptionist, a welfare officer, or a security guard? If it is difficult to measure the marginal revenue product, this may limit the value of demand and supply analysis.

- The output of some employees has no market value—for example, librarians, teachers, and priests—and so their marginal revenue product cannot be valued.

- There are many markets. Whilst the theory of supply and demand may work, actually analysing the determinants of wages can be difficult because there are so many different labour markets. The demand for taxi drivers in London is very different from the demand in Dundee. The supply of motorbike couriers in the south-east of England may be different from the supply in Wales. 'The' labour market is therefore made up of millions of labour markets, each with its own supply and demand conditions.

- In the public sector, the government determines the wage rate rather than market forces (although it is likely to compare public sector pay with private sector pay). In these cases, the wages that are determined by supply and demand will probably influence the wages paid for these jobs, but market analysis does not effectively explain what happens.

Minimum wages

On 1 April 1999, the UK government introduced a national minimum wage (NMW). This set an hourly rate below which employers could not go. There are three rates: a development rate for those under the age of 18; one for employees between the ages of 18 and 21; and one for those aged 22 and over.

The arguments for the NMW are that:

- it ensures a 'living' wage—that is, one that is perceived as fair;
- it should mean that fewer people have to receive benefits and this should help to shift the aggregate supply function in the economy to the right; and
- it should help to reduce the inequality between the low-income and high-income groups.

The arguments against the NMW include that:

- it raises costs and may reduce firms' profits, which may reduce funds for investment (the higher costs may also lead to higher prices for consumers) and may reduce their competitiveness overseas and
- it creates unemployment by raising the price of labour.

In Figure 15.14, imagine that the labour market is at equilibrium at the wage W0 and the quantity of labour L0. If a minimum wage above equilibrium is introduced, then the quantity of labour supplied is L1, but the quantity demanded is L2. Those who are in work are earning more, but the total number in work is reduced.

The impact of overall earnings depends on the wage elasticity of demand for labour. If demand for labour is wage elastic, then the higher wage leads to a proportionately higher

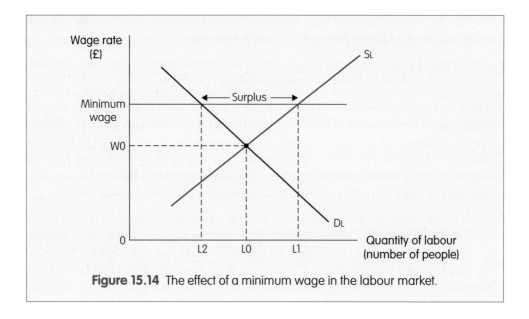

Figure 15.14 The effect of a minimum wage in the labour market.

fall in the quantity demanded and overall earnings decrease for those still in work (see Figure 15.15a). If demand is wage inelastic, then the higher wage leads to a proportionately lower fall in the quantity demanded and overall earnings increase for those in jobs (see Figure 15.15b) but there has been an increase in unemployment.

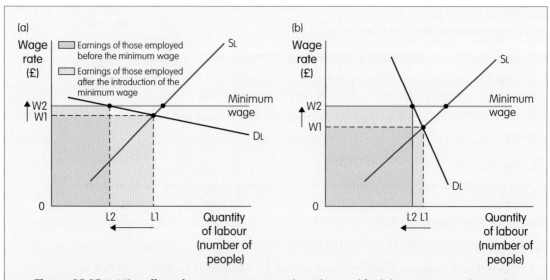

Figure 15.15 (a) The effect of a minimum wage when demand for labour is wage elastic (the introduction of a minimum wage above equilibrium leads to a fall in the overall earnings of those employed); (b) The effect of a minimum wage when demand for labour is wage inelastic (the introduction of a minimum wage above equilibrium increases the earnings of those employed).

Case study

According to a recent report wages in the UK have fallen more in real terms in the current economic downturn than ever before. On top of the rising cost of living, a third of workers who stayed in the same job saw a wage cut or freeze between 2010 and 2011 according to the Institute for Fiscal Studies. Average real hourly wages fell faster in the private sector than the public sector over the last few years.

In 2009, the average public-sector worker earned about £16.60 per hour, which dropped to about £15.80 in 2011. The hourly pay for private-sector workers in 2009 was just over £15.10 and fell to about £13.60 in 2011.

The IFS analysis looked at salaries in real terms, which takes the inflation rate into account. It showed many UK companies, particularly smaller businesses, have cut wages rather than lay off staff. Larger companies tended to reduce their workforce but maintain wages.

The report also said that lone parents and older workers were not giving up work, which may in part be due to changes to the welfare system. This means that workers may be experiencing greater competition for jobs and hence may be more willing to accept lower wages than before.

Also the IFS said fewer workers are unionised or covered by collective wage agreements and tended to see smaller wage increases.

Office for National Statistics (ONS) data indicated 2.51 million people were out of work in the three months to April.

❓ Questions

1   Why is the demand for labour a derived demand?

2   What is meant by real wages?

3   Using the data in Table 15.3 explain why households in the UK may have found themselves worse off between 2008 and 2013.

4   Analyse four possible reasons why real wages might have fallen. Illustrate your answer using diagrams.

5   Does it matter if real wages in the UK have fallen?

Table 15.3   Price increases on selected goods

Goods	Price (£) 2008	Price (£) 2013	Increase
Unleaded petrol (litre)	0.89	1.37	54%
Milk (pint)	0.45	0.46	2%
Bread (white loaf 800g)	1.13	1.40	19%
Oven ready chicken (kg)	3.03	3.08	2%
Wine 175ml glass	2.90 (2011)	3.25	11%
Heating oil (1,000 litres)	610.97 (2011)	643.39	5%
Average weekly wage	416.00	447.00	7%

Source: ONS

Review questions

1 Explain why the demand for labour is downward-sloping

2 To what extent does labour productivity determine the demand for labour?

3 Explain the effect on the market wage rate of an increase in demand for labour.

4 What is the effect on the market wage of an increase in the supply of labour?

5 Explain why merchant bankers are paid so much in comparison with teachers.

6 Explain the effect of a minimum wage above the equilibrium wage rate.

7 Why is the marginal cost of labour above the average cost of labour in a monopsony?

8 Is having a national minimum wage a good thing? Explain your reasons for or against.

Put into practice

1 Using a diagram show the effects on the equilibrium wage and number of people employed if the demand for labour falls. Assume the supply of labour is wage inelastic.

2 Using a diagram show the effect on the equilibrium wages and quantity of people employed of an increase in supply of labour.

Assignment questions

1 Research wage differentials in the UK between different occupations. Analyse the reasons why these differences exist.

2 Research the proposal for a Living Wage. Do you think employers should pay a Living Wage?

Key learning points

- The demand for labour is derived from the demand for the final product.
- Profit-maximizing firms employ workers up to the point at which the marginal revenue product of labour equals the marginal cost of labour.
- A monopsony occurs when there is a major employer in an industry.
- The wage and employment decisions depend on the nature of the labour market.
- In some markets, productivity may be difficult to measure; in other markets, there is no saleable output.

Learn more

There are many different forms of labour market. In the UK, for example, the National Health Service (NHS) employs a high proportion of doctors and nurses. To learn more about these labour markets, visit the Online Resource Centre.

 Visit our Online Resource Centre at **http://www.oxfordtextbooks.co.uk/orc/gillespie_ econ3e/** for test questions and further information on topics covered in this chapters.

Advise the Government

Whichever political party you are, being in government is no easy task. You are faced by many competing demands, limited resources, and lots to do in a restricted amount of time before the next election. In this section we consider some of the key microeconomic issues facing governments, and ask you to help advise whoever is power on what they should do.

1. SHOULD ENERGY BE PROVIDED BY THE GOVERNMENT?

In many countries in recent years households have suffered from high energy prices at a time when their incomes have not been growing quickly. This has squeezed their real incomes. In some cases private energy firms have been blamed for abusing their monopoly power. Some politicians believe essentials such as energy must be provided by the government, while others believe the market can lead to a better deal for consumers.

Research this issue and analyse the case for and against the government owning all energy providers.

Advise the government on whether to allow private providers of energy in its country.

In your analysis you might want to consider issues such as prices, consumer surplus, community surplus, private and social costs and benefits, fairness, efficiency, innovation, monopolies

2. SHOULD THE GOVERNMENT BAN TAKEOVERS?

Every year there are some high profile takeovers that cause a great deal of controversy in the media. Some analysts believe that takeovers can lead to more efficiency; others worry about issues such as monopoly power.

Research the issue of takeovers and analyse the case for and against the government banning them.

Advise the government on the policy you think it should adopt towards takeovers.

In your analysis you might want to consider issues such as allocative efficiency, productive efficiency, X inefficiency, dynamic efficiency, monopolies, oligopoly, community surplus, innovation, research and development, economies and diseconomies of scale.

SHOULD THERE BE A MINIMUM PRICE FOR ALCOHOL?

The UK government has been considering imposing a minimum price of alcohol sold in retail outlets.

Research this issue and analyse the case for and against this proposal. Advise the UK government on whether it should go ahead this proposal.

In your analysis you might want to consider issues such as negative externalities, demerit goods, indirect taxes, consumer surplus.

Macroeconomics

PART 2

Introduction to macroeconomics

Microeconomics focuses on individual markets. In this chapter we start to take an overview of the economy as a whole. The economy is made up of many individual markets. This chapter introduces some of the key issues in macroeconomics. We then analyse how the government might try to control the economy and examine the objectives it might have.

LEARNING OBJECTIVES

By the end of this chapter, you should be able to:

✓ explain the meaning of macroeconomics;

✓ explain government economic objectives;

✓ explain government policy instruments;

✓ explain the possible conflicts of government economic objectives.

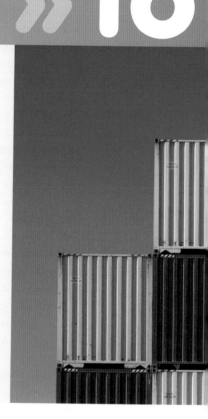

▓ Introduction

In the previous chapters, we have been studying microeconomic issues. We have looked at the demand for and supply of a particular product, and examined the different structures that can exist in various types of market. This form of analysis helps us to explain issues such as:

- why the price of a particular product is high or low;
- why someone working in one industry gets paid more than someone working elsewhere; and
- why firms in some industries can earn more profits than others.

These are all microeconomic issues.

However, we may also want to examine the economy on a larger (or macro) scale. For example, we may be interested in the general price level in an economy rather than the price of one product. We may want to examine the average wage rate in the economy as a whole or the total amount being produced in a country rather than focus on one industry.

Macroeconomics tackles all of these issues. Building on the analysis covered in microeconomics, macroeconomics takes more of an overview and focuses on big issues that affect the economy as a whole.

In microeconomics, we developed an understanding of a series of concepts and models, such as supply and demand analysis, and marginal cost and marginal revenue. We were then able to apply this understanding to a range of markets and market structures. We saw how supply and demand conditions affect the price of oil, housing, labour, and concert tickets. Using our economic tools, we could analyse many different markets to understand changes within them. The same is true in macroeconomics.

In the following chapters, we will develop an understanding of many different areas of the economy, such as households, government, and firms. We will put this understanding together to build a model of the economy that includes areas such as the money market, the labour market, the capital goods market, and the market for final goods and services. We will analyse how a change in interest rates, taxation, or government spending affects all of these markets, and we will be able to trace the effect through to the impact on national income, growth, prices, employment, the government's budget, and the trade position. In essence, we will be building a model of the whole economy, and learning how the different elements fit together and interact with each other. The analytical tools that you gain will allow you to analyse any economy in the world and to appreciate some of the fundamental issues within them.

By the end of these chapters on macroeconomics, you should be able to form a view on the policies that any government should consider adopting given the position of its economy. However, you will also come to realize how difficult it is actually trying to control an economy made up of millions of households, employees, and firms, all with their own objectives, constraints, expectations, and experiences. Sometimes, policy decisions do not lead to the result that you expected—especially when you are dealing with as many different complex relationships as there are within any economy.

Economic change has a real impact on people's lives. It affects whether they have a job, what they do, whether they can afford to buy a house, whether they have a good standard of living, and whether they can afford to start a family. Macroeconomic analysis is therefore important to governments because they have a responsibility for the state of the economy and are often assessed on their economic performance. In fact, how well the economy is doing is a very important factor in determining how people vote. A government will set objectives and then try to influence the economy to achieve these, using its policy tools.

▢ Government economic objectives

Typical government objectives include achieving the following.

- **Economic growth** Economic growth measures how much the income of an economy is growing over time. This is often seen as a very important target for governments. This is because, with more income in the economy, people can afford more products and may have a better quality of life. Interestingly, however, there is increasingly debate over whether having more money does necessarily lead to a better standard of living (if you work an 80-hour week, you may earn more, but not enjoy life much). This debate is discussed in Chapter 20. Even so, most governments still try to make sure that their economies are growing. Economic growth can provide more income, more jobs, and economic progress. Economic growth can be achieved by moving from inside the production possibility frontier onto the frontier or by an outward shift of the frontier.

- **Stable prices** In most economies, prices in general increase by a small percentage each year. For most firms and people, this is not a major problem; they can plan for it and take it into account when setting their own prices or bargaining for their wages. However, sometimes prices can increase unexpectedly or at fast rates. This can become a problem in many ways. For example, some people will find that they cannot afford products and will be worse off, and the country's products are likely to be expensive when they try to sell them abroad, which could limit sales. This is why governments usually try to keep prices relatively stable. An increase in the general price level is known as inflation, and governments usually try to keep this at a low and predictable rate. The causes, consequences, and possible cures of inflation are examined in Chapter 26.

- **Low levels of unemployment** If people are unemployed, then they are not working. This means that they are not generating output and are not earning money. This is inefficient and a waste of resources. It is also a drain on a government's own income, because it will probably have to pay benefits to the unemployed people. Unemployment can also lead to frustration and social discontent with the government, and so, not surprisingly, the government will usually try to reduce it! The causes, consequences, and cures of unemployment are examined in Chapter 25.

- **A favourable balance of trade** All countries are involved in trade. They buy goods and services from abroad (these are called imports), and they sell products overseas (these are called exports). The amount that a country buys and sells abroad depends on many factors, such as the relative price of products, their quality, and the incomes in the different countries. By trading abroad, a country can consume outside its own production possibility frontier (PPF) (see Chapter 28). A government is therefore likely to encourage trade, but may want to make sure that the imports and exports are reasonably balanced. If there are too many imports, then this leads to money leaving the economy; if there are too many exports, then this may mean that foreign governments retaliate because money is flowing out of their economies. Governments will monitor their country's balance of trade and ensure that it is at an appropriate level.

Put into practice

Which of the following statements are true and which are false?

a. Economic growth leads to an inward shift of the production possibility frontier

b. If prices rise faster than nominal wages real wages fall

c. Export revenue comes from products bought from abroad

d. The demand for labour is derived from the demand for products

Whilst these are the four main economic objectives that governments have, there will be others. For example, the government may be interested in the distribution of income in its economy and the relative income of different regions and the impact of the economy on the environment.

▇ Policy instruments

To achieve its objectives, a government may use economic tools such as the following (see Figure 16.1).

- Fiscal policy This involves changing the level of government spending and taxation and benefit rates.
- **Monetary policy** This involves controlling the money supply within an economy and changing interest rates.

By changing the different elements of fiscal and monetary policy, a government will try to influence the total level of demand in the economy (this is called aggregate demand) or the total level of supply in the economy (this is called aggregate supply). For example, the government might:

- cut corporation tax which is the tax on company profits, leaving firms with more money to invest (here, fiscal policy is affecting demand in the economy);
- increase its own spending in areas such as health and defence to generate more demand (again, raising demand);

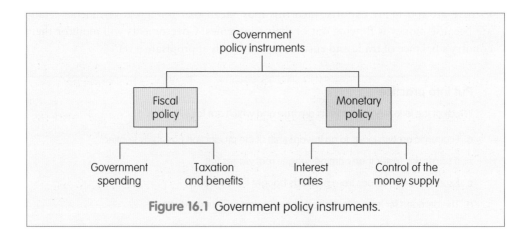

Figure 16.1 Government policy instruments.

In the 2013 Budget the government changed the remit of the Monetary Policy Committee of the Bank of England which would allow it to give explicit guidance on how long it will keep interest rates at a given level. This is intended to give reassurance to businesses and households rather than have the uncertainty of whether the cost of borrowing would go up or down. The hope is that this would stimulate spending and growth. The Bank retained its inflation target of 2 per cent but was given the powers to use a wider range of monetary instruments to achieve this.

❓ Questions

Analyse how changes in interest rates might affect demand in the economy

Analyse how greater confidence in the economy might help demand in the economy.

* make it cheaper for people to borrow money by lowering interest rates (this is an example of monetary policy);
* make it cheaper and easier for firms to borrow money to invest in new equipment (again monetary policy); or
* reduce unemployment benefits to encourage more people to work and increase the supply of labour (this is fiscal policy affecting aggregate supply).

Monetary and fiscal policy are examined in more detail in Chapters 23 and 22, respectively.

Aggregate demand and aggregate supply will interact with the price level bringing about equilibrium in the whole economy in the same way as it does in a particular market.

What do you think?

How important are changes in interest rates to you?

After several years where annual growth has been around 9 per cent India's economy has slowed rapidly recently to about half this. Indians are now facing rising prices and high interest rates as well as higher rates of unemployment.

Manufacturing has been particularly badly hit. Companies say they are struggling to cope with higher costs of supplies. They also claim they are being taxed too heavily which is deterring investment. Manufacturers are asking the government to invest more.

India needs high growth just to create jobs for new entrants to the labour market.

Its population of 1.2bn people is growing at 1.4 per cent a year, almost three times the rate for China.

Growth rates in Asia

- Australia 3.1%
- China 7.7%
- Indonesia 6.0%
- Malaysia 4.1%
- Thailand 5.3%
- Vietnam 4.8%

Source: OECD/IMF

? Questions

What macroeconomic problems are facing the Indian government?

What actions would you recommend that the Indian government takes to improve its economy?

▦ Policy debates

Inevitably, using government policy to affect the economy is quite complex and not a precise science. If we cut income tax, for example, and expect people to spend more, then we may be surprised and find that they decide to save it! Instead, they may spend it much later than we thought they would, so the impact does not occur at the right time. Alternatively, at the time that we cut taxes, other changes in the economy may offset the expected benefits of this. Changes in economic policy can therefore have unpredictable effects.

As well as the practical problems of intervention, economists often differ in their diagnosis of a problem and their views of how best to solve it. Common areas of debate include the following.

- How much should the government intervene in the economy? Can it effectively control the many different aspects of demand and supply, using a range of policy instruments? If so, the government can attempt to 'fine-tune' the economy. Or is it better to use only a few key instruments to try to bring about broad changes in the nature of the economy? In the 1950s and 1960s, there was a belief in the UK that fine-tuning could work. In the 1980s and the next 30 years many economists have favoured a broader, less interventionist approach, but there is still much disagreement about what this means in practice. The recent global economic crisis has, for example, led many economists and politicians to revert to a more interventionist approach to try to stimulate the economy.

- Which policy instruments are the most effective? Is it better to rely mainly on fiscal policy or monetary policy, or are they both as effective as each other? To boost demand in the economy, does a tax cut work better than reducing the cost of borrowing? Again, there is much debate here and views change over time. Generally, in the last decade, the UK government has favoured interest rates as the main policy tool to influence the economy, but obviously continues to use a range of other spending, tax, and benefit programmes to support this. More recently, much greater levels of government spending have been thought to be necessary in many economies to boost demand levels.

Put into practice

Which of the following are true and which are false?

a. Interest rates are part of monetary policy

b. Cutting taxes tends to decreases demand in the economy

c. Increasing growth is a typical government objective

d. An objective shows how to achieve a policy

▧ Policy conflicts

Even if it were clear which policy instruments were best, life would still be difficult for governments! This is because achieving all of their economic objectives at the same time may prove problematic. For example, to reduce unemployment, a government may want to encourage more spending in the economy (perhaps through lower taxes and lower interest rates). However, as we saw in our microeconomic analysis, an increase in demand may lead to higher prices, which could cause higher inflation: achieving one target has been at the expense of another. Similarly, if an economy were importing too much, then one possible solution to this would be to slow the economy's growth; with less growth in income, the amount of imported products that people were buying would probably fall. However, the consequence of this would be less demand, as well as more unemployment within the economy. Again, achieving one goal has had a negative effect on others. Of course, by using the right combination of policies, it may be possible to achieve all of the goals—or at least reach an acceptable compromise. However, the government may have to decide what the priority at any moment is and on its general focus in terms of policy instruments. Remember, any decision will have an opportunity cost.

What do you think?

What do you think should be the economic priority of the government at the moment? Justify your answer

---

Put into practice

Which of the following are true and which are false?

a. Increased spending may help growth but lead to higher prices

b. Increased spending may help growth but lead to more imports

c. Increased growth will cause more exports

d. Increased growth will tend to increase unemployment

Case study

The following is a description of the Greek economy taken from the CIA Factbook.

Greece has a capitalist economy with a public sector accounting for about 40% of GDP and with per capita GDP about two-thirds that of the leading european economies. Tourism provides 15% of GDP. Immigrants make up nearly one-fifth of the work force, mainly in agricultural and unskilled jobs. Greece is a major beneficiary of EU aid, equal to about 3.3% of annual GDP. The Greek economy grew by nearly 4% per year between 2003 and 2007, due partly to infrastructural spending related to the 2004 Athens Olympic Games, and in part to an increased availability of credit, which has sustained record levels of consumer spending. But the economy went into recession in 2009 as a result of the world financial crisis, tightening credit conditions, and Athens' failure to address a growing budget deficit. The economy contracted by 2.3% in 2009, 3.5% in 2010, 6.9% in 2011, and 6.0% in 2012.

Deteriorating public finances, inaccurate and misreported statistics, and consistent underperformance on reforms prompted major credit rating agencies to downgrade Greece's international debt rating in late 2009, and has led the country into a financial crisis. Under intense pressure from the EU and international market participants, the government adopted a medium-term austerity program that includes cutting government spending, decreasing tax evasion, overhauling the health-care and pension systems, and reforming the labor and product markets. Athens, however, faces long-term challenges to push through unpopular reforms in the face of widespread unrest from the country's powerful labor unions and the general public. In April 2010 a leading credit agency assigned Greek debt its lowest possible credit rating; in May 2010, the International Monetary Fund and Euro-Zone governments provided Greece emergency short- and medium-term loans worth $147 billion so that the country could make debt repayments to creditors. In exchange for the largest bailout ever assembled, the government announced combined spending cuts and tax increases totaling $40 billion over three years, on top of the tough austerity measures already taken.

Greece, however, struggled to meet 2010 targets set by the EU and the IMF, especially after Eurostat – the EU's statistical office – revised upward Greece's deficit and debt numbers for 2009 and 2010. European leaders and the IMF agreed in October 2011 to provide Athens a second bailout package of $169 billion. The second deal however, calls for Greece's creditors to write down a significant portion of their Greek government bond holdings. In exchange for the second loan Greece has promised to introduce an additional $7.8 billion in austerity measures during 2013-15. However, these massive austerity cuts are lengthening Greece's economic recession and depressing tax revenues. Greece's lenders are calling on Athens to step up efforts to increase tax collection, privatize public enterprises, and rein in health spending, and are planning to give Greece more time to shore up its economy and finances. Many investors doubt that Greece can sustain fiscal efforts in the face of a bleak economic outlook, public discontent, and political instability.

Source: https://www.cia.gov/library/publications/the-world-factbook/geos/gr.html

? **Questions**

1 Summarize the economic problems facing Greece.

2 What measures do you think the government might need to take to help the Greek economy recover?

Review questions

1   How does microeconomics differ from macroeconomics?
2   What are the four main economic objectives of a government and why do they matter?
3   Explain how the economic objectives of a government might conflict.
4   Explain what is meant by monetary policy.
5   What is meant by fiscal policy?
6   Outline the meaning of inflation.
7   What is meant by aggregate demand?
8   Explain what is meant by aggregate supply.

Put into practice

1   Visit the website of the Organisation of Economic Cooperation and Development and the International Monetary Fund and outline three significant economic issues facing the UK at the moment.
2   Outline two measures you would take if you were in power to improve the UK economy. Justify your choices.

Assignment question

1   Research the performance of your own economy over the last five years and consider any forecasts for the future. Compare your findings with one other economy of your choice (perhaps a near neighbour?). Summarize the performance of these economies in terms of meeting the key economic objectives outlined in this chapter. Overall how would you rate the performance of your own economy? Why do you think it is outperforming or underperforming the other economy you have chosen?

Key learning points

- Macroeconomic analysis focuses on the economy as a whole rather than one market within it.
- Typical economic objectives include stable prices, economic growth, a favourable trade situation, and low unemployment.
- The government uses policies such as monetary and fiscal policy to achieve its economic objectives.

- Achieving all of the government's objectives simultaneously may be difficult; at times, there may be a conflict of objectives.

Learn more

To learn more about the performance of the UK economy over recent years, visit the Online Resource Centre.

 Visit our Online Resource Centre at http://www.oxfordtextbooks.co.uk/orc/gillespie_ econ3e/ for test questions and further information on topics covered in this chapter.

Equilibrium in the economy

In this chapter, we examine how equilibrium in the economy is brought about. To do this, we consider what is known as the circular flow of income and the conditions necessary for equilibrium in the economy. In microeconomics, we examined supply and demand in one particular market. In macroeconomics, we consider the aggregate, or total, supply and demand for the whole economy.

LEARNING OBJECTIVES

By the end of this chapter, you should be able to:

✓ distinguish between injections and withdrawals;

✓ explain the conditions necessary for equilibrium in the economy and how the economy moves toward equilibrium;

✓ explain the factors that can influence aggregate demand;

✓ analyse the multiplier effect caused by a change in aggregate demand;

✓ explain the factors that can influence aggregate supply.

▓ Introduction

We will begin our study of macroeconomics by considering how equilibrium in an economy is determined—that is, what determines how much an economy is producing and earning. This analysis will help us to understand macro issues such as economic growth, unemployment, and the impact of government policy changes. Obviously, some economies generate more income than others. The USA, for example, earns much more than Papua New Guinea. This chapter examines the reasons why an economy settles at a particular level of income; with this understanding, we can then consider how a government might increase the income of a country.

Equilibrium in the economy

In microeconomics, we saw that equilibrium in a particular market occurs when demand equals supply. In macroeconomics, equilibrium in the economy as a whole will occur when the total (or 'aggregate') planned demand in the economy for all final goods and services equals the total (or 'aggregate') supply of these products. Thus, for equilibrium in the economy, we have:

Aggregate demand (AD) = Aggregate supply (AS)

To analyse how and why equilibrium occurs in an economy, we first consider the circular flow of income, which highlights how spending and income flow around an economy, and how equilibrium is reached.

The circular flow of income

Imagine a simple economy in which there are only firms and households. Firms are producing output. Households are employed by firms and earning income, which is then spent buying goods and services. This is called a two-sector economy because it contains only firms and households. In this scenario, the value of the output produced by producers equals the income earned by households. For example, if the economy produces £100 of goods, then the money for this is earned as income in some form by households (either as wages, rental on land or capital goods, or profit). In the simplest of models, this is then spent on buying the goods and services produced by the firms; this spending is known as consumption spending (C). Money flows around the economy from firms to households, and back again—hence the term 'circular flow' (see Figure 17.1). In this situation, we can see that the output of the final goods and services, the income earned, and the expenditure are all equal:

Output (Q) = Income (Y) = Expenditure (E)

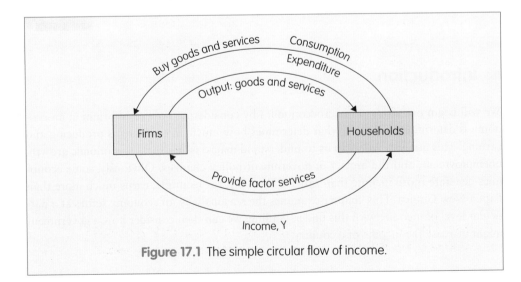

Figure 17.1 The simple circular flow of income.

Of course, this is a very limited model in which there are only two sectors and everything that is produced is sold. What we can now do is to extend the analysis by adding in other sectors of the economy (namely, the foreign sector and the government); this will introduce the concepts of injections and withdrawals into the circular flow of income.

Economics in context

Table 17.1   GNP per person in $ = income per person

Country name	2011
Norway	88,870
Qatar	80,440
Luxembourg	77,390
Switzerland	76,350
Denmark	60,160
Sweden	53,170
Australia	49,790
Netherlands	49,660
United States	48,620
Austria	48,170
Finland	47,760
Belgium	45,930
Canada	45,550
Japan	44,900
Germany	44,230
Singapore	42,930
France	42,420
United Arab Emirates	40,760
Ireland	39,150
United Kingdom	37,780

Source: World Bank

? Questions

Why do you think the income per person in Table 17.1 differs so much between countries?
What actions do you think a government could take to increase its income per person?

Injections (J)

Injections (J) into the economy represent spending on final goods and services in addition to households' spending. These represent demand for goods and services in addition to consumption spending (C). Injections include the following.

- **Investment (I)** This is spending on capital goods by firms. It includes the purchase of new equipment and machinery, which will be used to produce more in the future. Investment also includes stockbuilding: if stocks increase, then firms are assumed to have invested in these (intentionally or not). Note that investment in economics is referring to the purchase of items that will enable future production. It does not mean 'investing' money into banks; this is called savings in economics.

- **Government spending (G)** This is spending by the government on final goods and services, such as health and education.

- **Exports (X)** This represents the spending from abroad on an economy's final goods and services. If UK output is sold to US buyers, for example, this is export demand.

So, in summary, in addition to consumption spending in this economy, we have:

Injections (J) = Investment (I) + Government spending (G) + Exports (X)

All of these injections are assumed to be unrelated to the level of output or income, as shown in Figure 17.2. They are, therefore, exogeneous (or autonomous) of the level of income. This means that they are determined by factors other than the level of national income; the following are some examples of the influences on these factors.

- The level of investment in an economy (I) may be influenced by the cost of borrowing (interest rates) and expectations of future profits (which may be influenced by how the economy will do in the future), rather than the level of national income at the moment. Cheaper borrowing is likely to encourage more investment as is the expectation of higher profits, perhaps, as an economy recovers. (Investment is examined in greater

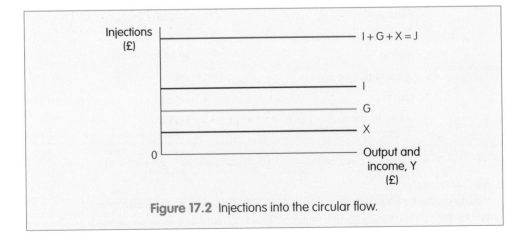

Figure 17.2 Injections into the circular flow.

detail in Chapter 21.) The level of investment depends on the returns that managers think will occur in the future rather than what the level of income is now. The economy may be doing badly, but managers may invest more in facilities and equipment if they think that it will grow quickly in the future.

- The level of government spending on final goods and services in an economy (G) may be influenced by government policy, and its view about the appropriate levels of government intervention and expenditure. A government may decide that it wants to boost demand and increase its spending (which is an expansionist policy) or it may decide to reduce demand by cutting its spending (which is a contractionary policy); these decisions depend on government policy and may depend on what it thinks is going to happen in the economy in the future. There is no definite, predictable relationship between the level of government spending and the current level of national income; the likely position of the economy in the future, rather than where it is now, determines government spending because changes in spending take so long to bring about and take effect. The government spending (G) considered is on final goods and services; it does not include

Economics in context

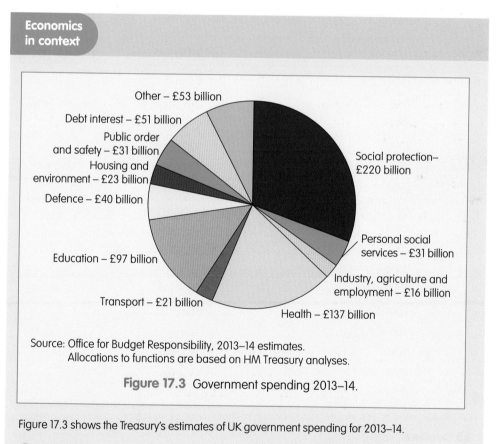

Source: Office for Budget Responsibility, 2013–14 estimates.
Allocations to functions are based on HM Treasury analyses.

Figure 17.3 Government spending 2013–14.

Figure 17.3 shows the Treasury's estimates of UK government spending for 2013–14.

? Questions

How would you change the way that the government spends its money? Why?

transfer payments (that is, payments such as benefits) because these simply redistribute income rather than create new demand.

- The level of spending on our exports (X) may be affected by income levels abroad and the exchange rate; it is not determined by the current level of UK income. Just because the UK earns more, for example, does not mean that it exports more; this depends on how much overseas buyers are earning. The influences on a country's level of exports are examined in greater detail in Chapter 28.

Planned injections refer to the amount that the government, firms, and foreigners intend to spend in a given period on final goods and services in an economy. These factors increase the level of aggregate demand in an economy.

Economics in context

Table 17.2 GDP at market prices ($ million) (National income)

	Current prices
1997	835,635
1998	882,718
1999	929,469
2000	975,294
2001	1,019,838
2002	1,068,599
2003	1,136,596
2004	1,199,881
2005	1,262,710
2006	1,333,157
2007	1,412,119
2008	1,440,931
2009	1,401,863
2010	1,466,569
2011	1,516,153

Source: The Blue Book

? Questions

Comment on the changes in UK national income in Table 17.2.

Why do you think these changes might have occurred?

What do you think?

On what do you think the government spends money?
What do you think are the main influences on the amount of government spending in an economy?
What do you think would make firms invest more in capital equipment?

Put into practice

Which of the following statements are true and which are false?

a. Injections are determined by the level of national income.

b. An increase in injections increases aggregate demand.

c. Lower interest rates might encourage spending and boost aggregate demand.

d. Higher exports increase injections into the economy.

Withdrawals (W)

In a four-sector economy, injections add to the demand of households to create the total (or aggregate demand) for final goods or services. However, not all of households' income will be spent on goods and services. This is because of withdrawals. Withdrawals (W) represent income that has been earned by households, but which is not spent on final goods and services in this economy. Withdrawals include the following.

- **Savings (S)** This is income earned by households that is saved rather than spent. People may save by putting money in the bank, for example, or by putting some of their salary into a pension scheme. In general, we would expect more to be saved as income increases. The determinants of consumption and savings are examined in greater detail in Chapter 20.

- **Taxation (T)** This represents revenue taken from firms and households by the government; it is withdrawn from the circular flow and therefore is not spent by them. There are many forms of taxation, such as taxes on income and company profits. Taxation is examined in greater detail in Chapter 22.

- **Imports (M)** This represents spending on foreign goods and services. This means that this spending leaves this economy to be spent elsewhere. It is withdrawn from this economy and creates demand overseas. The influences on a country's level of imports are examined in greater detail in Chapter 28.

So, in summary, we have:

Withdrawals (W) = Savings (S) + Taxation (T) + Imports (M)

Withdrawals are 'leakages' from the economy and reduce the level of demand in the domestic economy.

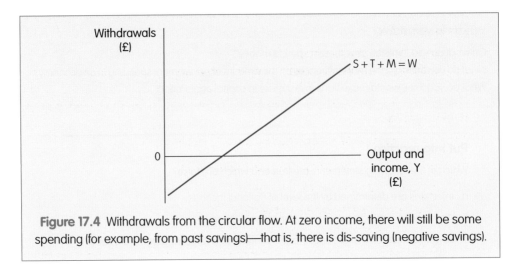

Figure 17.4 Withdrawals from the circular flow. At zero income, there will still be some spending (for example, from past savings)—that is, there is dis-saving (negative savings).

Unlike injections, withdrawals are assumed to be directly related to income (that is, they are a function of income), as shown in Figure 17.4. This is because, as income increases, the following occurs.

- The level of savings tends to increase because households can afford to save more
- The amount paid in tax will increase—for example, people will earn and spend more, so the government will gain more tax revenue from this and businesses will make more profits which lead to more corporation tax being paid
- The amount spent on foreign goods and services will increase. With more income, households will spend more, and some of this spending will be on foreign goods and services. This spending will therefore leave the UK economy.

The circular flow of income including injections and withdrawals is shown in Figure 17.5.

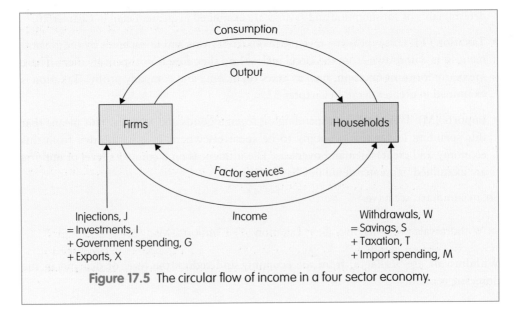

Figure 17.5 The circular flow of income in a four sector economy.

Put into practice

List as many types of tax as you can.

Why do you think all of these taxes exist? For what do they pay?

Put into practice

Which of the following statements are true and which are false?

a. An increase in withdrawals decreases aggregate demand

b. An increase in savings increases withdrawals

c. An increase in exports increases withdrawals

d. A decrease in taxation reduces withdrawals.

▓ Adding in injections and withdrawals to the circular flow

Let us now return to our simple economy with output and income of £100, but now assume that planned withdrawals are £40. This means that, of the £100 produced, £40 of this will not be demanded because households are saving, paying this in tax, or spending this money abroad. Withdrawals reduce aggregate demand. The economy is clearly not in equilibrium unless there is £40 of planned injection—that is, the £40 worth of products that households do not require are wanted by someone else (for example, the government, firms, or foreigners).

If the planned injections do equal the planned withdrawals, then the £40 worth of products produced, but not bought by domestic households, are bought by another group, such as the government. In this case, the aggregate demand in the economy will equal the aggregate supply and the economy will be in equilibrium. So, for equilibrium in the economy, we have that equilibrium will occur when

Planned injections (I + G + X) = Planned withdrawals (S + T + M)

The planned injections equal the planned withdrawals, so all of the output that is not demanded by households is bought by other sectors and the economy is in equilibrium (see Figure 17.6). Aggregate demand equals aggregate supply.

NOTE Individual elements of injections and withdrawals do not need to be equal (for example, the planned Savings does not have to equal the planned Investment), but the overall planned injections must equal the overall planned withdrawals for equilibrium.

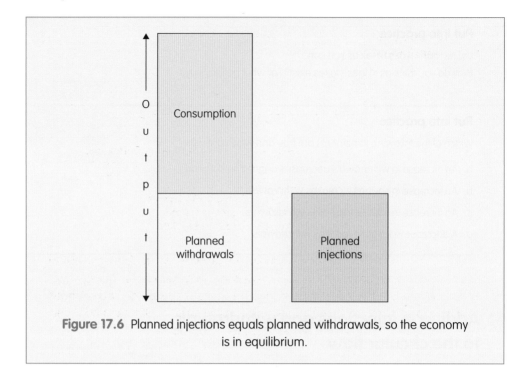

Figure 17.6 Planned injections equals planned withdrawals, so the economy is in equilibrium.

▦ Getting to equilibrium: The adjustment process

Imagine that planned injections are too low compared with planned withdrawals. This will mean that there is not enough demand in the economy. The amount that households do not buy is not completely bought by, say, the government or foreigner buyers. Firms will have to increase their stocks unexpectedly because there is unsold output. This increase in stocks is an unintended form of investment so the actual investment (planned plus unplanned) will equal the planned withdrawals. For example, if planned withdrawals are £40 but planned injections are £10 then there will be an unexpected £30 increase in stocks. Actual injections (planned plus unplanned) are £10 + £30 = £40 and equal planned withdrawals. However, although the actual injections and withdrawals are equal because firms are not doing what they planned they will change their behaviour next period. In this case in the next time period, they will cut back on output, because the demand had been lower than expected; this means that less income is earned in the economy. This will not affect the level of planned injections because they are assumed to be exogenous (independent) of income. However, with less income, there will be less in planned withdrawals, because savings, taxation, and import spending will fall with lower income levels. This process will continue, with income falling leading to lower planned withdrawals, until the levels of planned injections and planned withdrawals are equal. Changes in output and income therefore lead to a change in the level of the planned withdrawals, until the planned injections and the planned withdrawals are equal, and the economy is in equilibrium, as shown in Figure 17.7.

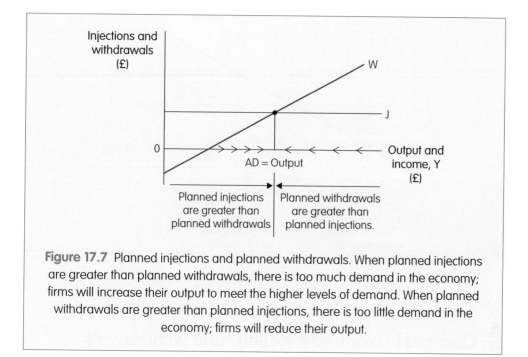

Figure 17.7 Planned injections and planned withdrawals. When planned injections are greater than planned withdrawals, there is too much demand in the economy; firms will increase their output to meet the higher levels of demand. When planned withdrawals are greater than planned injections, there is too little demand in the economy; firms will reduce their output.

On the other hand, if planned injections are too high compared with planned withdrawals, then there will be too much demand in the economy. The demand from the sectors other than households is greater than the output available that is not bought through consumption. Firms will have to de-stock (that is, use up more of their stocks than they intended). This means they will invest less than planned. Once again actual injections will equal planned withdrawals due to unexpected changes in stock levels but the economy is not in equilibrium because plans are not being fulfilled. In the next time period, firms will increase their output because demand was so high, leading to more income in the economy. This will not change the level of injections (because they are exogenous), but will change the level of planned withdrawals. These will increase with more income. This process continues, with firms increasing output, which increases income and therefore withdrawals, until equilibrium is reached where the planned injections and the planned withdrawals are equal.

Equilibrium in the economy is therefore brought about by changes by businesses in output which changes the income in the economy until the planned injections equal the planned withdrawals (see Figure 17.8)

Put into practice

- If planned injections are £300 million and planned withdrawals are £400 million, is the economy in equilibrium or not? Explain why actual injections will equal actual withdrawals.

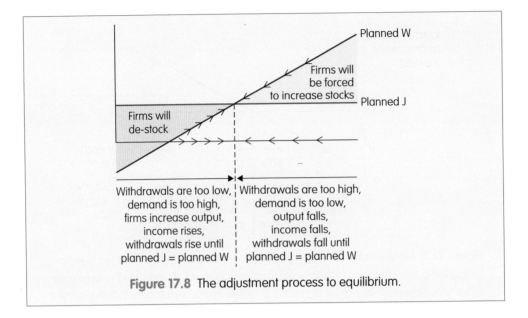

Figure 17.8 The adjustment process to equilibrium.

Changes in planned injections and withdrawals

If the level of planned injections in an economy increases this will lead to higher demand at the existing income level. Planned injections will be higher than planned withdrawals. This will lead firms to run down stocks in the short term. In the long term they will increase output and income. As income increases planned withdrawals will rise and this will continue until once again planned injections equal the planned withdrawals, as shown in Figure 17.9. At this output, the aggregate demand equals aggregate supply.

Government policy that aims to increase national income might therefore focus on increasing planned injections into the economy. For example, the government may do the following:

- offer incentives to encourage firms to expand or undertake more research and development boosting;
- increase its own government spending, perhaps by investing more in education; or
- promote UK goods and services abroad or influence the value of the exchange rate to boost export demand

By contrast if there was an increase in planned withdrawals (perhaps because greater uncertainty increases savings) this will reduce the level of demand in the economy. Businesses will unexpectedly increase stocks but next period will reduce their output. As output and income fall so will planned withdrawals until the new equilibrium is reached. An increase in withdrawals therefore reduces demand and will lead to a lower level of national income.

What do you think?

What type of incentive might a government offer to increase private investment by firms?
What other government actions might encourage investment?

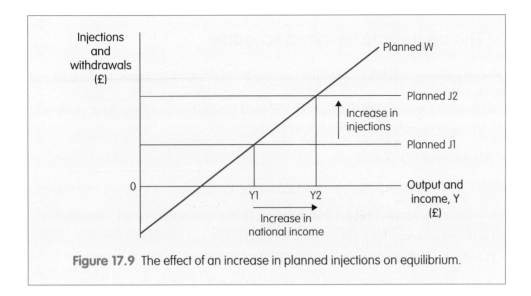

Figure 17.9 The effect of an increase in planned injections on equilibrium.

The changes in injections and withdrawals and their effects are summarized in Table 17.3.

Put into practice

Which of the following statements is true and which are false?

a. For equilibrium in a four-sector economy, savings must equal investment.

b. An increase in exports boosts aggregate demand.

c. An increase in taxation rates reduces aggregate demand.

d. If planned injections are greater than planned withdrawals, national income will fall.

e. If planned injections equal planned withdrawals, the economy is in equilibrium.

f. If aggregate demand increases, national income will increase.

Table 17.3   Changes in injections and withdrawals

Change	Meaning	Effect
An increase in investment	Higher injections	Higher aggregate demand
An increase in exports	Higher injections	Higher aggregate demand
An increase in imports	Higher withdrawals	Lower aggregate demand
An increase in savings	Higher withdrawals	Lower aggregate demand
A decrease in government spending	Lower injections	Lower aggregate demand
A decrease in taxation revenue	Lower withdrawals	Higher aggregate demand

▓ The aggregate demand schedule

How an economy reaches equilibrium can also be analysed using aggregate demand and supply schedules.

Aggregate demand (AD) is equal to the total planned demand for final goods and services in an economy, and is written as follows:

$$AD = C + I + G + X - M$$

where:

- C is the consumption (this is the demand for final goods and services by households);
- I is the investment (this is the demand for final goods and services by firms);
- G is the government spending on final goods and services; and
- X – M equals the exports minus the imports (this represents the overall demand for domestic goods and services resulting from international trade).

In Figure 17.10a, the level of aggregate demand is shown relative to national output and income. The schedule begins at the point F; it is assumed that even if national income were zero, there would still be some spending. For example, households, firms, or the government would use past savings to keep spending. As income increases, the aggregate demand increases, because of greater consumption spending; out of each extra pound earned, households will want to spend a proportion of this on goods and services in this economy.

Equilibrium

Equilibrium occurs when the aggregate demand is exactly equal to the output produced (i.e. aggregate supply). What is being produced is being demanded, so there is no excess demand or supply. This is shown where the aggregate demand schedule crosses the 45° line (this line represents all of the combinations at which demand equals supply)—that is, the equilibrium national income and output is Y1 (see Figure 17.10a). At this level of output, the planned injections must equal the planned withdrawals (see Figure 17.10b), as shown earlier.

At outputs below Y1, the level of aggregate demand is more than national output. This is because the planned injections are more than the planned withdrawals. Over time, firms will produce more output because of the high level of aggregate demand until Y1 is reached. With the higher levels of output and income, the level of planned withdrawals will increase, and at Y1, they equal the level of planned injections.

At outputs above Y1, the aggregate demand is less than national output. This is because the planned injections are less than the planned withdrawals. Firms will reduce output because demand is too low over time until Y1 is reached. As income falls towards Y1, the level of planned withdrawals falls, until it equals planned injections at Y1 and equilbrium occurs.

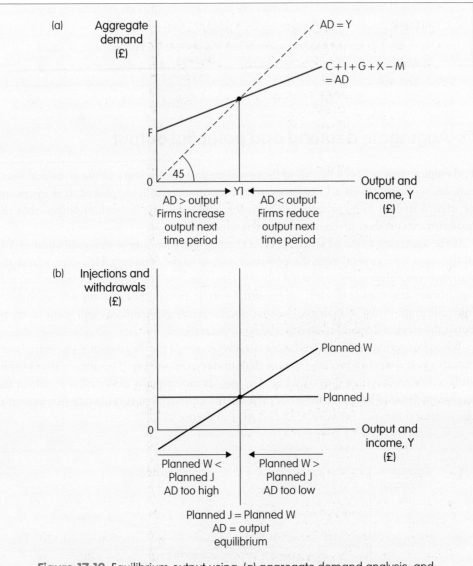

Figure 17.10 Equilibrium output using: (a) aggregate demand analysis; and (b) injections and withdrawals. In (a), the aggregate demand curve slopes upwards because with more income households spend more, and so consumption increases. At zero income, there will still be spending, for example by the government.

Put into practice

Suppose that Y1 is the equilibrium output.

- Below Y1, are the planned injections more or less than the planned withdrawals, or equal to them?

- Above Y1, are the planned injections more or less than the planned withdrawals, or equal to them?
- At Y1, are the planned injections more or less than the planned withdrawals, or equal to them?

Aggregate demand and potential output

Full employment occurs when all of those willing and able to work at the given real wage rate are working. When all resources in an economy are fully employed, it is operating at what is known as its potential output; this represents the maximum output that the economy can produce given its existing resources.

If the aggregate demand schedule is AD1, then the economy is in equilibrium at Y1; in this case, Y1 happens to be the potential output of the economy. However, whilst the economy may always move toward equilibrium, this does not necessarily mean that this equilibrium is always at this level of potential output. In fact, the economy will often settle in equilibrium below its potential output and therefore governments will want to try to boost the level of demand to change the equilibrium level.

When the aggregate demand is below the level required for the economy's potential output, this is known as a recessionary, or deflationary, output gap. This means that output and income are less than they could be. The 'gap' is measured by the amount by which the aggregate demand has to increase to reach the full employment equilibrium (for example, the vertical difference between AD2 and AD1 in Figure 17.11).

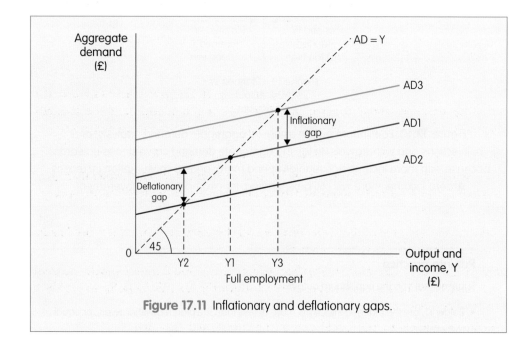

Figure 17.11 Inflationary and deflationary gaps.

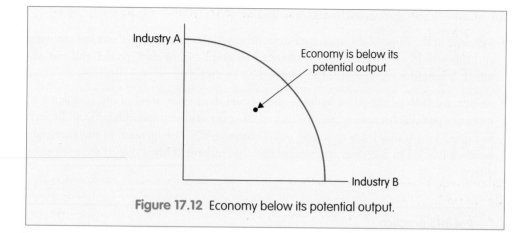

Figure 17.12 Economy below its potential output.

If an economy is below its potential output, then it is operating within the production possibility frontier (PPF). See Figure 17.12.

An inflationary output gap occurs when the aggregate demand is above the level required for potential output. The 'gap' is measured by the amount by which the aggregate demand has to decrease to reach the potential output (for example, the vertical distance between AD3 and AD1 in Figure 17.12). It is called an inflationary gap because, with excess demand, there will be upward pressure on prices—the economy cannot easily meet this level of demand and so firms are likely to put up prices. If there is a sustained increase in prices, this is known as inflation.

The causes and consequences of inflation are examined in greater detail in Chapter 26.

▓ Reflationary policies

Reflationary (or expansionist) fiscal policies occur when the government increases the level of aggregate demand in the economy. To do this, a government could use demand-side policies (that is, policies aimed specifically at changing aggregate demand) such as:

- increasing its own spending on goods and services (increasing G);
- reducing taxes to increase the incomes that customers and firms keep rather than give to the government, which should lead to greater spending (increasing Consumption and Investment);
- reducing taxes placed on goods and services, which should also encourage spending in the economy (increasing Consumption);
- reducing interest rates, which makes borrowing cheaper and therefore should increase spending. It should also discourage savings, because the rewards for doing so are less (increasing Consumption and Investment); and
- encouraging banks to lend, enabling more borrowing and spending.

An increase in the aggregate demand may lead to:

- a change in the slope of the aggregate demand schedule—if the rate of income tax were cut, this would mean that more is likely to be spent out of each pound and the AD schedule would pivot upwards (see Figure 17.13); and

- an upward shift of the AD schedule—this occurs if, at every level of income, demand increases perhaps because of an injection of more government spending. As can be seen in Figure 17.14, this leads to a new equilibrium at Y2. The increase in the aggregate demand has led to a greater increase in national income. This is due to the multiplier effect.

Put into practice

Do the following increase or decrease aggregate demand? Explain your answer.

- Higher taxes

- Lower interest rates

- More government spending

- More savings

- More imports

- Fewer exports

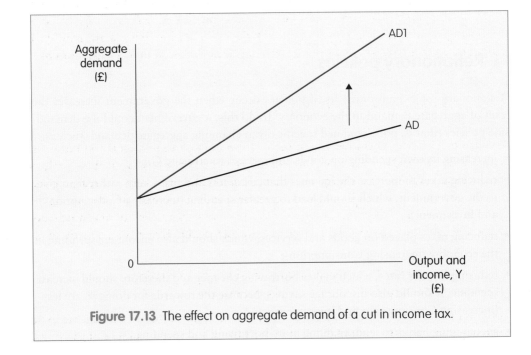

Figure 17.13 The effect on aggregate demand of a cut in income tax.

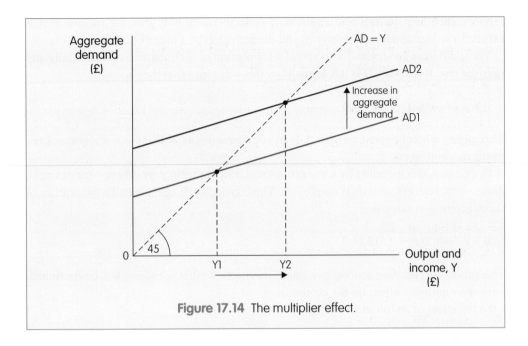

Figure 17.14 The multiplier effect.

▨ The multiplier effect

The multiplier effect explains how an initial increase in the planned injections into the economy increases national income by more than the initial amount of injection. For example, an increase in government spending by £1 million may increase national income by £5 million; in this case, the multiplier is five (5). The size of the multiplier shows how much output in the economy will increase relative to the initial increase in planned injections.

▨ How does the multiplier work?

Imagine that a government decides to spend £1 million on new schools and hospitals. This means that the construction companies and architects involved in these projects will be earning £1 million. A proportion of these earnings will be spent domestically and a proportion will be saved. The amount spent on domestic products will depend on the marginal propensity to consume domestically. The marginal propensity to consume domestically (MPCD) measures the amount of extra income that is spent on domestic goods and services:

$$\text{Marginal propensity to consume domestically} = \frac{\text{Change in consumer spending domestically}}{\text{Change in income}}$$

If the MPCD is 0.8, for example, then out of the extra income of £1 million, the extra spending domestically is £800,000. This £800,000 will be spent on a range of goods and services, such as materials and equipment. This spending will generate income that is earned by subcontractors, employees, and the providers of a range of other services.

These different groups will also spend a proportion of their earnings domestically and save the rest. If the MPCD is 0.8 again, then this will mean that they spend:

$$0.8 \times £800,000 = £640,000$$

This money might be spent on materials and components, as well as electrical goods, cars, meals out, and so on.

Once again, this spending by some groups will lead to earnings by others—for example, dealerships, retailers, and their employees. These groups will again spend a proportion of their income—in this case:

$$0.8 \times £640,000 = £512,000$$

This process of spending leading to income, leading to further spending, will be continued, having a multiplied effect on the economy.

So the effect of an initial spending of £1 million will be:

$$£1,000,000 + £800,000 + £640,000 + £512,000 + \ldots$$

The total effect of an increase in spending can be calculated using the following expression:

$$\frac{1}{1 - \text{MPCD}}$$

In this case, it would be:

$$\frac{1}{(1 - 0.8)} = \frac{1}{0.2} = 5$$

Thus any initial increase in spending will have five times the effect on the output; the multiplier has a value of 5. Therefore an initial increase in spending of £1 million will lead to an overall increase of £5 million—which is the sum of the series:

$$£1,000,000 + £800,000 + £640,000 + £512,000 + \ldots$$

The size of the multiplier

The size of the multiplier depends on the size of the marginal propensity to consume domestically. The higher the marginal propensity to consume domestically, the greater will be the size of the multiplier, because more of consumers' income is spent domestically at each stage of the process. For example, if the MPCD is 0.9, then the size of the multiplier will be:

$$\frac{1}{1 - 0.9} = \frac{1}{0.1} = 10$$

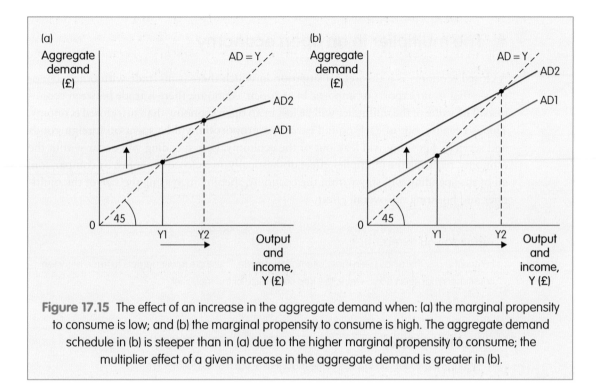

Figure 17.15 The effect of an increase in the aggregate demand when: (a) the marginal propensity to consume is low; and (b) the marginal propensity to consume is high. The aggregate demand schedule in (b) is steeper than in (a) due to the higher marginal propensity to consume; the multiplier effect of a given increase in the aggregate demand is greater in (b).

This means that an increase in spending of £1 million will lead to an overall increase in national income of £10 million. This is because, at each stage in the process, a greater proportion of income is spent, leading to a larger overall increase in demand.

A discussion of the determinants of the marginal propensity to consume domestically can be found in Chapter 20.

The impact of a higher marginal propensity to consume on the multiplier can be seen in Figure 17.15.

What do you think?

What do you think influences how much you spend out of each pound that you earn?

Put into practice

- If the proportion of each pound spent in the UK were 0.6, what would the size of the multiplier be?
- What if only 0.5 were spent in the UK out of each pound?

▇ The multiplier in an open economy

A closed economy is a theoretical situation in which there is no trade with other economies—that is, no exports or imports. In an 'open' economy, there is trade between economies. The value of the multiplier will be less in an open economy than in a closed economy. This is because, out of each pound earned, a proportion will be spent on foreign goods and services. Spending will leak out of the economy. Less spending will occur within the economy, reducing the multiplier effect domestically. In a closed economy, by comparison, all of the spending will stay within the economy, thereby increasing the size of the multiplier and boosting the overall effect.

> **What do you think?**
>
> In recent years, there has been more international trade. There are fewer barriers to trade between countries. What effect do you think this has on the size of the multiplier?

Put into practice

What is the impact on the size of the multiplier of each of the following?

- More spending out of each pound on imports
- More saving out of each pound
- A higher rate of income tax

The paradox of thrift

The paradox of thrift highlights the possible consequences of attempts to save more in an economy. Imagine a two-sector economy with only households and firms. For equilibrium, as we know, the planned withdrawals will equal the planned injections. In a two-sector economy, this means:

Planned savings = Planned investment

If households start to save more (to be 'thrifty'), this increases the level of planned withdrawals, which reduces aggregate demand. This leads to a fall in national income and equilibrium will occur once planned savings again equal the planned investment. Assuming that the planned injections have not changed, this means that households end up saving a bigger proportion of a smaller income and the absolute level of savings would be the same. (Hence the paradox: attempts to save more lead to a greater proportion of income being saved but do not actually lead to more savings in absolute terms.)

Using a simple savings function, imagine that savings are at 0.2 of income and planned investment is £500 million:

Planned $S = 0.2Y$

Planned $I = £500$ million

For equilibrium in a two-sector economy:

Planned S = Planned I

So:

$0.2Y = £500$ million

$$Y = \frac{£500 \text{ million}}{0.2} = £2,500 \text{ million}$$

Say households now save more and the savings function becomes:

$S = 0.5Y$

Then, for equilibrium:

$0.5Y = £500$ million

$$Y = \frac{£500 \text{ million}}{0.5} = £1,000 \text{ million}$$

What we can see is that households are saving a greater proportion of their income (0.5 rather than 0.2), but as a result, income has fallen to such a level (£1,000 million rather than £2,500 million) that the absolute level of savings remains at £500 million equal to the planned level of investment.

Put into practice

- If planned investment remains at £500 million, but savings increase so that $S = 0.8Y$, what is the equilibrium level of national income in a two sector economy?
- What if the savings were to fall to become $S = 0.1Y$?

Case study

The following discussion of consumption is taken from the Bank of England's quarterly bulletin.

Since mid-2008, the UK economy has faced an unprecedented series of large adverse shocks that have led companies and households to become more uncertain about future economic prospects. These shocks include one of the United Kingdom's largest ever financial crises, continuing headwinds from the euro-area debt crisis and the implementation of the Government's fiscal consolidation programme. The unusual size and nature of these shocks might have led households and companies to reassess their beliefs about the range of possible paths the economy can take. In other words, they may have become more 'uncertain' about the current and future economic climate.

Higher uncertainty can induce households to save more. Faced with uncertainty about their future labour income, households might build up a 'buffer stock' of savings to draw on in periods of temporarily low income (Carroll (1996), Romer (1990)). The flipside of increased saving for the future is a reduction in household consumption today. For example, Benito (2004) finds that a one standard deviation rise in unemployment risk for the head of the household reduces consumption in the United Kingdom by 2.7%. The effect on saving and spending is temporary, however, and will dissipate, once households have saved the amount they require as insurance against future fluctuations in their income.

The effect on consumption might also be skewed towards particular types of spending. For example, the decision to buy durable goods, especially big-ticket items such as cars, is particularly sensitive to uncertainty shocks because these purchases are costly to reverse (Romer (1990)). Buying a new car entails a particularly high fixed cost since there is a large drop in its value after being used for the first time. So households would rather wait to see the outcome of economic conditions before purchasing such durable goods. Benito's study of UK households suggests unemployment risk causes purchases of durables to be significantly delayed. For similar reasons, uncertainty faced by companies can lead them to postpone investment. Investing in new projects typically involves fixed installation costs, so companies value the option of delaying investment decisions until uncertainty about the viability of a project has been resolved (Dixit and Pindyck (1994)). Heightened uncertainty is likely to raise the value of this 'wait and see' option and therefore depress investment spending temporarily.

Source: http://www.bankofengland.co.uk/publications/Documents/quarterlybulletin/2013/qb130201.pdf

❓ **Questions**

1   Analyse the factors influencing consumption in the UK.

2   Analyse the possible consequences of less consumption in the UK.

3   What could the government do to boost consumption in the UK?

Review questions

1   What are the conditions necessary for equilibrium in an economy?

2   Explain two factors that might affect the level of injections in an economy.

3   What is the effect of an increase in injections on the level of national income?

4   Explain two factors that might lead to a decrease in aggregate demand.

5   Explain two factors that would increase the size of the multiplier.

6   What is the effect on national income if savings increase?

7   What is likely to happen to national income if aggregate demand is greater than aggregate supply?

8   Explain what is meant by a deflationary gap.

Put into practice

1   Using a diagram, show the effect on national income of a fall in planned injections.

2   Using a diagram show the effect on national income of a fall in planned withdrawals.

Assigment question

1   Research the present level of government spending in the UK economy. Analyse what the government spends its money on and where it gets it tax revenue from. Recommend two changes to the way it raises or uses finance. Justify your choices.

Key learning points

- Equilibrium in an economy occurs when the aggregate demand equals the aggregate supply.
- Equilibrium in an economy occurs when the planned injections equal the planned withdrawals.
- Equilibrium in an economy occurs when Planned $I + G + X$ = Planned $S + T + M$.
- If the planned injections are greater than the planned withdrawals, then there is excess demand in the economy and national income will rise until equilibrium is restored.
- If the planned injections are less than the planned withdrawals, then there is too little demand in the economy and national income will fall until equilibrium is restored.
- The aggregate demand measures the total planned expenditure on final goods and services in an economy, expressed as $C + I + G + X - M$.
- An increase in the aggregate demand can set off the multiplier process, which leads to a greater increase in national income.
- The size of the multiplier depends on the marginal propensity to consume domestically.
- The paradox of thrift means that attempts to save more may lead to a higher proportion of a smaller income being saved rather than a higher level of savings.

Learn more

If you want to learn more about the relationship between injections and withdrawals, and the difference between actual and planned withdrawals, visit the Online Resource Centre.

 Visit our Online Resource Centre at http://www.oxfordtextbooks.co.uk/orc/gillespie_ econ3e/ for test questions and further information on topics covered in this chapter.

»18 National income and the standard of living

In the previous chapter, we examined how an economy reached equilibrium. In this chapter, we examine how national income is actually measured and whether it can be used as a good indicator of a country's standard of living. Governments often seek to increase the income per person in their economies; this chapter considers whether or not this is a useful objective.

LEARNING OBJECTIVES

By the end of this chapter, you should be able to:

✓ explain the meaning of national income and how it is measured;

✓ discuss the value of national income as a measure of the standard of living;

✓ explain the Gini coefficient.

■ Introduction

National income measures the value of final goods and services produced in an economy over a given period—usually a year. Final goods and services include all of the intermediate products used in producing them. The final value of a car, for example, includes the value of all of the components and materials used in its production. Measuring the value of final goods and services therefore includes the value of all of the products used up in the supply and production process. Naturally, there is a large amount of interest in how high the level of national income is in an economy. If national income is high, then this suggests that there will be jobs and that the standard of living in a country will be high, because people will be earning more (assuming we believe that earning more improves our standard of living). On the other hand, a low national income will be associated with poverty and unemployment. In this chapter, we consider how national income is measured and whether it is, in fact, a good measure of the standard of living and the welfare of the citizens.

Measuring national income

As we saw in the previous chapter, the value of what has been produced in an economy must have been earned by one or other of the factors of production. If £100 million of output has been produced, then this money has been earned by one of the factors of production such as employees, owners, suppliers, or landlords. Therefore we can measure either the value of the output produced or the income earned by the different factors of production. Alternatively, we can measure the amount spent in an economy. Here, however, we have to make adjustments—for example, if we spend less than is produced, then firms will end up with unexpected stocks; provided that we include this stockbuilding as a form of spending, then the total expenditure will also equal the output, which will also equal the total income.

National income can, therefore, be measured in the following different ways which should all give the same figure:

- **Output** This measures the value of the final output of different sectors of the economy, such as agriculture, manufacturing, and services.

- **Expenditure** This measures the spending by all of the different sectors of the economy, such as households, the government, and foreign buyers, on a country's final goods and services.

- **Income** This measures all of the earnings in the economy—for example, the income earned by companies (corporations), employees, and the self-employed.

However national income is measured, it will give the same answer—that is:

Output = Expenditure = Income (Chapter 17)

Whichever method we choose to measure national income, there are several different indicators that can be used, including the following.

- **Gross domestic product (GDP)** This measures the value of final goods and services produced within an economy over a given period—usually a year. It shows how much has been earned within a country's national boundaries.

- **Gross national product (GNP)** This measures the value of final goods and services earned by a country's national citizens, as opposed to the amount of money earned within a country, over a given time period—usually a year. Some of the income measured by the GDP is earned by overseas producers or individuals who are not based in the UK. This money will leave the UK. At the same time, UK citizens and firms abroad will be earning money there and this will be counted as part of the GNP.

Thus we have:

GNP =

GDP
– Income earned by overseas firms and households located within an economy
+ Income earned by the country's households and firms working abroad
This can also be written as:

GNP = GDP + Net property income from abroad

where

Net property income from abroad = UK earnings abroad
– Foreign earnings within the UK

- **Net national product (NNP)** Some of the national income earned in a year is simply spent on replacing the depreciation of assets rather than genuinely adding new output to the economy. If, for example, you are buying equipment to replace old machines that have stopped working, then you are not increasing the productive capacity of the economy. Depreciation refers to the wear and tear of assets.

Thus we have:

Net national product (NNP) = GNP – Depreciation

- **GNP at market prices and factor cost** If we measure the value of spending on final goods and services, then these prices will include taxes placed on them by the government (which increase the price) and government subsidies (which reduce the price). The prices in the market do not therefore reflect the income (or cost) of the factors of production. To measure the value of the output at 'factor cost', you need to adjust the market prices.

Thus we have:

GNP market prices – Indirect taxes + Subsidies = GNP factor cost

---

Put into practice

Which of the following are true and which are false?

a. GDP measures the income of country's citizens over a given period

b. National income = value of output + value of income + value of expenditure

c. GNP = GDP plus net property income from abroad

d. The difference between GNP and NNP is depreciation

Given the data below what is the country's gross domestic product at factor cost

	£bn
Consumer expenditure	395
Government consumption of final goods and services	91
Investment spending	93
Exports	110
Imports	120
Taxes on expenditure	78
Subsidies	6
Depreciation	50

What do you think?

According to the Easterlin paradox (named after economist Richard Easterlin) higher incomes do not necessarily make people happier. Money does matter but at some point you become rich enough and more money no longer leads to greater happiness.
Do you agree with this? Why do you think it might be?

Economics in context   Data

GDP statistics in the USA are calculated every month of the year on the fifth floor of a modern office building in Washington, DC, where government economists review a large pile of data compiled by the Bureau of Economic Analysis, a part of the US Department of Commerce. For a whole day, the group is placed under 'lockup'. Phones have to be handed in and all Internet access is shut down; those entering and leaving the building are strictly limited. The work involves analysing 10,000 streams of data that describe recent economic activity in the USA. The goal is to arrive at a single figure for GDP. By tradition, no one in the room says the final number aloud—a throwback to the old days, apparently, when there was a fear of hidden microphones.

? Question

Why do you think it is so crucial that the GDP statistics are kept private until the day on which they are supposed to be officially announced each month?

> **Economics in context**
>
> ## Office for Budget Responsibility
>
> When the coalition government came to power in the UK in 2010, it created an Office for Budget Responsibility (OBR). The OBR was established as an independent body to ensure that the public sector financial figures are based on reasonable economic assumptions and explain where the numbers come from. It should mean that figures about the economy can be relied on and are not manipulated for political gain. In the words of George Osborne, chancellor of the exchequer:
>
> > We have changed the way Budgets are written, by establishing a new Office for Budget Responsibility, which will stop any chancellor fiddling the figures ever again in our history.
>
> ❓ **Question**
> Why might a government want to manipulate national income statistics?

▥ Real national income versus nominal national income

If the income of an economy has increased by, say, 2 per cent, then this is an increase in nominal income, but does not necessarily mean that firms and households are better off in terms of what they can actually afford to buy. This is because we need to know what is happening to the price level. If prices are growing by 2 per cent as well, then, in real terms, the economy is no better off: the nominal growth in income is cancelled out by the growth in prices. Nominal increases in income simply mean that the absolute number has increased. The real GDP and the real GNP measure the national income taking account of what is happening to prices. They show the purchasing power of a given level of income.

▥ National income and living standards

The standard of living in an economy is often measured by the real GDP per capita. The GDP is used (rather than the GNP) because it shows the income being earned in a region, regardless of who is earning it.

The real GDP per capita measures the national income per person adjusted for inflation—that is, in real terms, how much individuals earn. A higher average real income per person suggests a higher standard of living because, on average, people have more purchasing power.

The real GDP per capita is defined as:

$$\text{Real GDP per capita} = \frac{\text{Real GDP}}{\text{Population}}$$

However, this measurement simply shows an average figure—for example, £25,000 per person. A more detailed examination of a country's standard of living might consider the distribution of income in an economy. It might be possible to have a relatively high average income per person, for example, but then find that most of the income is being earned by relatively few people, whilst the rest live in poverty.

To analyse the distribution of income in an economy, we can use the Lorenz curve and the Gini coefficient.

What do you think?

How important do you think it is to have a relatively equal distribution of income in an economy?

The Lorenz curve and the Gini coefficient

The Lorenz curve shows the distribution of income within an economy (see Figure 18.1). The horizontal axis measures the percentage of the population from the poorest to the richest. The vertical axis measures the percentage of national income that they receive.

If income were distributed equally in an economy, then the Lorenz curve would be a straight line: 20 per cent of households would earn 20 per cent of national income; 60 per cent would earn 60 per cent; and so on. This would lead to a 45° line from the origin and this is called **the line of absolute equality**. In practice, the Lorenz curve will be below the 45° line. This is because the bottom 50 per cent of the population might earn only 20 per cent of the country's income.

The Gini coefficient measures the ratio of the area between the Lorenz curve and the 45° line to the whole area below the 45° line (see Figure 18.1).

If the income is equally distributed, then the Lorenz curve would be the 45° line and so the Gini coefficient would be equal to 0. The more unequal the distribution of income, the larger the Gini coefficient. The largest value that the Gini coefficient can have is one (1).

The Gini coefficient is sometimes expressed as a percentage between 0 per cent and 100 per cent.

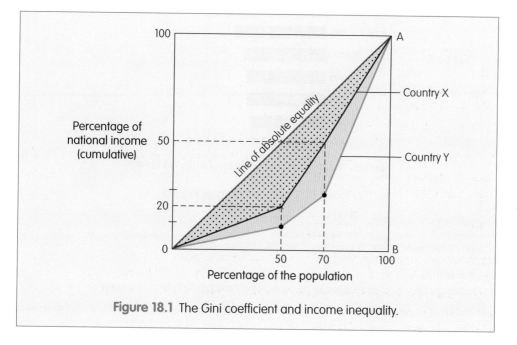

Figure 18.1 The Gini coefficient and income inequality.

In Figure 18.1, the Gini coefficient would be measured as follows:

$$\text{Gini coefficient} = \frac{\text{Shaded area}}{\text{Area OAB}}$$

From this, we can see that country Y would have a higher Gini coefficient than country X. This is because there is greater inequality: for example, in country X, 70 per cent of the population have 50 per cent of the country's income, whereas in country Y, they have a lower percentage.

Put into practice

If the Gini coefficient is 0.9, does this suggest that income is fairly distributed or not? Explain.

Economics in context

In 2013 for the first time in 12 years, the Chinese government reported its Gini coefficient for income inequality for 2012 and the previous ten years. The Gini coefficient for China was 0.474 in 2012, having been at its highest at 0.491 in 2008.

Figure 18.2 shows the Gini coefficients for various countries in 2012.

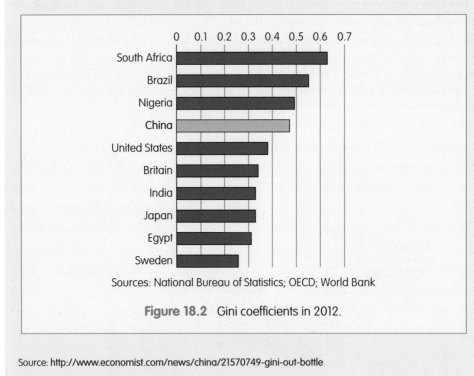

Sources: National Bureau of Statistics; OECD; World Bank

Figure 18.2 Gini coefficients in 2012.

Source: http://www.economist.com/news/china/21570749-gini-out-bottle

? Question

What might be the consequences for an economy of having a high Gini coefficient?

Economics in context

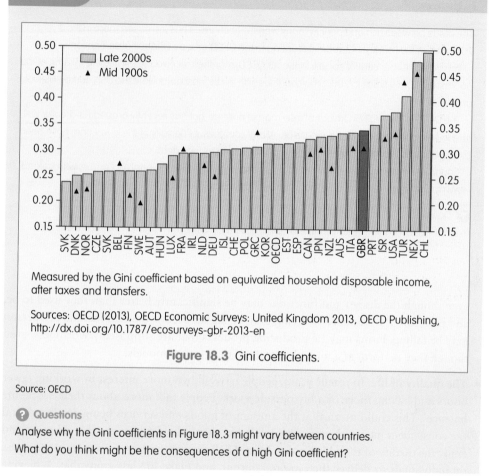

Measured by the Gini coefficient based on equivalized household disposable income, after taxes and transfers.

Sources: OECD (2013), OECD Economic Surveys: United Kingdom 2013, OECD Publishing, http://dx.doi.org/10.1787/ecosurveys-gbr-2013-en

Figure 18.3 Gini coefficients.

Source: OECD

? Questions

Analyse why the Gini coefficients in Figure 18.3 might vary between countries. What do you think might be the consequences of a high Gini coefficient?

Limitations of real GDP per capita as a measure of a country's standard of living

Although GDP per capita is the most common measure of the standard of living of an economy, many economists do not think that this provides a particularly good measure of the quality of life in economies, even if account is taken of the income distribution. There are many limitations of using GDP figures and other factors that may be important when considering a country's standard of living. The limitations of national income figures as an indicator of standard of living include the following.

- **The quality of goods and services provided** Over time, technology reduces the price of many goods—just think of the price of a laptop or flat-screen TV now compared with a couple of years ago, and then think how much better the quality is. These falling prices may reduce the value of the output produced and the income earned in an economy,

The divide between rich and poor in many wealthy economies has increased more in the 3 years to 2010 than in the previous 12 years according to the OECD group of industrialised nations.

The richest 10 per cent of society in the 33 OECD countries received 9.5 times the income of the poorest (up from 9 times in 2007) The countries with the biggest gaps were the USA, Turkey, Mexico, and Chile.

The OECD is generally in favour of free-market policies, but has recently argued for greater welfare to soften the impact of the recession. Many countries, especially in the eurozone, have been cutting back hard on welfare spending in an attempt to reduce debt.

Countries where the gap was least pronounced were mainly in the north of Europe, with Iceland, Norway, Denmark, and Slovenia the most egalitarian societies.

? Question

To what extent do you think it matters whether the divide between rich and poor is increasing?

even though the design and functions may be significantly better than they used to be, and therefore the standard of living may be higher even if the real income per person may be falling. Firms may be producing products that are supposedly worth less, even though they perform at a much higher level than earlier models.

- **The quality of life** In recent years, people have shown more interest in working fewer hours and having more of a life outside work. People talk more about their 'work–life balance'. This could mean that the amount of goods and services being produced, and the consequent income being earned, fall, but that individuals prefer this situation and enjoy the quality of their lives more. More GDP growth, by comparison, may put stress on individuals to deliver the required output, and make life less enjoyable. Achieving higher levels of GDP could mean more hours at work and fewer holidays. This could mean that the work–life balance shifts away from the home and toward the office or factory, and that satisfaction falls even if the GDP per person rises. Greater stress leading to more health care may increase incomes, but are we better off? More walking to work may reduce spending on transport, but with a healthier lifestyle and less pollution, are we actually worse off?

- **Non-marketed items** If work is undertaken but not paid for, then it will not be recorded in the official national income statistics. For example, if you hire a plumber, then this work will be paid for and will increase the recorded national income. If, however, you were to do the plumbing work yourself, then it would not be recorded or counted. Changes in the amount of work that people do for themselves will, therefore, distort comparisons of standards of living over time and between countries.

- **The 'black economy'** This refers to all of the work that may be done in an economy but which is not declared because people want to avoid paying tax to the government.

By definition, this income cannot be counted officially, even though it may be relatively high—particularly in some countries in which there is a culture of not declaring earnings to the government.

- **Environmental issues** Faster economic growth may be at the expense of damage to the environment. Although we may be richer, we may find that factors such as higher levels of pollution and global warming make growth undesirable.

- **Wealth** Income shows the stream or flow of earnings over a given period—usually a year. Wealth measures the value of all of the assets owned by a country at a given moment. It is known as a stock concept. The income of an economy may be low during a particular year, but because of previous earnings, its wealth may be high. Its citizens may benefit from this stock of assets accumulated in the past. This means that a country may have a lower income, but still have a high standard of living due to past wealth.

Traditionally, governments have been eager to increase the real GDP per person. This has been regarded as an important goal of government and a measure of its success or failure. Nowadays, some people argue that the government should not focus on increasing the real GDP per person, but should look at other targets. Many economists have developed their own measures of economic welfare rather than relied on the GDP per person. For example, Nordhaus and Tobin (1972) have produced a measure called the net economic welfare (NEW). This adjusts the GNP by deducting economic 'bads' (such as pollution), adding the value of non-marketed activities, and including the value of leisure. Similarly, Friends of the Earth suggests that an index of sustainable economic welfare (ISEW) is used instead. This attempts to:

> measure the portion of economic activity which delivers genuine increases in our quality of life—in one sense 'quality' economic activity. For example, it makes a subtraction for air pollution caused by economic activity, and makes an addition to count unpaid household labour—such as cleaning or child-minding. It also covers areas such as income inequality, other environmental damage, and depletion of environmental assets.

Obviously, with these other indicators, there is plenty of room for debate over what to include and the relevant weighting of the different factors.

Recently in the UK, there has also been increasing interest in measuring how happy people are within a country rather than simply measuring their income.

In 1999, Tony Blair, then UK prime minister, stated:

> Money isn't everything. But in the past governments have seemed to forget this. Success has been measured by economic growth—GDP—alone. Delivering the best possible quality of life for us all means more than concentrating solely on economic growth. That is why sustainable development is such an important part of this government's programme. All this depends on devising new ways of assessing how we are doing.

In 2006, David Cameron, then leader of the Conservative Party and who would go on to become prime minister in 2010, said:

> We should be thinking not just what is good for putting money in people's pockets but what is good for putting joy in people's hearts. When politicians are looking at issues they should be saying to

> **Economics in context**   Gross national happiness in Bhutan
>
> The remote Himalayan kingdom of Bhutan is the only country in the world that puts happiness at the centre of government policy. The government must consider every policy for its impact, not only on gross domestic product, but also on 'gross national happiness' (GNH). For example, the capital, Thimpu, has no advertising, because this is felt to promote consumerism. Bhutan has even banned plastic bags and tobacco on the grounds that they make the country less happy.
>
> ? **Questions**
>
> Do you think that a UK government should ban tobacco? Do you think that it would be able to do so?

themselves, 'How are we going to try to make sure that we don't just make people better off but we make people happier, we make communities more stable, we make society more cohesive?'

The issue of well-being has become such an important issue that the Office of National Statsistics in the UK has recently started measuring and publishing data on well-being.

Trying to achieve greater happiness has important implications for government policy. The following are some examples.

• Research suggests that one main reason why higher incomes do not automatically lead to happiness is that we tend to compare ourselves with people who are richer than we are. Therefore, even if we become better off, we do not necessarily get any happier. To produce a happier society, the government would need to reduce the gap between the rich and the poor. It can do this by redistributing wealth from the rich to the poor.

• Advertising may be a major cause of unhappiness because it makes some people feel less well off, and often promotes greed and envy. Perhaps advertising should be controlled to make us feel better.

• Research suggests that happiness is likely to be higher if more people get married and stay married. Marriage is typically so good for your happiness and general well-being that it adds an average of seven years to the life of a man and around four years for a woman. In this case, the government could use the tax and benefit system to make marriage more economically attractive.

Put into practice

Which of the following statements are true and which are false?

a. If the population size grows faster than national income GDP per capita increases

b. If inflation is higher than the rate of growth of national income real GDP falls

c. If the Gini coefficient gets smaller income distribution is more equal

d. An increase in real GDP per capita does not necessarily increase a country's standard of living

---

What do you think?

Do you think that people are more or less happy than they were 100 years ago? Why?

What do you think influences people's happiness?

To what extent do you think that government policy should aim to increase happiness rather than income?

If you were in government, what laws would you introduce to make people happier?

Case study

The ONS describes its Measuring National Well-being programme as follows.

The ONS recently launched the Measuring National Well-being (MNW) programme. The aim is to 'develop and publish an accepted and trusted set of National Statistics which help people understand and monitor well-being'. Traditional measures of progress such as Gross Domestic Product (GDP) have long been recognised as an incomplete picture of the state of the nation. Other economic, social and environmental measures are needed alongside GDP to provide a complete picture of how society is doing.

(i) The Economy

During the first part of the millennium, incomes and GDP were rising and debt levels were rising slowly. The recession in 2008 led to a sharp fall in GDP and impacted on income and debt levels at both the national and household level. Real income has fallen as inflation has grown faster than incomes, and the public sector debt ratio has increased. GDP has started to recover, but at a slower rate than before the recession.

- Real household actual income per head (RHAI) in the UK grew from £16,865 to £18,159 between 2002 and 2008, before falling to near 2005 levels in 2011 (£17,862).
- UK Public Sector Net Debt grew between 32.5% and 42.8% of GDP between 2003 and 2008 before rising to 65.7% in 2011.

(ii) People

The recession has led to a higher proportion who are unemployed, with a particular impact on the young, and in 2009/10 more than 1 in 8 (12.3%) of us were finding it quite or very difficult to manage financially. Life satisfaction presents a more resilient picture, having remained broadly stable throughout the last decade and the most recent figures for those who report being somewhat, mostly or completely satisfied with their social life and job standing at 67% and 77.8% respectively and satisfaction with our family life averaging 8.2 out of 10 (where 1 is very dissatisfied and 10 is very satisfied). In terms of our health which is one of the most important influences on our well-being, our 'healthy' life expectancy has increased as has our overall satisfaction with our health. Healthy life expectancy at birth in 2008-2010 was age 63.5 for males and 65.7 for females, in the UK, increases of 2.8 and 3.3 years respectively since 2000-02.

(iii) The Environment

Long term progress is being made with protecting our local and global environment. More than half of us visited our natural environment at least once a week in the 12 months prior to interview in 2011/12 and nationally, the proportion of protected areas, including land and sea has increased. Globally, emissions and energy consumption have fallen and use of renewable energy has increased during the last decade.

Background

The Measuring National Well-being programme began in November 2010 with a six month National Debate, asking, 'what matters', to understand what measures of well-being should include. Following 175 events, with 2,750 people and 34,000 responses received online or via other channels, ONS developed a framework for measuring national well-being. The framework consists of 10 areas or 'domains', including areas such as Health, Education and What we do; and 40 headline measures of well-being, for example, the unemployment rate, satisfaction with our health, or levels of crime. These measures and others have been used to describe life in the UK 2012, under the headings, the Economy, People and the Environment, and can be seen in the interactive wheel of measures.

Source: http://www.ons.gov.uk/ons/interactive/well-being-wheel-of-measures/index.html

❓ Questions

1   What are the limitations of GDP per person as a measure of the standard of living?

2   What else should be considered apart from income when assessing a country's standard of living?

3   How might Measuring Well Being affect government policy?

Review questions

1   Explain how income differs from wealth.

2   Explain how the gross domestic product differs from the gross national product.

3   If the Gini coefficient is close to one (1), is the income distribution fairly equal or not?

4   Why it is important to adjust national figures for inflation and the size of the population to measure the standard of living?

5   Explain two limitations to using national income figures to reflect the standard of living in a country.

6   Should the government focus on increasing the happiness of its people?

7   Explain what is shown by the Lorenz curve.

8   Explain the difference between GNP and NNP.

Put into practice

1   Produce a report proposing that the UK should aim to grow more slowly in the future.

2   Produce a report on recent trends in income distribution in the UK.

Assignment question

1   Choose two countries of your choice and compare and contrast their standard of living using a range of indicators.

Key learning points

- National income can be measured in terms of output, income, or expenditure.
- The gross domestic product (GDP) measures the income generated in a country. The gross national product (GNP) measures the income of a country's citizens.
- Real national income adjusts the nominal income for inflation.
- The standard of living in an economy is often measured by the real national income per person. However, this ignores the distribution of income.
- The Gini coefficient measures how equally income is distributed in an economy.
- The standard of living will depend on many factors apart from income, such as the quality of goods and environmental issues.

References

Gini, C. (1921) 'Measurement of inequality and incomes', *The Economic Journal*, 31(121): 124–6

Nordhaus, W. and Tobin, J. (1972) 'Is growth obsolete?', in National Bureau of Economic Research (ed.) *Economic Growth*, General Series No. 96E, Columbia University Press, New York

Learn more

In this chapter, we have focused on income rather than wealth. To learn more about the difference between these, and for more information on inequality in the UK and other countries, visit the Online Resource Centre.

Visit our Online Resource Centre at http://www.oxfordtextbooks.co.uk/orc/gillespie_econ3e/ for test questions and further information on topics covered in this chapter.

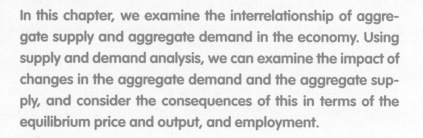

»19 Aggregate demand, aggregate supply, and the price level

In this chapter, we examine the interrelationship of aggregate supply and aggregate demand in the economy. Using supply and demand analysis, we can examine the impact of changes in the aggregate demand and the aggregate supply, and consider the consequences of this in terms of the equilibrium price and output, and employment.

LEARNING OBJECTIVES

By the end of this chapter, you should be able to:

✓ explain the shape of the aggregate demand curve relative to price;

✓ explain the shape of the aggregate supply curve relative to price;

✓ explain equilibrium in the economy in terms of aggregate supply and aggregate demand;

✓ examine the effect of changes in the aggregate supply and the aggregate demand in terms of price and output outcomes.

▨ Introduction

In our earlier analysis of aggregate demand in Chapter 17, we focused purely on the impact of changes in demand on output levels. For example, investigating the change in the aggregate demand using 45° diagrams simply showed the effect of demand changes on output; we did not consider the price level in any detail. In reality, any change in demand affects both output and prices. We now look at both aggregate supply and aggregate demand in the economy, and include changes in price in the analysis.

▦ Aggregate demand

The aggregate demand is the quantity of final goods and services that individuals and organizations in an economy are willing and able to buy at each and every price, all other things being unchanged. It is the total level of desired spending on final goods and services in an economy by households, firms, governments, and overseas buyers.

The aggregate demand curve is downward-sloping relative to price, meaning that more products are demanded in the economy as the price falls (see Figure 19.1). This is due to the following reasons.

- **The income effect** When the price level falls, this increases the real income and wealth of households. With lower prices, households and firms have more purchasing power, and can buy more with the same income. Therefore the quantity demanded increases.

- **The substitution effect** When the UK price level falls, there is a substitution effect. With lower prices, individuals and organizations are more likely to buy UK products than foreign products, thereby increasing the quantity demanded domestically.

The level of aggregate demand at any price will depend on factors such as:

- households' incomes—all things being equal, customers will usually spend more if their incomes are higher;

- households' and firms' expectations (which will affect their spending)—if households are confident that they will keep their jobs, and even anticipate a promotion or pay increase, they may spend more now; similarly, expectations affect levels of investment by firms;

- government spending on final goods and services—this is an injection into the economy and an expansionary government programme can boost demand; and

- the level of spending on exports and imports—an increase in demand for exports will increase demand, whilst more spending on imports should reduce it.

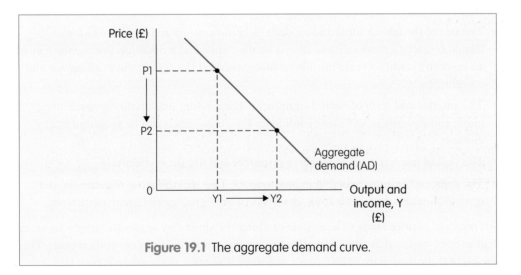

Figure 19.1 The aggregate demand curve.

Changes in these factors will change the level of injections into an economy and shift the aggregate demand curve; more or less will be demanded at each and every price.

Put into practice

Which of the following would increase aggregate demand? Explain your answers.

- An increase in investment
- A decrease in government spending
- A decrease in spending on exports
- A fall in import spending
- An increase in taxation rates
- A fall in the amount saved out of each extra pound

Aggregate supply

The aggregate supply is the quantity of final goods and services that firms in an economy are willing and able to produce at each and every price, all other things being unchanged.

The level of aggregate supply will depend on the following.

- **The price level** The amount supplied should increase if the price increases, because firms can afford to use less efficient methods of production and to pay more for resources. The effect of a change in the price level on supply in an economy is shown as a movement along the aggregate supply curve.

- **The level of technology and innovation in an economy** Improvements in technology may enable more to be produced at each price. This causes an outward shift in aggregate supply.

- **The size of the labour force and its skills** A better-trained and larger workforce should be able to produce more than a smaller, unskilled workforce. Immigration into an economy could increase the labour force, as could changes in the working age and retirement age.

- **The amount and state of capital equipment** The amount and quality of machinery, plant, and equipment will clearly influence the amount that can be produced at any moment.

- **The skill of management to combine resources and use them effectively**

- **The degree of entrepreneurship in an economy** This will influence the amount and quality of innovation, generating new ways of doing things and greater efficiency.

An increase in price leads to a movement along the short-run aggregate supply curve. A higher price means that firms can afford to produce more and can cover their costs. This means that the aggregate supply curve will slope upwards, as shown in Figure 19.2.

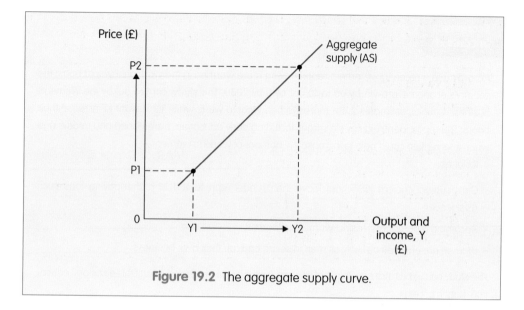

Figure 19.2 The aggregate supply curve.

A change in the other factors will shift the aggregate supply curve; with a larger or a better-trained workforce, for example, the aggregate supply curve will shift to the right (see Figure 19.3)—more will be supplied at each price. This is known as an increase in supply.

Put into practice

What factors would shift the aggregate supply curve inwards so that less is supplied at each and every price?

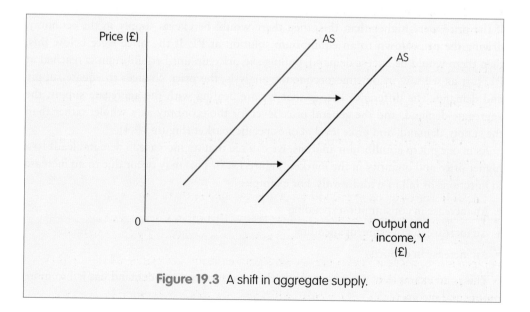

Figure 19.3 A shift in aggregate supply.

According to a recent government report having more wormen in the workforce would boost the country's economic growth by up to 10 per cent by 2030. The study, carried out by the Women's Business Council, estimates 2.4m more women want to work, while 1.3m want to increase their hours. The report identified key life stages including early education, parenthood and middle age when intervention could help to increase the number of working women.

It claims:

- Girl's subject choices at school leave them under-represented in higher-paying jobs such as science.

- Becoming a parent can restrict women's progress.

- Women are only half as likely as men to set up and run their own business.

The study calculates that two-thirds of women over the age of 50 work in just three sectors: education, health or retail.

? Questions

Why do participation levels of women in the economy matter?

Analyse the ways the government could increase the participation of women in the workforce.

▦ Equilibrium in the economy

Equilibrium in the economy will occur at the price and output for which the aggregate demand equals the aggregate supply. This occurs at the price P1 and output Y1 in Figure 19.4. If the price were higher than this, then there would be excess supply in the economy, driving the price down to an equilibrium solution at P1. If the price were below this, then there would be excess demand, pulling the price up until equilibrium is reached at P1. Just as we saw in our microeconomic analysis, the price changes to equate supply and demand. The difference here is that we are dealing with the aggregate supply, the aggregate demand, and the general price level for the economy as a whole, rather than the supply, demand, and price level in one specific market (Figure 19.4).

As in our micro equilibrium analysis, we can see that an increase in demand leads to a higher price and quantity in the market (Figure 19.5). This may occur due to an increase in injections or fall in withdrawals. For example:

- An increase in consumption spending

- An increase in government spending

- An increase in exports

This is an example of actual growth in the economy as more demand has led to more output and income.

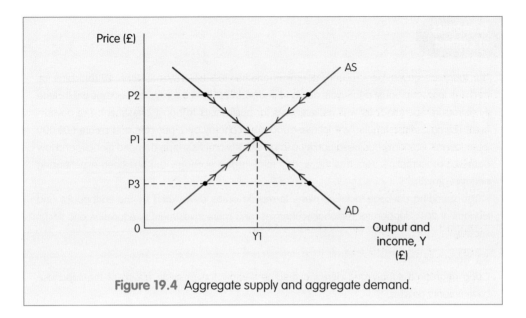

Figure 19.4 Aggregate supply and aggregate demand.

By comparison an increase in aggregate supply may occur due to factors such as:

• An increase in labour supply
• An improvement in technology
• An increase in investment

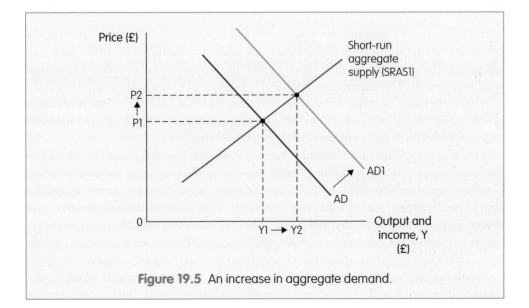

Figure 19.5 An increase in aggregate demand.

The Japanese government recently approved another 10.3 trillion yen ($116bn; £72bn) stimulus package to try and boost aggregate demand and supply in its economy. The package will include infrastructure spending, as well as incentives for businesses to boost investment. The government estimates this stimulus will increase Japan's economy by 2 per cent and create 600,000 jobs. Japan's economy has been hurt by a fall in exports amid slowing demand globally and low domestic consumption. Japan is the world's third-largest economy but has been experiencing negative growth.

The spending package includes plans to rebuild areas devastated by the earthquake and tsunami of 2011, support for regional economies, and more investment in education and social security.

❓ Questions

Using aggregate supply and demand diagrams show the possible effects of the Japanese government's policies.

What do you think might be the problems that could occur?

What do you think?

Do you think the main challenge facing businesses is increasing aggregate demand or aggregate supply?

■ The short-run and long-run aggregate supply curve

In the short run, we assume that wages are fixed in an economy; this can prevent the labour market adjusting back to the long-run equilibrium immediately. In the long run, we assume that wages are flexible which enables the labour market to return to long-run equilibrium easily. The importance of wage flexibility can be seen in the analysis below.

Imagine that an economy is at long-run equilibrium at P1Y1 in Figure 19.6. An increase in aggregate demand in the short run will lead to a movement along the short-run aggregate supply (SRAS1) and an increase in the price level to P2Y2.

In the short run, wages are assumed to be fixed—possibly because employees are locked into employment contracts and/or because they do not immediately notice that prices have gone up. Most of us buy a relatively limited range of goods and so do not necessarily appreciate the overall rate of inflation immediately. This means that we may suffer from **money illusion**—that is, we may not realize what the processes actually are. If prices are higher, but money (or nominal) wages are not, then, in real terms, employees are cheaper (so more are hired)—which is one reason why more products can be supplied.

Over time, however, employees will notice the higher prices and demand higher wages; wages will be pulled up by the increased demand for labour and the higher price level as

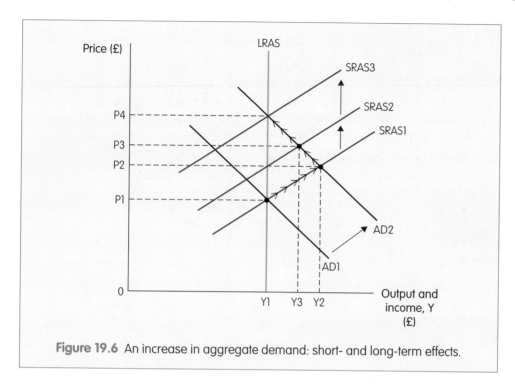

Figure 19.6 An increase in aggregate demand: short- and long-term effects.

contracts are renegotiated. This will increase a firm's costs and shift the short-run aggregate supply curve upwards. In the medium term, this might shift to SRAS2 and the new equilibrium would be P3Y3. In the long term, the wages would increase to compensate completely for the higher prices, further shifting the aggregate supply to SRAS3 and a new long-run equilibrium of P4Y1. This means that the long-run aggregate supply curve is vertical at LRAS. Higher aggregate demand in the long term has led to higher prices and higher wages, meaning that in real terms nothing has changed. The economy remains at its potential output, but with higher prices. More demand has simply created higher prices over time, although in the short and medium terms it has increased output and reduced unemployment.

Now imagine that the economy is in long-run equilibrium at P1Y1 again, but this time aggregate demand falls (see Figure 19.7). In this situation, prices will fall, but if wages are fixed, in the short term, employees are more expensive in real terms and likely to be laid off (or at least to have overtime cut). This would reduce the quantity supplied and the economy moves along the SRAS1 to P2Y2. Wages might be "sticky" downwards (i.e. slow to change) because of employment contracts which may have been negotiated for a year or more, because employees do not realize prices are generally lower (money illusion) and/or because employees do not want to accept a nominal pay cut.

However in the long term, there will be a fall in money wages as:

- employees realize prices are lower and so are more willing to accept lower wages as they renegotiate their wages; and

- there is pressure from an excess supply of labour.

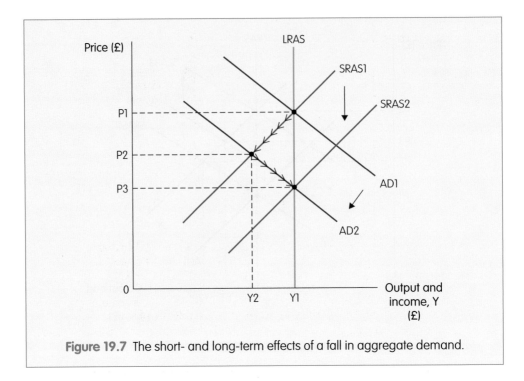

Figure 19.7 The short- and long-term effects of a fall in aggregate demand.

This leads to short-run aggregate supply shifting to the right to SRAS2 until a long-run equilibrium of P3Y1 is reached. Wages have fallen, reducing the real wage to its original level, and the economy is back at its potential output with full employment. The long-run effect of a fall in aggregate demand has been a fall in prices, but no long-term change in output. Again, it can be seen that the long-run aggregate supply is vertical at the maximum capacity of the economy; changes in aggregate demand change prices, but not output.

How long is the long run? Different economists' views

When deciding on the price elasticity of aggregate supply the key is the labour market and how flexible money wages are. If they adjust quickly both up and down, then the economy should reach the long-run situation rapidly and the economy is on the long-run aggregate supply most of the time. This is the position of new classical economists, who think that the economy is always at or close to full employment and supply is vertical. In this situation, demand-side policies are not especially effective, and governments should concentrate on supply-side policies and on shifting the long-run supply of the economy to the right.

If, however, the labour market does not clear rapidly, then for long periods of time the economy may be below full employment. If, for example, wages are very sticky downwards because employees will not take pay cuts or strong trade union bargaining power rejects pay cuts, then the real wage would not fall back to the long-run equilibrium level. In this case, even in the long run, the economy could be stuck below full employment and supply could be very elastic. This is the position of economists known as Keynesians (after

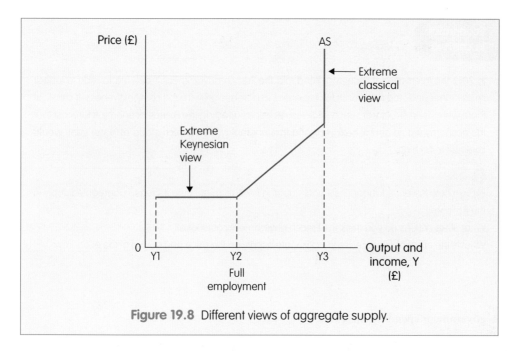

Figure 19.8 Different views of aggregate supply.

the work of John Maynard Keynes), who argue that the vertical supply curve might only ever occur in the very, very long run, but by then, according to Keynes, 'we are all dead'! In this case, there may be a role for demand-side policies to boost demand and output.

For much of our analysis, we will use Figure 19.8, which highlights the different positions of economists. Keynesians would argue that the economy is likely to be stuck well below the potential output with an elastic supply curve (that is, in Figure 19.8, between Y1 and Y2). Classical economists would argue that supply is price inelastic and that the aggregate supply is vertical as at Y3; most economists would argue that we are somewhere in between these two extremes.

NOTE In reality, we are really looking at changes in the rate of inflation rather than at absolute changes in the price level—that is, a fall in aggregate demand is likely to reduce the rate at which prices and wages grow in the long term, rather than their absolute level. Similarly, an increase in demand is likely to lead to higher inflation and wage-rate growth. However, these figures do provide a simplified illustration of what is happening in the economy to demonstrate the underlying issues.

The effects of a shift in the aggregate demand on the economy

Aggregate demand may shift due to changes in consumption, injections, or withdrawals. An outward shift may occur, for example if:

* consumption increases;
* investment increases;

In 2013 the International Monetary Fund told the French government it needed to reduce labour costs further and stop additional tax increases to increase growth and competitiveness. It said that there were deep structural supply-side issues issues affecting the French economy. It forecast that the economy would shrink next year and that unemployment (which stood at 11 per cent) would continue to be high.

? Questions

Explain how lowering labour costs and stopping tax cuts might help increase aggregate supply in the economy.

What other actions do you think the French government could take?

What is the effect of an increase in aggregate supply on the price and output of the economy?

- government spending increases;
- export spending increases; or
- savings fall;
- taxation revenue falls;
- import spending falls.

When the long-run aggregate supply is relatively price elastic, then an increase in the aggregate demand will have a relatively greater effect on output and income than prices. For example, in Figure 19.9, an increase in the aggregate demand from AD1 to AD2 increases the output from Y1 to Y2, but the price level only increases from P1 to P2.

If long-run aggregate supply is more price inelastic, a given increase in the aggregate demand has an increasingly greater effect on prices compared to output. When the aggregate demand increases from AD3 to AD4 (see Figure 19.9), prices increase from P3 to P4, and output increases from Y3 to Y4.

When the long-run aggregate supply is totally price inelastic, an increase in the aggregate demand increases the price level, but does not change output. An increase in the aggregate demand from AD5 to AD6 leads to a price-level increase from P5 to P6. These diagrams highlight the effect of aggregate demand changes depending on the price elasticity of the aggregate supply which in turn depends on your view as an economist. Neo Classical economists think we are further to the right near to the highest value of Y. Keynesian economists think we are below this and to the left nearer to the lowest value of Y.

The effect of a shift in aggregate supply: Short-run and long-run effects

Just as aggregate demand can shift, so can aggregate supply. Imagine that there is an increase in costs—perhaps due to employees demanding higher wages or higher imported costs of materials. This shifts the short-run aggregate supply inwards because at each price less can

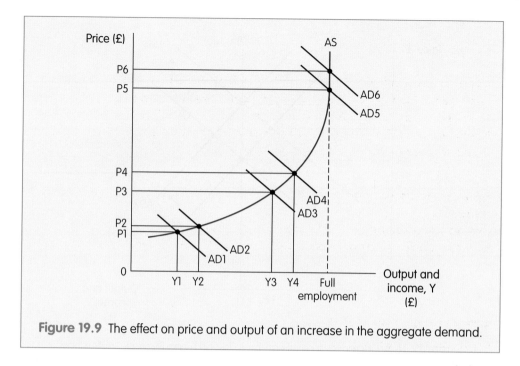

Figure 19.9 The effect on price and output of an increase in the aggregate demand.

be supplied due to higher costs. This leads to an equilibrium with a higher price and lower income in the economy in the short run (see Figure 19.10). In theory employment should fall, putting downward pressure on money wages. If money wages fall, this reduces costs, shifting the short-run supply back out, and the economy moves back down to the original equilibrium at P1Y1. There has been short-term unemployment, but no long-term effects.

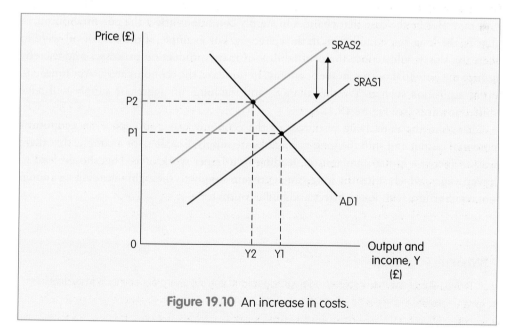

Figure 19.10 An increase in costs.

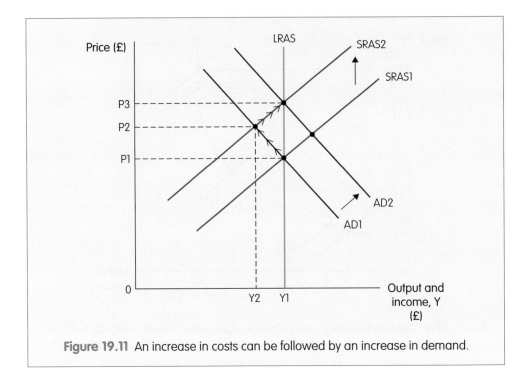

Figure 19.11 An increase in costs can be followed by an increase in demand.

However, the question again is how long it takes to get back to the long run. Would a government faced with high unemployment be tempted to boost aggregate demand, shifting this out and leading the economy back to its potential output, but with higher prices at P3 (see Figure 19.11)?

It may also be the case that changes in supply conditions affect the potential output—that is, the long-run equilibrium in the economy. For example, if the cost of oil were to increase, this would reduce the profitability of many production processes and thereby reduce the potential output in the economy. In this case, the economy may, over time, end up at a position such as Y rather than X, and the long-run aggregate supply will have shifted inwards (see Figure 19.12).

Change in the underlying resources of the economy can also change an economy's potential output and shift the long-run aggregate supply. Imagine, for example, that there was an increase in net immigration, leading to a larger workforce. This should lead to lower wages, which shifts the long-run aggregate supply to the right—leading to a long-run equilibrium, with lower prices and higher output.

What do you think?

Can you think of any major shifts in aggregate demand and supply in your economy in the last few years? Why did this occur do you think?

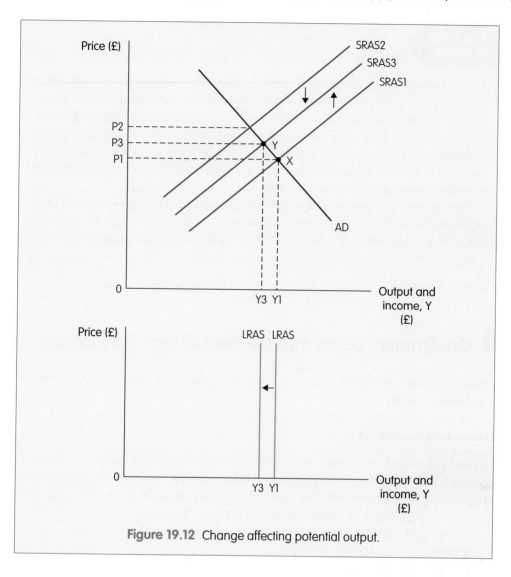

Figure 19.12 Change affecting potential output.

Economics in context

The price of oil

In the 1970s, the price of oil increased significantly, making energy much more expensive. This also made many pieces of capital equipment uneconomic to run. The effect of this was to shift the aggregate supply to the left.

❓ Question

Illustrate this, using an aggregate supply and demand diagram, and show the effect of this shift on the equilibrium price and output in the economy.

The Asian economy Cambodia has been growing at around 7 per cent in recent years with exports being a key driver of growth. The low cost of labour has helped the country to become an important manufacturer and exporter of garments and footwear to markets such as the USA and European Union (EU). Growth has been helped by increases in foreign direct investment in the country, which increased by 75 per cent last year to $1.5bn (£1bn). Foreign investment has not only been into traditional sectors such as garment manufacturing but also newer industries such as auto-parts manufacturing and agricultural products processing.

However there have been protests recently with employees demanding an increase in their wages and further growth in the economy may struggle due to skills shortages. The enrolment rate in tertiary education is only 14 per cent, which means the pool of skilled people is very small.

❓ Question

Discuss the possible consequences for the economy of a labour shortage.

Government policy and the level of national income

To influence the equilibrium of the economy, the government may use demand-side or supply-side policies.

Demand-side policies

Demand-side policies are policies used by the government to control the level of aggregate demand. For example, expansionist policies may include lowering the tax rates to boost spending, or an increase in government spending. Contractionary policies would aim to reduce aggregate demand—for example, by increasing interest rates to encourage saving to earn higher rewards.

The impact of a change in the aggregate demand in terms of its relative effect on price and output therefore depends on the price elasticity of supply. This, in turn, depends on how close the economy is to full employment. The nearer an economy is to its potential output, the more likely it is that expansionist demand-side measures simply lead to inflation and not to increases in output. If supply is price elastic, then an increase in demand is much more effective in terms of boosting output than it is in affecting prices.

Put into practice

Illustrate the impact of a fall in the aggregate demand on the equilibrium price and output.

Supply-side policies

As we saw in Chapter 17, supply-side policies focus on changing the aggregate supply, and influencing the amount supplied in the economy at each and every price.

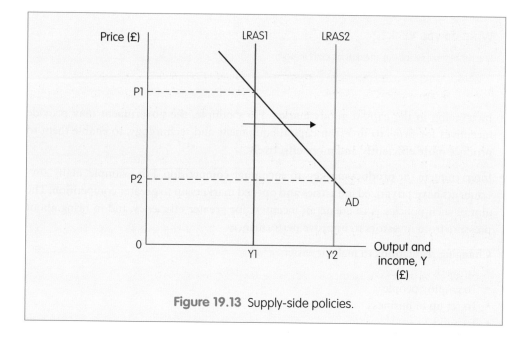

Figure 19.13 Supply-side policies.

Supply-side policies will be aimed at shifting the long-run aggregate supply to the right (see Figure 19.13). For example, the government may want to increase the potential output of the economy.

Supply-side policies could include the following.

- **Increasing the quantity of resources available** For example, a lowering of the school leaving age would increase the size of the available workforce. An introduction of an immigration system to limit the number of people entering a country, by comparison, would limit the growth of the workforce.

- **Increasing the quality of those resources** For example, a better-trained workforce would be more productive.

- **Increasing the efficiency in the way in which they are used** For example, if resources are managed more effectively, then they can produce more.

Supply-side measures might include the following.

- **Labour market measures** The government may invest in training schemes to provide employees with the skills that they need for the jobs that are available. In some cases, employees lack the appropriate skills which prevents them from getting jobs or being as productive as they could be.

  The government may also change the tax and benefit system to boost the rewards of working relative to being unemployed.

  The government may introduce labour market reforms to help the labour market to work more efficiently. For example, it may reduce trade union power to enable more flexible working practices, and to enable firms to hire people and change the number of people working for them more easily.

- **Intervening in the capital goods market** For example, the government may provide incentives for firms to invest in capital equipment and technology, to enable them to produce more efficiently and more effectively.

- **Intervening in the product markets to encourage competition** For example, many governments have privatized industries and opened markets up to greater competition. The aim of such policies is to create an incentive for greater efficiency and to bring about pressure from investors to improve performance.

- **Changing regulations to make it easier**
  - To work
  - To employ people
  - To set up in business
  - To build
  - To expand your premises

The planning regulations, for example, can slow up any development and investment plans that businesses have.

- **Improve the infrastructure of the country** The government can invest in sectors such as roads, communications and transport to make it easier for firms to do business. In the UK for example, the ability of businesses to develop trade links with the emerging markets may have been hindered by the lack of enough direct flights to these regions due to limits on airport capacity. Demands from businesses for another runway at Heathrow have been high. There have also been requests for more investment in broadband, in the motorway system and faster rail links.

Supply-side policies aim to increase the productive capacity of the economy. By increasing aggregate supply they lead to growth and lower unemployment. Increasing supply puts downward pressure on prices and can therefore offset inflationary pressures. Supply-side policies can also increase competitiveness which can boost exports.

Difficulties with supply-side policies

The difficulties with supply-side policies include the following.

- To create flexibility in the labour market, fewer employees may be offered permanent contracts and these short-term employees will therefore be less secure in their jobs. In an attempt to create a more flexible workforce, managers are less willing to guarantee jobs for life or to offer long-term contracts. They want flexible contracts that enable them to increase or decrease supply as demand dictates. This may be good for the firm, but not for employees.

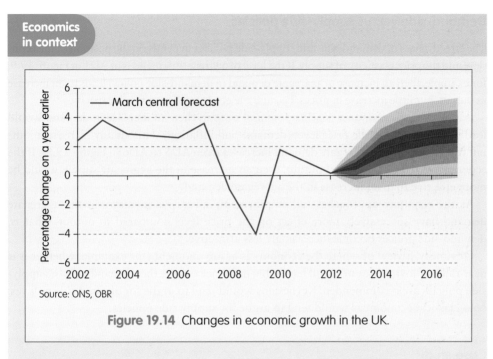

Source: ONS, OBR

Figure 19.14 Changes in economic growth in the UK.

? Question

Analyse the possible causes of changes in economic growth in the UK since 2002 (Figure 19.14) using aggregate demand and supply analysis.

- In an attempt to encourage people to work, those who are unemployed may become worse off—for example, the government may reduce the benefits available to those who are unemployed. This will widen the gap between the rich and the poor, and may be seen as unfair.

- An increase in supply is valuable only if the demand is there; otherwise, it simply creates excess capacity.

Supply-side policies

Supply-side policies focus on increasing the supply of goods and services in the economy. Supply-side policies came to prominence in the 1980s when they were advocated in the UK by Margaret Thatcher and in the USA by Ronald Reagan. The traditional approach to the economy of managing demand was seen to have failed and so the emphasis was now placed on supply-side issues.

? Question

Are supply-side policies likely to be more of a priority than demand-side policies when the economy is at, near, or well below full employment?

Demand-side versus supply-side policies

The effectiveness of demand-side and supply-side policies depends on the position of the economy and the price elasticity of supply. If the level of aggregate demand is at AD1 in Figure 19.9, for example, then an increase in aggregate demand (a demand-side policy) leads to an increase in output, but little increase in prices, because the economy has so much capacity.

If, however, the economy is at its potential output, then an increase in demand would lead to an increase in the price level (demand-pull inflation) without any increase in output (for example, the aggregate demand increases from AD5 to AD6 in Figure 19.9). If the economy were at its potential output, then an increase in the aggregate supply would be more effective than an increase in the aggregate demand.

As the economy approaches full employment, successive increases in the aggregate demand have successively more effect on the price level compared to output—that is, demand-side polices become increasingly less attractive.

Obviously, a view of where the economy is at any moment (for example, whether it is near full employment or not) will have a big influence on whether demand-side or supply-side policies are recommended. Keynesians would tend to argue for demand side policies. Neo-classical economists would tend to argue for supply side policies.

Case study

The United Kingdom could boost growth by bringing forward measures already included in its fiscal plan, such as spending on infrastructure and job skills, the International Monetary Fund said recently.

Despite recent improvements in some indicators of economic growth, the economy is still a long way from a strong and sustainable recovery. The economy also needs to rebalance, the IMF said, and make the transition to a high-investment and more export-oriented economy. After five years of relatively weak growth, investment is low and youth unemployment is high, and the IMF is concerned about the risk of permanent damage to long-term growth.

The complexity of the issues means policymaking has become particularly difficult. Conventional distinctions between demand and supply problems don't work so neatly—firms might give up on demanding credit lines if they think the terms supplied to them will be particularly onerous, for example.

This makes it all the more important to pursue a package of policies that support each other, the IMF said. Financial policies are needed to restore the health of the banking system, to ensure that monetary policy is fully effective, and fiscal and structural policies are needed to raise expectations of incomes and returns on investment. The government has shown flexibility in its fiscal programme to mitigate damage to growth, but planned fiscal tightening this year will be a drag on the economy, the IMF said.

With unemployment high and interest rates low, the government should take the opportunity to bring forward 'high value' spending that has big long-term payoffs. The government could do this within its current fiscal plan, such as

- Bring forward planned capital investment. This would help catalyse private investment.

- Further modify the composition of plans to reduce government debt and deficits. This could include growth friendly measures, such as reducing the marginal effective corporate tax rates to bring investment forward, and introducing tax allowances for raising equity.

The government's commitment to a medium-term plan has earned it credibility, and it has the advantage of good institutions and astute debt management practices. Raising growth expectations will do more to reassure financial markets about debt sustainability, the IMF said.

Making monetary policy more effective

The Bank of England has lowered short-term interest rates, bought government bonds and used other tools in its arsenal to help increase the flow of credit to help the economy. With the economy's output running below capacity and inflation pressures easing, the central bank can afford to keep in place policies that support the economy, according to the IMF.

But credit flows have continued to fall. The problem is the monetary stimulus is not fully getting through to the real economy. Restoring the health of the banks is crucial for restoring credit flow, according to the IMF.

Banks have improved the health of their balance sheets by raising capital, but the share of non-performing assets across some major banks remains at high levels. Banks will need to focus on building capital while not compromising the availability of credit, by some combination of new equity issuance, dividend reductions, remuneration constraints, and balance sheet restructuring.

Source: Adapted from IMF Survey article: "UK Should Restore Growth, Rebalance Economy", May 22, 2013 http://www.imf.org/external/pubs/ft/survey/so/2013/car052213a.htm

Questions

1 Summarize the position of the UK economy.

2 Discuss the role fiscal policy can play in the UK according to the IMF.

3 Discuss the role of monetary policy in the UK according to the IMF.

4 What difficulties does the government face when using fiscal and monetary policies to influence the economy?

Review questions

1 How might an increase in the aggregate demand affect the equilibrium price and output in the economy?

2 Explain two factors that might cause an outward shift of the aggregate supply curve.

3 Why might the aggregate supply be price inelastic?

4 Explain two supply-side policies to promote growth.

5 Explain two demand side policies to promote growth.

6 Explain why Keynesians think aggregate supply is price elastic.

7 Explain why Classical economists think aggregate supply is price inelastic.

8 Should demand-side policies always be used rather than supply-side policies when a government intervenes in an economy?

Put into practice

1   Show the effect of a decrease in aggregate demand on the equilibrium price level in the economy and the quantity; assume that aggregate supply is relatively price inelastic.

2   Show the effect of an increase in aggregate supply on the equilibrium price and quantity. Assume that aggregate demand is relatively price inelastic.

Key learning points

•   Equilibrium in an economy occurs when the aggregate demand equals the aggregate supply.

•   The aggregate demand is downward-sloping in relation to price. A higher price level for a given level of income reduces the quantity demanded.

•   The short-run aggregate supply is upward-sloping in relation to price.

•   The long-run aggregate supply is vertical.

•   An increase in the aggregate demand will usually lead to an increase in price and output. The relative impact on price compared to output depends on the price elasticity of the aggregate supply.

Learn more

Supply-side policies have a significant impact on the level of income in an economy and on economic growth. To learn more about supply-side policies that have been introduced in the UK, visit the Online Resource Centre.

 Visit our Online Resource Centre at http://www.oxfordtextbooks.co.uk/orc/gillespie_ econ3e/ for test questions and further information on topics covered in this chapter.

Consumption

The level of aggregate demand in an economy is made up of consumption spending, investment, government spending, and export and import spending. In this chapter, we examine the factors that affect consumption spending in particular. In the following chapters, we examine the other elements of aggregate demand.

LEARNING OBJECTIVES

By the end of this chapter, you should be able to:

✓ explain the factors that influence levels of consumption;

✓ analyse the impact of a change in consumption spending.

Introduction

We all like to spend money and, in so doing, we are consuming goods and services, and creating demand in the economy. This spending generates output and employment. Consumption, in macroeconomics, measures the total planned level of demand in the economy by households for final goods and services. Consumption spending is the largest element of the aggregate demand and therefore changes in households' spending can have a major impact on an economy. Economists are naturally interested in what determines the total level of consumption in the economy because this is such an important element of the aggregate demand and therefore has a big influence on how well an economy is doing. As we saw in Chapter 17 aggregate demand comprises $C + I + G + X - M$; consumption is a major element of aggregate demand.

The Keynesian consumption function

According to the economist John Maynard Keynes (1936), the level of consumption in an economy is given by the following equation (see Figure 20.1):

$C = a + bYd$

where:

- 'C' is the level of consumption spending;

- 'a' is the level of autonomous consumption—that is, the amount of spending that there would be even if incomes were zero. This is known as 'dis-saving' because households must be borrowing or using up past savings;

- 'b' is the marginal propensity to consume (MPC)—that is, the amount of extra spending out of an extra pound. For example, if the MPC is 0.8, then this means that 80 pence out of each extra pound are spent on the consumption of final goods and services.

The MPC is given by:

$$\frac{\text{Change in consumption spending}}{\text{Change in income}}$$

A change in the size of the MPC will alter the slope of the consumption function and therefore the aggregate demand schedule;

- 'Yd' is the disposable income, which consists of income from employment and selfemployment, pensions, investment income, and cash benefits *less* income tax, local taxes, and employees' National Insurance contributions (NICs). It represents the household income available to be spent or saved.

According to this equation, there is a direct relationship between the level of disposable income earned by households and the amount that they spend on consumption.

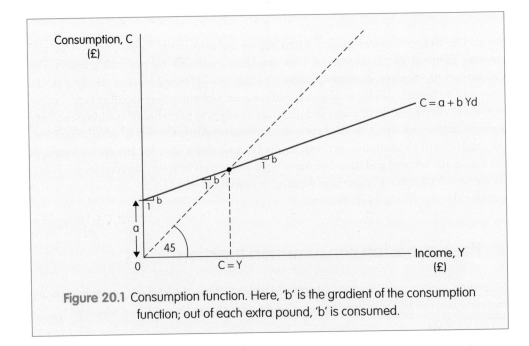

Figure 20.1 Consumption function. Here, 'b' is the gradient of the consumption function; out of each extra pound, 'b' is consumed.

The average propensity to consume

The average propensity to consume (APC) measures the average spending out of every pound of income:

$$APC = \frac{C}{Yd}$$

At any level of income, the APC can be measured by the gradient of a ray drawn from the origin to the consumption function (see Figure 20.2), whereas the MPC is shown by the gradient of the consumption function. Note how the APC falls as income increases (as shown by the fact that the rays become flatter); as income falls, the value of the APC approaches the MPC.

Imagine that the consumption function is

$$C = 100 + 0.8Yd$$

Out of each extra pound, we spend 80 pence; there is an autonomous element of spending of £100. If we earn only £1 of disposable income, then the consumer spending will be £100 + £0.80—that is, a total spending of £100.80 out of £1. The APC is 100.8. Due to the autonomous element, we are spending a lot, even though income is low, making the APC high. The average spending is much higher than the marginal spending.

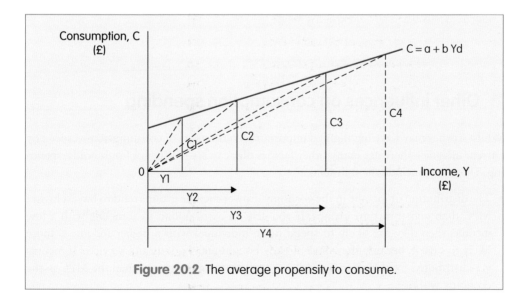

Figure 20.2 The average propensity to consume.

As income increases, the autonomous element becomes far less significant and the key factor of our spending becomes the MPC. For example, if income is £10,000, then:

$$C = £100 + (0.8 \times £10,000) = £8,100$$

Therefore:

$$APC = \frac{£8,100}{£10,000} = 0.81$$

The APC is now close to the MPC. The average spending is closer to the spending out of each extra pound. The autonomous element of consumption becomes almost irrelevant at high levels of income because most of the consumption is now linked to income.

Put into practice

Imagine that C = £10 billion + 0.5Yd
What is the MPC and the APC when:

- disposable income is £100 billion?
- disposable income is £200 billion?

What do you think?

Between 2009 and 2012, the savings ratio in the UK (i.e. the proportion of income saved) was around 7 per cent. By the start of 2013, it had fallen to 4.2 per cent. Why do you think this might be?

After the economic crisis of 2008 the UK economy was very slow to recover. In 2013 the government was pleased to announce some signs of growth but the rise in aggregate demand was due mainly to a rise in consumption, and a fall in savings. Exports were rising only slowly and investment was 25 per cent lower than in the boom years prior to 2008. Do you think it matters why aggregate demand is rising as long as it is rising?

▦ Other influences on consumption spending

Whilst Keynes may have highlighted important determinants of consumption—especially current income—there are many other factors that can also influence households' spending. These may include the following.

- **The distribution of income in the economy** Lower-income groups tend to have a higher MPC than higher-income groups. If you give an extra pound to someone with a low income, then they are likely to spend it; an individual with a higher income is more likely to save it, because they have already bought many goods and services. If income is redistributed from high-income earners to low-income earners, then the MPC in the economy will rise.

- **The availability and cost of credit** If it is easy and cheap to borrow, then households are more likely to spend money, so consumption will rise even if incomes have not increased. Think of all of the different ways in which you can borrow money, and you will realize how much spending is financed this way and how important credit is in the UK economy.

What do you think?

Over the last 20 years UK households have had high levels of debt. Do you think the government should encourage households to save more?

Economics in context

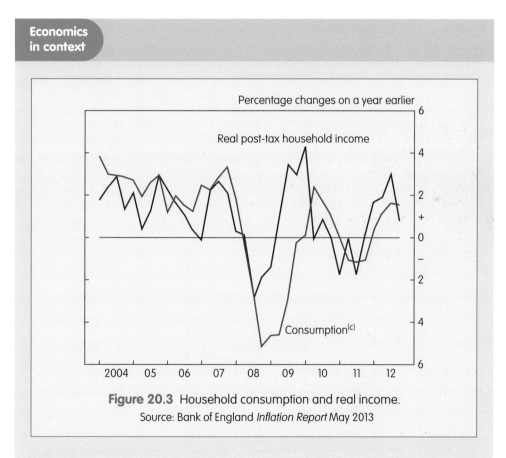

Figure 20.3 Household consumption and real income.
Source: Bank of England *Inflation Report* May 2013

? Question

How strong is the link between consumption and real household income based on the data in Figure 20.3?

Put into practice

There are numerous ways of borrowing money, such as overdrafts, loans, student loans, credit cards, and mortgages.

- Can you think of any more?
- How much do you owe?
- Could you borrow more if you were to want to do so?
- How easy would it be?

What do you think?

Do you think that it is the banks' responsibility to check whether people can easily afford to repay a loan or not?

- **Wealth effects** If households become wealthier—perhaps due to an increase in house or share prices—then this can allow them to borrow more to spend. Often, this will be spent on items such as holidays, cars, and other income elastic products.

- **The age distribution in the economy** In general, people will tend to spend more than their income when they are younger (for example, when they are just starting out in a job). We will tend to spend less than our income in our middle years (when we are building up savings) and more than our income in later life (when we are running down savings) (see Figure 20.4). The importance of the stage in the life cycle on consumption

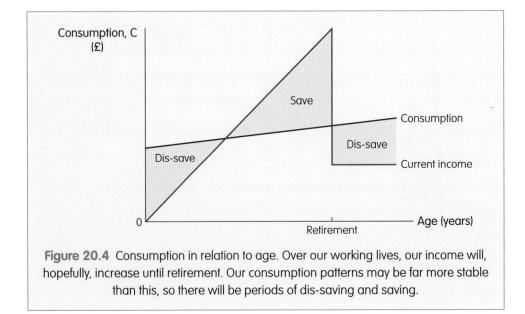

Figure 20.4 Consumption in relation to age. Over our working lives, our income will, hopefully, increase until retirement. Our consumption patterns may be far more stable than this, so there will be periods of dis-saving and saving.

spending was highlighted by Ando and Modigliani (1957). The UK has an ageing population, for example, which means that there may be more dis-saving.

- **The permanent income theory** This model was developed by Friedman (1957) and states that what matters to consumers when determining spending is not their present income, but rather their 'permanent income'. A household's permanent income depends on its view of what it will earn over its whole lifetime. Temporary unemployment may reduce the current level of income considerably (which, according to Keynes, would lead to a significant fall in spending), but its impact on the overall lifetime income is far less significant, assuming that the household thinks that the unemployment will not last long. Equally, a one-off bonus would not lead to a significant increase in present spending, because when this one-off increase is considered in the context of the whole

Economics in context

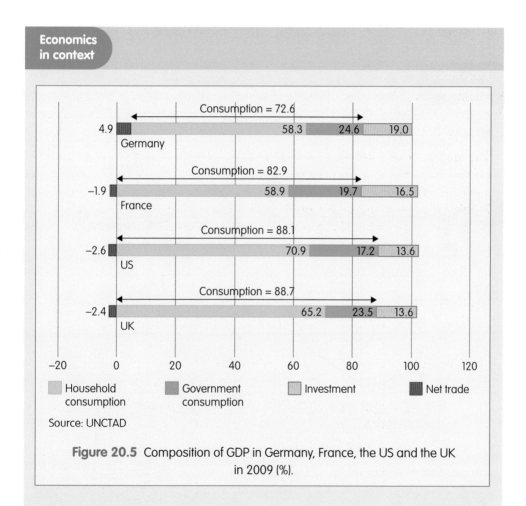

Source: UNCTAD

Figure 20.5 Composition of GDP in Germany, France, the US and the UK in 2009 (%).

? Question

In Figure 20.5 why do you think consumption in the UK is a bigger proportion of aggregate demand than in other countries?

lifetime's income of a household, its effect is less significant. According to the permanent income hypothesis, changes in disposable income that are not expected to last will not have much effect on current spending.

This has implications for government policy. A tax cut to boost spending will not affect consumers' view of their permanent income if they think that the tax cut is only for the short term. To have a real effect, the government would need to convince households that the tax cut would be large enough and long enough to have an impact on their average lifetime earnings.

What do you think?

What are the main influences on how much you personally spend and save? Are you typical do you think?

Economics in context

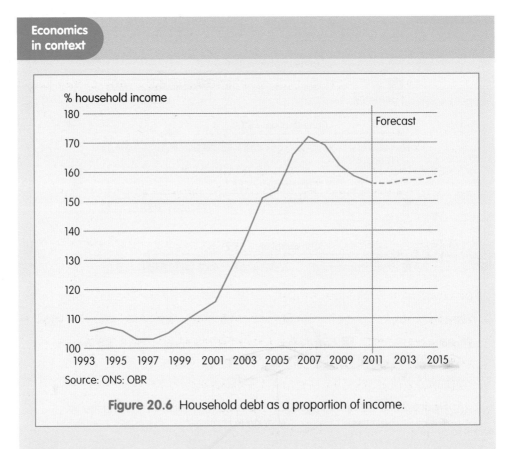

Figure 20.6 Household debt as a proportion of income.

? Questions

In Figure 20.6 why do you think household debt as a proportion of income has been rising?
Do you think these levels of household debt are a problem?

Case study

A recent report by the Ernst and Young Item Club suggests that UK consumers are ready to 'loosen their belts' due to a recovery in consumer confidence. Increases in personal tax allowances and a recovery in the housing market are expected to lead to an increase in consumer spending.

The Item Club predicts that the growth in consumer spending will reach 2.2 per cent by 2015, which will be back to the level it was before the financial crisis. The report said that the economy was essentially returning to a situation where growth in the economy was fuelled by consumer spending.

Spending on entertainment and leisure is expected to grow by 5.9 per cent in the coming year, as shoppers splash out on TVs, tablet computers, smartphones, and package holidays. Increases in personal tax allowances will sees basic rate taxpayers taking home nearly £300 extra this year.

The Item Club also noted that mortgage lenders, estate agents, and property websites are reporting an increase in activity, some of which has been helped by the government's Funding for Lending scheme which was designed to help people to borrow for housing.

Much of the increase in spending will be in the income elastic sectors, such as cars, hotels and restaurants. However, the report warned that any hint of adverse economic developments is likely to provoke an immediate blip in spending and a retreat from the local restaurant back to meal deals and nights on the sofa.

Source: http://www.ey.com/UK/en/Issues/Business-environment/Financial-markets-and-economy/ITEM—Forecast-headlines-and-projections

❓ Questions

1   What is meant by an income elastic product?

2   Analyse the influences on consumer spending identified above.

3   Does it matter if growth in the economy is fuelled by consumer spending?

Review questions

1   Explain what is meant by consumption.

2   What, according to Keynes, is the most important determinant of consumption spending?

3   What is meant by autonomous consumption spending in the Keynesian model?

4   Explain what is meant by the marginal propensity to consume.

5   Explain what is meant by the average propensity to consume.

6   How might a fall in interest rates affect consumption spending?

7   Explain what is meant by 'permanent income'.

8   Explain how the age distribution in an economy might affect the total level of consumption.

Put into practice

1   Draw a consumption function $C = £10bn + 0.6 Yd$; show what happens if autonomous consumption increases to £15bn

2   If the consumption function is given by $C = £5bn + 0.7 Yd$ what is the equation for the savings function? Draw the savings function.

Assignment questions

1   Research the age composition of the UK. Discuss the possible implications of this for the patterns and level of consumption in the UK.

2   Research the levels of consumption and savings in the UK. Analyse the possible causes for this pattern of consumption and savings.

Key learning points

- Consumption is an important element of aggregate demand.

- The level of consumption in an economy may be influenced by a range of factors, including current income, estimates of permanent income, interest rates, expectations of the price level, the availability of credit, and the age distribution.

- An increase in consumption increases the aggregate demand.

References

Ando, A. and Modigliani, F. (1957) 'Tests of the life cycle hypothesis of saving: Comments and suggestions', *Oxford Institute of Statistics Bulletin*, XIX(May): 99–124

Friedman, M. (1957) *A Theory of the Consumption Function*, National Bureau of Economic Research, Princeton, NJ

Keynes, J.M. (1936) *General Theory of Employment, Interest, and Money*, Harcourt, Brace, and Co, New York (first published by Macmillan, Cambridge University Press for the Royal Economic Society)

Learn more

This chapter has focused on the consumption function; this is clearly interrelated with the savings function. To learn more about this relationship, visit the Online Resource Centre.

 Visit our Online Resource Centre at http://www.oxfordtextbooks.co.uk/orc/gillespie_ econ3e/ for test questions and further information on topics covered in this chapter.

Investment

Investment is an important element of the aggregate demand. It is of particular importance because it is the most volatile element of the aggregate demand, and therefore an understanding of it is vital if a government is to be able to influence the level of aggregate demand effectively and influence the growth path of the economy. Investment is also important because it affects the level of aggregate supply in the economy. In this chapter, we examine the influences on the level of investment in an economy, and the consequences of it changing on the equilibrium price and output, and employment.

LEARNING OBJECTIVES

By the end of this chapter, you should be able to:

✓ analyse the determinants of investment spending;

✓ explain the impact of a change in investment spending on national income;

✓ explain the instability caused by the accelerator–multiplier model.

▨ Introduction

Investment occurs when firms make a decision to allocate resources into projects that will generate future returns—for example, investing in a new machine or a new information technology system. Investment involves sacrificing existing, present consumption for future expected benefits.

Investment may be in the following.

- **Fixed capital** This involves the purchase of assets that are expected to be used for a long period—for example, transport, factories, and production equipment.

- **Working capital** These are short-term assets that will be used up in the production process—for example, stocks and materials.

Investment spending is an injection into the economy and is a particularly volatile element of aggregate demand, as well as an influence on aggregate supply.

▨ Gross and net investment

The types of investment include the following.

- **Gross investment** This measures the total investment in an economy in a period.
- **Depreciation investment** This is investment undertaken to replace equipment or machinery that has worn out. Depreciation investment simply maintains the level and quality of the capital stock.
- **Net investment** This is new investment that increases the capital stock in the economy.

Therefore we have:

  Gross investment = Net investment + Depreciation investment

  or

  Net investment = Gross investment − Depreciation investment

Although, in the media, 'investment' often refers to buying shares or putting money into a pension scheme, these represent savings to an economist. 'Investment', to an economist, refers to capital goods. It is the purchase of items that increase output in the future.

What do you think?

Why do you think the level of investment matters in an economy?

▨ Factors affecting the level of investment in an economy

The amount of investment in an economy will depend on the following.

- **The initial cost of capital projects and availability of funds** Some projects may be attractive in terms of the possible rewards that they offer, but may not be affordable at the present time if firms do not have, or cannot raise, the necessary finance. Therefore the availability and cost of finance are an important issue. Following the global recession of 2008–09, one of the problems facing businesses was the difficulty raising finance for investment projects, because banks were worried about taking risks.

- **The expected returns from the investment** What are the expected costs and revenues from the project, and therefore what profits does the firm expect to be earned and over what period? These estimates of revenues and costs are, of course, only a forecast of the future net inflows. As a result, investment decisions inevitably have an element of risk and uncertainty. An investment into an oil project, for example, involves estimates of what the world oil price will be many years into the future—this involves a high degree of risk in terms of the accuracy of the forecast. The likely returns on a project will depend on firms' views about the likely level of sales, which are likely to be linked to economic growth and also to the likely inflation rates. The importance of expectations in the investment decision explains why this element of aggregate demand can be so volatile. Changes in our views of what might happen in the economy will affect the expected profits and therefore investment spending.

- **The alternatives available** A decision to invest in one project means that resources are being allocated to this area and away from something else. A decision is therefore being made about the best way in which to use resources and this involves an opportunity cost. If, for example, the returns available in other countries or in financial savings such as shares are high, then this is likely to reduce the level of investment in the UK.

- **Risk and culture** Any investment project will involve risk, because the outcomes are not certain. Different managers and organizations may have different perceptions of the risk of any particular project, and will have different attitudes to taking risks. This may affect their willingness to pursue a particular investment. If a country has a culture that is risk-taking, then this might affect the level of investment in one country compared to another. National culture can also be important in other ways. Japanese and German investors have tended to be more long-termist than UK firms; this means that they were willing to wait longer for the eventual rewards. This was partly because their investors tended to be linked to the firm in some way (such as being their suppliers) and so were willing to wait for the long-term benefits in which they would share. In the UK, investors do not tend to be directly linked to the business and look for shorter-term rewards. This has tended to reduce the number of projects in which UK firms might invest compared with those available to Japanese firms, because investors are less willing to wait for their returns.

- **Non-financial factors** When considering an investment, a firm may be interested in the expected profits, but it may also take into account non-financial factors. What will the investment do to the brand image? How will stakeholders in the firm react to the investment? Will it fit with any proposed policy on issues such as corporate social responsibility? Does it fit with the corporate strategy? Investing in a new product area may in itself appear profitable, for example, but may not fit with a corporate strategy that intends to focus on existing business areas. In recent years, for example, many firms have become more concerned with the environmental impact of their activities and this has diverted investment away from some projects that are perceived to be environmentally unfriendly. On a national scale, firms may be concerned about factors such as political stability when deciding whether or not to go ahead with a project.

- **Government policy** Changes to the tax system can provide incentives for firms to invest. For example, tax credits may enable firms to reduce their tax bill if they invest more in research and development; a reduction in corporation tax increases likely returns on a project, encouraging investment.

Put into practice

Show using a diagram the likely effect on investment of a fall in business confidence.

The importance of investment

Investment is an injection into the economy and is important for the following reasons.

- Investment tends to be very volatile, partly because it depends so much on expectations. Sudden changes in investment can lead to instability in the economy. The economist Keynes referred to firms's expectations as 'animal spirits' and highlighted how easily a decision to invest may change. Changes in managers' views on the future state of the economy can change the level of investment and therefore aggregate demand.

- Investment affects both the aggregate demand (because it involves spending) and the aggregate supply (because it increases the productive capacity of the economy and therefore, in the long run, the amount that can be produced) (see Figure 21.1). Investment is an injection into the economy and so an increase in it will boost the level of the aggregate demand. However, more investment will also increase the productive capacity of the economy and shift the aggregate supply over time.

Put into practice

Using an aggregate supply and aggregate demand diagram, show the effect of an increase in demand and an increase in aggregate supply due to an increase in investment.

What do you think?

Expectations are an important influence on investment decisions.

- Do you think the government can influence firms' expectations?
- In what other ways do you think expectations can influence decisions within an economy?

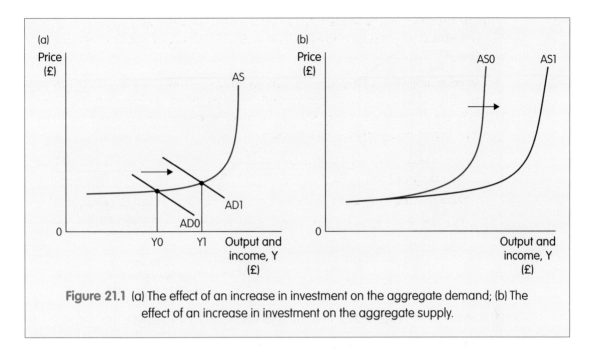

Figure 21.1 (a) The effect of an increase in investment on the aggregate demand; (b) The effect of an increase in investment on the aggregate supply.

▓ The marginal efficiency of capital

The marginal efficiency of capital (MEC) shows the rate of return on an additional invest-ment project. This return can be compared with the cost of borrowing to decide whether or not to invest in a project. If the return on the project (that is, the MEC) is greater than the rate of interest (which is the cost of borrowing), then the project should go ahead on finan-cial grounds. If the return is less than the cost of borrowing, then the project should not go ahead (for example, you should not invest in a project expected to generate returns of 8 per cent if the cost of borrowing is 9 per cent). Therefore, a profit-maximizing firm should in-vest up to the point at which the MEC equals the extra costs of borrowing (the interest rate). This is another example of the marginal condition under which, to maximize returns, man-agers undertake an activity up to the point at which the extra benefit equals the extra cost.

In Figure 21.2, for example, project I1 is expected to achieve returns of 18 per cent; project I2 is estimated to achieve returns of 6 per cent. If the cost of borrowing is 6 per cent, then all of the projects up to and including I2 are worth doing. The projects beyond I2 are not financially attractive, because the expected return (MEC) is less than the cost of borrowing. so profits would fall.

Changes in the interest rate therefore lead to movements along the MEC schedule. Higher interest rates usually lead to less investment as fewer projects become viable. The extent to which investment changes depends on the interest elasticity of demand for capital goods.

$$\text{Interest elasticity of demand for capital} = \frac{\text{percentage change in investment levels}}{\text{percentage change in interest rates}}$$

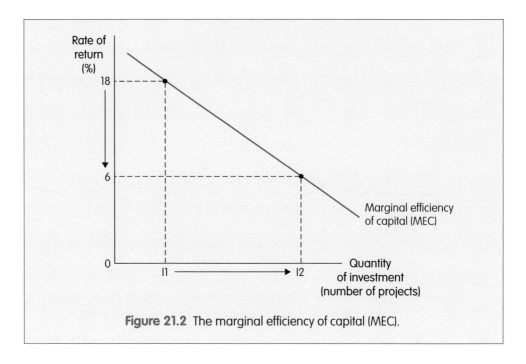

Figure 21.2 The marginal efficiency of capital (MEC).

Put into practice

- If demand for capital goods is very sensitive to interest rate changes, does this mean that it is interest elastic or interest inelastic?
- Calculate the interest elasticity of investment if investment falls 20 per cent when interest rates increase 4 per cent.

The MEC curve will shift if every project is expected to earn higher or lower returns. This may be due to more optimistic expectations about the future level of sales and therefore returns; this, in turn, may be due to a belief that the economy is going to grow faster. This would lead to an upward shift in the MEC as higher returns are expected on each project (see Figure 21.3).

In the media, you will often see reports on levels of business confidence and the views of business people about whether they think that orders will increase or not in the future. These surveys are a way of assessing business confidence. The level of business confidence is an extremely important factor in determining the level of investment in an economy. Given that people's confidence can change quite easily (for example, if the government is having problems or if there is an external shock, such as a natural disaster or a change in the oil price), investment levels can change quite dramatically due to shifts in the MEC. This can have a large impact on the aggregate demand.

The MEC might also shift due to changes in technology or the level of capital in the economy. An increase in the expected returns on projects will lead to more investment at any level of interest rate.

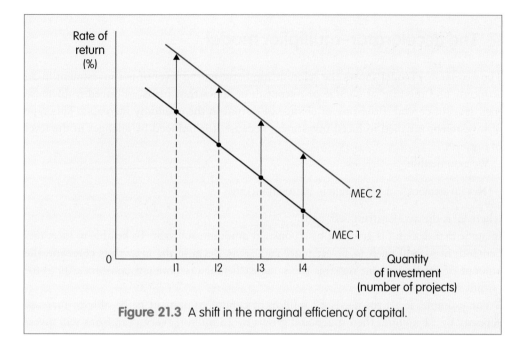

Figure 21.3 A shift in the marginal efficiency of capital.

What do you think?

What do you think influences firms' expectations of the future economic environment?
The Bank of England may start to provide 'forward guidance' about the interest rate i.e. it will announce what the interest rate will be for a set period of time in the future. How might this affect investment?

Put into practice

a. There will be a movement down a given marginal efficiency of investment schedule when:

  • managers become more optimistic.

  • managers become more pessimistic.

  • the rate of interest falls.

  • the rate of interest rises.

b. There will be an outward shift in the marginal efficiency of investment schedule when:

  • managers become more optimistic.

  • managers become more pessimistic.

  • the rate of interest falls.

  • the rate of interest rises.

The accelerator–multiplier model

The accelerator model shows the relationship between the level of net investment in an economy and the rate of change of output. It assumes that firms will need to increase their level of capital if the rate of change of output in the economy increases. This type of investment is called induced investment because it is induced by changes in the level of output.:

We assume that

Net investment = a × Change in national income

where 'a' is the accelerator coefficient.

Imagine that demand is growing by a constant amount each year. To be able to meet this demand, firms will need to invest more each year. Because the growth is constant, the amount of net investment remains the same each year (assuming a constant capital-to-output ratio).

For example, if a firm needs £2 million of capital equipment to be able to increase capacity by £1 million, then if demand grows by £5 million every year, firms will invest £10 million per year to be able to produce at this higher level. The level of net investment (that is, ignoring spending on updating and maintaining old equipment) will be constant each year at £10 million and this will increase the capacity of the economy by a constant amount.

If, however, demand begins to grow by more each year, then, to keep pace with this increasing rate of demand, firms must increase their annual level of net investment. This, in turn, boosts the aggregate demand and helps to stimulate even more spending due to the multiplier process. If this increased spending leads to a larger increase in demand than the year before, then this, again, increases the level of net investment to keep pace with it and a growth spiral has been created.

For example, if demand grows by £5 million one year, £6 million in the second year, and £7 million in the third year, then firms will want to invest £10 million, then £12 million, and then £14 million. The level of net investment is increasing because the growth in demand is accelerating (see Figure 21.4).

However, this investment–demand spiral is vulnerable to collapse. For example, if the demand grows again, but by less than the year before (for example, by £4 million rather than £5 million), then firms will need to invest to have the additional capacity to produce this output, but their investment will be at a lower level than the previous year. In this example, investment will fall to £8 million from £10 million. Because the rate at which demand has grown has slowed up, the amount of net investment will be less than before. This leads to a fall in the aggregate demand and sets off a downward multiplier. This may send the economy into a period of even slower growth and therefore another fall in net investment.

The accelerator model shows the link between net investment and the rate of growth of demand in the economy. It shows why the level of net investment in an economy may fall

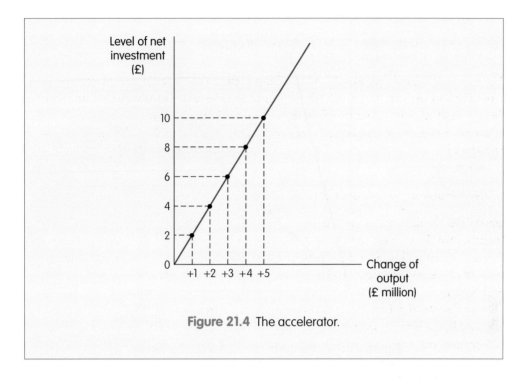

Figure 21.4 The accelerator.

compared with the year before, even if the economy is still growing. It is the rate of growth that is most important. Given that changes in net investment can set off the multiplier, it also highlights how significant swings in the aggregate demand can be caused by initial changes in the rate of growth of the economy. A small fall in the rate of growth of the economy leads to a fall in net investment, which can set off a downward multiplier and create much slower long-term growth.

According to the accelerator model, an increased level of net investment can only be achieved by accelerating increases in demand in the economy; this is not sustainable, which is one reason why economies swing from booms to slumps.

▪ Limitations of the accelerator model

The limitations of the accelerator model include the following.

- Some firms will have excess capacity and therefore will not need to undertake net investment to meet an increase in demand.
- Technology may change and this will change the accelerator coefficient—for example, less net investment may be required to meet a given increase in output. The effect of a change in the accelerator coefficient can be seen in Figure 21.5.
- There may be bottlenecks and constraints in the producer (capital goods) industry that prevent or delay the net investment from going ahead.

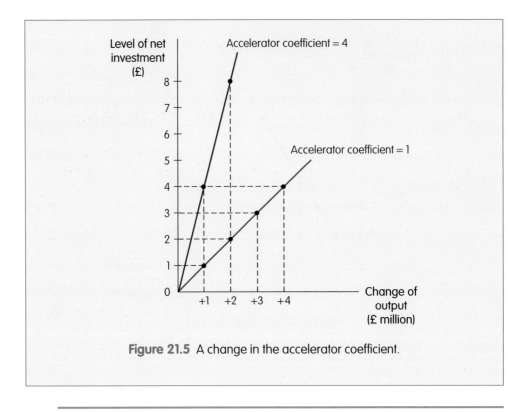

Figure 21.5 A change in the accelerator coefficient.

Put into practice

- Can you remember the equation for the multiplier?
- On what does the size of the multiplier depend?

▓ Cost–benefit analysis

Cost–benefit analysis is a technique used mainly by governments when assessing an investment project. It is a technique that tries to quantify the external costs and external benefits involved in any project. It is often used by governments, which are not only interested in the private costs and benefits of any activity, but also want to consider the full social impacts of any project. For example, it may be used when assessing a new council-house development or high-speed railway. The government may also ask private firms to undertake such an analysis when dealing with a major project with important social effects, such as a new airport terminal.

A cost–benefit analysis involves estimating the monetary value of external costs, such as pollution, congestion, noise, and the impact of a project on wildlife. It will also try to value external benefits, such as the benefits to society of improving the public transport system. Measuring such external costs and benefits can be difficult to do, but is likely to lead to different decisions being made from those that a private firm would make.

Traffic speed systems

In the 1990s, a cost–benefit analysis of traffic light and speed cameras was commissioned by the Home Office, working with the Association of Chief Police Officers (ACPO) Traffic Committee. The terms of reference were:

to provide a detailed and rigorous cost–benefit analysis in relation to traffic light and speed cameras by identifying and quantifying the whole range of relevant factors, and producing a comprehensive and clear account of the analysis process.

The types of cost and benefit considered relevant included:

- the costs of purchasing, installing, operating, and maintaining the cameras;

- the costs to the courts and the Crown Prosecution Service (CPS) resulting from the use of the cameras;

- the costs of associated publicity campaigns;

- savings in human life and injury, as well as those associated with reduced damage to property;

- savings experienced by the police and emergency services as a result of attending fewer traffic collisions;

- savings experienced by the health service as a result of dealing with fewer road accident victims;

- fine income generated as a result of camera use; and

- improved traffic flow, reduced journey times, and an 'improved environment'.

Source: http://rds.homeoffice.gov.uk/rds/prgpdfs/fprs20.pdf

? Question

A number of councils in the UK recently removed their traffic speed cameras because financial cutbacks meant that they could not afford to maintain them. Do you think that speed cameras should be maintained?

Case study

The following is an article by KPMG arguing for more investment into infrastructure in the UK.

Investment into infrastructure is crucial for stimulating economic growth. It will create jobs, raise incomes and lead to a virtuous circle of affordability and investment. If we deny that we could go on a downward spiral towards being a second tier economy.

Experts estimate that the UK needs at least £400bn investment into our ailing infrastructure over the next 10 years. Around 65% of the UK's infrastructure is already privately financed and with Government spending under pressure, the UK has no choice other than to look to the private sector for infrastructure investment. What we need from Government is a clear vision of the infrastructure development needs of the country and consistency between Government message and action in order to build confidence amongst developers and investors.

If anything the Government's infrastructure plans need speeding up. The Government needs to make more effective use of the guarantee scheme it introduced last year. It should also consider re-establishing tax relief on infrastructure investments in line with other G20 countries, a move that would have real and lasting impact on jobs and capital investment in the UK.

Richard Threlfall, KPMG's Head of Infrastructure, Building and Construction

http://www.kpmg.com/uk/en/issuesandinsights/articlespublications/newsreleases/pages/infrastructure-investment-will-lead-to-virtuous-circle-of-affordability-and-investment-says-kpmg.aspx

? Questions

1   Discuss how greater investment in infrastructure might lead to economic growth and less unemployment.

2   Discuss the role that the government can play in helping increase investment in infrastructure in the UK.

3   In what ways might investment in infrastructure create a virtuous cycle?

4   What do you think might prevent further investment in infrastructure?

Review questions

1   Is investment an injection or withdrawal from the economy? Why?

2   Explain how firms decide on the profit-maximizing level of investment.

3   Explain why expectations are such an important influence on the level of investment in an economy.

4   What is the likely effect of a fall in interest rates on the level of investment in an economy?

5   Explain the meaning of external costs and benefits in cost–benefit analysis.

6   Explain the accelerator effect.

7   Explain two factors that might shift the MEC curve inwards.

8   In what way can the accelerator–multiplier model help to explain the economic cycle?

Put into practice

1   Draw two Marginal Efficiency Capital curves; one that is interest elastic and one that is interest inelastic.

2   Show the effect of greater business optimism on the Marginal Efficiency of Capital and on aggregate demand and equilibrium price and output.

Research Assignment

Research the levels of private sector investment over the last ten years in the UK. Produce a report on the key determinants of private sector investment.

Key learning points

- Investment depends in part on expectations of the future and can be volatile.
- Changes in investment lead to changes in the aggregate demand.
- The marginal efficiency of capital shows the expected return on investment projects.
- Profit-maximizing firms will invest up to the point at which the interest rate equals the marginal efficiency of capital.
- An increase in interest rates is likely to decrease the level of investment and therefore the level of the aggregate demand in an economy, all other things being unchanged.
- The accelerator shows the relationship between net investment and the rate of change of national income. According to the accelerator, an increase in net investment requires the economy to grow at an increasing rate.
- A cost–benefit analysis uses social costs and benefits rather than private costs and benefits when assessing an investment.

 Visit our Online Resource Centre at http://www.oxfordtextbooks.co.uk/orc/gillespie_ econ3e/ for test questions and further information on topics covered in this chapter.

»22 Fiscal policy

Fiscal policy refers to decisions made by a government regarding its spending, taxation, and benefits policies. Changes in these policy areas can affect the level of aggregate demand and aggregate supply, and therefore the equilibrium levels of price and output, and employment. In this chapter, we examine the elements of government fiscal policy and analyse the importance of it in terms of the economy as a whole.

LEARNING OBJECTIVES

By the end of this chapter, you should be able to:

✓ understand the key elements of government spending;

✓ outline the different elements of taxation;

✓ analyse the impact of changes in taxation;

✓ assess the fiscal stance of a government.

▮ Introduction

Fiscal policy involves the use of changes in government spending, and the taxation and benefit systems to influence the economy. Fiscal policy can be used to affect the level of both aggregate demand and aggregate supply. At times in the past, the priority of fiscal policy in the UK has been to try to fine-tune the level of the aggregate demand. However, in the first decade of the twenty-first century, the UK government left much of the control of demand to the Bank of England via interest rates; fiscal policy was used more to influence the aggregate supply. The global recession of 2008 and 2009 brought debates about fiscal policy back to the fore. Some argued that expansionist fiscal policy was regarded as essential to try to sustain demand levels in economies around the world; others focused on the high levels of debt in many countries and argued that this needed to be brought under control by cutting government spending and/or raising more tax revenue.

First of all, in this chapter, we examine forms of government spending and taxation, then we consider how fiscal policy can influence demand and supply and then look at the debate over the role of fiscal policy in recent years.

Government spending

The government in the UK is made up of central and local government. Central government is responsible for the national provision of some goods and services, such as the National Health Service (NHS) and the police force. Local government is responsible for regional, city-based or town-based services, such as street cleaning and local amenities (for example, swimming pools).

Government spending covers a wide range of goods and services, including:

- defence;
- social security benefits (for example, government payments to people if they are ill or unemployed);
- education; and
- repayments on previous borrowing.

Governments need to spend money to intervene to solve the market failures and imperfections that arise in the free market. For example, government spending may be needed to:

- provide public and merit goods;
- subsidize greater production of positive externalities; and
- reduce instability in some markets with a buffer stock system.

A government may also intervene to try to bring an economy out of a recession and to stabilize economic growth. This could be achieved by increasing injections or decreasing withdrawals.

To finance its spending, the government raises funds from the following sources.

- **Taxation revenue** (see below) The government can raise revenue via taxes placed on products, households, and firms. When considering a tax system, it is important to examine the range of taxes, the thresholds at which taxes have to be paid (for example, at what level of income do households start paying income tax?), who has to pay the tax and the rates of taxation.

- **Borrowing** This might refer to borrowing from banks and individuals, for example. The government sells what are called bonds, or securities. These are 'IOU's that last for a variety of periods. Government bonds pay interest and are paid back on a specified date. Some government bonds are short term and some are long term. The interest rate that has to be paid depends on the number of years to maturity, the rates available elsewhere, and the risk associated with it.

An increase in government spending is an injection to the economy; it increases the aggregate demand and sets off the multiplier (see Figure 22.1a). It can be used to stimulate

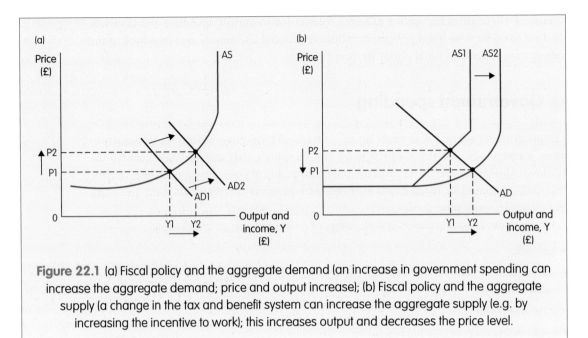

Figure 22.1 (a) Fiscal policy and the aggregate demand (an increase in government spending can increase the aggregate demand; price and output increase); (b) Fiscal policy and the aggregate supply (a change in the tax and benefit system can increase the aggregate supply (e.g. by increasing the incentive to work); this increases output and decreases the price level.

the economy. At times a government may use it to 'pump prime' the economy by investing in key sectors such as construction to have knock-on effects throughout the suppliers' industries.

Fiscal policy may also be used to provide incentives to increase the aggregate supply (see Figure 22.1b) and increase the potential output of the economy.

Put into practice

Which of the following statements are true and which are false?

a. Interest rates are part of fiscal policy

b. Government spending on final goods is an injection into the economy

c. Taxation revenue is a withdrawal from the economy

d. An increase in government spending boosts aggregate demand

---

▦ Taxation

Taxes are charges levied on individuals and organizations in an economy. Taxation is used to achieve the following.

• To raise revenue to finance government spending

• To change firms' and households' behaviour. For example, by making some goods more expensive, taxation can lead to households switching to other products or changing their consumption patterns (for example, taxes placed on fuel may reduce energy usage, whilst taxes on tobacco may reduce consumption).

The different types of taxes include the following.

- **Direct taxes** These are taxes placed directly on households' incomes and firms' profits, such as the following.
  - **Income tax** The primary forms of taxable income are earnings from employment, income from self-employment and unincorporated businesses, income from property, bank and building society interest, and dividends on shares. Income tax has different rates according to the amount of money being earned.
  - **National Insurance contributions (NICs)** These act like a tax on earnings, but their payment entitles individuals to certain ('contributory') social security benefits.
  - **Corporation tax** This tax is charged on the global profits of UK-resident companies. Firms not resident in the UK pay corporation tax only on their UK profits.
  - **Capital gains tax (CGT)** Introduced in 1965, CGT is charged on gains arising from the disposal of assets by individuals and trustees. Capital gains made by companies are subject to corporation tax (see above). As with income tax, there is an annual threshold below which CGT does not have to be paid.
  - **Inheritance tax (IHT)** This tax applies to transfers of wealth on or shortly before death that exceed a minimum threshold.
  - **Council tax** This is a largely property-based tax. Domestic residences are banded according to an assessment of their market value; individual local authorities then determine the overall level of council tax, while the ratio between rates for different bands is set by central government.
  - **Business rates** These taxes are levied on non-residential properties, including shops, offices, warehouses, and factories.

- **Indirect taxes** These are incurred when items are purchased. The producer is legally obliged to pay these taxes, but adds them onto the price to try to pass them on to the customer.
  - **Value added tax (VAT)** This is a proportional tax paid by businesses on sales. Before passing the revenue on to HM Revenue and Customs (HMRC), however, firms may deduct any VAT that they paid on inputs into their products; hence it is a tax on the value added at each stage of the production process, not simply on all expenditure. For example if you sell something for £200 and pay 20 per cent tax you owe £40. However if your inputs cost £120 and you paid 20 per cent on these (i.e. £24) then you only owe the difference £40–£24 = £16. In effect you are paying on the value you have added from £120 to £200 i.e you are paying 20 per cent on the difference of £80 i.e. £16. A reduced rate applies to some products such as domestic fuel, children's car seats, contraceptives, certain residential conversions and renovations, certain energy-saving materials, and smoking-cessation products. A number of goods are either zero-rated or exempt. Zero-rated goods have no VAT levied upon the final good and firms can reclaim any VAT paid on inputs as usual. Exempt goods have no VAT levied on the final good sold to the consumer, but firms cannot reclaim VAT paid on inputs.

- **Excise duties** These are levied on three major categories of good: alcoholic drinks; tobacco; and road fuels. They are levied at a flat rate (per pint, per litre, per packet, etc.); tobacco products are subject to an additional *ad valorem* tax of 24 per cent of the total retail price (including the flat-rate duty, VAT, and the *ad valorem* duty itself).
- **Licences** The main licence is vehicle excise duty (VED), levied annually on road vehicles.
- **Air passenger duty** On 1 November 1994, an excise duty on air travel from UK airports came into effect (flights from the Scottish Highlands and Islands are exempt).
- **Landfill tax** Landfill tax was introduced on 1 October 1996 to charge for the disposal of waste in landfill sites.

Economics in context

Table 22.1 Analysis of government receipts by tax type (billions)

Outturn	2011–12	2012–13	2013–14	2014–15	2015–16	2016–17
Income tax and NICs	16.7	16.5	16.4	16.5	16.7	17.3
Value added tax	6.4	6.5	6.5	6.5	6.4	6.4
Corporation tax	2.2	2.3	2.2	2.0	1.9	1.9
UK oil and gas receipts	0.7	0.4	0.4	0.4	0.3	0.3
Fuel duties	1.8	1.7	1.6	1.6	1.6	1.6
Business rates	1.6	1.7	1.7	1.7	1.7	1.7
Council tax	1.7	1.7	1.7	1.7	1.7	1.7
Excise duties	1.3	1.3	1.2	1.3	1.2	1.2
Capital taxes	1.1	1.0	1.2	1.3	1.3	1.4
Other taxes	2.5	2.7	3.1	2.9	3.0	2.9
National Accounts taxes	36.0	35.8	36.0	35.8	35.8	36.3

Source: Office for Budget Responsibility

❓ Questions

Review Table 22.1. Corporation tax is a relatively small percentage of government receipts. Should the government get rid of it do you think?

Do you think income tax rates should be reduced?

Should VAT rates be increased do you think?

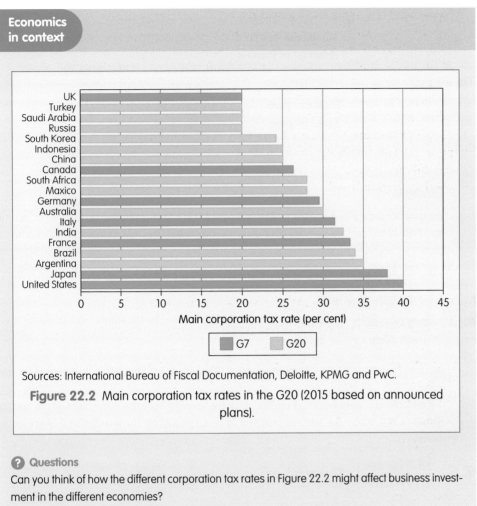

Sources: International Bureau of Fiscal Documentation, Deloitte, KPMG and PwC.

Figure 22.2 Main corporation tax rates in the G20 (2015 based on announced plans).

❓ Questions

Can you think of how the different corporation tax rates in Figure 22.2 might affect business investment in the different economies?

What do you think determines the corporation tax rate that are set in different countries?

- **Climate change levy** The climate change levy came into effect on 1 April 2001. It is charged on industrial and commercial use of electricity, coal, natural gas, and liquefied petroleum gas, with the tax rate varying according to the type of fuel used. The levy is designed to help the UK move towards the government's domestic goal of a 20 per cent reduction in carbon dioxide emissions between 1990 and 2010.

▓ Marginal and average tax rates

The marginal rate of tax is the extra tax paid when an additional pound is earned. For example, 40 pence may be paid on each extra pound of income earned.

The marginal rate of tax is calculated as:

$$\text{Marginal rate of tax} = \frac{\text{Change in tax paid}}{\text{Change in income}}$$

The average rate of tax is calculated as:

$$\text{Average rate of tax} = \frac{\text{Total tax paid}}{\text{Total income}} \times 100$$

that is, the average amount of tax paid per pound.

Example

Imagine, for example, that a tax system is 0 per cent tax on every pound up to £999 of income and then 40 per cent tax on every pound earned above this. This means that if £1,000 is earned, then:

- the marginal rate of tax (the extra tax on the last pound) is 40 per cent;
- the average rate of tax is

$$\frac{\text{Total tax paid}}{\text{Total income}} \times 100 = \frac{£0.40}{£1,000} \times 100 = 0.04\%$$

Because the amount of tax-free income relative to the actual earnings is low, the average tax rate is low.

If an individual were earning £1 million, then the tax paid would be 40 per cent on the taxable amount of £999,001. The total tax paid would be £399,600.40. The average rate of tax would then be:

$$\left(\frac{£399,600.40}{£1,000,000} \right) \times 100 = 39.96\%$$

What do you think?

What do you think the rate of income tax should be?
Do you think the UK should have a flat rate of tax?

Put into practice

An individual can earn up to £5,000 with 0 per cent income tax. The marginal rate of tax after that is 25 per cent.

- What is the total tax paid if the individual earns:
  - £20,000?
  - £50,000?

- What is the average rate of tax if the individual earns:

    - £20,000?

    - £50,000?

Taxation systems

The following are the different types of taxation system (see Figure 22.3).

- **Progressive** In a progressive taxation system, the average rate of tax increases as people earn more money. The income tax system in the UK is progressive; as people earn more, they move into higher marginal tax brackets. The increasing marginal tax rate pulls up the average amount of tax paid per pound.

- **Regressive** In a regressive tax system, the average rate of taxation falls as income increases. This can occur if, for example, the same amount of tax is paid regardless of individuals' or firms' income levels. For example, you might pay £10 VAT on an item whether your income is £10,000 or £50,000. On average, therefore, the more income you have, the lower the tax paid per pound earned.

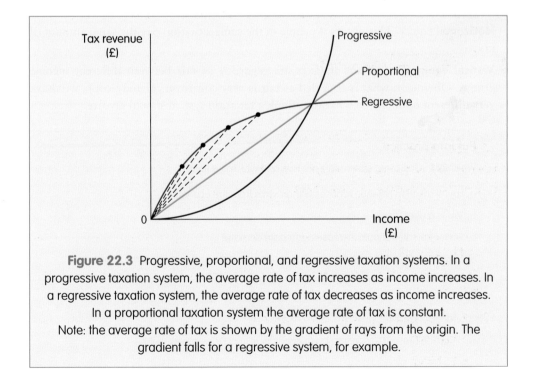

Figure 22.3 Progressive, proportional, and regressive taxation systems. In a progressive taxation system, the average rate of tax increases as income increases. In a regressive taxation system, the average rate of tax decreases as income increases. In a proportional taxation system the average rate of tax is constant.
Note: the average rate of tax is shown by the gradient of rays from the origin. The gradient falls for a regressive system, for example.

- **Proportional** A proportional tax occurs when the percentage of their income that people pay in tax stays constant whatever they earn—that is, the average rate of tax is constant.

What do you think?

Some economists and politicians have argued for a flat rate of income tax rather than having different tax bands with increasing rates of tax. Would you recommend this?

An effective taxation system should have the following features.

- **Understandable** Individuals and organizations should be able to understand how their tax is calculated or they will think that it is unfair.
- **Cost-effective to administer** If a taxation system is too complex, then too much will be spent administering it and collecting the tax, thereby wasting resources.
- **Difficult to avoid paying**
- **Non-distortionary** It should not alter market signals in an undesirable fashion—for example, it should not discourage the production or consumption of a product below the socially efficient level.

A 'fair' tax system

The fairness of a taxation and benefit system can be measurevd in terms of the following.

- **Horizontal equity** This occurs if people in the same situation pay the same amount of tax.
- **Vertical equity** This occurs if taxes are regarded as fair between different income groups. Obviously, what is regarded as fair is very controversial and people will have very different opinions on what they think a taxation system should involve.

Put into practice

Which of the following statements are true and which are false?

a. Lower taxation revenue reduces withdrawals from the economy

b. VAT is a direct tax

c. Lower tax rates should increase aggregate demand

d. Lower government spending on final goods reduces withdrawals into the economy

What do you think?

Do you think the present tax system in your country is fair? Does it work well?

Using taxation as a government policy instrument

The factors to consider when assessing the effectiveness of taxation as a government policy instrument include the following.

- Taxing people and firms can reduce their earnings, but cannot directly increase their income. This can only be done if the taxation revenue is redistributed in some way. It is therefore important to consider not only what taxes are charged, but also what is done with the money raised.

- There is always an incentive for tax avoidance and tax evasion.
  - **Tax avoidance** occurs when individuals or firms take legal steps to avoid paying as much tax—for example, by finding loopholes in the system.
  - **Tax evasion** is illegal and means that people are trying to get out of paying the tax that they are meant to pay.

- Increasing tax rates can have a disincentive effect. For example, increasing income tax can lead to there being less incentive for people to work (or at least to work more hours) because the amount that they earn is relatively little after tax. This is known as the **poverty trap**. On the other hand, a tax cut can have an incentive effect and, according to Laffer (see Wanniski, 1978), may increase tax revenue, as explained below.

What do you think?

What do you think would be one good tax to introduce? One tax to remove?

The Laffer curve

Professor Art Laffer advised President Reagan in the USA between 1981 and 1984. He highlighted that the total tax revenue depends on the tax rate and the income being earned; if cutting the tax rate encourages people to work and thereby increase incomes, then this can increase tax revenues—an effect known as the Laffer curve (see Figure 22.4).

If the average rate of tax were zero, then no tax revenue would be raised. As the average rate of tax increases, more tax revenue is raised. However, if the tax rate is set too high, then this might discourage people from working and firms from investing, therefore reducing the income and the tax revenue being earned. Laffer argued that the USA at that time had reached a point at which the tax rate was too high and was acting as a disincentive to firms and households to earn more. A tax cut would encourage more earnings and lead to an increase in revenue.

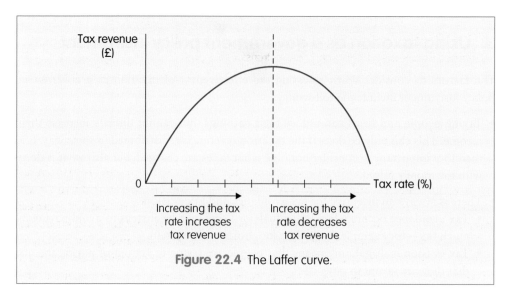

Figure 22.4 The Laffer curve.

What do you think?

At the moment, the government can use the money raised from any tax on whatever it decides. Some economists argue for **hypothecation**, whereby the tax from a particular source must be used for a specific purpose. For example, road tax would have to be spent on road improvements, or the revenue from National Insurance would have to be used for the health service.

Do you think that hypothecation would be a good idea?

Why do you think it has not been adopted?

▨ Types of benefit

The impact of fiscal policy is not only to do with the tax system or government spending on final goods and services; it also depends on the government's spending on benefits. Types of benefit include the following.

• **Means-tested benefits** These are benefits that are paid to people on low incomes, such as income support.

• **Universal benefits** These are available to everyone, such as State Pension.

• **Benefits in kind** These are not direct monetary payments, but provide free or subsidized goods or services, such as health care and education.

These payments are known as transfer payments; they are transferring money from one group to another (for example, taxpayers to non-taxpayers), and are not in return for final goods and services.

Fiscal drag

Fiscal drag occurs when individuals pay more tax because their nominal incomes have increased and this has moved them into higher tax brackets, even if in real terms their incomes have not increased. Imagine that someone receives a 2 per cent pay increase and inflation is also at 2 per cent. In real terms, this person is not better off; his or her real income has not changed—he or she can buy only the same amount of products. However, if the government does not move the tax brackets in line with inflation, then it is possible that this person may move from one tax bracket to another because of the increase in his or her nominal earnings. This means that he or she would end up paying more tax.

To avoid fiscal drag (if it wants to!), the government should move up the levels at which people enter different tax bands in line with inflation.

The public sector net cash requirement

The public sector net cash requirement (PSNCR) used to be known as the public sector borrowing requirement (PSBR). It measures the amount that the government has to borrow in a given year to meet its spending requirements. It occurs if the government spends more than it earns in revenue. The PSNCR can be measured in absolute terms (that is, billions of pounds) and also in relative terms, as a percentage of national income.

To finance its PSNCR, the government needs to borrow money. It can do this by borrowing from the Bank of England or by selling government securities. Government securities include Treasury bills and government bonds.

- **Treasury bills** are short-term loans to the government (they are paid back within three months).
- **Government bonds** are long-term loans (for example, they are paid back several years later).

Selling bonds incurs an interest charge, because the government will have to offer an inducement to get firms and households to lend to it.

150 days as a share of the year. In France, the equivalent date falls in July but in the USA and Australia it comes as early as mid-April. The calculations included every tax, including stealth taxes—income tax, national insurance, council tax, excise duties, air passenger taxes, fuel and vehicle taxes to name a few—and show just how long the average person has to work to pay their share of them all. Do you think it matters that that it takes 150 days of work just to pay your taxes?

The national debt

The national debt is the total amount of money that a government owes. If a government has a deficit in a given year, then this will increase the national debt. The debt needs 'servicing'—that is, the government will have to decide on how much it wants to pay off, if any, in a given year.

What do you think?

Is the government wrong to borrow?

Automatic and discretionary fiscal policy

Some changes in fiscal policy occur automatically as the level of income in the economy changes. In a boom, for example, more people will be employed and more people will be spending. All things being equal this will increase tax revenue. At the same time, unemployment benefits should not be needed as much, so government spending will fall. Therefore, in a boom, a government's fiscal position should automatically improve because its income will be higher, but spending will be lower, as shown in Figure 22.5. Similarly, in a deficit, a government's fiscal position will automatically worsen. With any given tax rate, less tax revenue will be generated in a slump and more will be spent on unemployment benefits.

In Figure 22.5, G – T shows the difference between the government's spending and revenue (the PSNCR).

Discretionary fiscal policy occurs when the government makes a deliberate attempt to change the level of economic activity. For example, it might:

• introduce new taxes and benefits, or withdraw existing ones;

• change the thresholds at which taxes are paid and change the rate of tax; or

• increase its spending in addition to any automatic changes in expenditure.

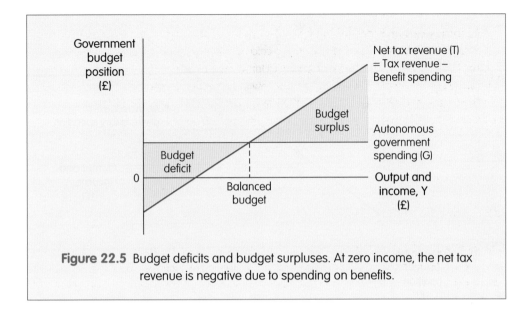

Figure 22.5 Budget deficits and budget surpluses. At zero income, the net tax revenue is negative due to spending on benefits.

These discretionary changes are shown on the diagram by movements in the government spending line (for example, more might be spent at every level of income) and the tax revenue line (for example, tax revenue may be cut reducing the tax revenue for any level of income).

Fiscal stance

A government's fiscal stance shows whether it is adopting an expansionist or deflationary policy. You cannot tell this simply by looking at the size of the PSNCR. This is because the budget position will not only depend on the discretionary decisions of the government, but will also be automatically affected by the level of national income. To identify the fiscal stance of a government, it is important to remove the automatic effects of national income changing in order to measure the discretionary changes.

Automatic changes to the government's fiscal position are shown as we move along a given budget line. If the government deliberately changes the tax rate or deliberately changes its levels of spending, then this is discretionary fiscal policy. This can be seen by a shift or pivoting of the line, as shown in Figure 22.6. As we can see from Figure 22.6a, an increase in government spending has increased the deficit at Y2 from B – A to C – A. Also, Figure 22.6b shows how a cut in the rate of tax increases the deficit at Y2 from A – B to A – C.

What do you think?

Do you think a government can spend more and end up with a lower deficit? Can a government cut spending and end up with a bigger deficit?

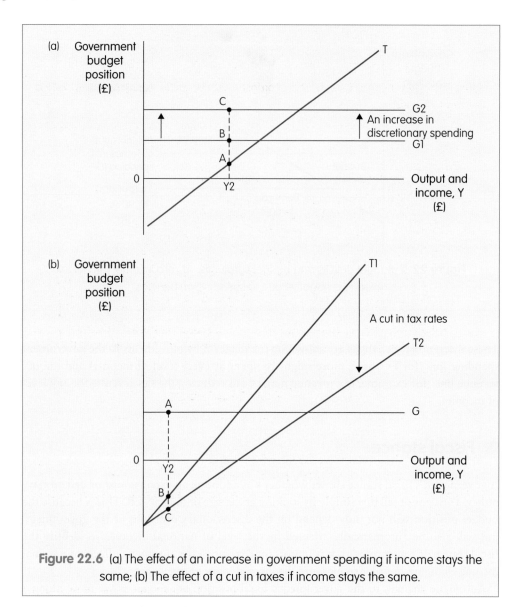

Figure 22.6 (a) The effect of an increase in government spending if income stays the same; (b) The effect of a cut in taxes if income stays the same.

▦ Changing taxes versus changing spending to affect the aggregate demand

When using fiscal policy, a government may use changes to the taxation system or changes in government spending to influence aggregate demand. Changes in government spending directly affect the aggregate demand. By comparison, reducing direct taxes increases disposable income, but the impact on the aggregate demand will depend on how much of the extra income is spent and how much is saved. A spending of £100 by the government will have a greater multiplier effect than giving £100 back to households because some of the latter will

Figure 22.7 shows the Public Sector Debt position for the UK. It was produced by the Office of Budget Responsibility in 2013.

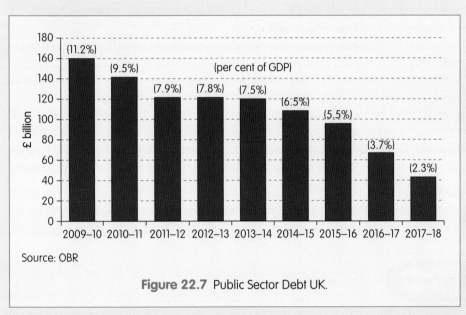

Source: OBR

Figure 22.7 Public Sector Debt UK.

❓ Questions

Analyse the possible reasons why the debt might be falling.

Analyse the possible impact of this fall on the UK economy

Explain why the figures for public sector debt do not in themselves reflect the fiscal position of the government

be saved and only a proportion will be spent—for example, only £80 may be spent. Also, by using spending, the government can target specific industries or regions quite easily.

On the other hand, taxes can usually be changed more quickly than spending programmes, can target specific products or forms of income, and are likely to have a faster effect on the economy. Changes in spending usually involve changing major government projects, which can take years to bring about. Furthermore, the government may have committed itself to particular projects and levels of spending. It may not be easy to alter these commitments.

Put into practice

If the government were trying to boost the aggregate demand, what changes might it make to the taxation system?

The Greek deficit

Attempts by the Greek government to convince its citizens of the need for austerity measures to cut its deficit met with riots in the streets. In Athens, demonstrators marched outside the government building where they were debating the cuts and called on the parliamentary 'thieves' to come out. Other protesters set fire to a bank building.

The deficit had grown during ten years of spending. A change of approach was clear with the announcement on 2 May 2010 of loans from the International Monetary Fund (IMF) and the European Union worth a total of €110 billion ($144 billion), plus an austerity plan to cut spending and raise more revenue. The government has announced major cuts in pay in the public sector, higher taxes, and plans to reduce the budget deficit from 13.6 per cent of GDP in 2009 to less than 3 per cent by 2014. However, this will almost certainly deepen the recession that is already hitting Greece. The Greek government needed to take action because its lack of financial controls was making it increasingly difficult to borrow and this was leading to real concerns about the government's ability to govern.

? Question

What difficulties are likely to be faced by the Greek government when making these cuts?

Economics in context **Global deficits**

On 26 and 27 June 2010, the leaders of the G20 countries met in Canada to consider how to protect the global economic recovery while also dealing with the large public sector deficits of most of the countries attending. (The G20 is an organization set up in 1999 for important industrialized and developing economies to discuss key economic issues.)

These deficits have increased significantly as a result of the recession of 2008–09, which reduced tax revenues and resulted in more people claiming benefits, and because of the expansionary fiscal policies adopted to bring countries out of recession.

However, the leaders were divided on how much to cut their deficits now. Some, such as the new coalition government in the UK, wanted to cut the deficit quickly in order to regain control of finances and avoid a lack of confidence in the government's ability to finance the debt. Others, such as the Obama administration in the USA, wanted to cut the deficit more slowly so as not to put the recovery in jeopardy. Nevertheless, cuts were generally agreed, although agreement about the timing was more vague.

However, if all countries cut their spending, this could lead to a second global recession (a double dip). Also, higher taxes and reduced government spending may make consumers nervous, reducing their spending as well as deterring investment.

? Question

Faced with deficits after a severe recession, some governments wanted to reduce their spending dramatically and fairly suddenly. Others wanted to wait to make cuts. What approach do you think is right?

The effectiveness of fiscal policy

The effectiveness of fiscal policy depends on the following.

- **The accuracy of government forecasting** Intervention will depend on where the government thinks that the economy is at any moment and where it thinks it is heading. If either of these estimations is wrong, then fiscal policy may not remedy the problems effectively; it may even make them worse! It can be difficult for a government to know the exact state of the economy at any moment because data is often slow to come in. Many individuals and companies, for example are slow to send in their tax returns and then these have to be checked. In June 2013, for example, the Office for National Statistics announced that the UK did not experience a double dip recession when national income figures did not fall in the first quarter by 0.1 per cent but stayed flat. Given the data problems that can exist government decisions can often be based on incorrect assumptions. Interestingly Google is now doing research based on the search times being used to try and produce better 'real time' estimates of what is happening in the economy.

- **The impact of any policy changes** The government may base a policy on a set of assumptions about the behaviour of households and firms, only to find that they do not react in the expected way or at the expected time. Not only are delays likely between the economy changing position and the government realizing this, but delays are also likely when it comes to agreeing a policy response to this change. For example, it may take years to get agreement to increase spending in the economy significantly. There will also be a delay in the policy change taking effect. For example, an income tax cut may not lead to an immediate increase in consumer spending; households may wait for a while before deciding to increase consumption. This is particularly likely if consumption is linked to permanent income rather than current income (see Chapter 20).

- **Funding desired spending** A government may wish to inject more money into the economy, but lack the necessary funds to do so. If the deficit is already high, then further borrowing could lead to extremely high interest rates to achieve the necessary funding, and a government may worry about the burden of debt and interest repayments.

- **The funding of government spending may also create problems** It is possible that fiscal policy by the government may lead to less private sector investment. This is called 'crowding out'. Crowding out can occur because, with higher levels of government spending, the Bank of England does not need to keep interest rates as low as it otherwise would to maintain the desired level of demand overall in the economy. As a result, the higher interest rates may deter private sector investment because borrowing is more expensive. The effect of this depends in part on the sensitivity of investment to changes in the interest rate. Also, if the government attracts private finance by selling bonds, then

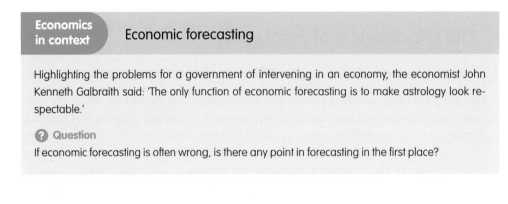

Economics in context   Economic forecasting

Highlighting the problems for a government of intervening in an economy, the economist John Kenneth Galbraith said: 'The only function of economic forecasting is to make astrology look respectable.'

? **Question**

If economic forecasting is often wrong, is there any point in forecasting in the first place?

these funds will not be available for other private sector projects; these projects have been 'crowded out', because the government has absorbed the funds that were needed to go ahead with them.

Supply-side fiscal policy

This involves the use of fiscal policy to influence the aggregate supply in the economy; the methods for achieving this include the following.

- In the labour market, the methods include:
  - offering individuals funding to help them with training and developing their skills;
  - helping the unemployed to get back into work—for example, with retraining schemes;
  - guaranteeing a minimum wage to encourage people to work;
  - reducing income taxes to act as another incentive; and
  - avoiding a poverty trap—that is, the situation that occurs when the benefits given up and the taxes incurred when an individual starts to work mean they are worse off than when they were unemployed.
- In the goods market, the methods include:
  - encouraging firms to invest by using tax incentives to undertake research and development to develop new products, and new production processes; and
  - helping start-ups with advice and financial aid, thereby encouraging new businesses, and increasing the supply of goods and services in the economy.

Put into practice

Show the effect of an increase in the aggregate supply on the equilibrium price and output in the economy.

Case study

The International Monetary Fund (IMF) recently urged the USA to repeal the major federal budget cuts that had been introduced this year, claiming that they were being made too rapidly. It argued that the deficit reduction programme would limit growth this year.

It forecast US growth would be 1.9 per cent this year, but said it could be as much as 1.75 percentage points higher without the rapid tightening of fiscal policy.

It did accept there was a recovery. It highlighted the increase in house prices and construction activity, stronger household confidence, an improvement in the labour market, and strong business profitability. However, the IMF claimed that spending cuts would damage the economy not just in the short term but if the cuts applied to areas such as education, science, and infrastructure this could reduce potential growth in the medium term.

❓ Questions

1 Discuss the reasons why the IMF wants the USA to cut its deficit.

2 Analyse why increasing house prices is a sign of a recovery.

Review questions

1 What is meant by fiscal policy?

2 How does the government raise revenue?

3 Can you tell a government's fiscal stance from its budget position?

4 Explain how cutting tax rates can increase tax revenue.

5 What factors might limit the effectiveness of fiscal policy?

6 Explain how the government finances its deficit.

7 Explain how fiscal policy can affect aggregate supply in the economy.

8 Explain what is meant by 'crowding out'.

Put into practice

1 Show using diagrams how an increase in government spending can increase income in the economy.

2 Show using diagrams the effect on national income and and output of fiscal policy that increases aggregate supply.

Assignment question

1   Research the present position of your economy and its approach to fiscal policy. Would you recommend a more expansionist fiscal policy than is being adopted at the moment? Justify your findings.

Key learning points

- Fiscal policy involves the use of government spending and taxation to influence the economy.
- Fiscal policy can be used to influence the aggregate supply and the aggregate demand.
- Fiscal policy acts as an automatic stabilizer on the economy; discretionary changes can also be used to try to influence the state of the economy.
- Fiscal drag occurs when the tax bands do not change in line with inflation or growth in the economy.
- A budget deficit occurs when government spending is greater than income over a year.
- The national debt measures the total borrowing of the government.

Reference

Wanniski, J. (1978) 'Taxes, revenues, and the "Laffer curve"', *The Public Interest*, 50(Winter): 3–16

Learn more

To learn more about the UK government's budget position, visit the Online Resource Centre.

 Visit our Online Resource Centre at http://www.oxfordtextbooks.co.uk/orc/gillespie_econ3e/ for test questions and further information on topics covered in this chapter.

Money and monetary policy

At the heart of an economy is money. We earn it, we save it, and we spend it! This chapter looks at the meaning of money and the functions that it performs. It examines the market for money and considers the consequences of an increase in the amount of money in the economy. It also examines monetary policy in the UK and the role of the Monetary Policy Committee.

LEARNING OBJECTIVES

By the end of this chapter, you should be able to:

✓ explain the key features of money;

✓ explain the factors influencing the demand and supply of money;

✓ outline ways of controlling the money supply.

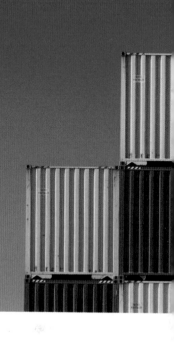

■ Introduction

'Money makes the world go around' according to one song, but what exactly do we mean by 'money'? Money is something of which we usually want more. It is something for which we work, that we try to accumulate, and something by which we measure success. But what exactly does money do? In most cases we don't want money just to sit and look at it—we want it because it is useful to us. The answer is that money performs a variety of functions, such as the following.

- **It is a medium of exchange** This means that it is something that the various parties involved in a transaction are willing to accept as payment. If we do not have money to buy products, then we have to exchange goods and services; this is what happens in a barter economy. The problem with a barter system is that it relies on a **double coincidence of wants**—that is, you must find someone who wants what you have and who has something that you want—and this is not always easy to find. With money you can trade your item, accept the money and then buy what you want from someone else at another time provided that other person accepts money as well.

- **It is a store of value** For it to be an effective medium of exchange, users of money must be confident that it will hold its value (they would obviously be reluctant to accept something that then became worthless). This, in turn, means that they are confident that others will accept this money in the future in return for products (otherwise it is not much use to them when they want to buy things later). If money is losing value quickly then people will not want to accept it in a transaction and will look for other ways of trading.

- **It is a unit of account** This means that money must be in a form whereby it can be used to measure the value of things—for example, the value of an item may be equal to £1, £2, or £10.

If someone asked you how much money you or your parents had, how would you calculate it? What exactly would you add up? You would get different answers depending on exactly what you include. For example, if you are asked how much money you have, then you may think of it in terms of the cash that you have in your pocket or the money in your bank account. What about any shares that you may have? What about other forms of savings? Which of these would you count? If you own property or other assets, such as a car, then are these also forms of money?

The answer is that it depends how you want to define 'money'. Some definitions of money are 'narrow'; these concentrate on cash or other items that can be quickly turned into cash (this means that they are 'liquid'). Other definitions of money are broader. This means that they include items that are less liquid (that is, less easy to turn quickly into cash), such as deposit accounts. The various definitions of money are all equally valid, but simply include different items; they highlight that actually defining what money is is not as simple as it may seem.

The narrowest definition of money is measured by M0. This comprises notes and coins (in circulation and in banks' tills), plus the balances that banks hold at the Bank of England. However, notes and coins only represent a relatively small part of what most of us would include when we think about what 'money' we have. Money in a broader sense

---

Economics in context   When 2 pence is 3 pence

A few years ago, the price of copper reached what was then an all-time high of $8,000 per tonne. This was due to major buying by commodity brokers and traders. Every 2 pence piece made before 1992 is 97 per cent copper—that is, it comprises 6.9 g of the metal. Approximately 145,000 coins would equal 1 tonne. The face value of these coins is just £2,900. However, given the level of copper prices at the time, this meant that they were worth around £4,400—that is, they could have been sold for a profit of £1,500. A 2 pence piece was therefore worth over 3 pence!

❓ Question

The value of the paper used in banknotes or the metals in coins is usually very low and nothing like the value of the money itself (except in the unusual case above). Why, then, are we willing to accept the face value of notes and coins?

will include what is held in bank and building society accounts. The measure of money that includes these is called M4.

The Bank of England

The Bank of England was established in 1694. It is the UK's central bank and plays a critical role in determining how much money there is in the economy. The role of the Bank of England (and, indeed, any central bank) is to:

- be the banker to the government;
- manage government finances;
- be the banker to commercial banks, such as Barclays;
- hold gold and foreign-exchange reserves that can be used when trying to influence the exchange rate;
- control the issue of notes and coins; and
- promote and maintain monetary and financial stability to contribute to a healthy economy.

Banks and financial institutions

The 1979 and 1987 Banking Acts defined the UK banking sector as consisting of a series of financial institutions the activities of which are supervised by the Bank of England. To be recognized as a bank, a financial institution must be granted a licence.

Financial institutions in the UK include the following.

- **Commercial (retail) banks** These banks, such as Barclays and HSBC, provide banking facilities for individuals as well as businesses. They provide facilities such as current accounts and loans.

- **Merchant banks** These specialize in receiving large deposits from, and lending to, businesses. They also help firms to raise finance.

- **Building societies** These are organizations that are owned by the people who save with them, as opposed to outside investors. However, many former building societies, such as Halifax and Abbey National, turned themselves into public companies owned by shareholders in the 1990s.

- **Finance houses** These organizations specialize in lending money to enable individuals to buy items, such as sofas and electrical goods.

- **Discount houses** These organizations specialize in the short-term lending of money to the government through the Bank of England and to local authorities. To do this, the discount houses obtain money from the banks by borrowing money on short notice that they then lend out.

The role of banks and financial institutions

Banks and other financial institutions exist to make a profit by investing and lending money. To do this, they need money in the first place, which they get via savings. To attract money, banks will offer interest. If you put money into a bank, then it will reward you by paying you interest on your savings. The amount of interest that it offers will depend on factors such as:

- for how long you are prepared to leave it in the bank (the longer you can tell the bank that the savings will be left with it, the longer it will have to earn profits with the savings, which should mean that it will pay you higher interest); and

- the amount that you put in the bank (the more money that it has to generate profits, the more that it can offer you).

If you are borrowing money from financial institutions, then the interest rate charged will depend on factors such as:

- how much you are borrowing;
- your track record (that is, whether you have a good credit rating; the better your rating, the lower the interest rate that banks can charge);
- for how long you want it; and
- what assets you have as security (collateral) (the lower the risk you are, the lower the interest rate that banks can charge).

There are therefore many different interest rates in an economy that depend on factors such as whether you are borrowing or saving. However, they will be linked to each other—for example, if one savings rate were significantly different from another, then savers would move their money to the institution with the higher rate if they could. Differences in interest rates are due to differences in factors such as the terms and conditions—for example, for how long you are borrowing the money and whether the interest rate is fixed or can fluctuate. A key measure of 'interest rates' generally in the UK is known as the **base rate**. This is the rate that the Bank of England will lend to other financial institutions and this will in turn influence the rate at which they lend to others. An increase in the base rate makes it more expensive for financial institutions to borrow if they need to which tends to make it more expensive for others to borrow from them. Changes in the base rate ripple though the economy.

What do you think?

What factors should a bank take into account before deciding how much to charge a business for a loan?

Why do you need to consider inflation to calculate the 'real' interest rate?

Zopa, a peer-to-peer lending service, explains its services as follows.

Zopa is the UK's leading peer-to-peer lending service. We reward savers and borrowers who are good with their money by providing lower rate loans and higher interest on savings.

Since Zopa was founded in 2005 we've helped savers lend more than £311 million in peer-to-peer loans.

Zopa's peer-to-peer lending bypasses banks and their high charges, to deliver better rates directly to both borrowers and savers.

Savers can lend their money safely and easily to borrowers and earn high interest on their savings. They are protected from risk by the Zopa Safeguard, which is designed to cover a saver if a borrower is unable to repay. Borrowers looking for a low rate loan to fund a purchase such as a car or home improvements can get a better rate than they can from the banks. Zopa borrowers have good credit ratings and our expert loans team helps them to make sure they can afford their loan. Zopa offers better rates to savers and borrowers, because peer-to-peer lending is more efficient than the traditional banking model. Banks have large overheads, with thousands of employees to pay and hundreds of branches to maintain. So they have to take large margins on the money that passes through them and this means worse rates on loans and savings.

Peer-to-peer lending is also known as social lending and lend-to-save, because it works by individual savers and borrowers coming together to get better rates. As well as getting a great financial deal, social lending helps you to cut out big banks. So you can help fellow borrowers and savers while knowing you are being smart with your money.

Source: http://www.zopa.com/about-zopa/about-zopa-home

? Question

Do you think peer-to-peer lending will replace the traditional banking system?

Changes in the interest rate will affect households and firms in many ways. They will affect:

- the amount that you have to repay on any existing borrowing such as loans or credit card borrowing, or on any money that you have borrowed via a mortgage to buy a property;

- the cost of any new borrowing (if you go to the bank to borrow money and the interest rate has increased, then this may deter you from borrowing; this will then reduce your spending); and

- the costs to firms of borrowing money and determining whether it is profitable to invest. Higher interest rates usually lead to less investment because there will be fewer projects where the expected returns now covers the costs. So interest rates obviously have a big impact on the level of spending in the economy. High interest rates will tend to reduce borrowing and spending by firms and households, thereby reducing the level of aggregate demand. Less investment will also reduce economic growth. An understanding of how interest rates are determined is therefore important. The interest rate is the cost of money (that is, the amount that you pay to borrow it), and, in a free market, would be determined by the supply and demand of money.

Put into practice

Show using diagrams the effect of higher interest rates on the price and output of the economy.

What do you think?

High interest rates can reduce the aggregate demand. What others factors might reduce demand in the economy?

Economics in context

In June 2013 it was announced that UK bank lending continued to fall, despite government attempts to promote lending through its Funding for Lending Scheme (FLS). Lending to individuals was up, but loans to businesses were down. The FLS was launched in August 2012 to try and boost lending and get the economy growing faster. Under this scheme, banks can borrow money cheaply from the Bank of England, providing they loan that money to individuals or businesses. By June 2013 the total amount that has been made available so far was £16.5bn. When FLS was launched, the government said it expected that up to £70bn would eventually be made available.

Changes in net lending by banks relative to the year before

LESS

- Santander –£8.6bn
- Lloyds Banking Group –£6.6bn
- RBS –£3.9bn

MORE

- Barclays +£6.8bn
- Nationwide +£4.8bn

Source: Bank of England.

? Questions

Why might banks not be lending more despite the Funding for Lending Scheme?
What might be the effect for the economy of less lending to businesses?

The market for money

The money market, like any other market, is made up of supply and demand. The interest rate is the price of money, which adjusts to equate the supply and demand of money. It is the price of money because it is the price paid when you borrow money and the price given to you if you save money.

The demand for money

There are various reasons why individuals and firms want to hold money—that is, factors that influence the demand for money. These motives include the following.

1. **The transaction motive** People hold money because they need it to live their daily lives. To pay our bills, pay for the bus, and buy a drink, we need money—that is, we need money to finance our transactions. Similarly, firms need money to buy their supplies, pay their rent, and reward their staff.

   The amount of transactions demand will be determined by the following.

   - **Real income levels** With more real income, we are likely to undertake more transactions (buy more things) and therefore need more money for this.

   - **How often people are paid** The less frequently that people are paid, the more they hold on average. Imagine that you are paid £500 per week. When you are paid, you have £500; by the end of the week, you have spent it and have £0. On average, you will have held £250 (see Figure 23.1a). If instead you were paid £26,000 once each year (equal to 52 × £500) and spent this over the year, then the average holding during the year would be £13,000 (see Figure 23.1b). The overall annual earnings are the same, but when you are paid less regularly, you hold more on average.

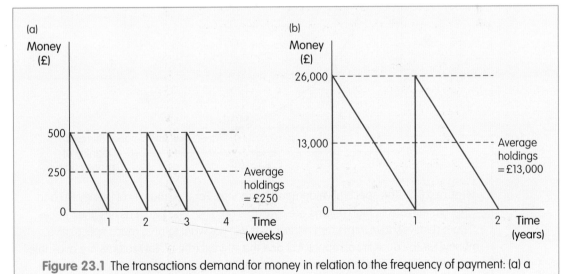

Figure 23.1 The transactions demand for money in relation to the frequency of payment: (a) a wage of £500 per week; (b) a salary of £26,000 per year.

- **The rate of interest** With higher interest rates, households will try to reduce the amount of money that they need for transactions because of the higher returns from saving. Whilst this might have some effect, it is not likely to be much. For simplicity, we assume that the transactions demand motives are not affected by the interest rate.

2. **The precautionary motive** This refers to the way in which people hold money 'just in case' something happens. For example, you may hold some money in case urgent repairs to your house are needed. Holding money for transactions and precautionary reasons is described as holding **active balances**. There is a positive reason why people hold money for these motives.

3. **The speculative motive** This is where people hold money whilst waiting to invest it in other assets. If, for example, you are worried that the price of shares is going to fall off, then you might sell your shares and hold the proceeds in the form of more liquid assets for the short term. This level of money holdings is therefore determined by expectations. If you think that the value of some assets are going to fall in the future, then you may hold more money now rather than these assets. If, however, you think that the values of assets are low at the moment, then you might hold less money and invest in other assets instead. This is shown in Figure 23.2. Speculative holdings are

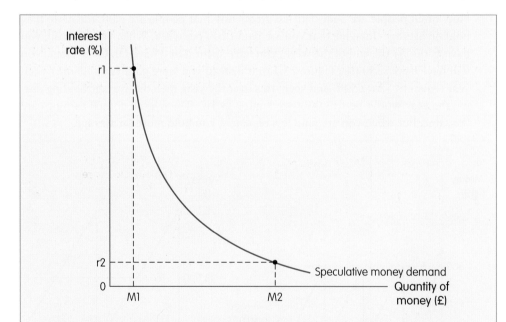

Figure 23.2 The speculative demand for money. For the quantity of money M1 and the interest rate r1, high returns are available on other less liquid assets (their prices are relatively low); firms and households will not want to hold much speculative money. For the quantity of money M2 and the interest rate r2, low returns are available on other assets (their prices are relatively high); firms and households are willing to hold high levels of money.

called **idle balances**; you are holding money because you feel that you have to do so, due to what you expect to happen in other markets.

The relationship between interest rates and asset prices

The speculative demand for money is inversely related to the interest rate. This is due to the relationship between interest rates and asset prices. Imagine that you buy a government bond (an 'IOU') for £100 and the government agrees to pay £10 per year as interest. The £10 per year represents a 10 per cent return on the £100 spending. If you had paid £200 for this bond, then the return would have been 5 per cent—that is:

$$\frac{£10}{£200} \times 100 = 5\%$$

The higher price of the asset means that the rate of return is lower. The same sort of analysis can be used with other assets. Imagine, for example, that you are going to buy a house to rent out for a given amount per month. The more you pay to buy the house, the lower the rental income will be as a percentage of the price i.e. the lower the rate of return.

Asset price and interest rates (rates of return) are therefore inversely related. The more that you pay for an asset, the lower the rate of return, and vice versa. This therefore affects the speculative demand for money; when asset prices are perceived to be low (that is, interest rates are high), individuals would rather hold assets than money, believing that they will increase in value. When asset prices are high and interest rates are low, individuals are more likely to want to hold money, because they will fear that asset prices will fall in the future.

The overall demand for money made up of transactions, precautionary, and speculative motives is known as the liquidity preference schedule. This is illustrated in Figure 23.3.

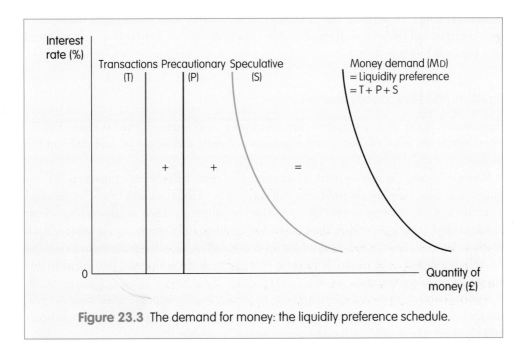

Figure 23.3 The demand for money: the liquidity preference schedule.

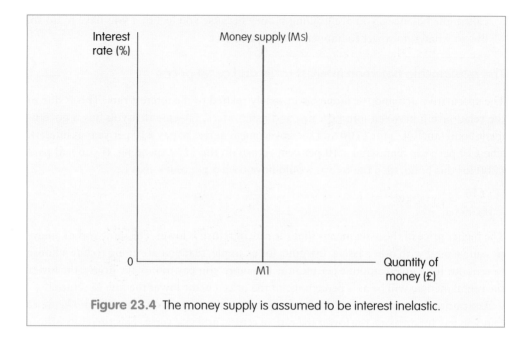

Figure 23.4 The money supply is assumed to be interest inelastic.

The supply of money

The supply of money at any moment is taken as a given amount—at any moment there is a certain amount of money in the economy. The money supply is, therefore, shown as being completely inelastic relative to the interest rate. Changes in the interest rate are assumed to have no impact on the supply of money available at any moment (see Figure 23.4).

Equilibrium in the money market

Equilibrium in the money market is brought about by changes in interest rates. The interest rate is the price of money and it adjusts to equate the supply of, and demand for, money.

When analysing the money market, we must also consider other asset markets. At any moment in time, households and firms will want to hold a certain amount of money and a certain amount of other assets (such as shares or property). Their decisions about how much to hold of each depend on their desire for liquidity and the returns available in each market. As we have seen the demand for money is called liquidity preference; firms and households should hold money because it is liquid and/or because the returns available elsewhere are not attractive.

At any moment, there is a given amount of money available in the economy—that is, the money supply. Imagine that we are at equilibrium at r0 (see Figure 23.5). Households and firms are happy holding the amount of money available.

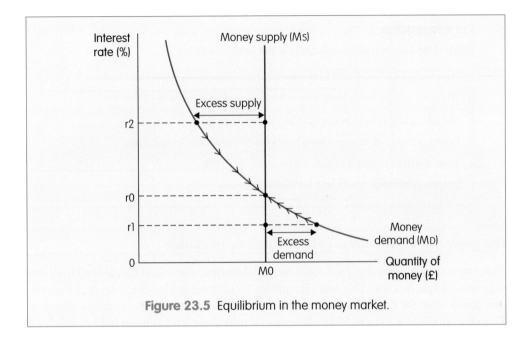

Figure 23.5 Equilibrium in the money market.

Now consider the situation at r1 in Figure 23.5. At r1, there is excess demand for money. At this low rate of return, there is more demand for money (which is liquid) than the amount that there actually is available. The return available on other assets is low (which means that their price is high), so households think that they might as well hold liquid money. They will want to sell their other assets and hold liquid money. As they start selling their other assets, this drives their price down and their rate of return up. This process will continue until the price of assets is so low and the return on them so high that households have no further incentive to hold more money, and are content holding the amount of money available M0.

Now consider the situation at r2 in Figure 23.5. At r2, there is excess supply of money. The rate of return on other assets is high, so households want to hold more of them rather than money. The excess supply of money means excess demand for other assets. This leads to more demand for other assets, thus bidding up their price. As their price increases (and therefore the return on them falls), this makes these other assets less attractive relative to money. With rising prices and falling returns, people become more willing to hold money, thereby reducing the excess supply. This process continues until equilibrium is reached at r0, and households and organizations are content to hold the amount of money M0.

As you can see, the money market and other asset markets are completely interrelated. An unwillingness to hold the amount of money available in the economy leads to excess demand in the other asset markets. This affects asset prices and returns until people are willing to hold the amount of money available. Similarly, excess demand for money means excess supply of other assets, which again leads to changes in asset prices and returns until equilibrium is restored.

Put into practice

Which of the following statements are true and which are false?

a. The precautionary demand for money is to purchase day-to-day items.

b. When the interest rate is high, demand for money is likely to be high.

c. The supply of money is assumed to be interest inelastic.

d. Excess demand for money is likely to lead to an increase in interest rates.

e. When the price of assets is high, the return on them falls.

f. Liquidity preference schedule is the supply of money.

The growth of the money supply: The money multiplier

When money is deposited in banks, the financial institutions would like to lend it all out or invest it all; in this way, they can earn profits by earning or charging interest. However, they know that the depositors may come and ask for some of it back at any moment. Therefore the banks have to hold some money in reserve. The amount held depends on how much they think is going to be asked for by depositors.

The money that is not kept back can be lent out. For example, it may be lent to individuals to go on holiday or to buy a new house. The money borrowed is therefore likely to be spent on goods and services. The people who receive this spending will deposit it in their banks. Once again, a proportion will be kept in reserve and the remainder will be lent out. Again, it is spent, and again a proportion will be kept back by the banks, and the remainder will be lent. This process continues and is known as the 'money multiplier'. It is equal to:

$$\frac{1}{\text{Reserve ratio}}$$

If, for example, the banks keep 10 per cent in reserve, then the money multiplier is:

$$\frac{1}{0.1} = 10$$

An initial deposit of £100 would therefore increase the total deposits and the overall money supply will grow to £1,000.

The money supply may therefore grow if:

• more money is deposited in banks and lent out; and

• the banks keep a smaller proportion of the money deposited in reserve and lend out more at any stage.

The money multiplier is similar to the consumption multiplier we studied in Chapter 17.

The effect of an increase in the money supply on the economy

The effect of an increase in the money supply can be analysed in the following series of stages.

Stage 1: Lower interest rates

Imagine that the money market is initially at r0 (see Figure 23.6a). If there were then an increase in the money supply, this would lead to an excess supply of money at the original rate. Households and firms will want to invest this 'excess money' into other assets. This will lead to more assets being bought, making them more expensive and reducing the return on them. As this happens, these assets become less attractive to invest in (as their price has gone up) and so people become more willing to hold the additional money in the economy. This process continues until the price of the other assets is so high that people are now willing to hold all of the extra money that is available. This happens when the interest rate is at r1 in Figure 23.6a. Equilibrium is restored with more money in the economy, higher asset prices and lower interest rates.

Stage 2: Higher aggregate demand

The fall in the interest rate is likely to increase the aggregate demand (see Figures 23.6b and 23.6c). This is because the increase in the money supply affects each of the following.

- **Consumption** With lower interest rates, it is cheaper for households to borrow money and there is less incentive to save. This should lead to extra consumption, thereby increasing the aggregate demand.

- **Investment** With lower interest rates, there will be more projects that have a higher rate of return than the cost of borrowing. This should lead to an increase in investment (how much depends on how sensitive the demand for capital goods is to changes in the interest rate). This will also increase the aggregate demand in the economy.

- **Exchange rates** Lower interest rates may lead to an outflow of money from the economy because investors will seek higher returns abroad. This is likely to reduce the external value of the currency. With more money in the economy, there will also be an increase in demand for foreign products and assets. This will lead to an increase in the supply of sterling in exchange for foreign currencies (see Figure 23.6d). Other things being unchanged, this will further decrease the external value of the currency. The effect of a weaker currency should make UK exports cheaper abroad in foreign currency, thereby boosting demand for exports. For example, if the pound falls from 1.5 euros in price to 1.2 euros then the price of a £2,000 product abroad falls from 3,000 euros to 2,400 euros. All other things being equal this should increase export revenue and further boosts the aggregate demand.

For more on exchange rates, see Chapter 27.

Put into practice

In addition to interest rates, what are the influences on consumption and the influences on investment?

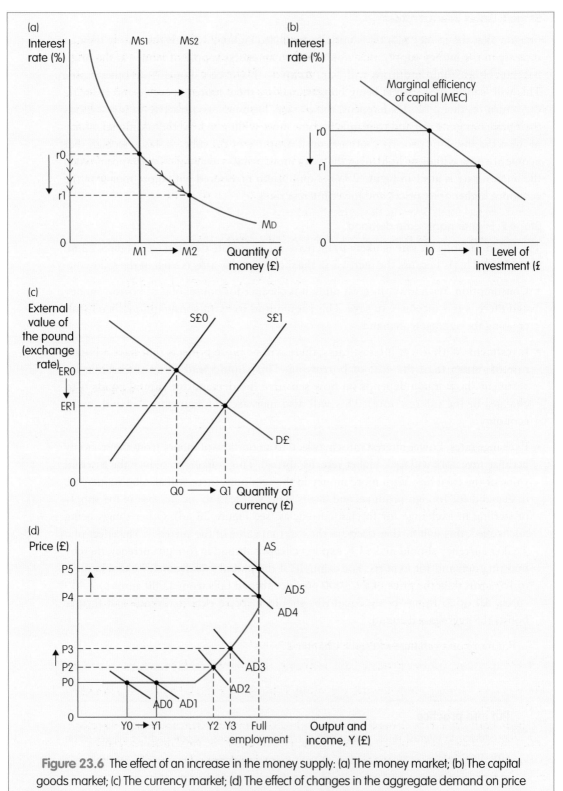

Figure 23.6 The effect of an increase in the money supply: (a) The money market; (b) The capital goods market; (c) The currency market; (d) The effect of changes in the aggregate demand on price and output will depend on the price elasticity of supply.

Stage 3: Higher prices and output

The consequences of an increase in the money supply are likely to be an increase in the aggregate demand either via interest rates boosting consumption, investment, and exports, or the exchange rate effect and the impact on exports. If the economy is well below its potential output, then this increase in the aggregate demand means that there is a high level of unused capacity and there are likely to be high levels of unemployment. An increase in demand would, in these circumstances, lead to more output, as shown in Figure 23.6e when the aggregate demand increases from AD0 to AD1. If, however, the economy is at full employment, then this means that the aggregate supply is completely price inelastic. An increase in demand will lead to an increase in prices (that is, inflation), as shown in Figure 23.6e when the aggregate demand increases from AD4 to AD5.

An increase in the money supply may therefore:

- increase output (if the economy is well below full employment);
- increase prices (if the economy is at full employment); or
- increase prices and output (if the economy is approaching full employment).

The effects of an increase in the money supply on prices and output can also be analysed using the quantity theory of money.

Put into practice

Using diagrams outline the possible impact of a decrease in the money supply on the aggregate demand.

Fisher's equation of exchange

Fisher's equation of exchange states that:

$MV = PT$

where:

- M is the quantity of money in the economy;
- V is the velocity of circulation—that is, this measures how often money moves around or is used in any given period;
- P is the average price level of goods and services; and
- T is the number of transactions—that is, the quantity of national output sold in a year.

The quantity PT is therefore equal to the money value of the national output sold in a year (basically, Price × Quantity).

The quantity MV represents the total spending on national output and must therefore equal PT because, unsurprisingly, total spending must equal the total amount spent!

For example, if the money supply is £100 billion and each pound is spent five times then the total spending is:

$5 \times £100 \text{ billion} = £500 \text{ billion}$

This means that the value of goods bought is £500 billion. If 25 billion goods were bought, then the average price level would be £20.

If the economy is at full employment, then the number of transactions in the economy cannot increase. If the velocity of circulation is also stable, then this means that an increase in the money supply leads to an increase in the price level—that is, more money in the economy leads to inflation. An increase in M leads to an increase in P.

For example, if the money supply were now £200 billion and each pound were still spent five times, then the total spending would be £1,000 billion. If the number of goods were still 25 billion, then this means that the price level would be £40. A doubling of the money supply has doubled the price level.

However, if the economy is below full employment, then this means that an increase in the money supply can lead to more output (that is, more transactions). In other words, an increase in M can lead to an increase in T. This means that the price level may not increase—that is, an increase in the money supply may not lead to inflation.

For example, MV could be £1,000 billion, but if the number of transactions doubles to 50 billion, then the average price level remains at £20.

Also, it is possible that the velocity of circulation may decrease. This could be because of lower interest rates, so there is less pressure to pass money on quickly (due to a lower opportunity cost). In this case, an increase in the money supply might lead to a decrease in the velocity of circulation. This means that there may not be any extra overall spending in the economy and therefore the price level may not increase.

■ The Quantity theory of Money and Monetarists

According to the Quantity Theory of Money V and T in the equation of exchange are relatively stable. This then means that an increase in the quantity of money (M) leads to an increase in prices (P). This theory is the basis of the Monetarist approach to economics. Monetarists argue that 'inflation is always and everywhere a monetary phenomenon in the sense that it is and can be produced only by a more rapid increase in the quantity of money than output' (Friedman, 1968)—that is, inflation is always due to growth in the money supply. Over time, the full employment level in an economy can increase due to, for example, developments in technology. This enables some growth in the number of transactions (T), so the money supply can grow in line with this without being inflationary. However, 'excessive money supply growth' will lead to more demand and higher prices.

The monetarists argued that the cause of inflation must ultimately be the money supply. Imagine that we have a situation in which

- quantity of money (M) is £100 billion;
- velocity of circulation (V) is 5 billion;
- overall spending (MV) is:

    $5 \times £100 \text{ billion} = £500 \text{ billion}$

- number of transactions (T) is 25 billion.

Therefore the average price level is £20.

Imagine that the price level now increases to £50, perhaps due to an increase in wages or imported components. If the money supply does not grow to accommodate this and the velocity does not change, then this means that the total spending is still:

5 × £100 billion = £500 billion

Because the price level is £50, the number of transactions must fall to 10 billion.

The higher prices without more money supply in the economy lead to fewer goods being bought and probably unemployment. This will put downward pressure on wages and prices, which will force the price back down to £20. Inflation has not persisted because the money supply was controlled. However to achieve this it has probably involved unemployment and a difficult period before prices and wages fall. Governments may not want to go through this difficult adjustment period if it is politically unpopular.

However, if the money supply had been allowed to expand, then the inflation could continue.

For example, if the money supply were to grow to £250 billion, then MV would become:

5 × £250 billion = £1,250 billion

Also:

PT = £50 × 25 billion = £1,250 billion

A growth in the money supply has allowed prices to stay higher.

According to monetarist theory, the temptation for governments is to let the money supply grow if prices increase. Although this leads to higher inflation, it avoids a difficult period of higher unemployment that is necessary to bring prices down if the money supply is not expanded.

Clearly, the growth of the money supply and, in fact, controlling its growth are key elements of the monetarist approach. However whether the link between money supply growth and inflation is that direct and that predictable is open to debate. According to the Bank of England:

> The amount of money in the economy and the level of prices are positively related in the long run. Without money, inflation could not exist. And, across many countries, persistently high rates of money growth have usually been associated with high inflation …
>
> … Although money and inflation are clearly linked over the longer term, the usefulness of money as an indicator of inflationary pressures in the short to medium term depends on there being a predictable relationship between money and the value of spending. For example, suppose money grew at the same rate as the value of spending over time. Then money growth of 4.0%–4.5% per year would be consistent with annual growth in economic activity of 2%–2.5%—the historical average in the UK—plus inflation of 2.0% per year, in line with the inflation target.
>
> In practice, however, the relationship between money and inflation has not been stable. Money growth has been influenced by many other factors, including financial innovations—such as the introduction of credit cards—changes in banking regulations, and developments in international capital markets. The effects of these changes have not always been easy to predict accurately. So rules of thumb like the one above have not usually been useful guides for policy.

Put into practice

Which of the following statements are true and which are false?

a. An increase in the money supply, other things unchanged, is likely to lead to a fall in the interest rate.

b. The monetarists assume that an increase in the money supply is deflationary.

c. A decrease in the demand for money is likely to lead to an increase in interest rates.

d. A decrease in the amount banks keep in reserve is likely to increase the money supply.

Factors that might limit the impact of an increase in the money supply on prices

The impact of an increase in the money supply on prices might be limited by the following factors.

- **The liquidity trap** At very low interest rates (which means very high asset prices), an increase in the money supply may not lead to a fall in interest rates (see Figure 23.7). Firms and households would simply absorb the extra money. The returns elsewhere are simply too low to appeal. The extra money is held with no impact on asset prices or interest rates; the demand for money is horizontal. The velocity of circulation falls as the money supply increases.

- The demand for money generally may not be very interest elastic, so any increase in the money supply might have a relatively small impact on interest rates (and therefore on the aggregate demand).

- The impact of lower interest rates on consumption and demand may be limited. Investment in capital goods is very dependent on expectations, for example, so a fall in interest rates on its own may have a limited effect.

- The economy may be below full employment, in which case output increases and the number of transactions (T) rises.

In any of these cases, an increase in the money supply would not have a significant impact on prices and inflation.

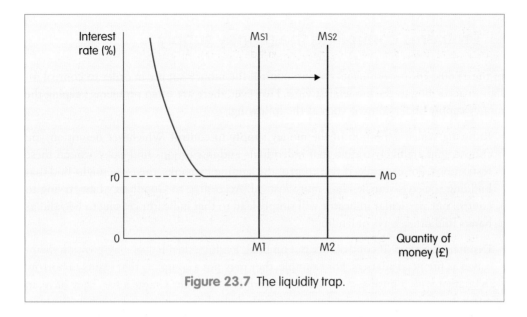

Figure 23.7 The liquidity trap.

Put into practice

Which of the following statements are true and which are false?

a. Lower interest rates should increase aggregate demand.

b. In the liquidity trap, an increase in the money supply does not affect interest rates.

c. An increase in the reserve ratio at banks should increase the money supply.

d. The quantity theory of money states that $MP = VT$.

Controlling the money supply

If an increase in the money supply does lead to inflation, then governments will want to try to control it to achieve their objective of stable prices if high inflation appears to be an issue. A central bank may attempt to reduce the money supply as follows.

- **Requesting that banks keep higher reserves and lend less out at any stage** The Bank of England, for example, can try to persuade other banks that this would be desirable for the economy. If the Bank of England can reduce the amount lent out at each stage by the banks, then this will slow the growth of the money supply.

- **Open market operations occur when a government buys or sells bonds** For example, to reduce the money supply, the government might sell bonds. To buy these bonds, households will use their money. This will usually be taken out of their banks. This reduces the amount that the banks have to lend out, thereby reducing the growth of the money supply.

▦ Problems controlling the money supply

In the 1980s, UK governments tried to control the money supply in order to control inflation according to the monetarist view. However, there are often problems keeping the money supply under control, such as the following.

- **Knowing which definition of the money supply to control** Whichever definition you choose, you are likely to find that individuals and institutions find ways around these restrictions. For example, if you control the lending by banks, then you might find that building societies start lending more instead. According to **Goodhart's Law**, trying to control one particular indicator will simply lead to that indicator ceasing to be valid as banks find other ways of lending!

- **Disintermediation** If controls are put on bank lending, then banks may position themselves as financial advisers. For example, they may put a company that wants to borrow in contact with a business that wants to lend. For this, they charge a fee. They have, in effect, lent a business money, but not directly (which is why this is known as disintermediation), so it is difficult to regulate. Financial institutions make their money from lending, so whatever a government does to stop this will be resisted and ways will be found to avoid control (for example, organizing more lending via overseas banks).

Put into practice

a. If the money multiplier is 5, the reserve ratio is:
   - 0.5 per cent.
   - 5 per cent.
   - 10 per cent.
   - 20 per cent.

b. A central bank may increase the money supply:
   - by increasing reserve requirements.
   - by increasing Bank Rate.
   - by means of an open-market purchase of government bonds.
   - by reducing the government deficit.

c. A decrease in reserve requirements _____ the money multiplier and _____ the money supply. Which of the following best completes this statement?
   - increases; increases
   - increases; decreases
   - decreases; decreases
   - decreases; increases

Monetary policy in the UK

After disappointing experiences trying to control the money supply in the 1980s, monetary policy in the UK in recent years has focused on controlling the interest rate set by the Bank of England (called Bank Rate) and using this to control the demand for money. Higher interest rates should reduce the quantity of money demanded; less will be borrowed from banks, thereby reducing the money supply (see Figure 23.8).

In May 1997, the Labour government gave the Bank of England's Monetary Policy Committee (MPC) the ability to set whatever interest rates it felt were necessary to achieve given inflation targets. This was made law with the Bank of England Act 1998. Price stability at present is defined by the government's inflation target of 2 per cent. By providing stable inflation rates, it is believed that this will encourage investment (for more on this, see Chapter 21). If inflation is more than 1 per cent above or below the 2 per cent target, the governor of the Bank of England must write to the Chancellor of the Exchequer to explain why.

Prior to the creation of the independent MPC, interest rates had been influenced by the government and were often used to achieve political, rather than economic, objectives. When an election was coming up, for example, the pressure was on to reduce the interest rate to make borrowing cheaper and therefore make the government more popular, even if it was not the right decision for the economy as a whole.

For much of the last decade, the MPC was trying to keep inflation down to achieve its target. This involved changing the interest rate to influence consumption, investment, and the exchange rate to achieve the desired levels of aggregate demand. If demand looked like it was going to be too high and pull up prices, the interest rate would be increased to dampen demand.

When the recession hit, the problem was that demand fell dramatically. At the same time the economy experienced significant increases in costs through oil and imports which

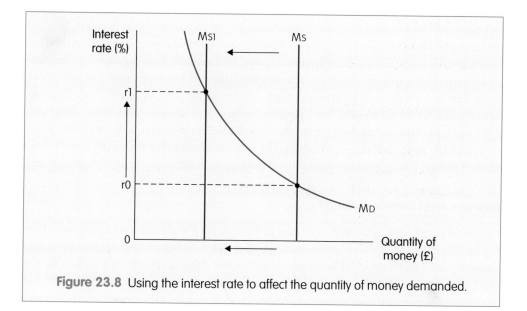

Figure 23.8 Using the interest rate to affect the quantity of money demanded.

pushed prices up. The economy was facing slow growth and relatively high inflation. To reduce inflation the Bank of England might be expected to increase interest rates to dampen demand. However, reducing demand would make growth even slower and might lead to another recession. On the grounds that the inflationary pressures pushing up prices were not long term the Bank of England justified keeping interest rates low; in fact they went to their lowest level ever when the base rate was set at 0.5 per cent. In 2013 the different pressures on the Bank of England were recognized when its objectives were slightly redefined—it still had to focus ultimately on keeping inflation around 2 per cent but also had to take into account the general state of the economy when making its decisions. To some extent this simply recognized what had been happening after the recession but it gave the Bank of England more flexibility when setting interest rates.

However, even with interest rates at their lowest level ever demand continued to remain low and the Bank of England looked for other ways of boosting the money supply including quantitative easing.

Quantitative easing

On 5 March 2010, the MPC reduced Bank Rate to 0.5 per cent and undertook what is called quantitative easing. This meant that it began purchasing public and private sector assets, using central bank money. The purpose of this was to inject money into the economy to provide an additional stimulus to spending.

The conventional way for the MPC to conduct monetary policy is by setting Bank Rate. The introduction of asset purchases has shifted the focus of monetary policy, but the objectives have not changed. The aim of the MPC remains that of achieving inflation of 2 per cent (within a band of 1 per cent either side). Asset purchases provide an additional tool to help the MPC to meet those objectives.

The Bank of England is the sole supplier of central bank money in sterling. As well as banknotes, central bank money takes the form of reserve balances held by banks at the Bank of England. These balances are used to make payments between different banks. The Bank can create new money electronically by increasing the balance on a reserve account. So when the Bank purchases an asset from a bank as part of quantitative easing, it simply credits that bank's reserve account with the additional funds. This generates an expansion in the supply of central bank money. Commercial banks hold deposits for their customers, which can be used by households and companies to buy goods and services, or assets. These deposits form the bulk of 'broad money'. If the Bank of England purchases an asset from a non-bank company, it pays for the asset via the seller's bank. It credits the reserve account of the seller's bank with the funds and that bank credits the account of the seller with a deposit. The expansion of broad money is a key part of the transmission mechanism for quantitative easing.

Why use quantitative easing?

The reduction of Bank Rate to 0.5 per cent in 2009 in the UK should have encouraged borrowing and spending, and thereby boosted aggregate demand; this should also have been supported by other factors, such as fiscal policy and a weak value of the currency (which should make exports relatively cheap and encourage export demand). Even so, the MPC felt that monetary policy needed to do even more (to be 'looser') in order to boost aggregate demand.

The decision to expand the money supply through large-scale asset purchases (or quantitative easing) shifted the focus of monetary policy towards the quantity of money, as well as the price of money. Asset purchases were intended to boost spending and so help to meet the inflation target.

However, there was considerable uncertainty about the strength and pace with which these effects would feed through. It depended in part on what sellers did with the money that they received in exchange for the assets that they sold to the Bank of England and the response of banks to the additional liquidity that they obtained. Despite injecting significant sums of money into the economy through quantitative easing there were still difficulties in terms of this leading to lending to businesses. Partly this was due to businesses being wary of investing in such uncertain times and therefore being reluctant to borrow. Also banks were reluctant to take risks with lending and so seemed reluctant to lend out the money they had. The Bank looked for other ways of encouraging lending to get the economy growing including the Funds for Lending Scheme. The Funds for Lending Scheme was intended to provide incentives for banks and building societies to boost their lending. It did this by providing funding to banks and building societies for an extended period, with both the price and quantity of funding provided linked to their lending performance.

What do you think?

Should the Bank of England pursue more quantitative easing?

Case study

In June 2013 the Bank of England kept its stimulus programme of quantitative easing (QE) unchanged and also held interest rates at 0.5 per cent. The decision, at the last Monetary Policy Committee meeting chaired by Sir Mervyn King, was widely expected.

The MPC had been divided over whether to increase Quantitative Easing from what was its current level of £375bn.

Three of the nine MPC members—including Sir Mervyn—had voted for an extra £25bn of QE at recent meetings. Recent economic data painted a mixed picture of the UK economy. Official figures showed retail sales fell recently, while unemployment rose. However, surveys of the services, construction, and manufacturing industries all pointed to a strong recent recovery in activity. Overall this meant there were signs of recovery which helped the MPC decide not to undertake further monetary stimulus.

Weeks before this decision the Bank upgraded its own forecast for growth, and recent data had confirmed that the UK had avoided a triple-dip recession. Inflation had also remained more subdued than expected.

❓ Questions

1   Why did the MPC decide to keep interest rates low?

2   Explain why the UK government sets an inflation target.

3   Explain what is meant by quantitative easing. What effect was it expected to have in the economy?

4   Why did the Bank decide not to undertake more quantitative easing?

Review questions

1 Explain two functions of money.
2 Explain two factors affecting the demand for money.
3 How might interest rates affect aggregate demand?
4 What is meant by MV = PT?
5 Explain the Monetarist view of inflation.
6 Outline the role of the Monetary Policy Committee.
7 Explain one way the Bank of England might control the money supply.
8 What is meant by Goodhart's Law?

Put into practice

1 Using diagrams compare the effect of an increase in the money supply on interest rates if (a) the demand for money is interest elastic and (b) the demand for money is interest inelastic.
2 Using diagrams show the effect of a fall in the money supply on interest rates, investment, aggregate demand, and national income and output.

Key learning points

- Monetary policy uses the money supply and interest rates to control the economy.
- The motives for holding money include the transactions motive, the precautionary motive, and the speculative motive.
- The interest rate in the UK is determined by the Bank of England's Monetary Policy Committee; it is used to achieve an inflation target.
- The quantity theory of money states that MV = PT. If V and T are constant, then an increase in the money supply leads to an increase in the price level. This is known as a monetarist view of the causes of inflation.
- The interest rate affects borrowing, saving, the price of assets, and the exchange rate.
- Quantitative easing is intended to inject money into the economy to stimulate spending.

Reference

Friedman, M. (1968) 'The role of monetary policy', *American Economic Review*, 58(Mar): 1–17

Learn more

To learn more about the UK government's approach to monetary policy over the years, visit the Online Resource Centre.

 Visit our Online Resource Centre at http://www.oxfordtextbooks.co.uk/orc/gillespie_ econ3e/ for test questions and further information on topics covered in this chapter.

»24 Economic growth and the economic cycle

In Chapter 17, we explained how an economy moves toward its equilibrium level of income. The level of consumption, and injections and withdrawals in an economy determine the equilibrium level of income. However, this level of national income is not static and will change over time. In fact, a key government economic objective is usually to increase the country's income over time. In this chapter, we examine the causes of economic growth, including productivity, research and development, and entrepreneurship. We also consider the pattern of economic growth over time, which is known as the economic cycle.

LEARNING OBJECTIVES

By the end of this chapter, you should be able to:

✓ outline the key stages and features of the economic cycle;

✓ explain the possible causes of the economic cycle;

✓ understand the meaning and significance of productivity;

✓ understand the meaning and significance of research and development;

✓ understand the meaning and importance of entrepreneurship;

✓ consider the possible problems of economic growth.

▓ Introduction

The level of national income is an important influence on a country's standard of living although, as we saw in Chapter 18, it is not its only determinant. Achieving economic growth and increasing national income are a common economic objective.

Economic growth can be measured by an increase in the real output or income of an economy over time. This may be measured in terms of the whole economy, or in terms of output or income per person. Economic growth is usually measured in terms of the percentage change in gross domestic product (GDP) or GDP per capita compared to the year before. This measures changes in the income generated in a given region.

Economic growth creates more income in the economy. This can lead to a higher average income per person (although the income may not actually be distributed equally). This is often linked to a higher standard of living. Greater earnings can contribute to greater welfare and a more content nation.

Remember, however, that a fast rate of growth is often achieved by economies that are industrializing quickly and starting from a relatively low base. More mature economies may have higher incomes per person, but relatively slow economic growth.

What do you think?

Do you think governments should focus on increasing growth rates in the economy?

▨ Types of growth

When examining economic growth, it is sometimes helpful to distinguish between actual and potential growth.

- **Actual growth** is the rate at which the economy is actually growing over a given period. It is measured by the annual percentage increase in national income.

- **Potential growth** measures how much the economy could grow were all of its resources to be employed fully—that is, it represents an increase in the capacity of the economy.

The difference between the two can be seen using a production possibility frontier (PPF). The movement from X to Y represents actual growth in the economy because more is produced; in this case, resources are being used more fully rather than there being increase in capacity (see Figure 24.1a), so this is not an increase in potential output. Actual growth may be caused by a boost in aggregate demand or the removal of inefficiencies in the markets for factors of production that make reallocating between industries easier.

Potential growth is shown by an outward shift of the PPF (see Figure 24.1b). This represents potential growth because the economy is increasing what it can produce, whilst still utilizing all of its resources fully. Potential growth may be caused by increases in supply which may be due to:

- an increase in resources—for example, a population increase, net migration, and a more skilled workforce would increase the labour input. The recent developments in fracking appear to have made far more gas available to economies which could help faster economic growth.

- improvements in technology or the way in which resources are used (for example, better management techniques). This increases the productivity of factors of production. The

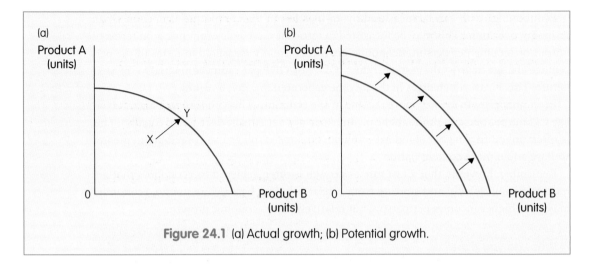

Figure 24.1 (a) Actual growth; (b) Potential growth.

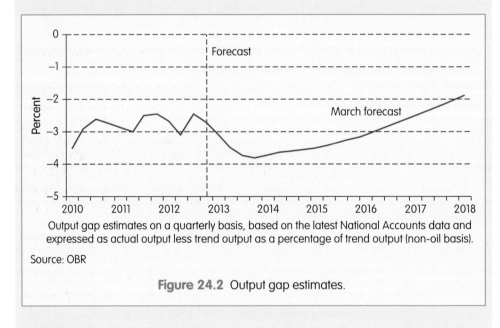

Economics in context

Figure 24.2 shows output gap estimates based on National Accounts data.

Output gap estimates on a quarterly basis, based on the latest National Accounts data and expressed as actual output less trend output as a percentage of trend output (non-oil basis).

Source: OBR

Figure 24.2 Output gap estimates.

? Questions

Analyse the reasons why the output gap exists.

Analyse the possible consequences of an output gap for the economy.

Analyse the reasons why the output gap may be expected to reduce.

rapid increases in technology in recent years has led to much more efficient processes fuelling economic growth.

An **output gap** occurs if there is a difference between an economy's actual and potential output.

- If an economy is operating below its potential output, then there is a negative output gap. The actual output of the economy is below what it could be. The economy is operating within the production possibility frontier.

- If the actual output of the economy is above the potential output, then there is a positive output gap. This would occur if firms were operating above their usual capacity levels—perhaps running additional shifts or working additional overtime hours.

What do you think?

In 1798 Thomas Malthus wrote the *First Essay on Population* and predicted that growth would lead to starvation. He argued that the supply of land was fixed and therefore as more people began to work on the land diminishing returns would set in and therefore there would not be enough food to feed the growing population. Why do you think he has proved wrong in many countries?

What can a government do to promote growth?

To promote potential growth (that is, to increase the capacity of the economy), a government could use supply-side policies.

These aim to boost the supply of resources such as labour, capital, land, and entrepreneurship, in the economy and shift the aggregate supply to the right (see Figure 24.3). The aggregate supply shows the amount producers are willing and able to produce in an economy at given price levels. At full employment in an economy, aggregate supply is perfectly price inelastic. For example, to increase aggregate supply the government might provide tax incentives to encourage more people to work, thereby reducing the number of people in the labour force but not working. Alternatively, it might increase the labour force by increasing the retirement age, or it might provide tax credits or subsidies for investment.

What is important in terms of government policy is providing a stable economic environment in which businesses feel confident about investing and households are willing to spend, confident of employment in the future.

The government might also try to improve the quality of resources. This could be through training, or by encouraging research and development to promote new products and processes. Supply-side policies are examined in more detail in Chapter 19.

To promote actual growth the government may try to increase aggregate demand using demand-side policies. It may seek to increase injections (investment, government spending, and exports) and/or reduce withdrawals into the economy (savings, import spending, and taxation revenue). To do this it may use fiscal or monetary policy. For example it might:

- Cut interest rates to encourage borrowing and then spending

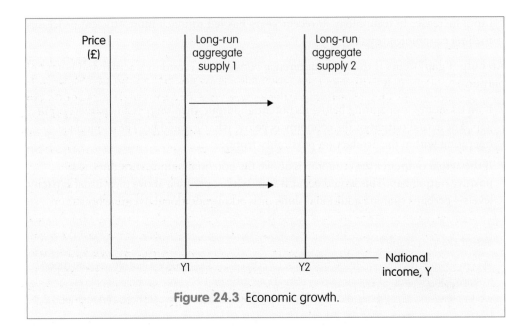

Figure 24.3 Economic growth.

- Cut taxation rates to leave firms with more profits to spend and households with more income to spend
- Increase its own spending on final goods and services

What do you think?

Is growth slow or fast in your economy at the moment? Why do you think this is?

Economics in context

India's economy grew at its slowest pace in a decade last year. The economy grew by 5 per cent over the year. India was typically recording a growth of 9 per cent per year until two years ago, but recently it has experienced a decline in its manufacturing and services sectors.

Foreign investors appear to have delayed investment because key reforms to open up markets have been delayed. The business community appears pessimistic and is worried about fast rising prices. The slow growth also means there are less profits to invest into the business.

? Questions

Analyse the reasons why India might be experiencing slow growth.

Why might the Indian government be concerned about slower growth?

Discuss the ways in which the Indian government might achieve sustainable growth.

The problems of growth

Although economic growth can bring benefits for society in that people, on average, have more income, it also brings with it problems, as we saw in our analysis of measuring the standard of living in an economy. For example, it may lead to more stress for individuals, who are pushed to work harder, and may well lead to a worse quality of life. Greater growth may also lead to greater inequality as some people gain more than others, thereby widening the differences between them. It may also damage the environment and lead to the loss of non-renewable resources, such as oil reserves. Fast growth may mean that these resources will be used up at a faster rate, leaving fewer for future generations. Indeed growth may have major environmental problems such as global warming. These effects may not be taken into account by the present generation because they will not necessarily be affected—the impact is on future generations. Whilst pursuing faster growth countries may not, therefore, be too concerned about the external costs. This is especially true when it is often the more developed economies these days who are trying to encourage emerging markets to adopt more environmentally friendly production techniques even if it leads to slower growth. Countries such as China and India are reluctant to sacrifice economic growth now in response to calls from developed nations, given that much of the environmental damage in the past has been done by those now calling for restraint and more investment in environmentally friendly technology. The *Stern Review on the Economics of Climate Change* for the UK government suggests that 1 per cent of global GDP needs to be invested in cleaner technology to avoid the worst effects of global warming and that failure to do this will only create more problems later. However governments seem reluctant to sacrifice present growth for future returns perhaps because they do not feel they can convince the voters.

Given the problems that can result from economic growth, some economists have called for a zero-growth policy by major economies. However, this may well be too extreme a solution; typically, economists would want a marginal solution. The best level of growth would be where the social marginal benefit of growth equals the social marginal cost. The problem lies in fully identifying and measuring the social costs and benefits.

What do you think?

Do you think that zero growth is a realistic policy option for governments? What do you think are the possible environmental costs of growth?

The economic cycle

The economic cycle shows the pattern of economic growth that tends to occur in economies over time. Whilst there may be an underlying steady long-run trend, most economies experience an economic cycle that is measured by changes in national income. Over time,

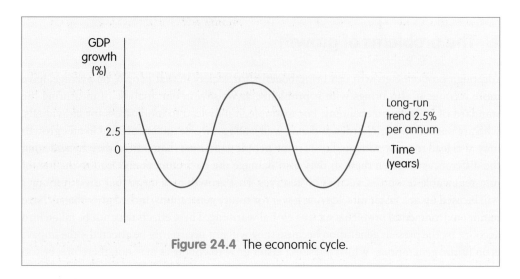

Figure 24.4 The economic cycle.

the stages through which economies typically go are growth, boom, recession, and slump, as shown in Figure 24.4. Whilst increasing national income is often an aim of government, so is stabilizing its growth path. Instability and uncertainty tend to make planning difficult and to deter investment. Firms may become wary of investing if they are not sure whether an economy is going to be doing well or not. Similarly, households may save more if there is greater uncertainty. If a government can provide stability, then it can actually help the economy to grow faster in the long run.

▥ The stages of the economic cycle

The four main stages of the economic cycle are as follows.

- **A boom** A boom is characterized by high rates of economic growth. The GDP will be growing relatively quickly. This should lead to relatively low levels of unemployment. Firms will have busy order books and may have to turn business away because they cannot keep up with demand. Prices may begin to rise due to demand growing so quickly that output cannot keep pace.

- **A recession (or downswing)** A recession occurs when there is a period of two successive quarters of negative economic growth. This means that the economy is shrinking. The GDP is growing at a negative rate.

  A recession is usually characterized by:
  - increasing levels of unemployment;
  - low levels of profits, reducing the amount of internal funds available for investment;
  - unused capacity;
  - downward pressure on prices to try to stimulate demand;

- less income, leading to less demand in the economy and equally less spending on imports;
- more business closures;
- less tax revenue for the government (because fewer people are earning and fewer products are being sold). At the same time, the government is likely to be paying more in subsidies and benefits, so overall, the government's financial position will be weakened and this may require more government borrowing.

- **A recovery (or upswing, or upturn)** In the recovery phase, demand begins to pick up, reducing firms' excess capacity and improving employment levels. With more demand for products, the demand for factors of production increases, which begins to pull up prices and wages. Machinery begins to be replaced or updated, and business confidence picks up, leading to more investment.

- **A slump (or depression)** In a slump, economic growth is slow and unemployment is high. There is downward pressure on prices (deflation) and profits, and business confidence is low. The point at which the slump flattens out is called the 'lower turning point' of the economic cycle. The 'upper turning point' is in the boom.

Whilst this general pattern of growth outlined in the economic cycle may typically be followed, there will be differences over time in:

- for how long each stage lasts; and
- how large each stage is—for example, how big the slump or boom is.

In fact, different economists have identified several different economic cycles. These include the following.

- **The classical trade cycle** This describes a pattern of boom and slump in which there is often around eight to ten years between one boom and another.
- **The Kuznets cycle** This is named after Simon Kuznets, a Nobel prizewinner, who identified a cycle of activity in the construction industry that took between 15 and 25 years.

Economics in context

Last year the US rock star Jon Bon Jovi and his band waived their fee at a concert in Madrid because of Spain's economic crisis. As a result the tickets were unusually cheap selling for between 18 (£15) and 39 euros. Madrid was originally left off the list of places the band would play but Bon Jovi decided to add it in and play for free so his Spanish fans could see him.

❓ Questions

What do you think is likely to happen to the price elasticity of demand for concert tickets in a recession?

What do you think is likely to be the sign and size of the income elasticity of concert tickets?

- **The Kondratieff cycle** This highlighted that, as well as a ten-year cycle, there was a major underlying cycle that takes 50 to 60 years to complete—that is, that there can be cycles within cycles.

> **What do you think?**
>
> How might different stages of the economic cycle affect a firm's marketing decisions?

What causes the economic cycle?

The causes of the economic cycle include the following.

- **Expectations** Changes in the expectations of firms and households can have a major effect on the state of the economy. If an economy is growing relatively fast and confidence is high, then firms may be more likely to invest, because they are more optimistic about future levels of demand. Households are more likely to spend because they are more confident about their employment and earning prospects. If expectations are positive, then this is likely to generate greater spending by firms and households, and this helps to stimulate further growth in the economy. However, at some point, households and firms may decide that growth cannot continue and may become more pessimistic. As this happens, spending falls, bringing about a recession. Changes in expectations may cause, or certainly exaggerate, the underlying economic cycle.

> **What do you think?**
>
> If you were in government, how could you influence people's expectations about the economy?

- **Stock levels** Stocks include raw materials, components, semi-finished goods, and finished goods waiting to be sold. They are also called inventory. Changes in stock levels can affect demand in the economy. When an economy starts to grow faster, managers may be reluctant to increase output in the short term in case the boom does not last. They will not want to invest and employ more people only to find that demand falls again. They are more likely to keep production at the same level as before and run down their stock levels. However, if demand does keep growing, then firms will now have too few stocks and managers will have to expand production. They may need to increase their production capacity, not only to meet the new higher level of demand, but also to replace the stocks that will have been run down. This leads to a relatively high increase in spending, which leads to even faster growth in the economy. This can create a boom in the economy.

  Once demand starts to grow more slowly, managers are likely to be reluctant to reduce their production levels immediately, because it may be only a temporary decline.

Rather than make people redundant and reduce capacity, firms are likely to maintain the existing output level in the short term. Given that demand is lower, producing at the old level leads to increasing levels of stocks. However, if demand continues to be low, then, in the long run, managers will cut back output. Because they have been building up stocks, they can now reduce output significantly. This leads to a large fall in demand for resources and may push the economy into a recession.

The sluggishness of managers to react to changes in demand therefore exaggerates the changes in demand, and creates booms and slumps.

- **Government policy** Governments will often intervene to try to stabilize the economy. However, policies that are intended to stabilize the economy can actually end up destabilizing it! This is because it is difficult for the government to fine-tune the economy effectively and attempts to do so may make things worse. One reason for this is that the information that the government uses to make decisions is inevitably out of date. By the time the government has determined what it thinks the level of national income actually is, the economy will have moved on. Policies intended to correct a particular problem may therefore not be relevant because the economic situation has changed.

This problem is made worse because economic policy changes take time to work through the economy and the effects are not always predictable. For example, a tax cut may not lead to an increase in spending if households decide to save the extra disposable income.

Imagine that the government thinks that the economy is at the point X in Figure 24.5 and therefore needs a boost in aggregate demand. It might then introduce reflationary policies. However, by the time the policies begin to have an effect, the economy may be at the point Y, in which case, the boost to aggregate demand leads to too much demand in the economy, causing excessive growth and then demand-pull inflation. Government attempts to reduce fluctuations in demand may therefore end up exaggerating them (see Figure 24.6).

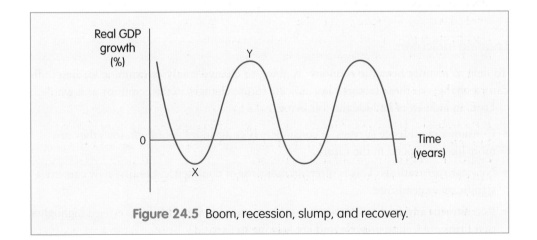

Figure 24.5 Boom, recession, slump, and recovery.

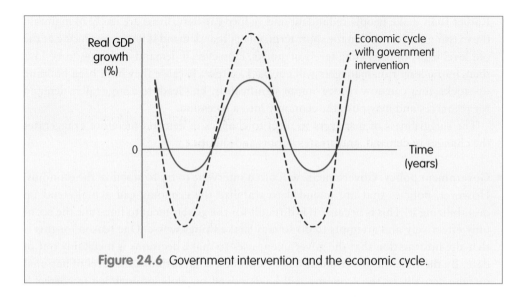

Figure 24.6 Government intervention and the economic cycle.

Put into practice

If the government were to think that the economy was in a recession, what type of policies would it adopt?

▮ Indicators of the economic cycle

As we have seen, one of the problems of government intervention is the difficulty of knowing when to intervene. If the government gets it wrong, then intervention can actually make the economic situation worse.

Leading indicators

To help to identify how the economy is going to change, analysts examine leading indicators; changes in these factors may indicate future changes in the economy as a whole.
Leading indicators include the following.

- **Consumer confidence surveys** If consumers become more confident, then they are more likely to spend in the future.

- **New car registrations** This is often an indicator of confidence, because new cars are a significant expenditure.

- **Recruitment advertising** An increase in the number of jobs being advertised highlights that firms are feeling positive and are looking to expand.

**Economics
in context**

Figure 24.7 shows growth figures for the UK over the last few years.

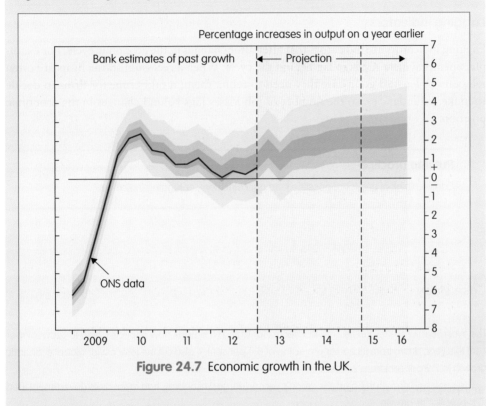

Figure 24.7 Economic growth in the UK.

Source: Bank of England *Inflation Report* May 2013

❓ Questions

Analyse the possible reasons why growth might have been relatively slow in the UK between 2010 and 2012.

Discuss the ways the government might boost economic growth in the UK in the future.

- **Mortgage applications** Mortgages are loans that households take out to buy a house. If the number of applications for these increases, then this, again, reveals something about the confidence of households.

- **Share prices** An increase in share prices suggests that there is more demand from investors to own companies. This suggests that investors believe that demand is going to be high in the future.

- **Amount spent at casinos** If people are feeling positive about the economy and their earnings they are more likely to gamble

Coincident indicators

Coincident indicators are indicators that happen as the cycle occurs—for example, changes in the real GDP and retail sales.

Lagging indicators

Lagging indicators are indicators that alter after changes in the economic cycle. For example, unemployment tends to lag behind the cycle. When a recession starts, firms are often reluctant to let staff go in case they need to rehire them; it takes time for firms to decide to make redundancies, so the number of job losses lags behind changes in the economic position.

Put into practice

Can you think of any more possible leading, coincident, or lagging indicators?

Case study

The World Bank recently cut its growth forecast for China. The bank now expects China to grow 7.7 per cent this year, down from its earlier projection of 8.4 per cent. It also cut the forecast for global economic growth to 2.2 per cent from 2.4 per cent.

The bank said growth in China, the world's second-largest economy, had fallen as its government tried to rebalance its growth.

Over the past few decades China has relied heavily on exports and government-led investment to boost its economy. However, a slowdown in key markets such as the USA and Europe has seen a decline in demand for Chinese exports, leading to concerns over whether China can maintain its high growth rate. This has led to calls to boost domestic demand to offset the effect of lower export demand.

The latest estimate reverses an earlier increase in its forecast when it claimed that the Chinese government's investment in infrastructure projects would boost China's growth to around 8.4 per cent. This was after Beijing had approved infrastructure projects worth more than $150bn (£94bn).

However, the World Bank now raises concerns over these investments. There are worries that these investments might not prove profitable and there would be a struggle to pay the interest on the loans needed to undertake them.

In response to concerns over growth the Chinese government recently introduced a number of measures including:

- suspending value-added tax (VAT) and turnover tax for small businesses with monthly sales of less than 20,000 yuan (around £2,000). This was intended to benefit more than six million small companies and increase the employment and income for millions of people;

- measures to streamline customs clearance procedures, reduce export costs, and help small and medium-sized private enterprises sell more abroad;
- greater investment in the country's railway network.

? Questions

1   Analyse the factors identified above that affect the growth of China's economy.

2   Discuss whether the actions taken by the Chinese government are likely to boost economic growth. What else might the government do?

3   Discuss the possible effects of slow economic growth in China.

Review questions

1   What is the economic cycle?

2   What is the difference between actual and potential growth?

3   Explain the difference between a boom and a recession. How might these stages affect a firm's decisions?

4   Explain how a government might promote faster economic growth.

5   What might cause the economic cycle

6   Explain what is meant by a leading indicator of the economic cycle.

7   Explain what is meant by a lagging indicator of the economic cycle

8   Explain what are the likely features of a recession.

Put into practice

1   A recession may be caused by a fall in aggregate demand. Show how a fall in aggregate demand leads to a fall in national income using a diagram.

2   Outline the actions a government might take to help an economy recover from a recession. Illustrate this with a diagram.

Assignment question

1   Research UK economic growth over the last twenty years. Can you identify any economic cycle? Analyse the key reasons for changes in UK growth over this period.

Key learning points

- National income growth does not follow a steady path, but tends to occur in cycles.

- The government often intervenes to stabilize growth in the economy, but mistimed intervention can create further instability.

- Leading indicators may be useful to identify future changes in the economy.

- Growth may bring a higher average income per person, but this does not necessarily mean that the quality of life is better or that growth is desirable.

- Growth in an economy occurs when income increases. This may lead to a higher standard of living, but there are many other factors that have to be considered to assess the quality of life.

- Potential growth in an economy can be shown by an outward shift of its production possibility frontier.

Learn more

To learn more about the economic cycle and economic growth in the UK over the last 20 years, visit the Online Resource Centre.

 Visit our Online Resource Centre at http://www.oxfordtextbooks.co.uk/orc/gillespie_ econ3e/ for test questions and further information on topics covered in this chapter.

Unemployment

Reducing unemployment is often seen as one of the major economic objectives of governments. This chapter examines the causes and problems of unemployment, and considers how it can be reduced.

LEARNING OBJECTIVES

By the end of this chapter, you should be able to:

✓ understand how unemployment in an economy might be measured;

✓ explain the possible causes of unemployment;

✓ outline the costs of unemployment;

✓ examine ways the government could reduce unemployment.

▦ Introduction

Unemployment is a measure of the number of jobless people who want to work, are available to work, and are actively seeking employment. It can be measured in different ways, including the following.

- **The claimant count** This measures the number of individuals who are actually claiming unemployment-related benefits at any moment. This is a relatively straightforward figure to gather, but may be misleading because governments can change the conditions under which people can claim such benefits. It is therefore open to abuse by governments because, to reduce unemployment, they can simply make claiming more difficult!

- **The Labour Force Survey (LFS)** This measure of unemployment is based on interviews with people to determine those who want to work, but who are not employed. This is now the official way of measuring unemployment in the UK.

Of the two measures, the claimant count is always the lower of the two, because some unemployed people are not entitled to claim benefits or choose not to do so. When employment is high, the gap between the LFS and the claimant count will tend to widen. This is because some jobless people who were not previously looking for work start to do so. By actively looking for work, they are counted under the LFS, but do not feature in the claimant count unless they also begin to claim benefits, which is not necessarily made easy for them.

As well as the overall number of people unemployed we should also be interested in the composition of this figure—how many have been unemployed for a long period of time? How many are young? How many are NEETS (not in education, employment, or training)? The flow of people into and out of the unemployment pool is significant. There is a difference between having 1 million people unemployed who remain unemployed for long periods of time compared to 1 million unemployed but only for short periods of time as people come in and out of the unemployment pool quickly.

Economics in context

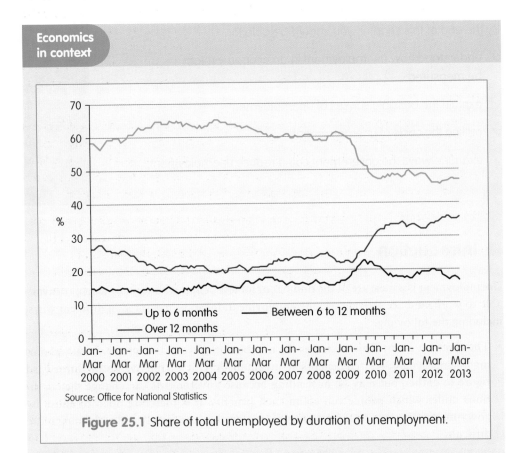

Source: Office for National Statistics

Figure 25.1 Share of total unemployed by duration of unemployment.

? Questions

Should the government worry about the changes in the composition of unemployment in the UK shown in Figure 25.1? Why?

Causes of unemployment

There are several causes of unemployment. These include the following.

- **Cyclical (or demand-deficient) unemployment** This type of unemployment occurs when demand is low throughout the economy. For example, there may be a recession with negative GDP growth. Demand for labour is a derived demand, so if demand for goods and services is generally low, then this will lead to less demand for employees and more unemployment.

- **Structural unemployment** This type of unemployment occurs when the structure of an economy changes. For example, an industry may lose its international competitiveness with the arrival of new global competitors. With the decline of a particular industry, some of those who are employed in it will lose their jobs. It may not be easy for these individuals to find alternative employment because they may have the wrong skills to work in other industries or may not easily be able to move to where the jobs are. These employees will need retraining. In the UK, for example, there has been a significant decline in many manufacturing sectors as other countries have come to dominate these markets.

- **Seasonal unemployment** This occurs in seasonal industries, such as staff in ski resorts and fruit picking. When the relevant season is over, people in that industry may be unemployed (unless they find work elsewhere). This does not usually involve large numbers of people. Seasonally unemployed workers are likely to find jobs again in the following season, so this type of unemployment is not usually a major concern.

- **Frictional (search) unemployment** This type of unemployment occurs when people have left one job and are looking for another. This may not be a concern if employees find another job easily. As long as people are passing through this period of frictional unemployment, this is not a major cause for concern; the problems occur if they get stuck and do not find work. As time goes on, it becomes increasingly difficult for employees to get re-employed.

- **Classical (real wage) unemployment** This occurs when the real wage remains too high for equilibrium. This will lead to an excess supply of labour (more people want to work than are demanded because of the relatively high real wages). Real wages may be too high because employees continue to demand high wages even when prices are falling. The downward stickiness of nominal wages in this situation (because employees resist nominal pay cuts) leads to higher real wages. Real wages may also be too high if trade unions push the wages above the equilibrium rate. This unemployment should put downward pressure on money wages to reduce the real wage, but this may take time to take effect. The extent to which real wage unemployment exists depends on whether you think that money wages are flexible upwards and downwards, or whether you think that factors such as negotiated contracts and trade unions mean that money wages can stay away from the real wage equilibrium for some time.

Put into practice

Which of the following statements are true and which are false?

a. Cyclical unemployment may be caused by high levels of aggregate demand.

b. A fall in export demand might cause cyclical unemployment.

c. To reduce structural unemployment may require retraining.

d. High real wages are associated with excess demand for labour.

▧ Voluntary and involuntary unemployment

Another way of categorizing unemployment is to distinguish between voluntary unemployment and involuntary unemployment.

- **Voluntary unemployment** is made up of those people who are in the labour force and are looking for work, but are not yet willing or able to accept work at the given real wage rate. This is shown by the difference at any real wage between the job acceptance and the labour force curves. The job acceptance curve shows the number of people who are willing and able to accept a job at a given real wage rate. It increases as the real wage increases because people will be less willing to wait around in the labour force as the rewards of taking a job increase. The labour force curve shows the number of people in work or looking for work at each real wage; this will also be slightly upward-sloping because, as the real wage increases, it is an incentive for more people to enter the labour force to start looking for work. In Figure 25.2, the difference between L2 and L1 represents voluntary unemployment. When the labour market is in equilibrium, this level of unemployment that still exists is known as the 'natural level of unemployment'.

- **Involuntary unemployment** measures the number of people who are willing and able to work at the given real wage, but who are not in employment. This is because there is a lack of jobs available. This is due to a lack of demand in the economy.

If, for example, the real wage is too high at W2, then L4 – L3 in Figure 25.3 represents employees who are willing and able to work, but are not demanded. This is involuntary unemployment.

L5 – L4 represents voluntary unemployment at this real wage.

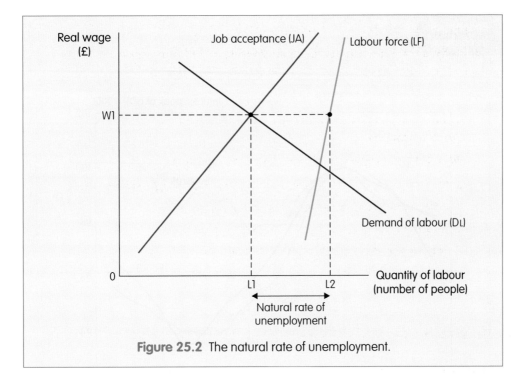

Figure 25.2 The natural rate of unemployment.

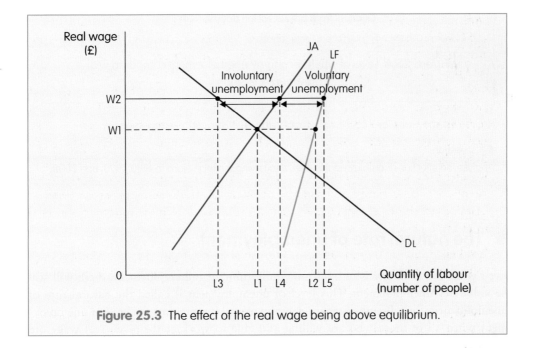

Figure 25.3 The effect of the real wage being above equilibrium.

Economics
in context

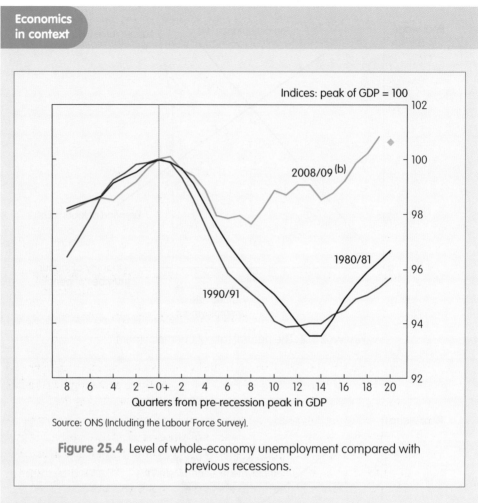

Indices: peak of GDP = 100

Source: ONS (Including the Labour Force Survey).

Figure 25.4 Level of whole-economy unemployment compared with previous recessions.

Figure 25.4 shows the level of unemployment in the UK in the last three recessions.

? Question

Analyse the effect on unemployment in the UK following the recessions in 1980, 1990, and 2008.

The natural rate of unemployment

Even when the economy is in long-run equilibrium, at full employment, there will still be voluntary unemployment. This level of unemployment is called the natural rate of unemployment (or full-employment unemployment). It represents the level of unemployment when all of those who are willing and able to work at the given real wage are working. This unemployment may be because people are simply between jobs or have no intention of working at the moment. To reduce the natural rate of unemployment, supply-side policies must be used. These can increase the number of people who are willing and

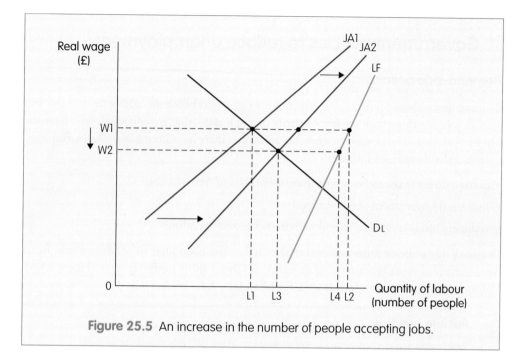

Figure 25.5 An increase in the number of people accepting jobs.

able to accept a job at each real wage. This shifts the job acceptance curve to the right and nearer to the labour force curve (see Figure 25.5). The natural rate of unemployment has fallen from L2 – L1 to L4 – L3 because the real wage has fallen from W1 to W2.

The natural rate of unemployment is the long-run equilibrium rate of unemployment; this means that there is no pressure for wages or prices to change. At the given real wage, the economy is settled for the long term. Some economists call the natural rate the non-accelerating inflation rate of unemployment (NAIRU); this is the rate of unemployment that occurs in long-run equilibrium when inflation is not accelerating.

What do you think?

Do you think that it is the government's responsibility to reduce unemployment? How low should the government try to get unemployment to be? What is the best way of achieving this?

The level of voluntary unemployment in an economy will depend on many factors, such as the level of benefits, the real wage, union power, and productivity. It also depends on how many people are in the labour force, and how many are willing and able to accept a job.

One interesting phenomenon following a period of unemployment is known as **hysteresis**. This occurs in the labour market if the occurrence of unemployment in the short term increases the long-term natural rate of unemployment. If people have been out of work for some time, they may lose the skills required as the world of work changes and/or they may lose the desire to work. They may also stop searching for jobs if this has proved unsuccessful in the past. The result is an increase in the level of voluntary unemployment.

Government policies to reduce unemployment

Demand-side policies

By using demand-side policies, the government can try to boost the aggregate demand and provide jobs for those who are involuntarily unemployed—that is, individuals who have the necessary skills and who want to work, but for whom there have been a lack of jobs available.

Demand-side policies include:

- cutting direct taxes to boost spending by firms and households;
- increased government spending; and
- reducing interest rates to stimulate borrowing and spending.

Demand-side policies raise the level of demand in the economy; to produce more, firms need to employ more labour, so the demand for labour shifts to the right (see Figure 25.6). Voluntary unemployment falls from L1 – L2 to L3 – L4.

Put into practice

Which organization has control of the interest rate in the UK? What are its objectives?

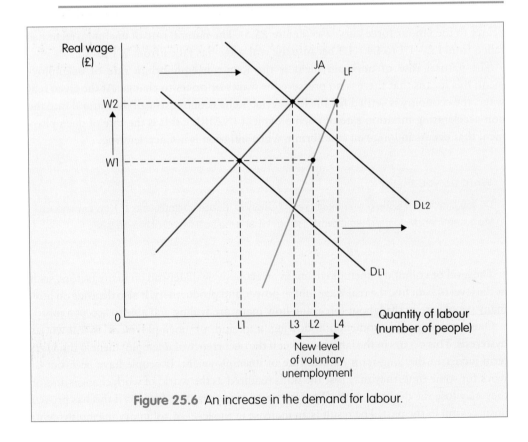

Figure 25.6 An increase in the demand for labour.

Supply-side policies

In the case of voluntary unemployment, the problem is not a lack of jobs; rather, it is a question of whether individuals have the required skills to work or want to accept a job. If the government were to intervene to increase spending to provide more jobs, then this would not solve the problem. What is needed here is help for individuals to get work that is actually there already—that is, supply-side policies.

To reduce voluntary unemployment, the government might do the following.

- The government could invest in training to provide the skills that people need to get jobs in other industries.

- It could change the benefits and tax system to make being unemployed less of an option—that is, to force people to accept a job by making the gains from being unemployed very low. The **replacement ratio** measures the levels of benefits available relative to the wages that can be earned when working. If this ratio increases, this may encourage more people to be in the labour force (because the benefits even if you are unemployed are higher), but at the same time, it may reduce the number accepting a job (because there is less incentive). This increases the amount of voluntary unemployment.

- The government could reduce the **tax wedge**. Taxes drive a wedge between the pay that employees receive and their take-home pay. In Figure 25.7, the equilibrium wage is W1. However, because the firm has to pay National Insurance Contributions (NICs) for employees, the actual cost to the firm is W2. After paying income tax, the employee will receive only W3. At this wage, the amount of voluntary unemployment will be L2 – L1. If the tax wedge could be reduced, then the level of voluntary unemployment would be less (L4 – L3).

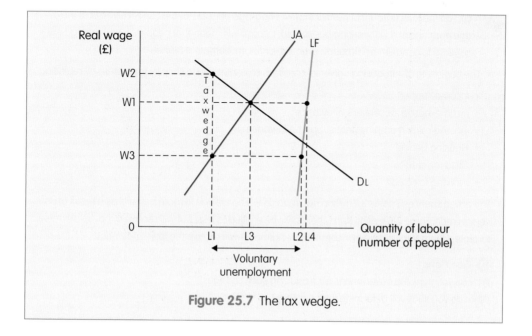

Figure 25.7 The tax wedge.

- The government could provide more information so that employees know what jobs are available; this could increase the mobility of labour.

Put into practice

Which of the following statements are true and which are false?

a. To tackle involuntary unemployment the government should focus on demand-side policies

b. To tackle voluntary unemployment the government should focus on supply-side policies

c. High levels of unemployment mean the economy is operating outside of the production possibility frontier

---

Economics in context

In 2013 the UK government introduced major changes to the welfare to encourage more people back to work. They include cuts to housing benefit for some social housing tenants with a spare room and changes to council tax. The aim according to the Work and Pensions Secretary was to make sure 'people find work always pays'.

The changes included:

- A cut in benefits for social housing tenants that had a spare room.

- Increasing working-age benefits and tax credits by just 1 per cent—a below-inflation cap—for three years from 2013–14. Historically benefits were increased in line with inflation.

- A cap on the total amount of benefit that working-age people (16–64) can receive. Set at the average earnings of a UK working household, the cap will mean that people of working age will receive up to a maximum amount, even if their full entitlement is higher.

- The beginning of introducing universal credit which is intended to simplify the system by replacing

  - Income support
  - Income-based jobseeker's allowance
  - Income-related employment support allowance
  - Housing benefit
  - Child tax credit
  - Working tax credit

The government estimates 3.1 million households will be entitled to more benefits as a result of universal credit. Some 2.8 million households will be entitled to less, but will receive a top-up payment to protect them from a drop in income. New claimants will receive the lower payment.

❓ Questions

Why do you think the government is introducing such changes?

What do you think will determine their success?

What do you think?

Should the government reduce the retirement age to create more jobs for younger people?
Is cutting benefits the best way to reduce unemployment?

▉ The possible costs of unemployment

One of the main problems with unemployment is that it is inefficient. If there are unemployed resources in the economy, then fewer goods and services are being produced than it is possible to produce. The economy is productively inefficient and is operating within the production possibility frontier (PPF)—for example, at the point X in Figure 25.8.

High levels of unemployment in an area are also likely to mean the following.

- There will be less income in a given region because fewer people are working. This, in turn, means less spending on local goods and services; this can then lead to more unemployment. This lowers living standards in the region due to a downward multiplier effect.

- There will be more social problems because people have more free time and lower incomes. It may, for example, lead to more crime.

- There will be more spending by the government on benefits, such as unemployment benefits.

- There will be less income for the government from taxation. The government will earn less from direct taxation because people are not earning and indirect taxation revenue will also fall because people are not spending as much. With less income and higher spending, the government's budget position will worsen.

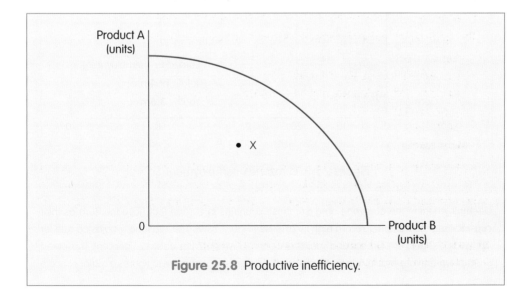

Figure 25.8 Productive inefficiency.

- Less investment may occur if firms lose confidence in the economy and so do not want to put money into longer-term projects until unemployment is seen to fall.

- Less consumption spending may occur as households who have people in employment worry whether they will also become unemployed in the future

The costs of unemployment can be divided into the following.

- **Private costs** These are the costs for the individual, such as lower morale and lower income.

- **Social costs** These are the costs that affect society as a whole—for example, higher levels of unemployment deter future investment in an area. This can reduce economic growth. High unemployment can also lead to higher crime levels, which can prove disruptive to society.

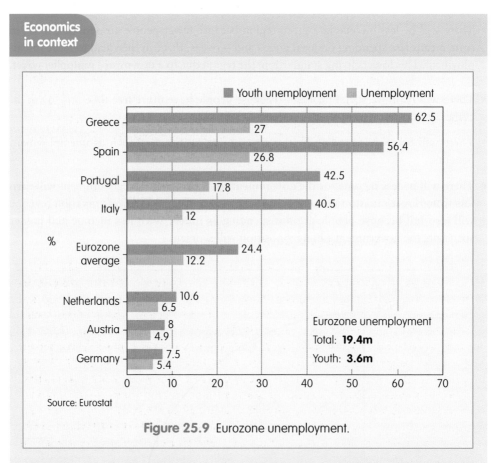

Economics in context

Figure 25.9 Eurozone unemployment.

Unemployment in the eurozone area (i.e. those countries in Europe that have the euro as their currency) reached another record high in 2013 (see Figure 25.9). The seasonally adjusted rate for April was 12.2 per cent. Greece and Spain have unemployment rates above 25 per cent. The lowest unemployment rate was in Austria where it was 4.9 per cent. Within these figures a major concern is the high levels of youth unemployment. In April, 3.6 million people under the age of 25 were out of work in the eurozone, which meant the unemployment rate for this age group was 24.4 per cent. In Italy 40.5 per cent of young people are unemployed.

Commentators are arguing for further cuts in the interest rate by the European Central Bank (ECB). However, this may not be enough—it is already at 0.5 per cent; it may need to pursue further quantitative easing.

Source: Adapted from http://www.bbc.co.uk/news/business-22727373

? Questions

Why do you think governments of the Eurozone should be concerned about higher levels of unemployment?

Explain how lowering interest rates might help reduce unemployment.

Explain how quantitative easing might help reduce unemployment.

What do you think?

Should reducing unemployment be a priority in the UK?

Do you think more government spending is the key to reducing unemployment in the UK?

Case study

The following survey of UK unemployment was prepared by the OECD.

The outlook for unemployment remains uncertain. Unemployment has been decreasing slightly over recent quarters despite sluggish activity. However, if output growth remains weak, which can be expected if headwinds from Europe persist, unemployment and under-employment could rise. Furthermore, fiscal consolidation involves large job cuts in the public sector. The Office for Budget Responsibility (OBR) projects a fall in general government employment of around 929 000 (excluding the impact of reclassifications in the education sector) between the start of 2011 and 2018, although it expects this to be more than offset over time by an increase in market sector employment of around 2.2 million over the same period (OBR, 2012). High uncertainty about the strength of the recovery is likely to hold back employment growth in the near term. As private sector employment is high in relation to output and involuntary part-time work is common, many firms may respond to higher demand by increasing hours worked by employees and using their workers at full potential, thereby increasing productivity, before hiring more workers. Weak external demand slows the rebalancing of the economy and the ability of export and investment goods industries to compensate the destruction of jobs in declining sectors.

Whilst unemployment overall may fall long-term; youth unemployment, and involuntary part-time work have increased markedly, now reaching about 900 000, 950 000 and 1.4 million. The long-term unemployment rate is slightly higher than the OECD average, but remains significantly below the European Union (EU15) average. Even though youth unemployment has fallen recently, it is somewhat higher than in the EU15 and well above the OECD average, although youth unemployment includes around 300 000 full-time students (about 30% of the total), which makes international comparisons difficult. The youth, as entrants to the labour market, are traditionally amongst the worst hit by recessions. But youth unemployment started to increase before the recession, and so it is unclear to what extent this represents a more structural problem. Furthermore, the number of youth not in employment, education or training (NEETs) has been on a rising trend and is among the highest in Europe, being surpassed only in some southern EU countries, Turkey and Ireland. NEETs face a risk of lasting exclusion from work causing permanent scars for the individuals involved, weakening the long-term economic growth potential as human capital erodes, and undermining social cohesion. High unemployment and inequality are likely to have adversely affected well-being.

Source: http://www.oecd.org/eco/surveys/UK_Overview_ENG.pdf

❓ Questions

1 Analyse the possible causes of unemployment in the UK according to OECD.

2 Why is it important to look at the composition of unemployment as well as the overall number?

3 Discuss the ways in which the government might tackle these issues and reduce unemployment.

Review questions

1 What is measured by the Labour Force Survey?

2 Explain the difference between voluntary and involuntary unemployment.

3 Explain what is meant by cyclical unemployment.

4 How might demand-side policies reduce unemployment?

5 How might supply-side policies reduce unemployment?

6 Explain why a government might be concerned about unemployment.

7 Explain the costs to the individual of unemployment.

8 Explain the opportunity cost of trying to reduce unemployment.

Put into practice

1 Show using a diagram the effect on unemployment of an increase in benefits leading to less incentive to work.

2 Show using a digram the effect of a fall in demand for labour on unemployment following a fall in aggregate demand in the economy.

Assignment question

1 Summarize changes to the level and composition of unemployment over the last five years. Analyse the reasons for these changes.

Key learning points

- There are different ways of classifying unemployment, such as structural, seasonal, frictional, and cyclical, or voluntary and involuntary.
- Unemployment may be reduced through demand-side or supply-side policies.
- The appropriate methods to reduce unemployment depend on the cause.
- Unemployment imposes both private and social costs.

Learn more

To learn more about levels of unemployment in the UK and government measures to influence these, visit the Online Resource Centre.

 Visit our Online Resource Centre at http://www.oxfordtextbooks.co.uk/orc/gillespie_econ3e/ for test questions and further information on topics covered in this chapter.

»26 Inflation

One common economic objective of government is to achieve stable prices. This involves controlling inflation. This chapter examines the causes and problems of inflation, and considers how inflation may be controlled. After this chapter we start to look in greater detail at exchange rates and international trade to give a global context to the economy.

LEARNING OBJECTIVES

By the end of this chapter, you should be able to:

✓ explain what is meant by inflation;

✓ outline the different causes of inflation;

✓ explain the costs of inflation;

✓ examine ways of reducing inflation;

✓ discuss the possible trade-off between inflation and unemployment.

■ Introduction

Inflation occurs when there is a sustained increase in the general price level over a given period. If annual inflation is 2 per cent, for example, this means that prices are generally 2 per cent higher than the year before.

Inflation measures the change in prices year on year—that is:

$$\text{Inflation} = \frac{(\text{Prices } t - \text{Prices } t\text{-}1) \times 100}{\text{Prices } t\text{-}1}$$

where:

- t is a particular moment in time; and
- t-1 is the year before.

In the UK, inflation is generally measured by the consumer prices index (CPI) and the **retail prices index (RPI)**. These both compare the price of a typical basket of goods and services of a household with the price of the same basket the year before. They differ in the items included in the basket: for example, the RPI includes council tax, mortgage interest payments, buildings insurance, and house depreciation. This means that lower or higher mortgage costs would reduce the RPI, but not affect the CPI.

Inflation increases the cost of living and reduces the purchasing power of a currency within its economy; it reduces its internal value. If prices are increasing in the UK, then £1 will not be able to buy as much as it did before the price increase.

Put into practice

Which of the following statements are true and which are false?

a. Inflation of 2 per cent means that the prices of all goods are increasing by 2 per cent.

b. Inflation increases the standard of living.

c. Inflation increases the cost of living.

d. If inflation falls from 3 per cent to 2 per cent, prices are falling.

e. If inflation is negative, prices are falling.

■ Calculating inflation

Inflation is calculated using a weighted index. The weight reflect the relative importance of the items in a shopping basket i.e. what proportion of consumers' spending is spent on that item.
For example:

Product	Price change	Weight	Price change * weight
A	5%	50	250
B	10%	20	200
C	10%	20	200
D	−10%	10	−100
		100	550

In the table above some items have gone up in price and one has actually gone down, We could just average these price changes but that does not take account of their relative importance. In this case product A is most significant in terms of our spending and has a weight of 50. The weighted index (price change multiplied by the weight) equals 550. We divide this by the total weights of 100 and derive a weighted percentage price change of $550/100 = 5.5$. Inflation is therefore 5.5 per cent reflecting the fact that the key item in our basket increased in price by 5 per cent.

Put into practice

Calculate the weighted price index for the data below.

Product	Price change	Weight
A	20%	30
B	10%	40
C	10%	10
D	−10%	20
		100

What do the weights in Table 26.1 tell us about spending patterns in the UK?
Do you think these weights might have changed over time? Why?

■ Why does inflation matter?

Inflation can cause a number of problems for an economy, such as the following.

- Inflation may damage business confidence because of fears about the future impact on costs. This may reduce levels of investment. Uncertainty about future inflation rates will make it difficult to estimate future profits and therefore may deter many investment projects, damaging economic growth. This is a key concern regarding inflation, because it can affect demand in the economy and its future growth.

Table 26.1 Allocation of items to CPI divisions in 2013

		CPI weight (per cent)
1	Food & non-alcoholic beverages	10.6
2	Alcohol & tobacco	4.4
3	Clothing & footwear	6.8
4	Housing & household services	13.7
5	Furniture & household goods	5.9
6	Health	2.5
7	Transport	14.8
8	Communication	3.1
9	Recreation & culture	14.1
10	Education	2.1
11	Restaurants & hotels	11.7
12	Miscellaneous goods & services	10.3

Source: ONS

- If prices are increasing, this creates costs for firms, because they may have to update their promotional material to reflect the higher prices. For example, this means reprinting brochures, updating price lists, and changing vending machines. These are called '**menu costs**'.

- With higher rates of inflation, individuals and firms may have to search more to find the best returns on their savings. This will be necessary to preserve the real rate of return (that is, the return adjusted for inflation). The costs of searching around are called '**shoe leather costs**'.

- Not all individuals will have the bargaining power to ensure that their own earnings rise at the same rate as prices are increasing. If their wages do not increase as much as prices, then, in real terms, they are worse off because they have less purchasing power. Their real income has fallen. The ability of an employee to bargain for higher wages in line with inflation depends on the extent to which they are in demand and/or whether they are well represented by trade unions. Unions represent employees collectively to give them more bargaining power. Inflation may therefore redistribute real incomes. Some groups, such as pensioners, may find that their earnings keep pace with inflation; others may not. This means that inflation has redistributive effects. Inflation will also redistribute income from savers to borrowers. If you are holding your money in savings the purchasing power of these savings will be reduced because, all other things being equal, it will not buy as much due to higher prices. However if you have borrowed money it may be easier now to repay. For example with inflation you may earn more per hour and this makes it easier to raise the finds needed to repay any given loan. Further redistribution occurs from the private sector to the public sector. If your earnings increase to keep pace with inflation then in real terms you are no better off but all other things being equal more people will now enter higher tax brackets and pay more revenue to the government. The government gains and employees lose. This occurs if tax thresholds do not increase in line with inflation. This is called fiscal drag (see Chapter 22)

- Internationally, if the prices of firms in the UK are increasing faster than those of their trading partners, then this may make the country's products uncompetitive compared with those of foreign firms. This may reduce the earnings from exports and increase the spending on imports. This will affect the balance of payments adversely. Domestically, the UK may also struggle to compete because imports will be relatively cheaper.

- If inflation is caused by increasing costs businesses may seek to reduce costs in other ways to remain competitive. This may affect employment with firms making redundancies or not replacing staff in an attempt to keep costs down.

Anticipated and unanticipated inflation

The effects of inflation will depend partly on whether it is 'anticipated' or 'unanticipated' inflation. If you know that prices are going to rise and you have strong bargaining power, then you can demand higher wages to compensate, for example. However, if you are locked into a 2 per cent pay increase and then inflation unexpectedly increases to

Economics in context — Measuring inflation

In 2013 eBooks were included in the basket of goods used to measure inflation for the first time to represent a significant and growing market and digital television recorders/receivers replaced the Freeview box to capture other types of set-top box including Personal Video Recorders (PVR).

Aside from new technology, a number of new items are introduced to represent specific markets where consumer spending is significant, and existing items in the basket may not adequately represent price changes for such goods. For example, continental deli type meat was introduced to reflect the increasing expenditure and shelf-space in supermarkets devoted to charcuterie. Blueberries and vegetable stir fry were also added to the basket for the first time.

Some items have also been removed such as soft contact lenses which were replaced by packs of daily disposable lenses.

? Question
What products do you think are likely to be added to the basket of goods used to measure inflation in the future?

5 per cent, then you will be worse off in real terms. If inflation levels are regularly unanticipated, then this will lead to high levels of uncertainty in the economy, which may deter investment and affect spending, and impact saving decisions. The impact also depends on the rate of inflation and how sustained it is; higher rates for a long time are more damaging than low rates for a short time.

What do you think?
What do you think inflation will be next year? How did you decide this?

■ What causes inflation?

The causes of inflation include the following.

- **Too much demand in the economy** This is shown by an outward shift of the aggregate demand curve. If demand is growing faster than supply, then this will pull prices up, causing demand-pull inflation. If firms cannot meet the demand, then they will increase their prices. Demand-pull inflation is characterized by shortages, low levels of stocks, long waiting lists, and queues. In this situation, firms will be eager to produce more as soon as they can. They may invest in extra capacity, but this can take time to come online. In the short term, supply is likely to be price inelastic because firms may not be able to recruit staff easily or produce more given the existing equipment. This means that an increase in demand will affect prices more than output. Inflation caused by an increase in demand is shown in Figure 26.1.

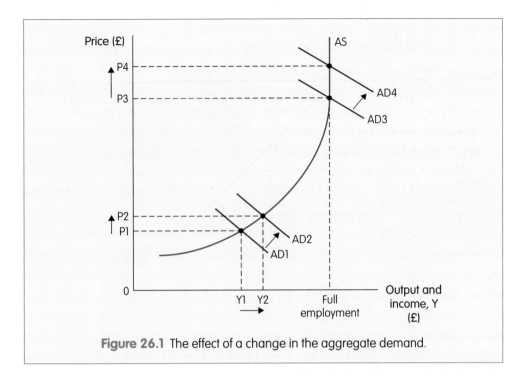

Figure 26.1 The effect of a change in the aggregate demand.

NOTE In Figure 26.1, an increase in demand simply leads to an increase in the price level; inflation measures the rate of growth of prices, so for inflation to be shown properly on this figure over time, aggregate demand would need to keep increasing.

- **Monetary inflation** According to monetarists, inflation occurs when there is too much money supply in the economy. With more money circulating, this leads to more demand in the economy, and then higher prices. This is a form of demand-pull inflation that is caused specifically by excess growth of the money supply.

- **Cost-push inflation** This type of inflation is caused by costs increasing—for example, this could be because of:
  - higher wages that are not related to productivity gains which therefore increases the costs per units;
  - higher import prices—perhaps because the exchange rate has fallen, meaning more pounds are needed to buy the same goods as before;
  - monopoly suppliers pushing up their prices; or
  - higher materials prices—for example, higher demand for oil might pull up its world price, increasing energy costs; a supply shock in agricultural markets might increase food prices.

Faced with higher costs, firms increase their prices to customers to maintain profit margins. This shifts the aggregate supply curve meaning a higher price is needed to supply a given output and causes cost-push inflation (see Figure 26.2). This shift of the aggregate supply will also lead to a fall in output and to firms operating under capacity. Again, to

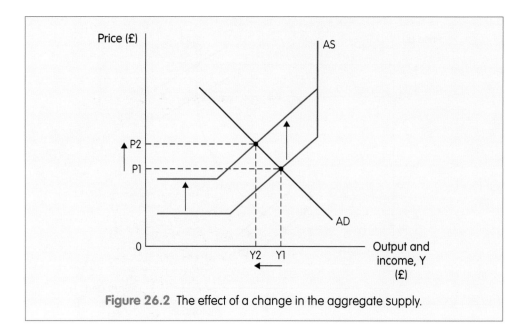

Figure 26.2 The effect of a change in the aggregate supply.

truly show inflation, aggregate supply would have to keep increasing so that prices are growing over time rather than only as a one-off increase. Much of the inflation in the last few years in the UK has been due to supply-side shocks, such as increases in food prices or oil prices, caused by shortages that have pushed up the prices of a typical shopping basket.

Put into practice

Which one(s) of the following might cause demand-pull inflation?

- An increase in export demand
- An increase in import spending
- An increase in savings
- A decrease in taxation rates

■ Controlling inflation

To control inflation, there is a variety of methods that the government may use, such as the following.

- **Reducing the aggregate demand** To control demand-pull inflation, the government will want to reduce the level of the aggregate demand in the economy relative to supply. This may be done using deflationary fiscal or restrictive monetary policies, such as reduced government expenditure, higher taxes, or higher interest rates. The government might want to reduce injections or increase withdrawals into the economy.

Economics
in context

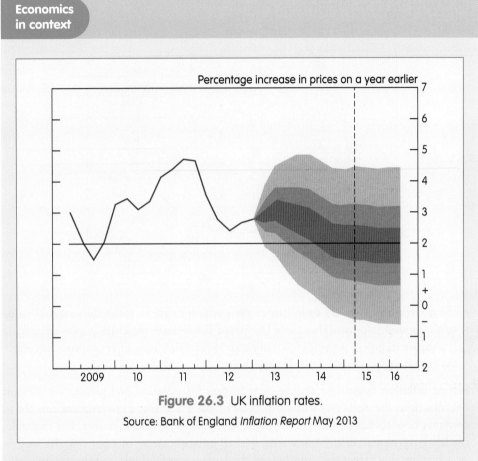

Figure 26.3 UK inflation rates.
Source: Bank of England *Inflation Report* May 2013

Figure 26.3 shows the rate of inflation in the UK over the last few years.

? Questions
Analyse the possible causes of high inflation in 2011.
Analyse the possible consequences of falling inflation forecast for the coming years.

- **Reducing costs** To control cost-push inflation, a government would not want to reduce demand because this would lead to even less output in the economy (see Figure 26.4). In this situation, the government may do the following.
  - Government may introduce wage restraint in the public sector, where it can control wages. It may also introduce wage controls across the economy to prevent wages from increasing too fast. This is known as an **incomes policy**. However, incomes policies can lead to frustration on the part of employers, who want to offer more money to reward and attract good-quality employees. Employees may also be frustrated and look for better-paid jobs abroad; this may lead to the loss of god employees and a loss of competitiveness.

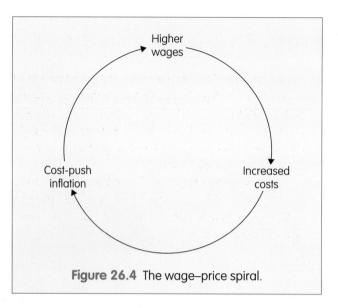

Figure 26.4 The wage–price spiral.

- the government may try to influence the exchange rate to make the external value of the pound stronger. This gives UK-based firms more purchasing power, making it cheaper to buy in supplies from abroad. However, it may affect exports adversely because it makes them relatively expensive.

- **Setting inflation targets** By setting clear targets for inflation and giving the relevant organizations the authority to take actions to achieve these, a government can try to convince households and business people that such targets will be met. For example, the UK government, in 2004 onwards, had an inflation target of 2 per cent. Its success in achieving this target early on helped to convince individuals and groups that this was going to be the level of inflation in the future. As a result, wage claims and price increases were linked to this level of expectations which helped keep inflation at this rate in the future. If, on the other hand, people think that inflation is going to be very high, then they will demand high wages. This could cause higher prices due to cost-push inflation. This inflation could then stimulate higher wages, higher costs, and higher inflation again. This is called the 'wage–price spiral' (see Figure 26.4).

- **Supply-side policies** The government may pursue supply-side policies to shift the aggregate supply curve outwards and drive prices downwards. The supply-side policies may focus on the labour market, the capital market, and the product markets and aim to increase productivity and competition. However, these policies are likely to take some time to take effect.

What do you think?

Do you think that the government should aim for an inflation rate of 0 per cent in the UK?

Do you think increasing interest rates is the best way to reduce inflation?

What supply side policies do you think could help increase the aggregate supply?

◼ The Monetary Policy Committee in the UK

As we saw in Chapter 23, in May 1997, the Labour government gave the Bank of England's Monetary Policy Committee (MPC) the ability to set whatever interest rates it felt were necessary to achieve given inflation targets. Price stability at present is defined by the government's inflation target of 2 per cent. If inflation is more than 1 per cent either side of this target, the Governor of the Bank of England has to write a letter to the government's Chancellor of the Exchequer explaining why.

The MPC meets monthly to assess the possible level of inflation and to decide on what to do about the interest rate. The Committee is made up of nine members; some are from the Bank of England, but others are outsiders who provide a different perspective. The Committee considers indicators such as:

- the growth in the money supply;
- national income figures;
- consumer confidence surveys and expectations of inflation (important because if people expect prices to rise, then they are more likely to demand larger wage increases, and so expecting higher inflation can be a self-fulfilling prophecy);
- lending by banks and building societies;
- consumer spending and credit;
- trends in the housing and labour markets, including average earnings, unit costs, and unemployment figures;
- developments in the foreign exchange market.

If, having looked at these indicators, the Committee believes that inflation will be outside its target in the future, it may then make changes to Bank Rate, which is the rate of interest charged by the Bank of England to other banks.

For example, if the MPC believes that aggregate demand is growing too fast and pulling up prices, then it will decide to raise its interest rates.

The effect of an increase in interest rates by the Monetary Policy Committee

An increase in the interest rates charged by the Bank of England is likely to have the following effects.

- It will increase the rates charged by other banks. Most banks will need to borrow from other financial institutions at particular times. The Bank of England is known as the 'lender of last resort'. For example, a high level of withdrawals may leave a bank short of liquidity. The Bank of England may be called upon to lend money to other institutions. They will be influenced by the rate that the Bank of England charges, because they will want to charge their own customers more to ensure that they make a profit. If the Bank of England therefore announces that Bank Rate is increasing, then other financial institutions will usually follow to cover any increased costs that they might have if they need funds. Higher interest rates offered by financial institutions will encourage saving and reduce consumption spending. There will also be less demand for other assets (leading to lower prices) because of the high returns from saving. Lower asset prices will reduce individuals' wealth and dampen demand.

- It will send a clear signal that the Bank of England is prepared to take action to control inflation. This should lead to wage demands in line with the stated inflation target. This in itself should help to ensure that the target is hit, because it discourages inflationary wage claims.

- It will lead to more demand for the currency from overseas investors, who will want to buy sterling to save in UK banks to gain higher returns. This should increase the external value of the pound. This makes UK exports relatively expensive overseas, thereby reducing the aggregate demand. It also reduces import prices in pounds, thereby reducing cost pressure. Both of these help to reduce inflation. (For more on this, see Chapter 27.)

The effect of changes in the interest rate can be seen in Figure 26.5.

Put into practice

1. Explain possible reasons for changes in inflation shown in Figure 26.5.
2. How might the projections of inflation above affect the behaviour of households, firms, and the government?

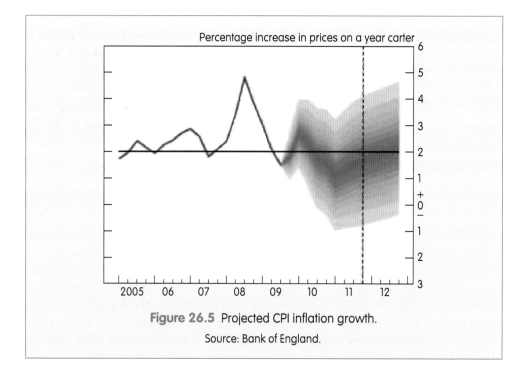

Figure 26.5 Projected CPI inflation growth.
Source: Bank of England.

In recent years, the recession in the UK led to concerns about inflation being below the given target rather than above it. Levels of aggregate demand were low in the economy, leading to negative growth and high unemployment. In this situation, the MPC cut the interest rate to its lowest level ever (0.5 per cent) to stimulate demand in the economy. At times during 2009 and 2010, inflation still exceeded the inflation target, but this was seen to be due to supply shocks, such as higher oil, commodity prices, or VAT increases, rather than the underlying inflation rate. Low interest rates have been seen as necessary to maintain demand and prevent deflation.

What do you think?

Do you think that the MPC should cut the interest rate at the moment in the UK?

Put into practice

Which one(s) of the following would be an appropriate response to reduce demand-pull inflation?

- Lower corporation tax rates
- Higher interest rates
- Increased government spending
- Higher income taxation rates

■ Real interest rates versus nominal interest rates

When analysing the effects of interest rates on the economy, it is important to consider the inflation rate. The rate that the Bank of England or high-street banks charge is the nominal rate. When this is adjusted for inflation this is the real interest rate.

Imagine the reward for saving is 5 per cent, for example, but prices are increasing by 5 per cent as well. This means, in real terms, the interest rate is zero. If you save your money, you will earn 5 per cent, but because prices have increased, you will not be able to buy more products.

The real interest rate can be calculated as:

Real interest rate = Nominal rate of interest − Inflation rate

For example, if the nominal rate of interest is 5 per cent and inflation is 5 per cent, this means the real rate of interest is:

5% − 5% = 0%

■ The Phillips curve: Inflation and unemployment

The Phillips curve shows the relationship between the rate of inflation and the rate of unemployment in both the short run and the long run.

In the short run, there appears to be a trade-off between the rate of inflation and the rate of unemployment; the government can reduce unemployment below the natural rate at the expense of faster-growing prices.

Imagine that the economy is at full employment equilibrium at X (see Figure 26.6). Wages and prices are growing in line with each other at 3 per cent, and the rate of unemployment in the economy is at the natural rate. All unemployment is voluntary.

If the government then increases spending, this will create demand-pull inflation. Prices will grow faster than wages—for example, prices may grow at 4 per cent, whilst wages are still increasing at 3 per cent. This is because wages are often 'sticky' in the short term. Individuals will have agreed their wages for a given period (for example, for the next year) and will not be able to renegotiate them. Also, employees are often slow to realize that inflation has changed; they tend to focus on the prices of things that they buy regularly and do not appreciate the overall trend with inflation. This is called money illusion. With prices growing faster than wages, real wages actually fall. This makes it cheaper in real terms to employ people, which should lead to a fall in unemployment (the point Y in Figure 26.6).

Over time, however, employees will notice that their purchasing power has been reduced and will want to bargain for higher wages to compensate for the inflation. If they manage to match wage increases to the price increases, then, in real terms, wages and the economy will be back to where they started, except that prices and wages are now growing at a faster rate of 4 per cent, not 3 per cent (the point Z in Figure 26.6). Unemployment is at the natural rate again, but with higher inflation. In the long run, therefore, there has been no trade-off between inflation and unemployment.

Conversely, if the government brings down spending in the economy, then, with lower demand, inflation may be reduced and, in the short run, prices will be growing slower than wages. This is again because wages are slow to change due to contracts and because it takes time for employees to notice fully changes in inflation. If prices are growing slower

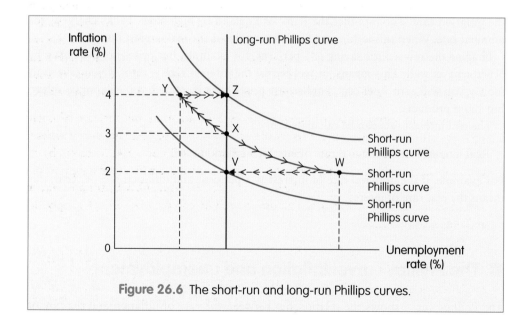

Figure 26.6 The short-run and long-run Phillips curves.

than wages, then real wages have increased and so employees are more expensive to hire. This will lead to fewer people being employed and unemployment rising. Imagine that the labour market is in long-run equilibrium at X, with prices and wages growing at 3 per cent (see Figure 26.6). Then prices start to grow at 2 per cent, so real wages have increased. Employees are more expensive and unemployment increases; the economy moves to W. In the long run, however, because of higher levels of unemployment and because they realize that inflation has fallen, employees would be willing to accept lower pay increases; this would mean that real wages were back where they were originally. All that has changed is that prices and wages are now growing at the lower rate of 2 per cent. The economy moves to the point V. Once again, there is no trade-off between the rate of inflation and the rate of unemployment in the long run.

Put into practice

- If the rate of inflation is higher than the rate at which nominal wages are growing, then what is happening to real wages? Why?

- What might be the impact of this on the quantity demanded and the quantity supplied of labour?

What do you think?

To what extent do you think employees are aware of the rate of inflation?

The Phillips curve suggests the following.

- There is a possible trade-off between the rate of inflation and the rate of unemployment in the short run, provided that prices grow faster than wages. If the government intends to keep unemployment below the natural rate, then it will always need to keep prices growing at a faster rate than wages. Obviously, if the government adopts such tactics, then employees might soon realize this; therefore, to keep fooling people, the government would need to create ever-larger increases in inflation so that employees do not anticipate this.

- There is no long-run trade-off between the rate of inflation and the rate of unemployment. This suggests that efforts by the government to use demand-side policies to manipulate inflation and affect unemployment levels will not work. Attempts by the government to reduce unemployment below the natural rate will, in the long run, simply lead to more inflation. The implication is that a long-run policy by the government would be to focus on changing the natural rate of unemployment through supply-side policies (see Figure 26.7).

What do you think?

Do you think the government should try to achieve inflation of 0%?

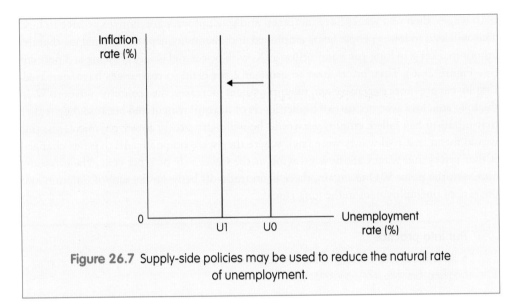

Figure 26.7 Supply-side policies may be used to reduce the natural rate of unemployment.

▥ Deflation

Deflation occurs when prices in an economy are generally falling over a given period. It means that there is negative inflation in the economy. This may be due to the following reasons.

- Supply may be growing faster than demand. In certain markets, such as some consumer electronics markets, supply is increasing rapidly due to developments in technology. This causes deflation in these specific markets.
- Aggregate demand may be falling, perhaps because interest rates are too high, or because there is a lack of household and business confidence. Deflation is often associated with a recession in the economy. If deflation is caused by a lack of aggregate demand, this is unwelcome because it is likely to be associated with high unemployment.

Deflation may lead to the following.

- There may be lower profits for firms because of lower prices. This means that there are fewer funds for investment, which may delay the purchase of new machinery.
- There may be redundancies as firms try to rationalize their production and make it more efficient; managers will be pressurized to cut costs to maintain profit margins.
- Businesses may close because they may not be able to make profits if prices are falling.

What is particularly worrying is the possibility of a **deflationary spiral**. This could be due to:

- households and firms delaying buying decisions because prices are falling, creating even more downward pressure on prices because it leads to even less demand in the economy; or

Economics in context

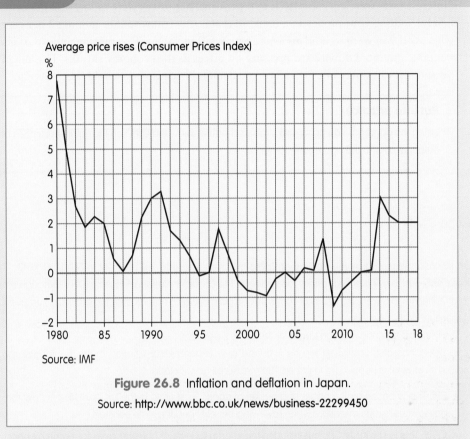

Average price rises (Consumer Prices Index)

Source: IMF

Figure 26.8 Inflation and deflation in Japan.
Source: http://www.bbc.co.uk/news/business-22299450

A key policy initiative by the Bank of Japan in recent years has been its decision to set a target inflation rate of 2 per cent. Unlike most other economies, Japan has experienced deflation for much of the past two decades. This has dampened demand in the country. The Bank of Japan has finally responded by boosting the country's money supply and buying government bonds, boosting their price and reducing interest rates. The aim is to stimulate borrowing and spending with lower interest rates. The Bank of Japan is undertaking one of the most aggressive injections of cash of any central bank in the world to try and avoid further deflation. This injection is part of a new set of economic policies introduced by Japan's Prime Minister, Shinzo Abe, which is known as Abenomics.

❓ **Question**

Why would the government in Japan be keen to prevent deflation?
How will the policies outlined above help remove deflation in Japan?

• the effect on real interest rates. If interest rates are cut to stimulate spending, but prices are falling, then it is still worth saving money because it is gaining in real terms. Even if interest rates were cut right back to 0 per cent, but prices were falling at 2 per cent, then by holding your money in a bank, in real terms you would be gaining 2 per cent (whereas if you were to hold an asset, it may fall in value). This may again lead to less spending and more downward pressure on prices as the economy shrinks. This means low interest rates may not help stimulate demand because households keep saving.

Put into practice

Using the aggregate demand and supply schedule, show the effect on the equilibrium price and output of a fall in the aggregate demand.

Case study

UK inflation measured by the Consumer Prices Index (CPI) rose to 2.8 per cent in February 2013. This was partly due to rising energy prices, according to the Office for National Statistics (ONS) although other contributing factors were the prices of cameras and games which had recently increased as competition in these markets reduced.

The Bank of England's inflation target for the CPI is 2 per cent.

The ONS has also published for the first time new experimental inflation measures to give more indicators of what is happening to prices. The measures now include:

• CPI: This is based on the prices of a basket of goods. First used in the UK in 1996, it is now the government's main measure when reviewing benefits and the state pension.

• CPIH: This is similar to CPI, but includes the changing level of housing costs for home owners, such as mortgage interest and buildings insurance.

• RPI: Unlike the CPI, this measure excludes the spending of the wealthy and pensioner households mainly dependent on the state pension and benefits—some 13% of the population.

• RPIJ: A new version of the RPI index but using the same methods as CPI for calculating average prices.

Most economists think price rises will continue climbing in the future, partly due to the weakness of the pound, which has fallen 7 per cent so far this year and makes buying goods in other currencies more expensive.

❓ Questions

1 Analyse the potential causes of inflation highlighted above. Use a diagram to illustrate your argument.

2 Why does the Bank of England have an inflation target?

3 Does inflation matter?

4 Which is the best way to measure inflation do you think?

5 Do you think inflation or economic growth will be the key issue for the UK government in the future?

Review questions

1   Explain the meaning of inflation.

2   Explain what is meant by demand-pull inflation.

3   Explain what is meant by cost-push inflation.

4   What is meant by menu costs in relation to inflation?

5   Explain how inflation might affect a country's international competitiveness.

6   What is meant by an incomes policy?

7   What is meant by deflation?

8   Explain the relationship between inflation and unemployment according to the long-run Phillips Curve.

Put into practice

Using diagrams show the effect of higher levels of unanticipated inflation on investment and aggregate demand.

Assignment question

1   Visit the Bank of England website and find the last letter from the Governor of the Bank of England to the Chancellor of the Exchequer explaining why the inflation target was missed. Summarize the reasons given. What has happened to inflation since then and why?

Key learning points

- Inflation is usually measured by the consumer prices index (CPI) in the UK.

- The possible causes of inflation include demand-pull and cost-push.

- Stable inflation rates help to stimulate economic growth.

- The appropriate cures for inflation depend on the cause.

- The Phillips curve suggests that there is a trade-off between inflation and unemployment in the short run, but not in the long run.

Learn more

To learn more about rates of inflation in the UK over the years, visit the Online Resource Centre.

 Visit our Online Resource Centre at http://www.oxfordtextbooks.co.uk/orc/gillespie_ econ3e/ for test question and further information on topics covered in this chapter.

Exchange rates

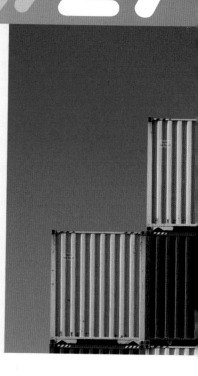

All economies are involved in international trade to some extent. The exchange rate is a key factor in determining the amount and value of trade between countries. This chapter examines the determinants of exchange rates and the effects of changes in exchange rates on an economy.

LEARNING OBJECTIVES

By the end of this chapter, you should be able to:

✓ explain the determinants of the external value of a currency;

✓ distinguish between a floating and a fixed exchange rate system;

✓ explain the possible impact of a change in the external value of a currency.

Introduction

If you have ever gone on holiday abroad, you will have had to change your pounds sterling into another currency. The amount of foreign currency that you received in return for your pound depends on the exchange rate. Sometimes, you might have felt that you received a lot of money in return for your pound; other times, you might have felt that the money you received did not go very far. The value of the exchange rate clearly matters to tourists and this is a very important sector of the UK economy. It also matters to any firm buying or selling products abroad. Given that the UK is a very open economy, which means that there is a high proportion of exports and imports, and that trade is very significant to the economy, changes in the exchange rate have a big impact on jobs, prices, and growth.

Exchange rate

An exchange rate measures the value of one currency in terms of another—for example, the value of one pound sterling in terms of US dollars or Japanese yen. It measures the external value of a currency. The external value of a currency is important because of its impact on trade, and its impact on export revenue and import spending.

▦ What determines the external value of a currency?

If a government does not intervene in the currency market, then the value of the exchange rate is determined by the supply of, and demand for, this currency—that is, by market forces. This is known as a floating exchange rate system. Currency markets are often referred to as forex (foreign exchange) markets.

The demand for the UK currency will be influenced by the following.

- **Demand for UK goods and services from abroad** To buy UK products, overseas buyers will need pounds. Overseas buyers will have to give up their own currency and change it into pounds. If demand for UK products increases, then, all other things unchanged, the demand for pounds will increase as well.

- **Relative interest rates** If UK interest rates are higher than interest rates elsewhere in the world, then, all other things being unchanged, the demand for pounds will rise. Overseas investors will look to buy pounds to save in UK banks and earn higher returns. High UK interest rates will attract what is called 'hot money' flowing into the country.

- **Relative inflation rates** If UK goods and services are relatively expensive, then this is likely to reduce demand for the products and therefore for pounds. With less demand for the currency, it will fall in value, all other things being unchanged.

- **Expectations** If currency speculators believe that the pound will rise in value in the future, then they may buy now so that their investment will become worth more. This increase in demand will in itself increase the value of the currency, all other things being unchanged.

The demand for pounds is downward-sloping. As the exchange rate increases, the price of UK goods and services will become greater in foreign currencies, all other things being unchanged. For example, at \$1:£1, a £10 UK product is \$10; at \$2:£1, it is \$20. This will lead to a fall in the quantity demanded of UK products and therefore a fall in the quantity demanded of pounds. The greater the price elasticity of demand for UK products abroad, the greater the fall in the quantity demanded of pounds (that is, the more price elastic the demand for pounds will be) following an increase in the exchange rate (see Figure 27.1).

What do you think?

What do you think is the most important exchange rate for the UK? The dollar? The yen? Explain your reasoning.

Example

Imagine that a UK firm produces a product for £100 and sales abroad are ten units. Imagine that the exchange rate now rises from \$1.5:£1 to \$2:£1. The price of the product abroad rises from \$150 to \$200. Originally, the firm earned:

10 × £100 = £1,000

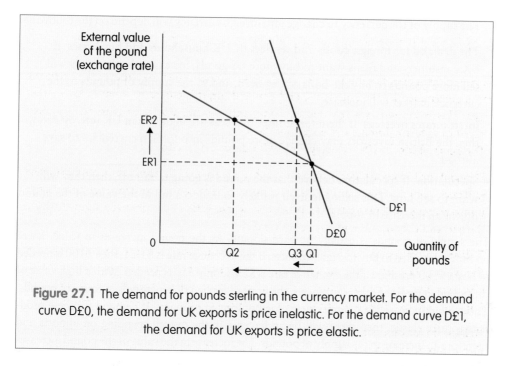

Figure 27.1 The demand for pounds sterling in the currency market. For the demand curve D£0, the demand for UK exports is price inelastic. For the demand curve D£1, the demand for UK exports is price elastic.

If demand is price elastic, then demand falls to, say, two units. This means that earnings fall to:

$2 \times £100 = £200$

If demand is price inelastic, then sales may fall to nine units. The earnings are now:

$9 \times £100 = £900$

The more price elastic demand is for UK products abroad, the greater is the fall in the quantity of pounds demanded given an increase in the external value of the pound.

A change in the exchange rate leads to a movement along the demand curve for pounds. Changes in other factors, such as demand for UK products or UK interest rates, will shift the demand curve for pounds in the currency market.

Put into practice

a. Imagine that a UK firm produces a product for £200. What would the price in dollars be:
  • if the exchange rate is $1.5:£1?
  • if the exchange rate is $2:£1?

b. Suppose that the original level of sales was 500 units and then sales fell to 450 units.
  • Calculate the original and new value of sales in dollars.
  • Calculate the original and new value of sales in pounds.

The supply of UK currency to change into foreign currency will depend on the following.

- **The demand for foreign goods and services by UK households and businesses** If UK consumers and firms want to buy more US goods, for example, then they will sell more pounds to buy the dollars they need, and so the supply of pounds to the currency market will increase.

- **Interest rates overseas** If the interest rates overseas are higher than UK interest rates, then the British investors may change more pounds into foreign currencies to save abroad.

- **Speculation** If speculators believe that the pound is going to fall off, then they will want to sell now. This selling in itself is likely to lead to a fall in the value of the pound due to an increase in supply.

The supply of pounds is usually upward-sloping. As the pound increases in value, fewer pounds are needed to buy foreign products. If the exchange rate is $1:£1, then £100 is needed to buy a $100 product; if the exchange rate is $2:£1, only £50 is needed. With a high value of the pound in terms of other currencies, the price of foreign products falls in terms of pounds. This should increase the quantity demanded of foreign products. If demand for these products is price elastic, then there will be an increase in the overall spending on imports and therefore an increase in the supply of pounds. The increase in the value of the pound increases the quantity supplied and the supply curve is upward-sloping (see Figure 27.2).

If, however, the demand for imports is price inelastic, then a fall in price in pounds will lead to a relatively smaller increase in the quantity demanded. This will lead to a fall in the overall spending on imports. An increase in the value of the currency in this case leads to a fall in the supply of pounds. This means that the supply curve for pounds is downward-sloping (see Figure 27.2).

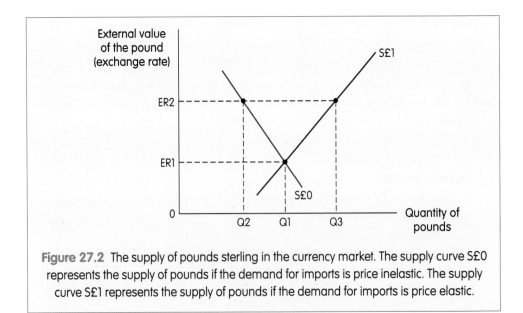

Figure 27.2 The supply of pounds sterling in the currency market. The supply curve S£0 represents the supply of pounds if the demand for imports is price inelastic. The supply curve S£1 represents the supply of pounds if the demand for imports is price elastic.

Example

Imagine that a US firm produces a product worth $300. A UK business imports ten of these. The exchange rate is $1.5:£1, so the US product costs:

$$\frac{\$300}{\$1.50} = £200$$

The UK firm spends:

10 × £200 = £2,000

If the UK exchange rate now rises to $2:£1, then the US product now costs:

$$\frac{\$300}{\$2} = £150$$

Suppose that demand for the import is price inelastic and the firm now buys, say, 11 units. This means that it spends:

11 × £150 = £1,650

Because the price is lower and the increase in quantity demanded is relatively low, the amount spent abroad (that is, the supply of pounds) falls. The supply of pounds falls as the exchange rate rises, as shown in Figure 27.3.

Suppose that demand for the import is price elastic and the firm now buys, say, 30 units. The firm spends:

30 × £150 = £4,500

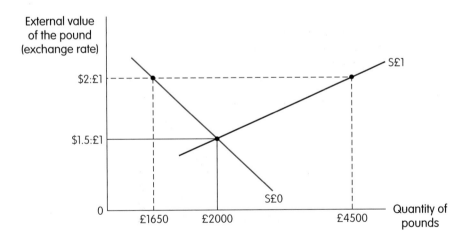

Figure 27.3 Upward-sloping and downward-sloping supply curves for a currency. The supply curve S£0 represents the supply of pounds if the demand for imports is price inelastic. The supply curve S£1 represents the supply of pounds if the demand for imports is price elastic.

The increase in the quantity demanded is so great that, even with the lower price, there is more spending in pounds on foreign goods and so the supply of pounds rises, as shown in Figure 27.3.

Put into practice

The exchange rate appreciates from $1.5:£1 to $2:£1. The US price of a product is $300. A UK consumer buys 20 units initially and then, when the exchange rate changes, 40 units. What happens to the amount of pounds spent on this import?

The US dollar devalues by 10 per cent and US firms keep the dollar price of their exports the same. The price elasticity of demand for US exports is −0.5. What will happen to US export earnings?

a. They will rise by about 20 per cent

b. They will stay the same

c. They will fall by about 5 per cent

d. They will fall by about 20 per cent

e. They will rise by about 5 per cent

▌ Equilibrium in the currency market

In a floating exchange rate system, the value of the currency will change to bring about equilibrium automatically, so that the supply of the currency equals the demand for the currency. The exchange rate is the price mechanism that equates supply and demand in currency markets. There are, of course, many different markets for any currency (such as the pound against the yen, the US dollar, and the euro); in each market, the exchange rate will fluctuate to bring about equilibrium.

For example, if the value of the pound is at ER2 in Figure 27.4, then there is excess demand for the currency (equal to Q3 – Q2). This means that overseas buyers want to buy more pounds than others want to sell and convert into other currency. This will pull up the value of the pound. As the value (price) increases, the quantity demanded will fall, whilst the quantity supplied increases (assuming that the price elasticity of demand for imports is price elastic and the supply of currency is upward-sloping). This process will continue until equilibrium is reached at ER1. At this value, the supply of the currency equals the demand for the currency.

This means that the number of pounds demanded by overseas buyers equals the number of pounds sold. This is equilibrium in the currency market.

If the exchange rate is at ER3 in Figure 27.4, then there is excess supply of the currency (equal to Q5 – Q4). This means that the sellers want to change more pounds than buyers want to buy in exchange for foreign currency. This means that the value of the pound will fall. As it does so, the quantity demanded of this currency will increase and the quantity

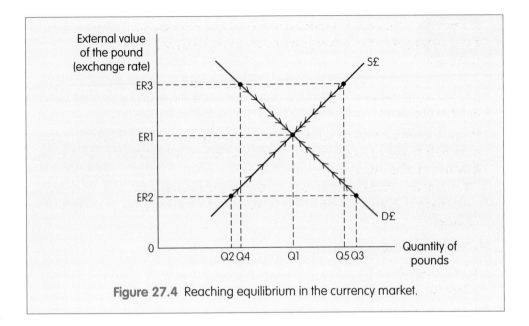

Figure 27.4 Reaching equilibrium in the currency market.

supplied will decrease (assuming an upward-sloping supply curve) until equilibrium is reached at ER1.

Given that there are so many different exchange rates showing the value of the pound against many different currencies, it is useful to be able to use one indicator that reflects the overall movement of the pound against these, taking account of their relative importance. If the UK trades a great deal with countries using the euro, then changes in the value of the pound against this currency are particularly important. The **effective exchange rate** is a weighted average of an exchange rate against its trade partners; this means that it takes account of the relative importance of different currencies depending on the relative amount of trade with these countries.

Put into practice

Which of the following statements are true and which are false?

a. Each country has one exchange rate.

b. An increase in domestic interest rates is likely to increase the value of the currency.

c. High domestic inflation is likely to increase the value of the currency.

d. A fall in the value of a currency makes its exports cheaper in foreign currencies, all other things being equal.

Which of the following is not likely to lead to a fall in the external value of the pound?

a. a fall in UK interest rates

b. more spending by overseas tourists in the UK

In 2013 the pound fell sharply after the Bank of England warned that markets were wrong to assume that it would start raising interest rates in the near future. The external value of the pound dropped a cent and a half against the dollar to $1.5141. It occurred as the Bank held interest rates at 0.5 per cent and kept its quantitative easing programme unchanged. Share prices rallied in London in anticipation of the further continuation of cheap borrowing costs. The statement by the Bank's Monetary Policy Committee highlighted that the country's economic recovery remained weak and stated that a rise in the Bank Rate was not warranted by the state of the economy. With the announcement that interest rates were likely to remain lower the pound became less attractive on currency markets.

? Questions

Explain why the Bank of England may have kept interest rates low.

Analyse why the external value of the pound might have fallen in value.

c. UK citizens buying more imported cars

d. an increase in UK aid to developing countries

e. an increase in UK military spending abroad

■ Appreciation and depreciation of the exchange rate

An appreciation of the exchange rate means that it has increased in value. It is more expensive in terms of other currencies. For example, if the value of £1 rises from $1.50 to $1.60, then this is an appreciation of the pound. This might be because of an increase in the demand for the currency or a fall in the supply (see Figure 27.5). If a currency has increased in value, then it is sometimes called a 'strong' currency.

A depreciation of the exchange rate means that it is less expensive in terms of other currencies. For example, the pound depreciates if its value falls from $1.50 to $1.40. This might be because of a fall in demand for the currency or an increase in the supply (see Figure 27.6). If a currency falls in value, then it is said to have become 'weaker'.

What do you think?

Do you think that a strong pound is better than a weak pound?

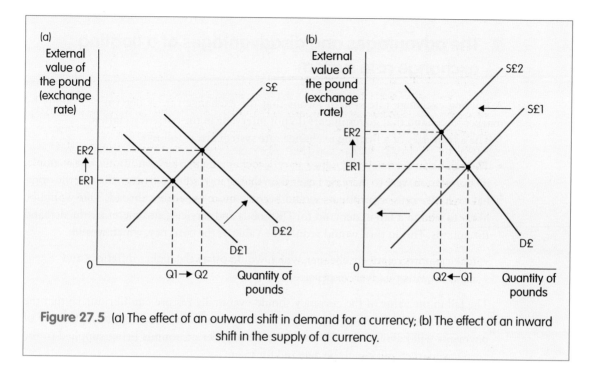

Figure 27.5 (a) The effect of an outward shift in demand for a currency; (b) The effect of an inward shift in the supply of a currency.

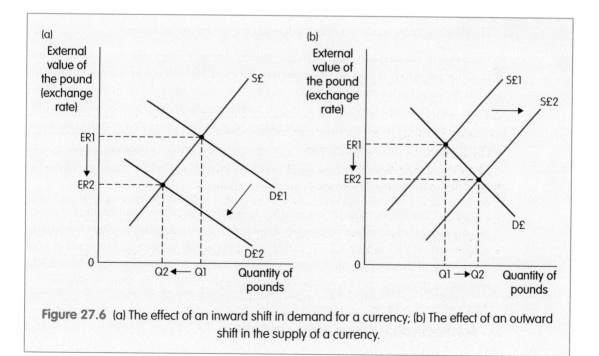

Figure 27.6 (a) The effect of an inward shift in demand for a currency; (b) The effect of an outward shift in the supply of a currency.

The advantages and disadvantages of a floating exchange rate system

A floating exchange rate system means that the exchange rate is determined purely by market forces and that governments do not intervene in the currency market.

The advantages of a floating exchange rate system are as follows.

- The value of a currency will adjust to reflect changing market conditions. For example, if UK inflation were to increase faster than that of its trading partners, then, at the original exchange rate, its products would become more expensive abroad. This would be likely to lead to a fall in demand for UK goods and services, and therefore the demand for pounds. This in turn would reduce the value of the currency, which would:

  - make exports relatively cheaper, which would offset the higher inflation; and
  - make imports relatively expensive.

  The fall in the value of the currency should eventually restore equilibrium, so that the supply of, and demand for, the currency will be equal. This means that the balance of payments will balance (see Chapter 28); the number of pounds being supplied to the currency market will equal the demand for them.

- There are no costs of intervention. The government will not have to use its resources to buy and sell currency. This enables the government to focus on internal domestic economic issues.

The disadvantages of the floating exchange rate system are as follows.

- The value of the currency will change regularly (literally every minute), making it difficult for firms to plan ahead. UK exporters, for example, will not know at any moment what the actual price of their products will be to overseas buyers; UK importers will not know what they will have to pay to buy in foreign products. This makes planning difficult and will deter investment. It may lead to resources being invested in other countries.

- Given that the value of the currency can change all of the time as demand and supply conditions alter, this encourages speculation. By buying and selling currency in the belief that it will change, this leads to greater instability.

- In reality, the exchange rate may not be able to adjust to bring about equilibrium. For example, if the supply of pounds is downward-sloping, then the currency market may not settle in equilibrium. At ER1 in Figure 27.7, there is an excess supply of pounds. This leads to a fall in the value of the currency. In this case, the excess supply increases (for example, to ER2). Changes in the exchange rate in this situation move the market away from equilibrium.

A fixed exchange rate system

In a fixed exchange rate system, a government intervenes to maintain the value of a currency at a fixed value or within a given range.

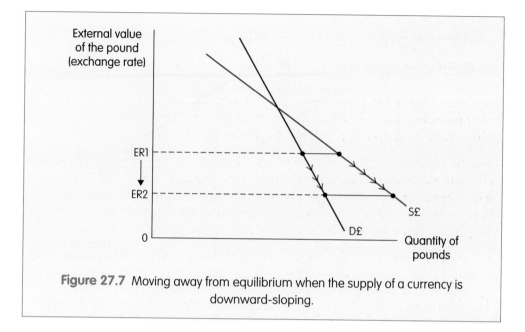

Figure 27.7 Moving away from equilibrium when the supply of a currency is downward-sloping.

A government can intervene in the currency market as follows.

- The government may buy or sell its currency. If it wants to increase the value of its currency abroad, then it can buy it in return for foreign currency that it holds. To decrease the value of its currency, it would sell it in return for foreign currency. This type of intervention involves transaction costs to monitor the possible currency movements and to exchange currency.

  - Suppose that equilibrium in the market is at ER1 in Figure 27.8. If this is below the rate that the government is trying to achieve, then it could increase demand for the currency by buying it in return for selling foreign reserves.
  - Suppose that equilibrium is at ER1 in Figure 27.9. If this is above the rate at which the government would like it to be, then it can sell pounds in return for foreign currency.

- The government may change the interest rate. An increase in the UK interest rate is likely to attract investment (hot money) from overseas, which increases the demand for pounds; this should increase the external value of the currency, all other things being unchanged.

- The government may use reflationary or deflationary policies to affect the level of demand and spending in the UK. Deflationary policies, for example, would reduce aggregate demand spending. This would reduce spending on imports. With less spending on imports, there is less demand for foreign currency and therefore less need to change pounds. This reduces the supply of pounds.

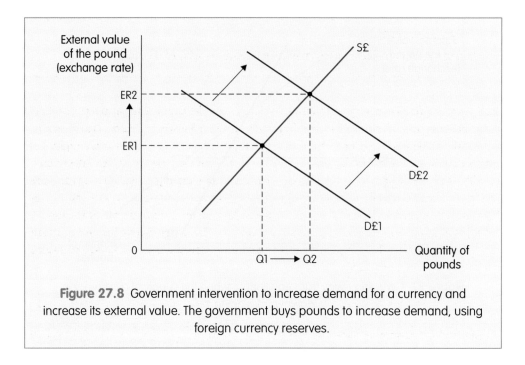

Figure 27.8 Government intervention to increase demand for a currency and increase its external value. The government buys pounds to increase demand, using foreign currency reserves.

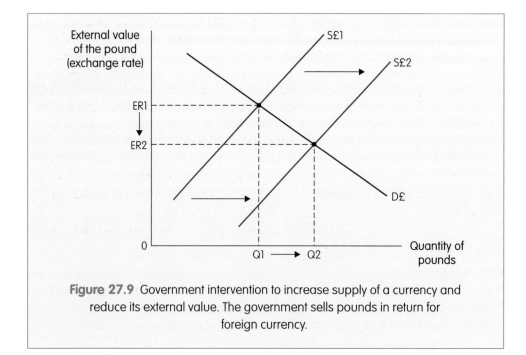

Figure 27.9 Government intervention to increase supply of a currency and reduce its external value. The government sells pounds in return for foreign currency.

Put into practice

Outline two ways in which a government might reduce the value of its currency.

The benefit of a fixed exchange rate system is that it provides stability for importers and exporters because they know at what rate they will be trading. However, decisions to intervene to affect the value of the currency have an opportunity cost and side effects that might disrupt other policies. For example, higher interest rates might increase the value of the pound, but will also have an impact on domestic savings and borrowings. High interest rates are likely to decrease domestic demand, and may cause slower economic growth and unemployment. The external value of the pound may be kept stable at the expense of UK jobs.

Also, as market conditions change, the fixed value of the currency may become too high or low. This will affect the competitiveness of a country's products abroad and a country's balance of payments position.

What do you think?

Do you think a stable currency wuld help the UK economy? Why?

Economics in context

The International Monetary Fund (IMF) recently downgraded its forecast for China's growth to 7.75 per cent and asked for 'decisive' reforms. The major reforms include relaxing its control of the exchange rate. The IMF said that the Chinese currency is 'moderately' undervalued. However the Chinese government was able to point to a rise in the currency to 6.1 yuan to the US dollar and claim this meant it was no longer undervalued. It was also able to highlight the fact that its trade surplus had fallen to below 3 per cent of national income suggesting its currency was no longer providing a major competitive advantage. Other countries still argue that given its growth rates and size China should be importing not exporting and the yuan is too cheap.

To get there would require reforms of the financial system, including the banks and the fiscal system. It would then pave the way for greater opening of trade too, which can help China's ambitions to establish global companies. Ultimately, these reforms would help to stabilize and sustain growth.

Until there is reform, the value of the exchange rate is unlikely to be settled. And, we can expect more reports from the IMF along these lines.

❓ Questions

Analyse the possible effects of the yuan being undervalued. Why are other countries complaining about this?

How might the Chinese government keep the value of the yuan low?

Put into practice

Which of the following statements are true and which are false?

a. An increase in demand for a currency is likely to lead to an appreciation of the currency in a floating exchange rate.

b. To increase the value of its currency, a government might sell its foreign currency reserves.

c. A decrease in supply of a currency to the currency markets is likely to decrease its value.

d. A floating exchange rate makes planning more difficult than a fixed exchange rate.

The exchange rate mechanism

The exchange rate mechanism (ERM) was a system in which member European countries fixed their exchange rates against each other. The aim was to stabilize exchange rates in Europe and thereby encourage trade. The currencies of member countries were given an upper and lower limit on either side of a given central rate within which their currencies could fluctuate. The UK joined the ERM at a rate of DM2.95 to £1 in October 1990.

The system collapsed on 16 September 1992, when countries could not keep their currencies within the set limits. On what became known as 'Black Wednesday', the British pound was forced to leave the system; it was then followed by the Italian lira. The UK government had fought against speculators who were selling pounds, believing that the fixed rate of the pound had been set too high. In a floating exchange rate system, this sale of pounds would drive the value of the pound down. However, because it was in the ERM, the UK government had to try to keep the value of the pound constant; it did this by buying billions of pounds with its foreign currency reserves and increasing domestic interest rates. In the end, the UK government recognized that it could not keep intervening like this (not least because of the impact of such high interest rates domestically) and left the ERM. Speculators such as George Soros made a fortune because they had been selling pounds; once the pound fell, they could buy them back much more cheaply.

The single European currency: The euro

The euro is a currency that has been adopted by a number of European Union (EU) members, which collectively are known as the eurozone. It was introduced on 1 January 1999, with the notes and coins being released at midnight on 31 December 2001, when national currencies started to be withdrawn from circulation. The transition period was needed to allow time to print the 13 billion banknotes and produce the 52 billion euro coins that went into circulation.

In 1997, the UK government set out five tests that would have to be met before the UK would join the euro. These were:

- that UK and European economies were converging, so that, for example, one interest rate would suit all countries;
- that the economies were flexible enough to cope if things were to go wrong;
- that joining the euro would encourage companies to invest in the UK;
- that joining the euro would be good for financial services; and
- that joining the euro would be good for jobs.

There is still debate over whether these criteria have been met and, at the time of writing, much of the pressure to join the eurozone has reduced in the UK. Economic problems of member countries, such as Greece, have highlighted the potential problems of a currency the value of which will affect the position of economies that could be performing very differently. For example, concern over some economies might lead to a fall in the value of the euro, making imports very expensive for members with economies that are relatively still strong.

The advantages of being a member of the euro include the following.

- Firms and households do not need to change currency when visiting or trading with another euro country. This saves on transaction costs (for example, the fee paid to change currency), which should lead to lower prices for consumers.

- It becomes easier to plan ahead. If the exchange rate is constantly changing, then managers and households cannot be certain of the value of a pound; they will not know what they will get when they change their currency to go on holiday, or when they want to buy products from abroad. Equally, they will not know what the price of the products that they want to sell abroad will be in terms of the foreign currency. This can add further risk to any spending or investment decision, which may prevent the decision from being made. Within the eurozone, all other things being unchanged, the price is more predictable, which makes trading easier and less uncertain.

- It becomes easier to compare prices. This is known as 'price transparency'. If a firm is searching for possible supplies in several countries with different currencies, then managers will have to convert the prices into pounds and try to estimate possible changes in the future. It is simpler to operate and choose a supplier if the prices are all in the same currency.

- Competition between firms in the member countries will be greater because of price transparency. This may lead to greater efficiency, which should lead to a better use of resources and an outward shift of the aggregate supply.

- There may be less need to control inflation domestically. If the UK were to have higher inflation than other countries, then this would automatically affect its price competitiveness (it cannot be offset by a fall in the external value of the currency within the eurozone). This is likely to make it harder to export, which dampens demand and therefore brings down inflation again in line with other countries.

- It creates the possibility of internal economies of scale. With trade being easier due to prices being easier to predict, this could lead to higher outputs and internal economies of scale, thereby reducing unit costs.

The disadvantages of joining the euro include the following.

- **One-off changeover costs** Changing the currency from pounds to euros would inevitably incur costs, because brochures have to be rewritten, price lists updated, and vending machines changed to accept new coins.

- **One-off inflationary effects** These are likely to happen because, when changing prices, firms are likely to round up rather than down.

- **Emotional costs** Some people are attached to their national currency, and see this as a sign of independence and heritage. Changing to the euro is sometimes resisted on the basis of national pride rather than economics.

- **Loss of economic policy control** The value of the euro will be influenced by changes in the levels of interest rates within those member countries. Decisions about interest rates must therefore be made in terms of the 'right' rate of the euro for all countries involved. At any particular moment, what is right for the euro members as a whole may

---

Economics in context **Members of the eurozone**

There are 18 members of the eurozone at the time of writing: Austria; Belgium; Cyprus; Finland; France; Germany; Greece; Ireland; Italy; Latvia; Luxembourg; Malta; the Netherlands; Portugal; Slovakia; Slovenia; and Spain. The most recent member was Latvia. The European Commission confirmed in 2013 that the Baltic state had met the criteria for joining the single currency. Latvia is eager to become a fuller part of Europe and be less dependent on Russia. Latvia started using the currency at the beginning of 2014 after meeting the criteria for membership, including low inflation and long-term interest rates, as well as low public debt. Latvia underwent one of Europe's most severe austerity programmes following the 2008–2009 financial crisis which reduced its GDP by around 20 per cent.

The euro entry criteria are:

- Low inflation
- Low long-term interest rates
- A stable exchange rate
- Low public debt
- Low public deficits

? Question

Why might countries want to join the euro?

Why do you think they might not want to join the euro?

not be right for a particular member—for example, a weak euro may stimulate demand generally within the eurozone, but cause problems in an area in which there is already demand-pull inflation. By joining the euro, the UK government and people would have to accept that interest rate decisions would be less UK-focused and more eurozone-focused. Interest rates are set by the European Central Bank (ECB) and not the Bank of England. The ECB is the central bank for the euro. The ECB's main task is to maintain price stability in the eurozone; it would not focus specifically on the UK's economic position. The significant differences between relatively strong economies (such as Germany's) and economies such as those of Portugal, Ireland, Greece, and Spain have put real pressure on the euro in recent years.

What do you think?

Do you think the UK should join the euro?

Put into practice

Which of the following statements are true and which are false?

a. All members of the EU have the euro as their currency.

b. If the pound falls in value against the euro, the euro must rise in value against the pound.

c. Higher interest rates in eurozone countries are likely to lead to an increase in the value of the euro.

d. If the euro is weak, this makes goods from these countries expensive in foreign countries, all other things unchanged.

The real exchange rate

When analysing the effect of exchange rate changes, it is important to consider what has happened to prices in the countries involved. If, for example, a currency were to fall in value, then, everything else unchanged, this would mean that a country's products were relatively cheaper in foreign currency. If, however, prices in this country were rising faster than in its trading partner, this would offset the effect of the falling exchange rate. If a currency halves in value, but prices double, then, in real terms, the exchange rate is the same. The real exchange rate therefore adjusts the nominal exchange rate for the relative prices in different countries.

For example, if there is a £100 UK product and the exchange rate is originally $2:£1, but falls by 50 per cent to $1:£1, then the product would sell for $100 rather than $200. The UK products are more competitive because of the fall in the currency. If, however, prices in the UK were to double, so that the product now costs £200, then this would mean that, even with the fall in the currency, it was selling for $200. Assuming that nothing has changed with the US prices, the product is exactly as competitive as it was originally.

The real exchange rate can be calculated as:

$$\text{Real exchange rate} = \frac{(\text{Nominal exchange rate} \times \text{UK prices})}{\text{Overseas prices}}$$

For example, imagine that the nominal exchange rate is $2:£1, but a pair of jeans sells for £10 in the UK, whilst jeans generally sell for $12 in the USA.

This means that the UK jeans would sell for $20 in the USA (given the nominal exchange rate), which is the top line of the equation:

$$\text{Real exchange rate} = \frac{(\$2 \times £10)}{\$12} = \frac{\$20}{\$12} = \$1.67$$

The real exchange rate is therefore $1.67:£1.

Put into practice

a. The nominal exchange rate is €1.5: £1. A product sells for £5 in the UK and typically sells for €4 in the eurozone. What is the real exchange rate?

b. What is the effect on the real exchange rate if:
  • the price in the UK increases to £10?
  • the price in the eurozone increases to €8?

▨ Purchasing power parity (PPP)

Purchasing power parity (PPP) is the exchange rate that gives one currency exactly the same purchasing power when converted into another—for example, £1,000 when converted into the other currency could purchase the same goods and services. If, for example, £1,000 of goods in the UK costs $1,700, then the exchange rate that would lead to PPP would be $1.7:£1. Thus we have:

$$\text{PPP exchange rate} = \frac{\text{Consumer price index in other country}}{\text{UK consumer price index}}$$

$$\text{PPP exchange rate} = \frac{\$1,700}{£1,000} = \$1.7 : £1$$

To maintain PPP, the value of a currency must move to offset differences in inflation rates. If UK inflation is relatively high, then the pound will need to fall; £1,000 will buy less in the UK because of domestic inflation and, when converted into other currencies, it needs to buy less there as well.

> **Economics in context**
>
> ## Burger index
>
> *The Economist*'s exchange-rate scorecard, the Big Mac index, is an attempt to gauge how far currencies are from their fair value. It is based on the theory of purchasing power parity (PPP), which argues that in the long run exchange rates should move to equalize the price of an identical basket of goods between two countries. *The Economist* basket consists of a single item, a Big Mac hamburger, produced in nearly 120 countries. *The Economist* then calculates the exchange rate that leaves burgers costing the same in America as elsewhere, and compares this with the current market exchange rate to decide if it is overvalued or undervalued.
>
> Asia remains the cheapest place to enjoy a burger. China's recent decision to increase the 'flexibility' of the yuan has not made much difference yet. A Big Mac costs $1.95 in China at current exchange rates, against $3.73 in America. Our index suggests that a fair-value rate would be 3.54 yuan to the dollar, compared with the current rate of 6.78. In other words the yuan is undervalued by 48 per cent.
>
> Other Asian currencies such as the Thai baht and the South Korean won are also undervalued. The Brazilian real is one of the few emerging-market currencies that is trading well above its Big Mac benchmark. With interest rates high—the policy rate now stands at 10.75 per cent—Brazil has attracted lots of attention from yield-hungry investors. Burgernomics suggests that the real is overvalued by 31 per cent.
>
> ### ❓ Questions
>
> What is meant by PPP?
>
> Analyse the possible effects of the currency valuations relative to the Big Mac index discussed above.
>
> Why might the euro have been 'overvalued by 29 per cent'?

▦ Does a strong pound matter?

A strong pound sterling means that the pound is relatively expensive in terms of other currencies. All other things being unchanged, this means the following.

* UK goods and services become relatively more expensive in other currencies. This may reduce demand for them and reduce UK export earnings. If the pound increases in value from £1:$1.5 to £1:$1.6, then a £100 good now costs $160, not $150, in the USA. This is likely to reduce the volume of, and earnings from, exports from the UK.

* Overseas products become relatively cheap in pounds. This may lead to cheaper costs for UK firms and therefore an increase in firms' profit margins. However, it also means that overseas final products are cheaper, which may threaten some UK sales domestically. If the pound increases in value from £1:$1 to £1:$1.5, then a $300 good now costs £200, not £300, in the UK.

The extent to which a strong pound has these effects depends on:

- how much the pound increases in value and for how long;
- the time period being considered (many prices are fixed for some periods, for example, until brochures are updated or contracts renegotiated); and
- how sensitive demands for imports and exports are to price (it may be that the quality of the products means that demand is not that sensitive).

▣ Effect of a falling pound: Depreciation and the current account

If the pound depreciates, then, all other things being unchanged, UK products become cheaper abroad in terms of foreign currency, whilst imports become more expensive in pounds. The cheaper exports should lead to more sales and greater income for UK firms. The extent to which sales abroad increase depends on how price sensitive demand is for UK products abroad. If demand is price elastic, then the increase in sales is greater than the fall in export prices (in percentage terms) and spending on UK exports rises relatively significantly. If demand is price inelastic, then the increase in sales will be less than the increase in price (in percentage terms) and so the increase in the number of UK products sold will be relatively low; therefore the increase in UK export earnings in pounds will also be relatively low.

Meanwhile, the increase in the price of imports in pounds is likely to lead to a fall in the quantity demanded. If demand for imports is price elastic, then this will lead to a larger fall in sales than the increase in price (in percentage terms); this will lead to a fall in the total spending on imports. However, if demand is price inelastic, then this means that the fall in sales is less than the increase in price (in percentage terms); this leads to an increase in the total spending on imports.

The effect of a depreciation in the value of the currency on the current account of the balance of payments therefore depends a great deal on the price elasticity of demand for imports and exports. This is examined in more detail in the next chapter.

Case study

The following describes the concerns that small businesses have over the value of the pound.

Small companies in the UK have warned that the value of the pound is hurting their business, as concerns over the health of the UK economy and expectations the Bank of England will restart its printing presses have caused a sharp slide in sterling this year.

More than half of UK small and medium sized businesses said that they would like to see the pound get stronger, while just 16 per cent said they would like it to fall, according to research carried out by the Financial Times and Western Union Business Solutions.

The pound has lost nearly 7 per cent of its value against the dollar this year and has slid more than 4 per cent against the euro. While the Bank of England opted not to do more monetary easing at its monthly meeting last Thursday, it is widely expected to restart its bond-buying programme after incoming BoE governor Mark Carney starts at the Bank of England.

The Federation of Small Businesses raised concerns over the impact of the weaker pound on smaller businesses in the UK, in particular importers, who face higher bills when paying overseas suppliers in a foreign currency.

'Depreciating sterling has the effect of making UK goods and services cheaper for overseas buyers, boosting the competitiveness of small UK exporters and potentially helping to strengthen expectations,' said Mike Cherry, national policy chairman at the FSB.

'However, this depreciation also has associated risks – a lower pound increases the cost of importing inputs for businesses which could lead to increased costs for manufacturers.'

Officials at the Bank of England hinted earlier this year that they were happy to see a weaker pound help the country's exporters. Less than a fifth of the 666 businesses surveyed by WUBS were importers, while more than 60 per cent had both import and export arms.

Lee Gardiner, founder of Northampton-based Sky Pet Products, which imports animal housing such as bird cages and rabbit hutches from China, warned that the weaker pound was squeezing profits and harming its ability to hire new people.

'We're only able to change our prices once a year with our clients – once we've set our price it means if the dollar moves against us our margin is squeezed and our ability to be profitable is quickly affected,' he said.

'We're stable and growing but where we've lost on the dollar rate we're not able to invest in training new people which is exactly what we'd like to do.'

The survey by WUBS found that just 29 per cent of companies thought the business environment in the UK would improve over the next six months, while 20 per cent predicted it would worsen and half said it would stay the same.

The small and medium-sized businesses said their top concerns were the overall health of the global economy, followed by cheaper competitors, currency volatility and eurozone instability.

Source: http://www.ft.com/cms/s/0/65cd24e8-9ded-11e2-9ccc-00144feabdc0.html#axzz2WJ9LNtLi

❓ Questions

1   Why might the pound have fallen in value?

2   Analyse how a weak pound might help UK businesses.

3   Analyse how a weak pound might have a negative impact on UK businesses.

Review questions

1   What is a floating exchange rate?

2   Explain two determinants of an exchange rate in a floating exchange rate system.

3   How can a government control the external value of its currency?

4   Explain two reasons why the value of a currency might increase.

5   Does controlling the value of the currency conflict with other economic objectives?

6   Explain the likely impact of a strong pound on spending on UK imports.

7 Explain two possible benefits of the UK joining the euro.

8 Explain two possible problems of the UK joining the euro.

Put into practice

1 Using a diagram show the possible effect of a falling value of the pound on national income and prices.

2 Assume the demand for UK exports is price inelastic and demand for UK imports is price inelastic. Illustrate the demand curve for and supply curve of pounds in the foreign currency market; explain your diagram.

Assignment question

1 Summarize changes in the value of the pound against one other major currency over the last five years. Analyse the reasons for any significant changes over this period.

Key learning points

• The value of a currency is determined by supply and demand in a floating exchange rate system.

• In a fixed exchange rate system, the government intervenes to keep the external value of a currency stable.

• The euro is a single currency used by members of the eurozone (most members of the European Union) that removes the problem and cost of converting currency.

Learn more

To learn more about the value of the pound over time and the impact on the UK economy, visit the Online Resource Centre.

 Visit our Online Resource Centre at http://www.oxfordtextbooks.co.uk/orc/gillespie_econ3e/ for test questions and further information on topics covered in this chapter.

International trade, balance of payments, and protectionism

»28

All countries engage in international trade, buying and selling from abroad, and this has a large impact on their economies. This chapter examines the reasons why international trade occurs and the benefits that can be gained from it.

LEARNING OBJECTIVES

By the end of this chapter, you should be able to:

✓ explain the theory of international trade;

✓ explain the elements of the balance of payments;

✓ outline the key elements of the European Union (EU);

✓ examine the benefits of belonging to the EU;

✓ examine absolute and comparative advantage;

✓ examine ways of of curing a current account deficit on the balance of payments.

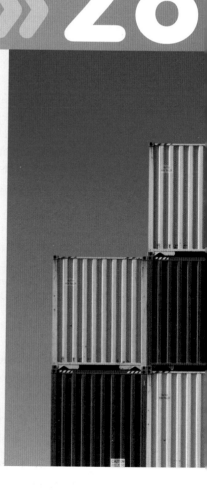

▨ Introduction

Whenever you go shopping, you are likely to be buying goods from all over the world. Clothes produced in China, wine from France, oranges from Spain, ham from Italy—the shops are full of products imported into the UK. You are also likely to make use of foreign services on a regular basis: your phone enquiry may be directed via a call centre in India; your bank may be based in Hong Kong; and your energy provider may be from continental Europe. At the same time, UK firms are busy exporting a range of products, including music, films, and education. To some extent we now live in a global village, buying products from, and selling products to, countries all over the world, and in which travel and tourism into and out of the UK are routine. International trade therefore has a massive influence on the economies. This could be seen in the global recession in 2009 when recessions in one country triggered a fall in demand for products from trading partners, contributing to a recession in those partner countries as well. To understand how one economy performs we need to look at its trading partners and how they are doing as well.

▓ Exports

The value of a country's exports measures the value of the goods and services that it sells abroad. In the case of goods, these may actually be transported abroad. In the case of services, they are more likely to have been consumed in the UK—for example, international students coming to study at a British university are UK exports. Exports are an injection into the economy and are an important element of the aggregate demand. The level of exports from a country may depend on the following.

- **The quality of the goods and services produced relative to those of international competitors** This in turn will depend on a range of factors, such as the levels of investment in technology, the training of staff, and the investment in research and development. It will also depend on the level of competitiveness domestically; high levels of domestic competition may force domestic firms to improve the quality of their products, which will improve their ability to export.

- **Ease of access to markets** The extent to which standards, policies, rules and regulations differ as well as language and cultural differences will determine the extent to which trade is likely and possible. Countries often trade most with their nearest countries geographically because these are the ones they are most similar to culturally and therefore they understand these markets best.

- Protectionism Protectionism occurs if a government protects its own firms from foreign competition. The ways in which this may be done include placing taxes (called tariffs) on foreign products coming into the country or limiting the number of foreign products allowed in (a quota). In some cases, political disputes may lead to a complete ban (embargo) on products from a particular country, with the aim of putting pressure on the government there to change its policies. If other governments introduce protectionist measures, then this may reduce the export opportunities for UK firms.

- **Exchange rates** The exchange rate is the value of one currency in terms of another. If, for example, the pound is expensive to buy in terms of US dollars, then, all other things being equal, this is likely to reduce the sales of UK products to the USA, because they will be relatively expensive. The relative price of one country's products compared to those of other countries will affect sales. The impact on sales will depend on the price elasticity of demand (see Chapter 4).

- **Customer preferences** The tastes and preferences of overseas buyers will obviously influence levels of demand for UK products.

- **Income levels abroad** If incomes are relatively high and growing abroad, then this may increase demand for UK products. With more disposable income, foreign buyers may buy more products in general, including UK products. The amount of UK goods purchased will be influenced by the other countries' marginal propensity to import (MPM) and the income elasticity of the products involved. This highlights the importance of other economies to the UK. If countries abroad are in recession, then this will hit UK exports and may lead the UK into recession as well. Equally, if countries abroad are prospering, then this offers the UK export opportunities.

Put into practice

Which of the following statements are true and which are false?

a. Export spending is an injection into an economy.

b. An increase in export spending reduces aggregate demand.

c. If a currency is cheap, this is likely to increase exports.

d. Higher incomes domestically lead to an increase in exports.

What do you think?

In 1990 Britain was the 5th largest goods exporter in the world. It now stands 11th, behind Belgium, Italy, and Russia. What do you think could have caused this change in position? Does it matter?

▨ Imports

Imports are a withdrawal and reduce the level of the aggregate demand. The level of import spending into a country will also depend on factors such as the exchange rate, customer preferences, and the quality of products abroad. Import spending will also depend on the UK's MPM and the level of income in the UK. With more income, there will be more spending, and this will increase the spending on imports.

The difference between the amount earned by selling exports abroad and the amount spent on imports is measured in the balance of payments.

Put into practice

Which of the following statements are true and which are false?

a. Import spending is an injection into an economy.

b. An increase in import spending reduces aggregate demand.

c. If a currency is cheap, this is likely to make imports more expensive, all other things unchanged.

d. Higher incomes domestically lead to an increase in imports, all other things unchanged.

▇ Absolute and comparative advantage

In theory, an economy can be closed and not open to trade. This would mean that it would have to produce all of the products that it wanted by itself. In this case, production would be restricted by the resources of that one country. However, by engaging in trade, it is possible to benefit from the skills and resources of other countries. To understand how and why trade occurs it is necessary to understand absolute and comparative advantage,

Absolute advantage occurs when one country can produce a product using fewer resources than another—that is, it is more efficient than the other country. If one country has an absolute advantage in product X and another has an absolute advantage in product Y, then trade may clearly be beneficial, with each country specializing and trading with the other.

However, even if a country has absolute advantage in all products (for example, because it was more efficient at producing generally), then trade may still be possible, and indeed beneficial, due to differences in comparative advantage. This theory was developed by Ricardo (1817). For example, the USA may be more efficient than another country in all products and therefore would have an absolute advantage in these. However, this does not mean that trade cannot be beneficial between the USA and other countries. Although the USA is more efficient in all products, there will still be some product categories in which another country has a lower opportunity cost and therefore a comparative advantage. The key to trade is to consider what you have to sacrifice to produce a product relative to what another country has to sacrifice.

Comparative advantage lies at the heart of international trade. Firms in a particular country or region have a comparative advantage in producing particular products if the opportunity cost of producing these products is less than in other regions. When producers in certain industries in one country sacrifice less than firms in other regions, then they are relatively efficient at producing these products. This means that they should be able to export them. At the same time, other areas will be more efficient at producing other products and therefore the first country can buy these in from abroad at a lower price than that for which it could make them itself.

▇ The benefits of trade

Trade can enable more output in the world, as economies specialize in products where they have comparative advantage.

Consider two economies, X, and Y, in which resources are split equally between two products, A and B. In these economies, the outputs produced are as in Table 28.1, and so this two-country economy produces seven units of A and three units of B in total.

Table 28.1   The outputs of two products, A and B, produced by two countries, X and Y

	Product A (units)	Product B (units)
Country X	4	1
Country Y	3	2
Total	7	3

The opportunity costs show what is being sacrificed to produce one unit of A or one unit of B. In country X, for example, the country can produce four units of A or one unit of B, so the opportunity cost of one unit of A is $\frac{1}{4}$ unit of B and the opportunity cost of one unit of B is four units of A. The opportunity costs for countries X and Y are shown in Table 28.2.

From Table 28.2, we can see that country X has the lower opportunity cost in the production of A and therefore should specialize in this product. Meanwhile, country Y has the lower opportunity cost when it comes to producing product B and should specialize in this product. If, instead of splitting resources, these economies now put all of their resources into one product, then, all other things being equal, output in these products should double.

The output levels would now be as shown in Table 28.3. Compared to the original situation, world output has increased by one unit of A and one unit of B. Focusing on an industry in which there is a comparative advantage has led to more production of both products.

Table 28.2   The opportunity costs of producing the products A and B in the two countries X and Y

	Opportunity costs of one unit of A	Opportunity costs of one unit of B
Country X	$\frac{1}{4}$ unit of B	4 units of A
Country Y	$\frac{2}{3}$ unit of B	$\frac{3}{2}$ units of A

Table 28.3   The output levels for the products A and B in the two countries X and Y

	Product A (units)	Product B (units)
Country X	8	0
Country Y	0	4
Total	8	4

The model in the above example assumes constant returns to scale—that is, that by doubling the resources in an industry, the output doubles. In reality, there may be further gains because, by specializing in one product, the country's firms may be more productive due to economies of scale and output may more than double (that is, benefit from increasing returns to scale). This would further increase the benefits of specialization.

Put into practice

Consider two economies, X and Y, for which the outputs produced of products A and B are as shown below.

	Product A (units)	Product B (units)
Country X	6	2
Country Y	2	3
Total	8	5

- Calculate the opportunity cost of each product for each country.
- Identify which product each country would specialize in and the total output if all of the resources focus on this industry.
- What has happened to the world output of A and B as a result of specialization and trade?

What do you think?

The model above assumes that resources can move easily from one industry to another. What barriers to mobility might exist?

▨ Terms of trade

In Table 28.2 above, each country ends up specializing in one product, so what is needed to enable them to consume both products is for them to engage in trade. For this to happen, it must be cheaper for a country to buy products from abroad than to produce them itself and it must achieve a profit from exporting the products in which it specializes.

If we consider country Y, then it is now specializing in producing product B. Each unit of B has an opportunity cost of $\frac{3}{2}$ units of A. Provided that it can sell its units of B for more than this, its firms will make a profit.

Meanwhile, in country X, one unit of B costs four units of A to produce; provided that its firms and households can buy units of B for less than this, it will be beneficial to trade.

For both countries to benefit from trade, one unit of B must sell for more than $\frac{3}{2}$ units of A, but less than four units of A—that is:

$\frac{3}{2}$ units of A < 1 unit of B < 4 units of A

The following are known as the terms of trade.

- Provided that one unit of B costs more than $\frac{3}{2}$ units of A, then country Y will be willing to export because it will make a profit from selling them.

- Provided that one unit of B costs less than four units of A, then country X will be willing to import because this is cheaper than it could produce this product itself.

For example, possible terms of trade that would prove mutually beneficial for both countries would be for one unit of B to cost the same as two units of A; exporters would then make a profit. Importers would benefit from buying from abroad, where the opportunity costs are lower than those of producing the product itself.

Put into practice

Calculate the possible terms of trade for the Put into practice example shown above for which you calculated the opportunity cost of each product.

The terms of trade index

The terms of trade index measures the prices of exports compared with the prices of imports. It is usually calculated as follows:

$$\text{Terms of trade index} = \frac{\text{Index of export prices}}{\text{Index of import prices}} \times 100$$

It shows how many exports can be bought relative to imports. For example, if the average price of exports is £200 and the average price of imports is £100, then one export buys two imports.

An increase in export prices relative to import prices is known as an improvement in the terms of trade. It means that if a product is sold abroad, then more imports can be bought in return than before. However, an improvement in the terms of trade does not necessarily mean that it is good for the economy (even though it sounds like it is); this is because if exports are more expensive relative to imports, then fewer may be sold. The balance of trade may worsen.

Put into practice

What are the likely effects of a fall in the terms of trade?

The dangers of specialization

Trade is therefore based on the idea that a particular country is likely to be good at some things, but not at others. By engaging in trade, a country can benefit from the skills,

Last year car production in Thailand reached 2.45m vehicles of which 1m were exported. This made Thailand the seventh largest car exporter globally. The rise of Thailand's car industry has not happened by accident. After a financial crisis in Asia in 1997 the Thai government removed much of the regulation in the sector making it easier to invest in the country; for example, unlike in India or Malaysia, foreign firms do not need to enter joint ventures with local partners. The Thai Board of Investment also offered generous incentives to companies who produced eco-friendly cars. The government cut the corporate tax rate from 30 per cent to 20 per cent, below that of Indonesia, Malaysia, and even Vietnam.

In addition to this the government provided help to first-time car buyers within the country which boosted domestic demand. In 2012 Thailand again became the biggest car market in South-East Asia with 1.44m new vehicles being sold.

The 'big three' manufacturers in Thailand are Toyota, Isuzu, and Honda. Other brands are now following these Japanese firms and shifting their production from higher cost areas, such as Australia, to Thailand. Ford set up a new plant there last year.

Thailand is not just an assembly location. Around 80 per cent of the parts used are from local companies. Thailand also exports parts worth about $5 billion—more than all the other members of the Association of South-East Asian Nations (ASEAN) put together.

However, some believe that producton will eventually shift to Indonesia due to lower costs even though at the moment according to a study by the Boston Consulting Group, Thailand beats Indonesia as a production centre on almost all important measures: competitiveness, infrastructure, business environment, and tax incentives.

? Question

How does the above item illustrate the benefits of international trade?
What does it suggest about comparative advantage over time?

abilities, and resources of others. Why do something yourself if you can buy it more cheaply from abroad? Free trade should benefit all of those involved.

However, there may be problems caused by specialization, such as:

• Firms may suffer from decreasing returns to scale, in which case, the overall world outputs may not gain as much as suggested in Table 28.3.

• Countries may become overspecialized and reliant on a limited number of products. This makes them vulnerable to changes in that market or to political problems with other countries supplying key products.

The balance of payments

The balance of payments is one of the UK's key economic statistics. It measures the value of economic transactions between UK residents and the rest of the world over a given time period usually a year.

These economic transactions include:

- exports and imports of goods such as oil, agricultural products, other raw materials, machinery and transport equipment, computers, and clothing;
- exports and imports of services such as international transport, travel, and financial and business services;
- income flows such as dividends and interest earned by non-residents on investments in the UK, and by UK residents investing abroad;
- transfers, such as foreign aid and funds brought by migrants to the UK; and
- financial flows, such as investment in shares, debt, and loans.

A surplus on the balance of payments occurs if the inflows are greater than the outflows. A deficit occurs if the outflows are bigger than the inflows over a given period.

The balance of payments is made up of the following.

- **The current account** This comprises the following.
  - **Visible trade** This records the value of imports and exports of physical goods. The balance of trade measures the difference between the value of exported goods and the value of imported goods.
  - **Invisible trade** This records the value of imports and exports of services, and interest profits and dividends, into and out of the country.
- **The capital account** Ths records payments of flows associated with the disposal of assets, the transfer of funds by migrants, and the payment of grants by governments for overseas projects.
- **The financial account** This measures the flows resulting from changes in the holdings of shares, property, bank deposits, and loans. Whereas the current account measures the income flows such as dividends and interest, the financial account measures the actual purchase and sale of assets. The purchase of shares abroad would be an outflow on the financial account; when dividends are paid, this is an inflow on the current account.

The balance of payments also records intervention by the government, such as buying and selling of foreign currency reserves (see Figure 28.1)

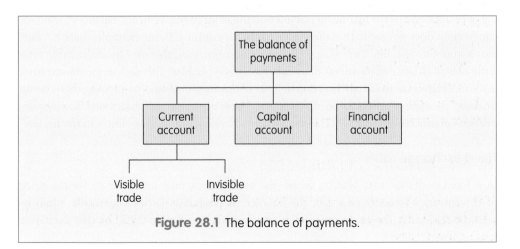

Figure 28.1 The balance of payments.

Economics in context **Japan trade deficit**

Japan's monthly trade deficit recently hit a record after the government's very aggressive monetary policy stance weakened its currency's value. The weak yen helped exports to increase by making them cheaper in foreign currencies but demand was not as buoyant as might be expected given the slow growth in many economies around the world. However, the weak yen increased the price of imports resulting in a trade deficit of over £11bn in one month. Japan has also suffered from more fuel imports because most of its nuclear reactors remain closed after the 2011 tsunami.

? **Questions**

Analyse the causes of the Japanese deficit outlined above.

Should Japan worry about the trade deficit do you think?

A balance of payments surplus means that a country's revenue from exports is greater than its spending on imports. This leads to extra demand in the economy because more money is coming in from abroad than is being spent on foreign products. A balance of payments deficit means that a country's export revenue is less than its import spending. This leads to less demand in the economy because less money is coming in from abroad than is being spent on foreign products.

The balance of payments and exchange rates

Floating exchange rates

In a floating exchange rate system, the external value of the currency changes to equate the quantity of pounds supplied to change into foreign currency and the quantity of pounds demanded in exchange for foreign currency. This means that the number of pounds being given up is exactly equal to the number being bought, so overall the balance of payments equals zero. This does not mean that each element is in equilibrium, but overall the spending in pounds equals the income in pounds and the balance of payments 'balances'. Even so, equilibrium does not mean that there is no cause for concern. If, for example, there is a current account deficit, but surplus in the financial account, then this may be undesirable even if the overall balance of payments does balance. This is because, although in the short term it leads to a higher standard of living due to more consumption thanks to imports, this is being financed by capital inflows into the country. These represent purchases of UK assets by overseas organizations and will lead to dividends flowing out of the country in the future.

Fixed exchange rates

In a fixed exchange rate system, where the government may intervene to fix the price of the currency (see Chapter 27), the balance of payments is not necessarily equal to zero. Imagine that the exchange rate is fixed at ER1 in Figure 28.2. At this exchange

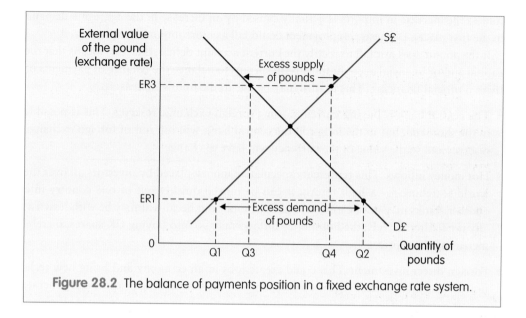

Figure 28.2 The balance of payments position in a fixed exchange rate system.

rate, the number of pounds demanded (Q2) is greater than the number supplied (Q1). There is a balance of payments surplus equal to Q2 – Q1. More pounds are demanded to buy UK goods and services and to pay for other inflows that are supplied to buy or invest in items abroad. In a floating exchange rate, the external value of the pound would rise.

To keep it fixed at ER1, the government must sell pounds to meet the excess demand Q2 – Q1. It will sell pounds in return for foreign currency reserves. This is known as official financing. For example:

Balance of payments surplus = + £300 million (excess quantity demanded of pounds)

Official financing = – £300 million (selling pounds)

If the pound is fixed at ER3 (see Figure 28.2), then there is an excess supply of pounds equal to Q4 – Q3. The quantity supplied exceeds the quantity demanded and there is a balance of payments deficit. More pounds are supplied to the currency market for spending abroad than are demanded for spending in the UK. In this case, the government buys pounds equal to Q4 – Q3 to prevent the value from falling. To buy pounds, the government uses its foreign currency reserves. For example:

Balance of payments deficit = – £200 million (excess quantity supplied of pounds to the foreign currency market)

Official financing = + £200 million (buying pounds)

A current account deficit on the balance of payments

A current account deficit on the balance of payments means that the value of goods and services exported is less than the value of goods and services imported into a country. This may lead to a fall in the aggregate demand because money is leaking out of the economy (unless the increase in imports is actually caused by an increase in the aggregate demand in the first place). Domestic employment could fall as more imports are purchased.

If the pound does not fall to rectify the current account deficit, then this means that the capital and/or financial account must be in surplus to balance the balance of payments or there is official financing. This in turn may be due to the following reasons.

- **The central bank is buying currency, using foreign exchange reserves** This is possible in the short run, but in the long run the central bank will run out of foreign exchange reserves and so the value of the currency will have to change.

- **Hot money inflows** This represents speculative money placed by investors all over the world searching for a high return. It can be moved quickly out of one country into another. Banks may not be able to lend this money out because it may be withdrawn at any time. Alternatively, the hot money inflows may go into buying UK shares, thereby increasing share prices.

- **Foreign direct investment** This could create jobs in an economy and bring new technology. The investment may set up companies in the UK that then export and generate export earnings. The increased competition may also help to create greater efficiency domestically. However, the foreign investment may bring competition that destroys jobs domestically. Also, the profits earned in a country are often repatriated to the country of origin and do not remain in the domestic economy.

A government may worry about a current account deficit if it reflects a fundamental problem with the competitiveness of a country's producers.

Curing a current account deficit

To remove a current account deficit, a government may do the following.

- **Use demand-switching policies** This involves methods of protecting domestic firms from foreign competition, so that consumers switch to domestic firms. For example the government might limit the number of foreign imports (which is called a quota) or impose a tax on them (which is called a tariff). These protectionist measures should reduce the spending on imports relative to exports. However, protectionism may not be possible (for example, because of trade agreements within the European Union) or may lead to retaliation.

- **Use demand-reducing policies** This involves policies to reduce the total spending in the economy (for example, by increasing taxes). With less demand, there will be less spending on imports. However, these policies also lead to less spending on domestic products, which can slow the growth of the economy.

- **Use supply-side policies** These policies, such as training schemes and incentives to invest in research and development, should help domestic firms to become more competitive internationally and therefore to export more.

- **Allow the exchange rate to fall** There may be downward pressure on the currency anyway due to less demand for exports or the government can intervene to reduce the value

**Economics
in context**

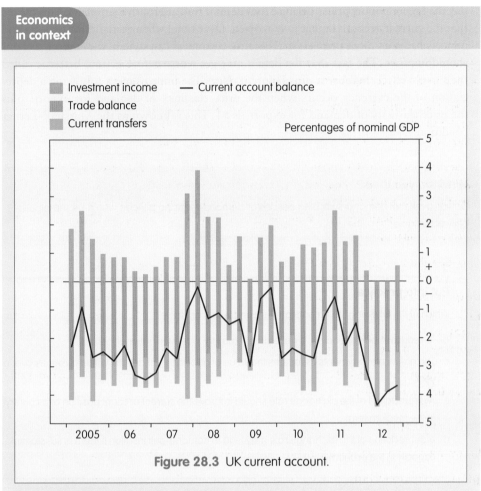

Figure 28.3 UK current account.

Source: Bank of England *Inflation Report* May 2013

❷ Question

Analyse the possible causes of the changes in the UK current account shown in Figure 28.3.

of the currency (for example, by lowering interest rates, which reduces demand for the currency as the returns of saving in the currency are lower). If the currency depreciates, then this should make exports relatively cheaper in foreign currencies and imports relatively more expensive in pounds. This should encourage exports and reduce the volume of imports. However, the precise effect in terms of spending depends on the price elasticity of demand for imports and exports, and may need time to take effect. In the short term, for example, demand for exports may not respond very much (perhaps because contracts have already been signed with existing suppliers); also importers may have to pay the higher import prices because they cannot find alternative suppliers. This means that the current account deficit may worsen. Over time, when demand for exports and imports becomes more price elastic, because customers can switch, the currect account should improve. The fact that the deficit may get worse before getting better is called the J-curve effect (because it dips before it rises). The improvement following a depreciation of the currency occurs when the price elasticity of demand for exports plus the price elasticity of demand for exports is >1. This is known as the Marshall–Lerner condition.

What do you think?

Do you think that demand-switching policies or demand-reducing policies would be more politically acceptable?

Put into practice

Which of the following statements are true and which are false?

a. To reduce import spending, a government may try to reduce national income.

b. The balance of payments measures the value of all of the transactions within a country over a year.

c. A depreciation of the exchange rate should improve the current account position of a country in the medium term.

d. A depreciation of the exchange rate may lead to demand-pull inflation if there is substantial capacity in the economy.

▨ Free trade

Free trade occurs when there are no barriers to trade. This means that products, money, and even people can move freely between one country and another. Free trade offers opportunities to businesses and consumers. Households and firms have a greater choice of goods and services because they can now buy from other countries, and are able to benefit from lower prices by importing from countries that have a comparative advantage.

This is why some countries join together to agree to remove barriers to trade between each other. However, there are different types of agreement, such as:

• In a free trade area, countries remove barriers such as tariffs and quotas on goods and services, but are free to determine their own trade policy with non-members.

• In a customs union, such as the European Union (EU), there is free trade between members and a common tariff on non-members.

The European Union

The EU is a group of countries that have joined together to form a customs union. It was created with six members in 1957, but has grown in numbers ever since and has 27 members at the time of writing. The EU is now the largest single market in the world. There are over 450 million people in this market and its GDP is greater than that of the USA. The EU is the main exporter in the world and the second-biggest importer. The USA is the EU's most important trading partner, followed by China. The EU is also an important trading partner for less-developed countries, most of the exports of which enter the EU duty-free or at reduced rates of duty. This preferential access to the EU market is aimed at boosting the economic growth of poorer countries around the world.

Within the EU:

- standards have been agreed between member states so that if a product can be sold in one country, then it can also be sold in another member country—there do not have to be changes made to the product and no additional taxes can be placed on it; and

- member countries must stick to common agreed tariffs (taxes) placed on products from non-member countries.

The UK joined the EU in 1973 and, as one of the world's largest economies, it is obviously a key member. Over half of the UK's trade is with other EU countries and the UK government estimates that over 3 million jobs are linked to exports to EU members. Around 100,000 Britons work in other EU countries and another 350,000 live in those countries.

The potential advantages to the UK of being within the EU are as follows.

- Being within the EU makes it easier for UK firms to access customers in other European markets. UK firms may therefore be able to sell more products. Given that standards are agreed across the Union, UK firms are not forced to change their product for each market to meet different regulations; this makes it possible to have longer production runs and possibly to gain from economies of scale.

- UK firms and households have easier access to products from other member countries. This may enable firms to find cheaper and better-quality supplies, and to have more choice. This can lead to better value for customers.

- There are lower costs due to the removal of technical and administrative barriers. Trade within the Union becomes easier, which should encourage investment.

- Greater competition within the EU stimulates competition and efficiency; UK firms can learn from their competitors and have to provide good value for customers to compete.

- The UK can benefit from the skills, expertise, and comparative advantage of other nations more easily.

Joining a customs union can lead to trade creation and trade diversion.

- **Trade creation** This occurs when firms and consumers can switch from higher-cost producers to lower-cost producers. With the removal of tariffs, UK firms could

The growth of the European Union

At present, there are 28 members of the EU, with more eager to join. The history of their accession to the Union is as follows.

Year	Member
1958	Belgium, France, Germany, Italy, Luxembourg, the Netherlands
1973	Denmark, Ireland, UK
1981	Greece
1986	Portugal, Spain
1995	Austria, Finland, Sweden
2004	Cyprus, the Czech Republic, Estonia, Hungary, Latvia, Lithuania, Malta, Poland, Slovakia, Slovenia
2007	Bulgaria, Romania
2013	Croatia

Croatia joined the European Union in 2013. Its population was around 4.3 million. At the time it was in recession for the fifth year and had high unemployment of over 20 per cent. More than 60 per cent of Croatia's exports go to the EU.

? Questions

Why do you think Croatia wanted to join the European Union?

Will this create opportunities or threats?

get supplies within the Union more cheaply than they could buy them before from anywhere in the world.

- **Trade diversion** This occurs when firms and households switch from a lower-cost producer outside the Union to a higher-cost producer within it. This can happen because of tariffs placed on non-Union members that raise the price of their products. It may now be cheaper to switch to firms within the EU, even though those outside were cheaper before the tariff.

Put into practice

Would you accept any country that wants to join the EU? Why? Or why not?

European Union institutions

Being a member of the EU involves agreeing to European regulations and directives, and being accountable to European institutions.

Economics in context

Four of the fastest growing economies in Latin America recently agreed to remove most of the tariffs on trade between their countries. Chile, Colombia, Mexico, and Peru, who are the founder members of the Pacific Alliance trading area, claimed that the deal would remove 90 per cent of tariffs on products traded between the nations. The remaining 10 per cent are due to go by 2020. The countries also agreed to remove the need for tourist and business visas. This means their 210 million citizens can now travel more easily between the four countries.

Together the four countries have the ninth biggest economy in the world (which is nearly 3 per cent of world output). They account for a third of Latin American gross domestic product (GDP).

The Peruvian and Chilean economies have grown by around 6 per cent in recent years. All four countries are looking to export more especially to Asia. The success of the Alliance in opening up trade in a short time (it was only set up in 2011) is very different from the experience of the other major trading bloc in the area, Mercosur.

Mercosur was set up in 1991 by Argentina, Brazil, Paraguay, and Uruguay but in recent years has not been very successful at opening up trade opportunities.

❓ Question

What benefits do the countries of the Pacific Alliance hope to gain by being members?
Why might countries resist attempts to become more open to trade?

The main institutions within the EU are as follows.

- **The European Commission** This consists of commissioners appointed by each member state; they propose new policies and administer existing policies.

- **The European Council of Ministers** This is made up of ministers from member countries. The Council receives proposals from the European Commission and can decide on all EU issues.

- **The European Parliament** Members of the European Parliament (MEPs) are elected within their own countries and represent them in Europe. The Parliament discusses proposals from the Commission.

Being a member of the EU also involves agreeing to common economic policies between member states, such as the following.

- **The Common Agricultural Policy (CAP)** This sets prices for food produced within the EU and places tariffs on imports (see the next section).

- **The EU's Monopoly and Restrictive Practices Policy** EU competition policy applies primarily to companies operating in more than one member state. Article 85 of the EC Treaty prohibits agreements between firms, such as overpricing, that adversely affect competition in trade between member states.

The World Trade Organization

The World Trade Organization (WTO) is an international body the purpose of which is to promote free trade by persuading countries to abolish import tariffs and other barriers. The WTO oversees the rules of international trade. It monitors free trade agreements, settles trade disputes between governments, and establishes trade negotiations. WTO decisions are absolute and so, when the USA and the European Union are disagreeing over products such as bananas or beef, the WTO decides.

The WTO was set up in 1995 and is based in Geneva. It replaced the General Agreement on Tariffs and Trade (GATT). WTO agreements cover goods and services, such as telecommunications and banking, as well as other issues, such as intellectual property rights. The membership of the WTO now stands at 149 countries. China joined in December 2001.

Economics in context

In 2013 the UK Prime Minister David Cameron announced plans for the biggest bilateral trade deal in history between the EU and the USA. Negotiations had started on a trade deal that will be worth hundreds of billions of pounds and which is aimed at boosting exports and increasing economic growth. According to Mr Cameron this agreement would have a greater impact than all other world trade deals put together. He claimed the deal could be worth £100bn to the EU economy, £80bn to the USA, and £85bn to the rest of the world. It could create two million jobs, and lead to more choice and lower prices in shops. The EU has said the deal will focus on bringing down remaining tariffs and other barriers to trade, and standardize technical regulations and certifications.

Although the USA and EU impose relatively low tariffs on goods traded between them, other barriers are in place to prevent European companies competing in the USA and vice versa. For example in the car industry, the EU and the USA both employ strict—but differing—safety standards, meaning that European car makers must meet both before they can sell cars in the US market, which puts them at a disadvantage.

Agriculture will be a particularly tricky area of discussion. The European farming industry is heavily subsidized through the Common Agricultural Policy, and the European agriculture minister has already expressed concerns about the impact a free-trade deal might have. The French, for example, are worried that they cannot protect their film industry from Hollywood.

The US government is also likely to come under pressure from domestic businesses who may want protectionist measures to prevent the market from being attacked from Europe.

❓ Questions

Analyse why this trade deal could create growth and reduce unemployment.

Analyse the possible reasons why European and US governments might resist such a deal.

Economics in context

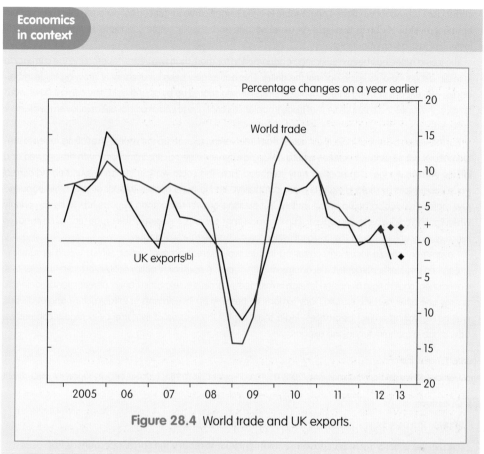

Figure 28.4 World trade and UK exports.

Source: Bank of England *Inflation Report* May 2013

? Questions

Discuss the factors that you think influence the volume of world trade.

Discuss the factors that you think influence the value of UK exports.

Consider Figure 28.4 What do you think this shows about the performance of UK exports over time?

Case study

The following is an article on the low value of the rupee from the *Times of India*.

The official view on the sharp depreciation of the rupee is that this is a temporary phenomenon, that there is no cause for panic. After all almost all developing country currencies have been experiencing downward pressure because the dollar is gaining, with a reviving US economy pushing the Federal Reserve to taper quantitative easing earlier than planned. But the fact is that the rupee is the most battered of the Asian currencies, its broader weakness attributable to India's significantly larger current account deficit. So the government must abandon its business-as-usual attitude and actually create conditions to narrow the deficit, instead of just talking about this.

The falling rupee has been a sustained phenomenon for more than two years now, forcing the currency to lose almost a third of its value against the dollar. This has largely been on account of growing trade imbalances, with exports slowing sharply while imports remain shored up by oil and gold. The current downward spiral of the rupee indicates either that trade imbalances continue to widen or that dollar inflows have further softened.

But the Reserve Bank of India must desist from intervening to prop up the rupee. The falling rupee is emblematic of our economy's troubles where dollar payments exceed dollar inflows, growth has slowed and inflation grown. Further depreciation may lie ahead. First, this could work in India's favour, helping correct trade imbalances by making exports more competitive and imports costlier. Bills for oil and other imported raw materials will also go up unfortunately. But pushing growth rather than imports has to be the priority when fighting back a serious imbalance on the trade front. Second, the scale of the rupee market now makes it increasingly unfeasible for the RBI to influence the exchange rate sustainably.

Government should focus on controlling its runaway current account deficit, which would organically strengthen investor sentiment, the economy and the rupee. A number of policy options are available for this. Government could begin by easing foreign investment restraints in retail, insurance, pension funds, defence, energy and other sectors. It could buoy exports by pushing up investments in infrastructure and utilities as well as expediting project clearances. India must exploit the erosion of its currency to regain competitive advantage in manufacturing and exports.

Source: Times of India

http://articles.timesofindia.indiatimes.com/2013-06-12/edit-page/39899985_1_dollar-inflows-rupee-account-deficit

❓ Questions

1 Analyse the possible reasons why the rupee might be falling.

2 Discuss the actions the Indian government might take to reduce the current account deficit.

3 Discuss the possible impact of a low value of the rupee on the Indian economy.

Review questions

1 Explain the meaning of comparative advantage.

2 Explain what is meant by free trade.

3 What is shown by the balance of payments?

4 Explain the J-curve effect.

5 Explain the difference between demand-reducing and demand-switching policies.

6 Explain how a government might reduce demand in the economy.

7 Explain the difference between a floating and a fixed exchange rate.

8 Outline the potential problems of free trade.

Put into practice

1   If the price elasticity of demand for exports is −0.4 and the price elasticity of demand for imports is −0.3 will a fall in the external value of the pound improve the current account of the balance of payments?

2   If the opportunity cost of 1A is 3B in one country and 5B in another country calculate possible terms of trade.

Assignment questions

1   Summarize the changes in the UK current account over the last five years. Analyse the reasons behind these changes.

2   In May 2013 the ex Chancellor of the Exchequer Nigel Lawson said that the UK should leave the European Union because the economic gains 'would substantially outweigh the costs'. Research the case for and against the UK leaving the European Union and reach a justified conclusion.

Key learning points

*   International trade is based on the principle of comparative advantage.

*   International trade enables countries to benefit from more efficient production overseas; this can lead to more consumption and lower prices domestically.

*   The European Union is a customs union.

*   The Union offers opportunities and threats to member countries. It offers more customers to whom to sell, but also more competition.

Reference

Ricardo, D. (1817) *On the Principles of Political Economy and Taxation,* John Murray, London

Learn more

To learn more about the UK balance of payments over time, visit the Online Resource Centre.

 Visit our Online Resource Centre at http://www.oxfordtextbooks.co.uk/orc/gillespie_econ3e/ for test questions and further information on topics covered in this chapter.

»29 Protectionism and globalization

In the last chapter we examined the reasons why international trade occurs and the benefits that can be gained from it. However, not everyone supports free trade—some argue for protectionist measures to try to limit trade between countries. In this chapter we consider the arguments for and against protectionism. We then consider the benefits and problems caused by a more global economy and what the implications are for developing economies.

LEARNING OBJECTIVES

By the end of this chapter, you should be able to:

✓ outline the possible elements of protectionism;

✓ analyse why governments might protect industries;

✓ examine the possible consequences of protectionism;

✓ understand the potential gains of globalization;

✓ understand the potential dangers of globalization;

✓ appreciate some of the barriers to growth in less developed economies.

▨ Protectionism

Despite the apparent benefits of free trade, such as benefiting from comparative advantage and having access to more suppliers and markets, not all governments believe in it or believe that it is always appropriate. There are often instances in which governments try to restrict trade. This is known as protectionism. Protectionism occurs when governments try to protect their domestic firms from foreign competition. It prevents free trade and introduces barriers to trade.

The methods of protectionism include the following.

- **Tariffs** These are taxes placed on selected goods and services from overseas. The tax revenue raised from tariffs goes to the government that placed them on overseas products.

- **Quotas** These are limits placed on the number of products from a particular country. For example, a limit might be placed on the number of sales or the market share of new cars from a foreign country.

- **Legal restrictions** A country may impose certain regulations or standards on products from abroad to make it more difficult for them to be allowed in.

- **Voluntary export restraints (VERs)** These are agreements negotiated between governments to restrict exports.

- **Government intervention to keep its currency low in value** A government may sell its own currency on the foreign exchange markets to reduce its value and make its products more competitive abroad. The US government has accused the Chinese government in recent years of deliberately keeping its currency low in value to help to promote its exports.

Why do governments protect domestic firms?

Given the arguments for free trade, the idea of protectionism may seem odd. However, the reasons why a government may protect its domestic firms include:

- to retaliate against the protectionist measures of other governments;

- to protect industries that are regarded as strategically important—for example, a government may target certain defence industries or food producers, and protect these in case of times of emergency;

- to enable small and new firms to grow and benefit from the economies of scale and experience that might be needed to compete worldwide (known as the 'infant industry argument');

- to protect certain selected industries to keep jobs safe within them and to protect a way of life (for example, agriculture); and

- to protect jobs if a particular industry is struggling.

> **What do you think?**
>
> Do you think that protecting a domestic industry is the right thing to do if it is struggling?

The appeal of protectionism

Protectionism is quite popular politically because a government is seen to be taking action to protect domestic firms. Domestic producers often organize themselves into

In 2013 the European Commission announced temporary anti-dumping charges on Chinese solar panel imports. This was despite fears it would spark a trade war.

The Commission claimed that Chinese firms are unfairly undercutting rivals. It argues that China is selling panels below cost and damaging competition. The charges will be around 11.8 per cent initially but reach around 47.6 per cent after two months, if no compromise with China can be found.

China is the world's largest producer of solar panels. Its exports of panels to Europe totalled 21bn euros ($27bn; £18bn) in 2011.

The Chinese could appeal against the EU's decision to the European Court of Justice in Luxembourg and to the World Trade Organization.

Source: http://www.bbc.co.uk/news/business-22766639

? Question

Do you think the EU's approach can be justified?

effective lobbying groups to influence government policy and to try to bring about measures that will safeguard them from foreign competition. As comparative advantage changes over time, certain industries may be particularly affected and there may be high levels of structural unemployment in these industries as they struggle against world-wide competitors. Over time, individuals will be able to transfer to other industries or retrain, but in the short term, unemployment could be high. Governments—particularly if they are coming up to an election—may protect these industries to keep these people in work.

The stakeholder group that suffers most from protectionism is the consumer; consumers end up paying higher prices for goods and services that are being provided by inefficient domestic producers. However, consumers are from individual households and do not usually form pressure groups. They tend to have little effective representation in government; therefore they are less likely to influence government policy than the well-organized producers.

▦ The effect of tariffs

In Figure 29.1, the world price for the product is shown at a given level P1. Consumers in the country can buy as much as they want at this price on the world market. The result is that the quantity Q1 is demanded and bought. Of this, the domestic supply curve shows that, at this price, domestic firms can supply the quantity Q2. No more can be supplied domestically because, at this price, local suppliers cannot cover their costs at quantities beyond Q2. The quantity Q1 – Q2 is therefore imported from other countries.

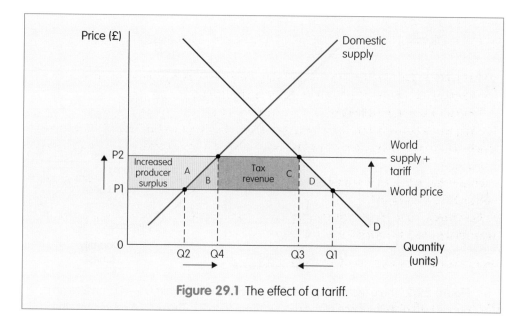

Figure 29.1 The effect of a tariff.

If the government now imposes a tariff on the product, then this will raise the price to P2. This means that domestic suppliers can now produce Q4. With the higher price, more local suppliers can cover their costs and afford to supply. With the higher price, the quantity demanded falls to Q3. This means that the quantity imported falls to Q3 – Q4.

The results of introducing the tariff are as follows.

- Consumers pay a higher price and buy less.
- The government earns a tax revenue, represented in Figure 29.1 by the area C. This is a transfer of money from customers to the government.
- Inefficient domestic producers who could not supply at the old price are able to produce at the higher price. The area B in Figure 29.1 represents the money paid to keep inefficient domestic producers in business.
- There is more producer surplus (equal to the area A in Figure 29.1) for local producers. This represents earnings over and above the price that they needed to supply.
- The area D in Figure 29.1 represents a loss of consumer surplus; these units were consumed before the tariff, and this area shows consumers' utility over and above the price—that is, consumer surplus that is now lost.

What do you think?

Who wins and who loses from the introduction of a tariff?

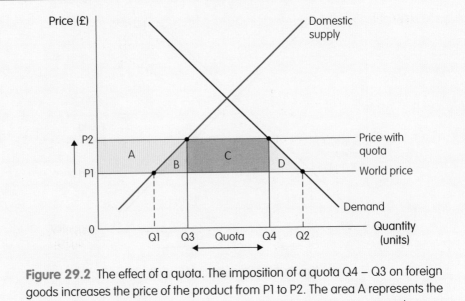

Figure 29.2 The effect of a quota. The imposition of a quota Q4 – Q3 on foreign goods increases the price of the product from P1 to P2. The area A represents the increased producer surplus for domestic producers. The area B represents the money paid to keep inefficient domestic producers in business, thus allowing inefficient domestic producers to supply. The area C represents the extra earnings for foreign producers. The area D represents the loss of consumer surplus due to the higher price.

The effects of quotas

In Figure 29.2, there is a limit of Q3 – Q4 on the number of products sold in the country. This quantity will be demanded only if the price is P2, which is above the world price. The producer surplus of domestic producers has now increased by area A. Domestic customers have fewer products at a higher price in comparison to the equilibrium price and output.

The effects of subsidies

One form of protectionism is to subsidize domestic producers. This is shown in Figure 29.3. The result is that more domestic producers can now supply the product. At the world price of P1, the quantity that domestic producers can supply increases from Q2 to Q4. The government is enabling inefficient producers to compete. The amount of subsidy paid by the government is equal to ABCP1. To finance the subsidies, the government will have to raise revenue—for example, by raising taxes—which may have a negative impact on other sectors of the economy. The effect of the subsidy is to reduce imports by Q2 – Q4; the world price remains unchanged at P1.

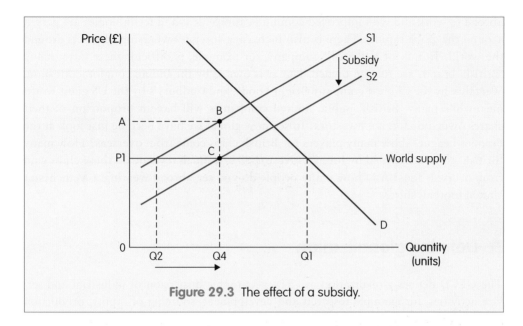

Figure 29.3 The effect of a subsidy.

Put into practice

Which of the following statements are true and which are false?

a. A tariff is a restriction on the quantity of imports into a country.

b. All countries in the world belong to the WTO.

c. Members of the EU have free trade amongst themselves, but agree their own trade policies against non-members.

d. In the EU, all member countries have the same taxation and government spending policies.

What do you think?

Do you think the UK government should introduce more protectionist measures against foreign importers?

■ Globalization

One development in world trade that has come under scrutiny in recent years is that of globalization. This is quite a broad term that can mean different things to different people but refers to the increasingly open borders across the world in terms of trade and the greater integration of economies. More and more businesses are producing abroad, are based abroad or are selling abroad. It is generally easier for people to relocate abroad to work and with improved communications ideas and technologies are passed around the globe rapidly. There is also increasing foreign ownership of assets around the world. To talk of a 'British' company, for example, is difficult these days: many 'British' brands are foreign owned. Jaguar is owned by the Indian conglomerate Tata, Weetabix by the Chinese company Bright Foods, and Cadbury's by the US giant Kraft; meanwhile many 'British' public limited companies will have a proportion of their shares owned by foreign investors. To see how global we have become just look at the Premier League—how many players for British clubs come from overseas? How many 'British' clubs are owned by foreign investors? How much revenue do these clubs gain from overseas fans? And how many people do you see abroad wearing a Manchester United football shirt?

■ Defining globalization

The OECD defines globalization as: 'The geographic dispersion of industrial and service activities, for example research and development, sourcing of inputs, production and distribution, and the cross-border networking of companies, for example through joint ventures and the sharing of assets.' Increasingly companies sell in markets across the world products that have been produced all over the world with staff located and recruited globally.

By comparison the International Monetary Fund defines globalization as: 'a historical process, the result of human innovation and technological progress. It refers to the increasing integration of economies around the world, particularly through the movement of goods, services, and capital across borders. The term sometimes also refers to the movement of people (labour) and knowledge (technology) across international borders. There are also broader cultural, political, and environmental dimensions of globalization.' Notice how this definition focuses on the idea of a process—something that is ongoing.

There are many indicators that show how open the world has become, how far this process has progressed, and how much we have moved towards a 'global village'. For example

- The value of trade (goods and services) as a percentage of world GDP has increased from around 42 per cent in 1980 to well over 60 per cent nowadays.

- Foreign direct investment increased from 6.5 per cent of world GDP in 1980 to over 30 per cent now.

- The number of minutes spent on cross-border telephone calls, on a per-capita basis, increased from 7.3 in 1991 to 28.8 in 2006.

Globalisation is a process of change in the world which brings with it benefits but also dangers and problems. In the words of the writer Theodore Levitt 'The Earth is round, but for most purposes it is sensible to treat it as flat' or perhaps it might be better to say that it is getting flatter as economies and societies converge.

■ What benefits can globalization bring ?

Globalization can bring a number of benefits to businesses, employees and consumers. For example:

- With access to more markets it is possible for businesses to source better quality, lower cost inputs. By offshoring and outsourcing production, firms can benefit from more efficient production and can pass these savings on to consumers

- It is possible to have access to a wider range of inputs (including staff and finance) and products providing greater variety for domestic customers

- The opening up of overseas markets creates new sales opportunities. Brands such as Sony, Nike, Marlboro, and Coca Cola are now recognized all over the world

- New competitors provide an incentive for innovation and change. This can increase efficiency and lead to better products for consumers

- More trade can encourage economic growth and provide jobs. Many argue that in fact globalization is the key to economic growth. As we have seen trade can enable countries to consume outside their production possibility frontier and the influx of money, skills, and ideas can promote further growth in the future. Ernesto Zedillo, the former president of Mexico, argued that, 'In every case where a poor nation has significantly overcome its poverty, this has been achieved while engaging in production for export markets and opening itself to the influx of foreign goods, investment, and technology.'

Put into practice

Show how trade can enable an economy to consume outside of its production possibility frontier.

- It enables information and knowledge to be shared all over the world. Multinational Enterprises (MNEs) are hugely important when it comes to investing in Research and Development and this can bring important ideas and processes to developing economies. Joseph Stiglitz, a Nobel Prize winner and frequent critic of globalization, has nonetheless commented that globalization 'has reduced the sense of isolation felt in much of the developing world and has given many people in the developing world access to knowledge well beyond the reach of even the wealthiest in any country a century ago' (Stiglitz, 2003).

What do you think?

In 2008, the aggregate spending of the world's eight largest MNEs on research and development was larger than the R&D investments of all individual countries, except for the United States and Japan. What do you think might be the benefits of attracting MNE investment into your country?

Globalization therefore has the potential to increase prosperity around the globe, provide more employment, and provide better (and more) goods and services for consumers. It can lower prices, create jobs, improve quality and choice and lead to faster growth and higher incomes. As the IMF states

> There is substantial evidence, from countries of different sizes and different regions, that as countries 'globalize' their citizens benefit, in the form of access to a wider variety of goods and services, lower prices, more and better-paying jobs, improved health, and higher overall living standards. It is probably no mere coincidence that over the past 20 years, as a number of countries have become more open to global economic forces, the percentage of the developing world living in extreme poverty—defined as living on less than $1 per day—has been cut in half.

> http://www.imf.org/external/np/exr/ib/2008/053008.htm

However globalization should not be seen as a miracle cure. It may be a 'necessary' but 'not sufficient' condition for growth and greater prosperity. Even with more trade the success of a country in this more open world will still depend on factors such as the level and quality of investment in a country, the education of its workforce, the business environment it provides, and the infrastructure that develops. Not all countries will benefit equally and not all citizens will benefit equally.

▉ What are the dangers of globalization?

There are many critics of globalization, based on economic, environmental, political, and social and cultural arguments. For example, there are people who argue that the differences in cultures are being eroded as globalization brings a Starbucks and McDonald's to every street corner of major cities. The history and traditions of countries may be removed to make way for global brands, making capital cities look increasingly similar.

Other objections to some of specific aspects of globalization include:

- The loss of jobs in some sectors overseas as businesses look for cheaper production opportunities and domestic businesses face more competition from abroad. Greater globalization exposes the comparative disadvantages of a country in some sectors—employees in these sectors may oppose more foreign competition.

- The foreign ownership of domestic businesses; some people want to keep 'British businesses British' for political reasons.

- The loss of jobs to overseas workers. Again this tends to be a political argument as some in society want to keep jobs for 'local workers'.

- The exploitation of cheap labour overseas. Businesses may produce abroad because of lower safety standards and weaker labour protection laws. It may be regarded as unethical to produce under such conditions even if costs are lower.

- The growth of major multinational companies which may have too much political power and put their own interests above those of the countries in which they operate.

- The impact on the environment as multinationals exploit lax regulation in some countries leading to adverse environmental effects such as high carbon emissions or deforestation.

- Greater interdependence. Whilst interdependence is the basis of trade and brings many advantages it also brings risks as shown by the recent economic crisis. What began as a financial crisis in the United States turned rapidly into a global economic crisis, leading to a massive collapse of international trade and foreign direct investment. The interlinking of financial institutions meant the collapse of the sub prime mortgage market in the USA had reverberations across the world as banks in many countries were exposed to this risk. This hit stock exchanges in many countries and damaged consumer and business confidence, which in turn affected demand and investment and led to falls in aggregate demand worldwide. The reduction in production following the fall in demand also had knock-on effects as supply chains have become increasingly global; less demand for Apple iPhones in the UK for example will affect firms in many countries such as South Korea, Taiwan, Mexico, and China.

These complaints against globalization have led to calls for protectionism or at least more controls over the way in which globalization occurs.

Why has globalization been occurring?

Globalization has become increasingly possible due to:

- The opening up of countries to trade; for example, with more trade agreements and the growth of customs unions such as the European Union as governments see the benefits of trade and as organizations such as the World Trade Organization negotiate a reduction in protectionism.

- The developments in information and communications technology which have made it easier to find businesses and customers abroad and to manage overseas operations. It has also enabled people all over the world to share information and follow trends that are emerging. The latest fashion in New York may be on the streets of Beijing quite quickly. Frances Cairncross refers to the 'Death of Distance' due to the communications revolution that has occurred in recent years with developments in information and communications technology such as the Internet.

- Developments in transportation such as containerization which make it cheaper to move products around the world

What do you think?

'Despite different cultures, middle-class youth all over the world seem to live their lives as if in a parallel universe. They get up in the morning, put on their Levi's and Nikes, grab their caps and backpacks, and Sony personal CD players and head for school' (Klein, 1999).
Do you think this is a bad thing?

▨ Rich vs poor?

One of the big debates over globalization relates to its effect on income inequality around the world. Some argue it helps to raise incomes of poorer countries; others argue it helps richer countries exploit poorer ones—for example, multinational enterprises of richer countries may use cheap labour and extract the minerals of less developed countries whilst investing little and not sharing technology or training local staff. Arundhati Roy writes about the negative impact of globalization in his book *Not Again*:

> In a country like India, the 'structural adjustment' end of the corporate globalisation project is ripping through people's lives. 'Development' projects, massive privatisation, and labour 'reforms' are pushing people off their lands and out of their jobs, resulting in a kind of barbaric dispossession that has few parallels in history. Across the world as the 'free market' brazenly protects Western markets and forces developing countries to lift their trade barriers, the poor are getting poorer and the rich richer.

It is undoubtedly true that regional disparities persist in the world: while poverty has fallen in East and South Asia in the last twenty years, it actually rose in sub-Saharan

Economics in context

In 2013 a building in Bangladesh in which many workers in the garment industry were working collapsed killing hundreds of people beneath the rubble. The owner of the building, Rana, was later caught trying to escape to India. Rana had links with local political parties and this is said to have allowed him to ignore rules and regulations to cut costs. Rana reportedly bought several government-owned properties at a discount and in 2010 constructed Rana Plaza on the site of a pond. The building was supposed to be five storeys high; Rana added an extra three. Two local engineers and the mayor—a political ally—signed off on the project. Just before the collapse of the building Rana insisted the building was safe, despite the discovery of ominous cracks. He told 3,200 workers employed by five garment companies that they had nothing to worry about and should return to their jobs.

Bangladesh's garment industry accounts for 80% of the country's total exports, and last year generated $20bn (£13bn). There is said to be great pressure placed on managers to deliver orders for western companies. The owners of garment factories are reluctant to send their workforces home.

The director at War on Want claims the Rana Plaza disaster was a tipping point—when the brutal truth of what lies behind our £2 T-shirts was finally revealed.

> The link between poverty and cheap clothes made in Bangladesh has been well established, What is important about this tragedy is that it has thrown into stark relief the fact that this is an industry where the workers are not just exploited and forced to work in an environment of harassment, violence and abuse, but where basic guarantees of safety have been thrown to the wind, where corners have been cut to the extent that a building can collapse on top of thousands of workers.

Source:http://www.theguardian.com/global-development/poverty-matters/2013/may/16/bangladesh-garment-workers-exploitation-slavery

❓ Question
Do you think this disaster was an inevitable consequence of globalization?

Africa. The UN's *Human Development Report* states there are still around 1 billion people surviving on less than $1 per day—with 2.6 billion living on less than $2 per day. However, those in favour of globalization argue that this is not because of too much globalization, but rather too little. They claim that it is the people of developing economies who have the greatest need for globalization, as it provides them with the opportunities that come with being part of the world economy.

One of the most authoritative studies of globalization has been carried out by World Bank economists David Dollar and Aart Kraay. They concluded that since 1980, globalization has contributed to a reduction in poverty as well as a reduction in global income inequality. They found that in 'globalizing' countries in the developing world, income per person grew three-and-a-half times faster than in 'non-globalizing' countries, during the 1990s. In general, they noted, 'higher growth rates in globalizing developing countries have translated into higher incomes for the poor'.

Although over the past two decades, income inequality has increased in most regions and countries it is also true that at the same time, incomes per person have risen across virtually all regions for even the poorest segments of population, suggesting that greater globalization has helped the poor be better off in absolute terms although incomes for the relatively well off have increased more quickly. In particular those with skills seem to do well as globalization develops. Whilst in general everyone benefits, those with skills benefit more according to the IMF. So therefore there may be a case to try and develop the education and training in less developed economies to share the rewards of globalization more equally.

What do you think?

Do you think the process of globalization can be reversed?

Some commentators point to those parts of the world that have achieved few gains during this period and highlight it as a failure of globalization. But this may be misdiagnosing the problem. While Secretary-General of the United Nations, Kofi Annan stated that 'the main losers in today's very unequal world are not those who are too much exposed to globalization. They are those who have been left out' (http://www.imf.org/external/np/exr/ib/2008/053008.htm).

Martin Wolf of the *Financial Times* highlights the dangers of trying to halt globalization, pointing out that this charge amounts to arguing 'that it would be better for everybody to be equally poor than for some to become significantly better off, even if, in the long run, this will almost certainly lead to advances for everybody' (Wolf, 2005).

Critics of globalization

The critics of globalization come from many different areas but in general the view seems to be not that globalization is inevitably bad (indeed it may not be possible to stop it over time) but that it needs to monitored and perhaps more regulated to influence the nature of it. Whilst it may not be true that all multinationals exploit cheap labour and damage the environment it is a risk that needs to be taken into account. Whilst it is true that trade may stimulate growth and that the benefits of this may trickle down to low income groups this cannot be assumed and needs appropriate measures to bring it about.

A major concern of many protesters is that globalization can be unfair—big multinationals can get richer at the expense of low income workers abroad and the demands of consumers in developed economies encourage the exploitation of resources in lower income countries. In particular there is a sense that the developed economies are exploiting the developing. They use up natural resources with little investment in the domestic economy and without helping domestic producers to benefit from their own resources. The big producers buy the coffee or cocoa beans, and turn this into coffee or chocolate, gaining most of the profits in the process. Farmers in the developing economies lack the finances or resources to undertake the transformation process of the beans themselves and so gain relatively small rewards.

Those against globalization generally want a fairer process in which richer nations are not abusing their power and not preventing poorer nations sharing the rewards of growth appropriately.

A summary of views for and against globalization is given in Table 29.1

What do you think?

What do you think can be done to make globalization fairer?

Table 29.1   Summary of views on globalization

Strongly in favour of globalisation	Reservations about globalisation
Globalization is good for the poor	Globalization can be bad for the poor
Inequality is not the key issue as long as poverty is falling	Inequality matters
The proportion of the population in poverty matters	The absolute number of people in poverty matters
Free trade is always good	The potential social and environmental costs mean trade needs regulating
All countries should open up access to markets and resources	Developing economies should only open up access to their markets if developed economies allow more access to their markets
Governments should allow free movement of Foreign Direct Investment (FDI)	Governments should control FDI to maximize benefits to the domestic economy
Multinational enterprises should be encouraged as they brings jobs and investment	The growth of multinational enterprises should be controlled as it can exploit the low income and damage the environment
Greater openness leads to more competition and efficiency	Greater openness of markets leads to greater oligopoly power of MNEs and reduces the ability of smaller local firms to survive

Emerging markets

Emerging markets are countries that still have relatively low incomes per person but where the growth rate of the economy is fast. Some of these markets have been labelled the BRIC economies, referring to Brazil, Russia, India, and China. Some of the next set of emerging economies have been labelled CIVETS referring to Cambodia, Indonesia, Vietnam, Egypt, Turkey, and South Africa. These markets provide enormous opportunities for businesses in terms of lower cost production but also consumer markets. Unilever, for example, has built its business model for the future on the sales of its products (from soaps to shampoos) to these emerging economies some of which are growing at rates of over 7 per cent a year. When domestic markets are mature then these rapid growth economies with a growing middle class are very appealing, whether you are selling washing machines, cars, or mobile phones.

? Questions

What might determine the attractiveness of an emerging market for UK exporters?

Why might helping emerging markets to grow help the UK to grow?

■ What limits the growth of some developing economies?

The World Bank places all economies in one of four categories: low income, (in 2012 this was $1,035 per person or less); lower middle income, ($1,036–$4,085); upper middle income, ($4,086–$12,615); and high income, ($12,616 or more). It classifies low-income and middle-income economies as 'developing economies', although it recognizes that there are many differences in the nature of these economies and that 'it is not intended to imply that all economies in the group are experiencing similar development or that other economies have reached a preferred or final stage of development'.

Whilst many developing economies such as China have grown rapidly in recent years some countries are still struggling to 'take off' in terms of economic growth; these are known as Less Economically Developed Countries (LEDC). There is no fixed definition of what constitutes a LEDC but the features include a low income per person, slow growth, and a low score on the Human Development Index (HDI). Less Economically Developed Countries include Afghanistan, Angola, Benin, Burkina Faso, Burundi, Chad, Congo, Gambia, Malawi, Niger, Rwanda, Senegal, and Zambia.

Although the situation of each developing economy is different, the barriers to growth in the LEDC countries typically include:

• **An overdependency on primary products** Many of the LEDCS generate a significant proportion of their national income from primary products such as agriculture or mining. In 80 per cent of Burundi's export earnings come from coffee, for example. This reliance on primary markets can cause problems because of

The Human Development Index

The basic purpose of development is to enlarge people's choices. In principle, these choices can be infinite and can change over time. People often value achievements that do not show up at all, or not immediately, in income or growth figures: greater access to knowledge, better nutrition and health services, more secure livelihoods, security against crime and physical violence, satisfying leisure hours, political and cultural freedoms and sense of participation in community activities. The objective of development is to create an enabling environment for people to enjoy long, healthy and creative lives.

Mahbub ul Haq (1934–1998)

The work of Haq led to the creation of the **Human Development Index (HDI)** by the United Nations each year. This is a composite statistic of a range of factors such as life expectancy, education, and income used to rank countries in terms of Human Development.

VERY LOW HDI score (out of 186 countries) 2013	
176.	Guinea-Bissau
177.	Sierra Leone
178.	Burundi
178.	Guinea
180.	Central African Republic
181.	Eritrea
182.	Mali
183.	Burkina Faso
184.	Chad
185.	Mozambique
186.	Congo (Democratic Republic of the)
186.	Niger

? Question

Do you think the Human Development Index (http://hdr.undp.org/en/reports) is more useful than national income as an indicator of how well a country is doing in relation to its citizens?

a. Price instability. Supply and demand for these products tends to be price inelastic. Shifts in supply can occur due to natural factors (e.g. changes in the weather) and demand can shift with changes in the growth of the world economy. A change in supply or demand conditions can lead to significant shifts in price which will affect the income of producers (and their employees if they have them). This variability in earning can affect the ability to consistently pay for services such as education and health.

Put into practice

Show using supply and demand diagrams the effect on price of a fall in supply in agricultural markets due to bad weather. Show the effect on farmers' incomes.

---

b. The danger of higher exchange rates affecting other sectors of the economy. If commodity prices rise this will increase demand for a currency pulling up the value of the currency making it more difficult for, say, manufacturing to export because its products may become price uncompetitive.

- **Lack of investment** Economic growth relies on higher productivity and this in turn requires investment by businesses. However investment in LEDCs is discouraged for a number of reasons such as corruption. This means multinationals may be expected to pay bribes—something they will not generally want to be seen to do and something which raises the costs of doing business. Corruption also deters other governments funding aid or infrastructure development programmes because they worry where the funds will end up. Business investment will also be discouraged by a lack of stability that exists in some countries—uncertainty about the economy and the government makes long-term planning difficult. A further issue is the rule of law in some countries or the lack of it. Companies operating in a country want to know that the law will be upheld and that it will be done so fairly and efficiently. If it is perceived that contracts can easily be ignored or broken, for example this will deter foreign investment. To operate and grow, businesses need clear rules and the ability to enter into agreements and resolve disputes quickly and affordably. In Sierra Leone, for example it used to take an average of six years for a commercial case to move from being filed to receiving a judgment. The UK government is working with the judiciary in Sierra Leone (and also other countries such as Rwanda and Zambia) to speed up the process; the target is six months.

- **Problems with the labour market** The supply of an economy will rely not just on technology but also the number of people available to work and the skills they have. Better education is vital for more growth. A problem of many LEDCs is a lack of skills. In countries such as Ethiopia and Chad, for example, adult literacy is only around 25 per cent. Disease such as HIV/AIDS is also a major problem in sub-Saharan Africa. High HIV infection rates affect the number of people available to work and their productivity; it also places a strain on health resources diverting resources away from other sectors of the economy such as education. In Botswana over 25 per cent of the population is HIV positive.

- **A lack of government investment** Many governments in LEDCs have accumulated high levels of debt over the years and are burdened with higher interest repayments. Much of this debt occurred in the 1970s and 1980s when oil prices were particularly high. LEDCS had to borrow to pay for energy and in a number of cases are still living with this debt. In addition if incomes are low tax revenue is also low and the result is less funds available to the government to invest in the economy.

Economics in context

Transparency International

Transparency International describes itself as the country's leading anti-corruption organization. It produces the Corruption Perceptions Index which ranks countries and territories based on how corrupt their public sector is perceived to be. A country's rank indicates its position relative to the other countries and territories included in the index.

Rank	
1st equal	Denmark
	Finland
	New Zealand
173rd	Sudan
174th	Afghanistan
174th	Korea (North)
174th	Somalia

http://www.transparency.org/cpi2012/results

? Question

What effect do you think perceived corruption has on the development of an economy?

Put into practice

Show using aggregate supply and demand diagrams how more government spending can help the growth of an economy.

- **Protectionism by more developed economies** More developed economies have often adopted quite protectionist policies against agricultural products from overseas—they have been keen to protect their own farmers. Japan, the EU, and the USA all heavily subsidize domestic producers and/or have very high tariffs on imported products. This is because these farming groups have strong lobbying power and because governments want to protect a way of life. Far more money is spent by developed countries on subsidizing their own producers than is spent on aid.

- **Bureaucracy** The UK is often criticized for the number of regulations and forms required to set up and run a business. This can act a deterrent to growth. However the situation is worse in some countries. In Bangladesh, for example, the UK government has worked with the government there to help streamline the business registration process from 35 days to 1 day; the process can now be completed online. This and other

Economics in context **Heavily Indebted Poor Countries (HIPC) Initiative**

The HIPC Initiative was launched in 1996 by the IMF and World Bank, with the aim of ensuring that no poor country faces a debt burden it cannot manage. Since then, the international financial community, including multilateral organizations and governments have worked together to reduce to sustainable levels the external debt burdens of the most heavily indebted poor countries.

In 2005, to help accelerate progress toward the United Nations Millenium Development Goals, the HIPC Initiative was supplemented by the Multilateral Debt Relief Initiative (MDRI). The MDRI allows for 100 per cent relief on eligible debts by three multilateral institutions—the IMF, the World Bank, and the African Development Fund (AfDF)—for countries completing the HIPC Initiative process.

To benefit from HIPC countries must meet certain criteria, commit to poverty reduction through policy changes and demonstrate a good track-record over time.

Of the 39 countries eligible or potentially eligible for HIPC Initiative assistance, 35 are receiving full debt relief from the IMF and other creditors after reaching their completion points.

Source: http://www.imf.org/external/np/exr/facts/hipc.htm

❓ Question

Do you think debt relief makes good economic sense?

Economics in context

When discussing the problems facing developing economies the UK government states that

Firms' willingness to invest depends on the business environment - the extent to which the laws, regulations and infrastructure within a country support or limit enterprising activities. Businesses need a degree of certainty and an acceptable level of risk. To achieve this, countries need:

- a strong rule of law
- enforceable property and land rights
- better regulations
- reduced trade barriers
- proper infrastructure
- a functioning tax system
- increased transparency

❓ Question

What role, if any, do you think outside governments can play in helping developing economies provide the environment outlined above?

(https://www.gov.uk/government/policies/helping-developing-countries-economies-to-grow)

work has resulted in over 19,000 new businesses being registered in two years. Further simplifications with regards to regulations are expected to generate $30 million in savings for business.

▓ The future?

Despite the problems faced by developing economies stated above there has been progress and in fact the growth of the more successful developing economies such as the BRIC countries is changing the balance of global economic power. The 2013 Human Development report by the United Nations stated that the rise of economies in the southern hemisphere (which is where the developing economies are largely based) has been unprecedented in its speed and scale in recent years. Indeed most developing countries have done well and some of the larger ones have done particularly well—for example, Brazil, China, India, Indonesia, Mexico, South Africa, and Turkey. There has also been significant progress in smaller economies, such as Bangladesh, Chile, Ghana, Mauritius, Rwanda, and Tunisia. These developments are encouraging in terms of lifting people out of poverty and are so significant that for the first time in 150 years, the combined output of the developing world's three leading economies—Brazil, China and India—is approximately equal to the GDP of the major economic powers of the north—Canada, France, Germany, Italy, United Kingdom, and the United States combined. In 1950, Brazil, China, and India together represented only 10 per cent of the world economy, while the six traditional economic powers of the north accounted for more than half. According to projections in the UN Report, by 2050, Brazil, China, and India will together account for 40 per cent of global output which will outweigh by far the projected combined production of the northern economies.

The southern developing economies are now emerging alongside the north as a source of technical innovation and entrepreneurship and also trading more amongst each other. Newly industrializing economies have developed the facilities to efficiently manufacture complex products for developed country markets. But what is also happening is more trade amongst developing economies. For example, Indian firms are supplying medicines, medical equipment, and information and communications technology products and services to countries in Africa. Between 1980 and 2011, south–south trade as a share of world merchandise trade rose from 8.1 per cent to 26.7 per cent.

Of course not all developing economies have done this well yet but increased trade, better education, and investment are helping many to progress economically. According to the UN the pace of change is slower in most of the 49 least developed countries, especially those that are landlocked or distant from world markets. Nevertheless, many of these countries have also begun to benefit from more trade with other developing nations and from investment, finance, and technology transfer. One region in particular to watch in the next twenty years is sub-Saharan Africa. This is likely to be an area of rapid economic growth. For example, a recent Accenture report highlighted that

- In 2010, sub-Saharan Africa (SSA) was populated by more than 856 million consumers. The region will have more than 1.3 billion consumers by 2030.

- While the global economy is predicted to grow by two percent to three percent between 2011 and 2020, SSA is poised to grow by five percent to six percent, making it one of the world's fastest-growing regions.

- African countries received $72 billion in foreign direct investment in 2008, which is five times the amount received in 2000.

- Consumer expenditure in SSA equaled nearly $600 billion in 2010, accounting for almost eight percent of all emerging-market spending, and is expected to reach nearly $1 trillion by 2020.

- Poverty in SSA is decreasing rapidly—from 40 percent in 1980 to less than 30 percent in 2008—and is expected to fall to 20 percent by 2020.

- By 2050, almost 60 percent of people in SSA will live in cities, compared with 40 percent in 2010. This means 800 million more people will live in urban environments.

These developments create huge economic opportunities not only for the countries themselves but for their trading partners.

Source: http://www.accenture.com/SiteCollectionDocuments/Local_South_Africa/PDF/ Accenture-The-Dynamic-African-Consumer-Market-Exploring-Growth-Opportunities-in-Sub-Saharan-Africa.pdf

What do you think?

Faster population growth, less poverty, and greater urbanization are creating huge markets for businesses. What factors do you think could have led to these developments in sub-Saharan Africa?

▓ Conclusion

The developments in emerging economies highlight the importance of economics in determining the welfare and development of countries and the impact of economics on citizens. Issues such as trade and investment affect all of us and can make the difference between living in a highly developed or lesser developed economy—between wealth and poverty. Hopefully, having read this book you are in a better position to analyse the role of governments, of international trade, of education, and the importance of not only demand but also aggregate supply in an economy. This may help you not only to understand the changes happening around you but also encourage you to bring about economic change either directly as an employee, consumer, investor, or protester or through voting for or lobbying others. As you can see from the financial crisis of 2008 and by the rise of economies such as China the world of economics does not stand still and there is still much to learn but hopefully this book will have helped you make more sense of the events occurring around you.

Case study

According to this article from the OECD trade is the key to economic growth:

> One thing is for sure: No country has ever lifted itself out of poverty without international trade. Trade is key to help countries develop. So we need to make sure that people in the world's poorest countries have access to markets, to create jobs and encourage growth as a result. But trade needs the right conditions to flourish. Bottlenecks and inefficiencies – whether at border crossings, or in the way the economy is regulated, or even within the private sector – get in the way of progress and prosperity. This is where Aid for Trade comes in: as financial assistance to build new infrastructure, improve ports or customs facilities in developing countries – in short: we want to help developing countries "trade" their way out of poverty.
>
> Today, the EU and its Member States provide more trade-related development assistance than the rest of the world put together. We contributed a third of world-wide Aid for Trade assistance, or €10.7 bn, in 2010 – that's a quarter of our own total official development assistance (ODA) budget. And the results speak for themselves: a 10% increase in Aid for Trade spending on infrastructure has been shown to lead to a 6.5% increase in goods exports.

Source:OECD

http://oecdinsights.org/2013/01/14/aid-for-trade-helping-developing-countries-trade-their-way-out-of-poverty/

❓ Questions

1 Do you think more free trade is desirable?

2 Do you think trade is the key to economic prosperity?

3 How can more aid help developing economies?

4 How can this then help developed economies?

Review questions

1 Outline two possible reasons put forward for protectionism.

2 Explain the effect of a tariff on (a) the market price (b) the quantity consumed (c) domestic supply (d) government revenue.

3 Explain the effect of a quota on (a) the market price (b) the quantity consumed (c) domestic supply (d) government revenue.

4 Give two arguments against protectionism.

5 Give one reason why companies become multinational.

6 Explain two benefits multinational companies may bring to an economy.

7 Outline two possible problems of globalization.

8 Explain two reasons why some countries remain lesser developed at the moment.

Put into practice

1 Show the benefits of free trade using numerical data.

2 Draw a diagram to show how free trade might enable an economy to consume outside of its production possibility frontier

Assignment questions

1 Research the UK's spending on International Aid. Outline the arguments for and against international aid. Would you increase the amount the UK provides?

According to the campaigning organization Make Poverty History (www.makepovertyhistory.org)

Rich countries and the institutions they control must act to cancel all the unpayable debt of the poorest countries. They should not do this by depriving poor countries of new aid, but by digging into their own pockets and providing new money. The task of calculating how much debt should be cancelled must no longer be left to creditors concerned mainly with minimising their own costs. Instead, we need a fair and transparent international process to make sure that human need takes priority over debt repayments.

International institutions like the IMF and World Bank must stop asking poor countries to jump through hoops in order to qualify for debt relief. Poor countries should no longer have to privatise basic services or liberalise their economies as a condition for getting the debt relief they so desperately need.

2 Research the case made by Make Poverty History and outline the case for and against cancelling the debt of poor countries. Recommend what actions you think the governments of developed economies should take in relation to cancelling debt.

Key learning points

- Protectionism can take several forms, such as tariffs, quotas, and legislation.

- Protectionism can encourage inefficiency, and lead to less consumption and higher prices for consumers.

- Globalization offers the possibilities of growth, more products, lower prices and better quality goods and services.

- Globalization can lead to exploitation if not regulated.

- Limits to growth in some developing countries include a lack of investment, poor infrastructure and lack of a good education and training system.

References

Klein, N. (1999) *No Logo: Taking Aim at the Brand Bullies*, Picador, London

Stiglitz, J. (2003) *Globalization and Its Discontents*, W.W. Norton & Company, New York

Wolf, M. (2005) *Why Globalization Works*, Yale University Press, New Haven and London

 Visit our Online Resource Centre at http://www.oxfordtextbooks.co.uk/orc/gillespie_ econ3e/ for test questions and further information on topics covered in this chapter.

Advise the Government

Whichever political party you are, being in government is no easy task. You are faced by many competing demands, limited resources, and lots to do in a restricted amount of time before the next election. In this section we consider some of the key macroeconomic issues facing governments and ask you to help advise whoever is power on what they should do.

1. HOW DO WE REDUCE YOUTH UNEMPLOYMENT?

Youth unemployment has become a major concern across the world. The level of youth unemployment in many countries has increased, even when overall unemployment figures have fallen.

Research this issue and analyse the causes and consequences of youth unemployment in your country. Recommend to the government three actions it should take to help reduce this problem. Justify your choices.

In your analysis you might want to consider issues such as voluntary and involuntary unemployment, supply side and demand side policies, economic growth and government deficit.

2. SHOULD THE UK LEAVE THE EUROPEAN UNION?

There is much debate at the moment about the UK's relationship with the European Union. One view put forward by the former Chancellor Nigel Lawson is that the economic gains of leaving are greater than the benefits of staying as a member.

Research this issue and analyse the case for and against the UK leaving the European Union. Advise the UK government on whether to leave the European Union.

In your analysis you might want to consider issues such as customs unions, trade creation and trade diversion, economic growth, exports and imports.

3. SHOULD THE UK MAKE GOOGLE PAY MORE TAX?

A number of high profile business such as Amazon and Google have been criticised in recent years for paying low amounts of corporation tax. The UK government has been eager to make such companies pay more tax.

Research the case for and against new legislation to make big companies pay more tax. Advise the UK government on whether more action is needed and, if so, what actions should be taken. Justify your recommendations.

In your analysis you might want to consider issues such as tax revenue, budget position, investment, economic growth, and employment.

Index